Fundamentals of Islamic Philosophy

Fundamentals of Islamic Philosophy

Sharif Ahmed

CYBER TECH PUBLICATIONS
4264/3, Ansari Road, Daryaganj, New Delhi-110002 (India)
Ph.: 011-23244078. Fax: 011-23280028
E-Mail: cyberpublicationsdelhi@yahoo.com

FUNDAMENTALS OF ISLAMIC PHILOSOPHY

Sharif Ahmed

First Edition 2009

Published by :

G.S. Rawat for **Cyber Tech Publications**
4264/3, Ansari Road, Daryaganj, New Delhi-110002 (India)
Ph.: 011-23244078. Fax: 011-23280028
E-Mail: cyberpublicationsdelhi@yahoo.com

Printed at : Asian Offset Printers

Preface

Although Islamic philosophy represents one of the most important philosophical traditions in the world, it has only recently begun to receive the attention it deserves in the non-Islamic world. This important text provides a concise and accessible introduction to the major movements, thinkers and concepts within that tradition, from the foundation of Islam to the present day. Ever since the growth of Islam as a religious and political movement, Muslim thinkers have sought to understand the theoretical aspects of their faith by using philosophical concepts. Leaman outlines this history and demonstrates that, although the development of Islamic philosophy is closely linked with Islam itself, its form is not essentially connected to religion, and its leading ideas and arguments are of general philosophical significance. The author illustrates the importance of Islamic thought within philosophy through the use of many modern examples. He describes and contrasts the three main movements in Islamic philosophy - Peripatetic, Sufi and Illuminationist - and examines the Persian as well as the Arabic philosophical traditions.

Comprehensive coverage is given to key aspects of Islamic philosophy, including epistemology, ontology, politics, ethics and philosophy of language, providing readers with a full and rounded view of the discipline. The main markets for this book are in the areas of philosophy, Islamic studies, Middle Eastern studies, cultural studies, religious studies and theology.

—Author

CONTENTS

1

PRE-ISLAMIC INDIAN THOUGHT

Maurice Bloomfield says paradoxically in The Religion of the Rig Veda that "Indian religion begins before its arrival in India." By this he means to imply that Indian religion is a continuation of the primitive faith of the IndoEuropean race to which the Aryans that came to India belonged. "The Sanskrit word deva (to shine) for God is similar to the Latin word deus; yaj a Sanskrit word for worship is common to more than one Indo European language; while the Vedic god Mitra has his counterpart in the Iranian god Mithra." From a comparative study of the beliefs and practices of the Teutonic, Hellenic, Celtic, Slavonic, Italian, Armenian, and Persian peoples which all sprang from the Indo European race, it has been established beyond the slightest doubt that the basis of their religion was an animistic belief in a very large number of petty gods, each of which had a special function. They were worshipped with sacrifice, accompanied with potent formulas and prayers. Magic was highly regarded and much used.

It is greatly regretted that there is neither any formal history nor any archaeological remain to throw light on the early home of this ancient race or on the time when the great historical people hived off from it. Our principal source for the history, religion, and philosophy of the Indian branch is the Vedas besides the Epics and the Puranas.

The Vedas: Among the Vedas, the oldest is Rg Veda which consists of more than a thousand hymns composed by successive generations of poets during a period of many centuries. The hymns are connected in various ways with the sacrifices, the domestic ceremonies, and the religious speculation of the time, and are concerned chiefly with the worship of gods, who represent personification of natural forces, and the propitiation of demoniac beings.

In the Indo Iranian period the refreshing drink prepared from the somaplant was offered to gods in a special ritual and the singing of a hymn was a necessary part of the ritual. The Aryans brought this custom with them and continued to compose verses for the sama ritual and for the occasions of annual sacrifices in their new homeland. As the hymns were to be sung, a class of priests arose whose duty it was to recite poems of praise in honour of gods. The priests who could sing better hymns and were in possession of a secret lore, which enabled them by conducting sacrifices in the right way to win the favour of gods for their patrons, were in great demand. Consequently, a number of priestly families vied with one another in composing hymns in the best language and metre then available. The Rg Veda gives evidence of seven such families each bearing the name of a patriarch to whom the hymns are ascribed. At first the hymn collections of six families were brought together and then of nine. At a much later stage some scholars collected one hundred and ninety one poems which were taught as the last section of the oral curriculum of hymns. Thus, there became ten books of the Rg Veda.

The mantras of the Atharva Veda consist largely of spells for magical purposes and advocate pure and unalloyed polytheism. The other Vedas are entirely sacrificial in purpose. The Sama Veda consists of verses borrowed from the Rg Veda to be applied to soma sacrifice. The Yajur Veda consists of ritual formulas of the magical type.

For a long time the number of the Vedas was limited to three, the Atharva Veda being totally excluded from the group of the Vedas. In support of this contention the following verse from Manu can be cited: "From Agni, Vayu, and Ravi, He drew forth for the accomplishment of sacrifice the eternal triple Veda, distinguished as Rik, Yajush and Saman." Similarly, in Satapatha Brahnmanas it is said, "The Rik Yajush Saman verses are the threefold science."

A probable reason for the exclusion of the Atharva Veda from the Vedas is that "it consists mostly of magic spell, sorcery, and incantations which were used by the non Aryans and the lower classes to achieve worldly goods such as wealth, riches, children. health, freedom from disease.... The Atharva Veda was recognized later on when hymns relating to sacrifices seem to have been added to it to gain recognition from the orthodoxy."

Vedic Conception of God: The religion of the Vedas is polytheism. It has not the charm and grace of the pantheon of the Homeric poems; but it certainly stands nearer the origin of the gods. All gods whether great or small are deified natural phenomena. The interesting thing about them is that they are identified with the glorious things whose deifications they are and are also distinguished from them. They are still thought of as being sun, moon, rain, wind, etc., yet each god is conceived as a glorious being who has his home in heaven and who comes sailing in his far shining car to the sacrifice and sits down on the grass to hear his own praise recited and sung and to receive the offerings. The hymns sung by the priests were mainly invocations of the gods meant to accompany the oblation of soma juice and the fire sacrifice of the melted butter.

The Vedas are not consistent in their account of the gods. In one myth the sun is a male, in another a female. The sun and the moon are mentioned in one place as rivals, elsewhere as husband and wife. The dog is extolled in one place as a deity and in another mentioned as a vile creature. Again the sun, the sky, and the earth are looked upon sometimes as natural objects governed by particular gods and sometimes as themselves gods who generate and control other beings.

In the Rg Veda, heaven and earth are ordinarily regarded as the parents of gods, pitra or matra. In other passages heaven (dyaus) is separately styled as father and the earth (prithivi) as mother. At other places, however, they are spoken of as having been created. Thus it is said, that he who produced heaven and earth must have been the most skilful artisan of all the gods. Again, Indra is described as having formed them, to follow him as chariot wheels do a horse. At other places the creation of the earth and the heaven is ascribed to Soma and Pushan. Thus, while the gods are regarded in some passages of the Rg Veda as the offsprings of heaven and earth, they are at other places considered independent of these deities and even their creators.

In various texts of the Rg Veda the gods are spoken of as being thirty three in number. Thus it is said in the Rg Veda: "Come hither Nasatyas, Asvins, together with the thrice eleven gods, to drink our nectar." Again, "Agni, the wise gods lend an ear to their worshippers. God with the ruddy steeds, who lovest praise, bring hither those three and thirty." In the Satapatha Brahmanas this number of thirty three gods is explained as made up of eight vasus, eleven rudras, and twelve adityas, together with heaven and earth, or, according to another passage, together with Indra and Prajapati instead of heaven and earth.

The enumeration of gods as thirty three is not adhered to throughout the Vedas. In the Rg Veda, the gods are mentioned as being much more numerous: "Three thousand, three hundred, thirty and nine gods have worshipped Agni." Thus verse which is one of the many shows that the Vedic Indian believed in the existence of a much larger number of supernatural beings than thirty three.

The gods were believed to have had a beginning; they were stated to be mortal, but capable of overcoming death by the practice of austerity. The Rg Veda says that the gods acquired immortality by drinking soma. Still the gods are not self existent or unbeginning beings. It has been seen that they are described in various passages of the Rg Veda as offsprings of heaven and earth. In various texts of the Rg Veda the birth of Indra is mentioned, and his father and mother are also alluded to.

The Vedic gods can be classified as deities of heaven, air, and earth:

Celestial Gods: The oldest god is Dyaus, generally coupled with Prithivi when the two are regarded as universal parents. Another is Varuna, the greatest of the Vedic gods besides Indra. It is he who sustains and upholds physical and moral order. In the later Vedas, when Prajapati became creator and supreme god, the importance of Varuna waned, and in the post Vedicperiod Varuna retained only the dominion of waters as god of the sky. Various aspects of the solar activity are represented by five gods, namely, Mitra, a personification of the sun's beneficent power; Surya, the proper name of the sun, regarded as the husband of dawn; Savitri, the life giving activity of the sun; Pusan, a pastoral deity personifying the bountiful power of the sun; and Visnu occupying the central place in this pantheon.

Atmospheric Gods: The most important of these gods is Indra, a favourite national deity of the Aryan Indians. He is not an uncreated being. It is said of him, "Thy father was the parent of a most heroic son; the maker of Indra, he also produced the celestial and unconquerable thunder... was a most skilful workman." Again, "A vigorous (god) begot him, a vigorous (son), for the battle; a heroic female (nari) brought him forth, a heroic soul." His whole appearance is golden; his arms are golden; he carries a golden whip in his hands; and he is borne on a shining golden car with a thousand supports. His car is drawn by two golden steeds with flowing golden manes. He is famous for slaying Vrta after a terrific battle, as a result of which water is released for man and light is restored to him. Certain immoral acts are also attributed to him. He occasionally indulges in acts of violence such as slaying his father or destroying the car of Dawn. Less important gods of this group are Trita, Apamnapat and Matarisvan. The sons of Rudra, the malignant deities of the Vedas, are the Maruts (the storm gods) who help Indra in his conflicts. The god of wind is Vayu while that of water is Apah.

Terrestrial Gods: Rivers are deified. Thus Sindu (Indus), Vipas (Bias), and Sutudri (Sutlej) are invoked in the Rg Veda. The most important god is Sarasvati, often regarded as the wife of Brahma. Another very important god is Agni, the god of fire. The number of hymns addressed to him far exceed those addressed to any other, divinity with the exception of Indra. In the Rg Veda he is frequently spoken of as a goblin slayer. Another god is Soma, the divine drink which makes those who drink it immortal. A priest says in the Rg Veda: "We have drunk Soma, we have become immortal, we have entered into light, we have known gods."

In addition to these, there is a host of abstract deities and also deities of less importance which cannot be described here for want of space. Suffice it to say that an attempt was made by the sages (rsis) to introduce order in the bewildering multiplicity of gods. As several gods had similar functions, they were in some cases bracketed together, so that it might be said that when Indra and Agni performed identical functions, Agni was Indra or Indra was Agni. Hence arose many dual gods. A farther effort in the direction of systematization was made through what Max Miller has called henotheism a tendency to address any of the gods, say, Agni, Indra, Varuna, or any other deity, "as for the time being the only god in existence with an entire forgetfulness of all other gods." Macdonell has a different theory to explain the so called henotheism by ascribing to it exaggeration, thus retaining the charge of polytheism against the Veda.

Some modern Hindus under the influence of Swami Dayananda repudiate both these theories as inconsistent with the true spirit of the Vedas " He is One, sages call Him by different names, e.g., Agni, Yama, Maarishvan." No doubt, a few verses of this nature can be found in the Vedas; but the consensus of scholars is that monotheistic verses are a product of the later Vedic period and that they do nt express the dominant strain of the Vedic thought. Shri Krishna Saksena in his chapter "Indian Philosophy" in A History of Philosophical Systems edited by V. Ferm says that the early mantras contain a religion of nature worship in which powers of nature like fire (agni)and wind (vayu) are personified. In later hymns and the Brahmanas, monotheistic tendencies began to crop up a little. Swami Dayananda was a product of Hindu Muslim culture and his insistence on monotheism shows the extent to which Muslim thought has influenced Indian religious beliefs.

Vedic Eschatology: The Rg Veda makes no distinct reference to a future life except in its ninth and tenth books. Yama, the god of death, was the first of the mortals to die. He discovers the way to the other world; guides other men there, assembles them in a home, which is secured for them for ever. He grants luminous abodes to the pious and is an object of terror for the wicked. Yama is said to have two insatiable dogs with four eyes and wide nostrils who act as his messengers and convey the spirits of men to the abode of their forefathers. After a person's dead body has been burnt, his spirit soars to the realm of eternal light in a car or on wings and enters upon a more perfect life which fulfils all of his desires and grants him unending happiness. Since the Vedic gods did not have purely spiritual pleasures but were often subject to sensual appetites, it can be said that the pleasures promised to the pious in the world to come were not altogether spiritual. Yama is described as carousing with the gods, Gandharvas, a class of gods who are described as hairy like dogs and monkeys, often assume handsome appearance to seduce the earthly females. Indra is said to have had a happy married life.

Brahmanas: Each of the four Vedas has three sub divisions: the Samhitas (sacred texts), the Brahmanas (commentaries),and the Aranyakas (forest books): The Brahmanas are, therefore, an integral part of the Vedas. Sayana, a great scholar of the Vedas, says, "Veda is the denomination of the Mantras and the Brahmanas." (Swami Dayananda differs on this point.) By the Mantras are meant hymns and prayers; and the Brahmanas are intended to elucidate objects which are only generally adverted to in the hymns. The Brahmanas comprise precepts which inculcate religious duties, maxims which explain those precepts, and arguments which relate to theology.

Considering the fact that the Brahmanas often quote from the Vedas and devote themselves to the clarification of the ritualistic and the philosophical portions of the Vedas, it may be concluded that the Samhitas must have existed in their present form before the compilation of the Brahmanas was undertaken. In fact in the Brahmanass, we find fully developed the whole Brahmanical system, of which we have but faint indications in the Vedas. We have the whole body of religious and social institutions far more complicated than the simple ritual of the Samhitas; four castes with the Brahmins at the top and the Sudras at the bottom have been recognized both in theory and in practice all this shows that the Brahmanas must have been composed a long time after the Vedas. It is, however, obvious that the Brahmanas were a kind of a scriptural authority for the Brahmanical form of worship and social institutions.

Upanisads: The third integral part of the Vedas, namely, the Aranayakas, intended for the study of the anchorites in the forests in the third stage of their life, led ultimately to the Upanisads or Vedantas as the concluding portion of the Vedas. These were meant for the ascetics in the fourth stage of their lives called the Sannyasa Asrama. Literally, the word Upanisad means "a sitting besides." i. e., a lesson taught by the teacher to the pupils sitting by his side. These discourses expounded in enigmatic formulae a series of esoteric doctrines to the selected few students, mainly Brahmins, who were deemed fit to receive such a course of instruction.

Considering the age which gave birth to the Upanisads for understanding some of the major problems of life, one marvels at the depth and insight of the early Hindu seers. Their attitude towards the Vedas was not one of veneration; it was on the contrary an attitude of doubt and disrespect. While they considered Vedas to be of divine origin, they felt at the same time that the Vedic knowledge was inferior to the true divine insight and could not liberate them. They were not concerned with the world of phenomena and denounced with all the force at their disposal the rich and elaborate ritualism then prevalent. Sacrifice, an integral part of the Vedic faith, had no significance for then. Their interest lay not in the outer world but in the inner and, within that, in the mystery of the self. The introverted Brahmins were accordingly carried far beyond the realm of the anthropomorphic deities of the early Vedic period and devoted attention to that all transcending principle from which all natural forces and events were supposed to proceed.

The Upanisads, however, fall short of offering a coherent presentation of the Brahmanic doctrine of the Universal Soul in all things. "This is only found in them in fragments, some small, some large. And in addition these fragments are the work of various schools and various ages. Those who have described the Upanisads as chaotic are not altogether wrong." It would be hard to say what philosophical opinions might not be supported on their authority, for the most part contradictory statements find a place in them, yet the tendency is on the whole towards pantheism. The Upanisads teach the identity of the soul of all beings both animate and inanimate with the Universal Soul. Since the Universal Soul dwells in all, one finds one's own self in all things, both living and nonliving. In this light alone can the meaning of the famous tat tvam asi (That art thou) of the Upanisads be understood. The human self is not a part of the Divine Self, but is the Brahman Atman whole and undivided. The Self is consequently a single principle, which, philosophically speaking, can offer an explanation for the entire spectacle of nature.

It is often said that the pillars on which the edifice of Indian philosophy rests are Atman and Brahman. These terms have no fixed connotation in the Upanisads. Generally speaking, Atman is used to designate self or soul, while Brahman is used to denote the primary cause of things. What is remarkable about these terms is that though their significance is different, one denoting an inner world of subjectivity and the other an objective principle of explanation, yet in course of time the two came to be used interchangeably both signifying an eternal principle of the universe. The notion of the self was arrived at through introspection and it was thought by the Upanisads thinkers that the outer reality should correspond exactly with the psychical reality within. In this way what was simply a psychical principle came to be recognized as a world principle.

This strain of thought was supported by another which objectively traced the visible universe to a single source, namely, Brahman, and Brahman was identified with the Atman. Thus, two independent currents of thought met together and paved the way to monism of an idealistic type which has remained till now the hallmark of Indian philosophy. By combining subjective and objective principles into one, the ultimate principle partook of the characteristics of both it became infinite as well as spiritual. All this is very well expressed in Chandogya Upanisad in a dialogue between a father and a son. The sum and substance of the story is that the primal spiritual principle is all comprehensive and that the principle is no other than the self of the person then engaged in the discussion. With regard to the nature of Brahman (the Absolute) there is a great divergence of opinion.

At some places He is conceived as cosmic, i.e., all comprehensive, at others acosmic, i.e., all exclusive. Further, at some places Brahman is imagined as the impersonal Absolute without attributes; at other places he is recognized as the highest spiritual Being that unites all forms of perfection in Himself. Hence it would be no exaggeration to say that though the Upanisads contain flashes of insight, yet they are not a self contained homogeneous system and that they also lack completeness. It is for this reason that Samkara believes that there are two types of doctrines in the Upanisads: esoteric, understanding God as the impersonal, unknowable Absolute without attributes, and the other exoteric, regarding God as a Person who manifests Himself in the various divinities.

The second interpretation of the Absolute as a Person led to the development of a theology largely theistic in spirit yet polytheistic in practice, since it sanctioned symbol worship which expressed itself in various forms of idolworship. The Upanisads are not, however, responsible for the excesses of later theology. In them breathes a spirit of monism. They preach a cult of mystical union with the Absolute, and suggest practical methods for its realization. In the main the stress is laid upon complete detachment from all that is mundane and belongs to the world of phenomena. Accordingly, one finds in the Upanisads a whole series of sayings in which complete renunciation is recommended. "When all desires which are in his heart disappear, then man becomes immortal. Here he has already reached Brahman. As the old slough of a snake lies on an ant hill, so now does the body lie there."

According to the Upanisads, the highest merit called Preryas, which consists in the realization of one's true self, can be reached through knowledge alone. The purpose of ethics, on the other hand, is quite distinct, namely, mundane good called Preyas which is reached by moral actions. The two ends are consequently poles apart, one concerned with the timeless good and the other with the temporal and evanescent good. It is said in Katha Upanisad that the ethical and the spiritual goals are opposed to each other as light and darkness and cannot co exist. A man has to renounce all activity for worldly goods if he wants to achieve spiritual unity with the Supreme Being. One cannot, therefore, select both knowledge and action as two ends of life, since the highest end must be one and not many.

The ideal of detachment was emphasized by the Indian thinkers not only for the reason that it was necessitated by their theory of human deliverance, but also because they regarded the whole phenomenal world of names, forms, and plurality as maya or a mere unreality, an illusion having only a temporary reality which is transcended ultimately in the being of the Supreme Self. The Upanisads demand the votaries of Brahma to ponder over the illusoriness and unreality of the world of senses and to extricate themselves from its temptations and enchantments by contemplation of a transcendental reality within the soul of each person. Thus can a person get to spiritual heights and achieve mukti or salvation. Hence along with the renunciation of the phenomenal world another thing required is the concentration of the spirit on the supersensible reality. The Upanisads contain detailed instructions on this subject.

The aim is to reach a stage of ecstasy in which a person has the psychical experience of feeling one with the Ultimate Reality.

The ethics negating tendencies, however, could not be maintained consistently in face of the demands and concrete realities of life. The ideal of human salvation as outlined by the Upanisads cannot be achieved easily and so many are destined to fail. This is realized by the Indian sages. "What is hard for many even to hear, what many fail to understand even though they hear: a marvel is the one that can teach it and lucky is its obtainer; a marvel is he that knows it when taught by the wise." The majority are born again after death and can win release from the cycle of births and deaths through the performance of good deeds. Thus ethics rejected by Brahmanic mysticism enters through the doctrine of the Transmigration of Souls a doctrine unknown to the Vedas.

The doctrine referred to above appears in connection with a myth. "All who depart from this world go to the moon. The waxing half fills itself with their lives; in the waning half it is effecting their rebirth. The moon is the gate of the heaven. He who knows how to reply to it, him it allows to pass by. He who cannot reply, it sends him as rain down to the earth; he is reborn here and there according to his deeds and knowledge as worm, moth, fish, bird, lion, wild bear, jackal, tiger, man, or whatever it may be. For when a man comes to the moon, the moon asks: `Who art thou ? 'Then he ought to answer: Iam thou....' If he speaks thus, then the moon lets him get away, out above itself." One finds no reference to the myth in the Vedas. From this it is concluded that it is not Aryan in origin but belonged to the religious world of the aboriginal inhabitants of India.

The law which governs the kind of birth a soul is destined to have after each death is the law of karma, which signifies that nothing can happen in the moral world without a cause.

But the recognition of the fact that moral events are caused by antecedent factors cannot explain the palpably indemonstrable and poetic way in which the moral causes are believed to operate. That moral causes can work in smsara, that is to say, in a series of births and deaths, all of which do not necessarily pertain to human beings, is a hypothesis of a very doubtful nature and utility. That the doctrine of reincarnation is inconsistent with the Brahmanic mysticism of the identity of the individual with the Universal Soul goes without saying. Instead of the doctrine that every individual soul returns to the Universal Soul after inhabiting the body once, we are required to believe in a theory which starts from new premises altogether.

This theory is based on the supposition that souls are prisoners in the world of sense and can return to their Primal Source not at once after their first death, as required by the theory of mystical absorption of the Brahmins, but after undergoing a long process of reincarnation necessitating a series of births in the animate and inanimate realms. Schweitzer thinks that the acceptance of this doctrine created insuperable difficulties for Hindu thought. On the older hypothesis of mystical reunion with the Divine Source it was easy to explain world redemption on the assumption that all souls returned to their Source after their death. But if the theory of reincarnation is accepted, world redemption becomes possible only if all souls reach the level of human existence and become capable of acquiring that knowledge and conduct which is required for liberation and of which human beings alone are capable.

The Epic Period: Twogreat events belong to this period. The first is the expedition of Rama from Oudh to Ceylon to recover his wife Sita who had been carried off by Ravana, the king of that island, and the second is the struggle for supremacy between two rival Ksatriya groups, the Pandavas and the Kauravas, in which Lord Krsna played a significant part.

Rama is an avatar, i. e., a divine incarnation of Visnu, who being the preserver of the universe had to leave his celestial abode very often and to assume different forms in order to destroy evil and establish truth. The purpose of this avatar was to kill the ten headed Ravana, who had pleased the mighty gods through his austerities and as a result had received a boon from them which was that he could not be killed by any god. Feeling secure, he started a campaign of terror against both gods and men. The gods approached Brahma who had granted immunity to Ravana. He remarked that Ravana could be killed by a god assuming the form of a man since Ravana had not been granted immunity from mankind. Visnu undertook to be born as a man to rid the world of evil. He was accordingly born in the house of a king, Dasaratha by name, who ruled over Ayodhya and bore the name of Rama. As he came of age he married Sita, who "was an incarnation of Laksmi, Visnu's wife, and was born of no woman but of mother earth herself, and was picked up by Janaka from a paddy field."

Rama became the victim of court intrigues, and for fourteen years had to suffer exile in jungles from where Sita was carried off by Ravana. To rescue Sita from the clutches of Ravana, Rama contracted military alliance with ganuman, the king of monkeys, with whose active support he reached Ceylon and learnt the secrets of Ravana's power from a brother of Ravana. Then ensued a fierce battle in which the armies suffered losses. At last Ravana came out and met Rama in a single combat. "Each like a flaming lion fought the other; head after head of the ten necked one did Rama cut away with his deadly arrows, but new heads ever rose in place of those cut off, and Ravana's death seemed no wise nearer than before. The arrows that had slain Maricha and Khara and Bali could not take the king of Lanka's life away. Then Rama took up the Brahma weapon given to him by Agastya, the Wind lay in its (weapon's) wings, the Sun and Fire in its head, in its mass the weight of Meru and Mandara. Blessing that shaft with Vedic Mantras, Rama set it with his mighty bow and loosed it and it sped to its appointed place and cleft the breast of Ravana and, bathed in blood, returned and entered Rama's quiver."

The most popular avatar of Visnu is Lord Krsna, whose main object was to kill Kansa, a demon born of a woman, and who was well known for his childish tricks and many practical jokes on milk maids. He was, however, a great warrior and a strategist. He killed many demons and kings.

Bhagavad Gita: It was Lord Krsna who sang the Bhagavad Gita (the song celestial) to Arjuna, giving the most widely accepted view of life among the Hindus. Says Mahatma Gandhi,

"I find a solace in the Bhagavad Gita that I miss even in the Sermon on the Mount. When disappointment stares me in the face and all alone I see not a ray of light, I go back to the Bhagavad-Gita. I feel a verse here and there and I immediately begin to smile in the midst of overwhelming tragedies, and if they have left no scar on me I owe it all to the teachings of the Bhagavad Gita."

According to Sankaracharya, a great scholiast, the main function of the Gita is to epitomize the essentials of the whole Vedic teachings. A knowledge of its teachings leads to the realization of all aspirations. The real purpose of this great song, as Zimmer thinks, is to harmonize the non Brahmanical pre Aryan thought of aboriginal India with the Vedic ideas of the Aryan invaders. The Gita, therefore, "displays a kaleidoscopic interworking of the two traditions that for some ten centuries had been contending for the control and mastery of the Indian mind. Its teachings are founded upon the Upanisadic principle of an all unifying, transcendental reality, but they also accommodate not only the gods of the earlier Vedic pantheon but also the philosophic and devotional formulae of the non Aryan and aboriginal tradition. It was not an easy task.

The Gita had to pick up scattered and heterogeneous material to reconcile the irreconcilable tendencies of that age and to present a unified view of life. Little wonder that the attempt has appeared to the Western scholars as no better than an `ill assorted cabinet of primitive philosophical opinions.' There were the Vedas with their belief in multiple divinities; there were the Upanisads with their revolt against the ritualism of the Vedas and their anthropomorphic conception of gods; there was the doctrine of renunciation; and finally there were the Sanikhya and the Yoga principles. And if we add to them the heretical tendencies, particularly those represented by Buddhism, we realize how confusing the situation was and what an uphill task Lord Krsna had before him.

It would be futile to look for a consistent and neat metaphysical system in the Gita, for the Gita is not primarily a book of recondite and abstruse thinking, written with the object of presenting a world view. It has a much loftier purpose, which is to relate the broad principles of metaphysical reality to the fundamental aspirations of mankind. This is not accomplished through abstract reasoning which only a few can understand but by selecting a specific situation involving a moral dilemma and pointing out how it is overcome.

The occasion was a battle between the Kauravas and the Pandavas. The latter were led by Arjuna whose spirits were unmanned and who felt reluctant to start the battle seeing on both sides his friends, relations, and teachers who were likely to be killed in the event of a war. At this juncture his charioteer who was none other than Lord Krsna himself addressed to him the Song Celestial, propounding to him as well as to the whole of mankind the Yoga of selfless action (karma yoga).

The significance of this teaching will become obvious if we refer to the two ideals which were prevalent then: one, the negative one of renunciation and the other, the positive one, of active life. The first recommended complete withdrawal from the work a day world and the second encouraged living in society undertaking all the obligations implied thereby. The object of the Gita is to discover a golden mean, to reconcile as it were the claims of renunciation and active participation in the affairs of society. This is done through the doctrine of karma yoga which means doing one's duty without the thought of consequences.

"Giving up or carrying on one's work, both lead to salvation; but of the two, carrying on one's work is the more excellent," says Lord Krsna in the Bhagavad Gita. He also says, "Neither does man attain to (the state of) being without work by undertaking no work, nor does he reach perfection by simply shunning the world." What is required is a spirit of detachment where the heart of a person is free from the outward motives to action. "Thy interest shall only be directed to the deed, never to the fruits thereof," says Lord Krsna.

A natural consequence of this theory is that even what is judged as evil from human standards can be approved of, if the agent feels that the task selected by him is one which must be fulfilled. "Even if a thorough scoundrel loves me and nothing else, he must be deemed good; for he has well resolved." "Even if thou wert the most sinful of all sinners, yet thou wouldst pass over all guilt with the boat of knowledge alone." With these words Arjuna is urged to fight against his relations, for his killing would not be an evil: it would be a necessary consequence of the duty he has to discharge.

The ethics of detachment as preached by the Gita is laudable no doubt, but, as Schweitzer says, "It grants recognition to activity, only after activity has renounced natural motives and its natural meaning." An action loses its significance when it ceases to be purposive. The Gita raises a voice of protest against the soul killing and life negating cult of renunciation, but it has not gone far enough. Renunciation remains when the end of an activity is no concern of a person. "The Bhagavad Gita has a sphinx like character. It contains such marvellous phrases about inner detachment from the world, about the attitude of the mind which knows no hatred and is kind, and about loving self devotion to God, that we are wont to overlook its non ethical contents."

The Heterodox Systems: Among the systems which defied the authority of the Vedas may be mentioned the Carvaka, Jainism, and Buddhism:

The Carvaka: This system seems to be fairly old. It is mentioned in the Rg Veda, the Epics, and the Bhagavad Gita. The main work on the system, the Brhaspati Sutra (600 B.C.), is lost and its teachings have to be reconstructed from criticism of it in other works.

The Carvaka is a non Vedic, materialistic, and anti supernaturalistic doctrine which holds that only this world exists and there is nothing beyond. There is no future life. Madhava Acharya says in Sarvadarsanasangrgha, "The efforts of Carvaka are indeed hard to be eradicated, for the majority of living beings hold by the refrain:

While life is yours, live joyously;

None can escape Death's searching eye:

When once this frame of ours they burn,

How shall it e'er again return?"

"The mass of men, in accordance with the Sastras of policy and enjoyment are found to follow only the doctrine of Carvaka. Hence another name for that school is Lokayata a name well accordant with the thing signified."

The four elements alone are the ultimate principles and these are earth, water, fire, and air. Only the perceived exists; the unperceivable does not exist, simply for the reason of its never having been perceived. The only source of knowledge and the criterion of validity is perception. Every other source including that of inference is rejected. Inferential knowledge involves inductive relations and can never be demonstrably certain. Empirical generalizations may possess a high degree of probability, but their operation in unknown cases can never be guaranteed. To avoid this difficulty, if it is maintained that the empirical laws connect the common features of the particular instances observed by a person, the Carvaka objects to it by saying that such a course would leave the particulars unrelated and that it is the particulars alone which matter.

As against the Upanisads which postulated five elements, the Carvaka admits of only four discarding the fifth one, viz., space. The whole universe including souls is interpreted strictly in terms of these elements. The self is nothing but the physical body as characterized by sentience. "The soul is but the body characterized by the attributes signified in the expressions, I am stout, I am youthful, I am grown up, I am old, etc. It is not something other than that body)."

The Carvaka rejects outright all types of spiritual values and has faith in the present world only. "There is no world other than this; there is no heaven and no hell; the realm of Siva and like regions are invented by stupid impostors of other schools of thought.... The wise should enjoy the pleasures of this world through the proper visible means of agriculture, keeping cattle, trade, political administration, etc." The authority of the Vedas is repudiated not only on the ground that their teachings are irrational, but also because of the inconsistencies which render it impossible to know what they really teach.

The Carvaka is a protest against the excessive spirituality of the early Brahmanic thought. It recognizes neither god nor conscience. It cares not for a belief in the life to come. Hence the ethical ideal is pleasure in this life and that too of the individual.

Since the main trend of Hindu thought: has been idealistic, the Carvaka system has contributed very little to the sum of

Indian thought, and this is rather unfortunate. In view of the fact that the Vedas, the Upanisads, and the Gita reject the evidence of the senses as illusory, the Carvaka contention might have served as a corrective.

Jainism: Jainism, according to Tomlin, is the most perplexing of all religions, for it is not only incredible but also impracticable. It denies life to the extent of recommending suicide as the most sacred act of which man is capable, and yet it has survived for two thousand years.

The founder of Jainism, Mahavira, was born in a Ksatriya family. His father was a wealthy person belonging to a religious sect which was opposed to the Vedas. This school of thought had materialistic tendencies and sceptical attitude very much akin to that of Carvaka. But it was not a thoroughgoing materialism. It shared with the masses the horror of rebirth and advocated slow suicide through starvation as a remedy against transmigration. Mahavira's father got his wife converted to his viewpoint and in due course shared with her the martyrdom they desired.

Before following the example of his parents, Mahavira embarked upon a quest of wisdom and adopted an ascetic life. After two years of abstinence and self denial he withdrew himself from civilized life and dispensed with all the amenities of life including those of clothing. During the first six years of his peregrination, he observed frequent fasts of several months duration. He voluntarily exposed himself to be maltreated by the Mlechcha tribes of Vajrabhumi and Lat who abused and beat him, and shot arrows at him, and baited him with dogs, to all of which he offered no resistance. At the end of the ninth year, Mahavira relinquished his silence, but continued the practice of self mortification. The whole of the time spent by him in these preparatory exercises was twelve years acid six months, and of this he fasted nearly eleven years.

The Jains have a tradition that saviours are sent to the world whenever mankind is plunged in corruption and sin. Mahavira was twenty fourth in the line.

Mahavira denied the divine origin and infallible authority of the Vedas. His religion is, therefore, reckoned as a heterodox religion. Its cosmology and anthropology is non Aryan. While

Brahmanism is the representative of Vedic Aryan thought and beliefs, Buddhism; Jainism, and a host of other doctrines relate themselves to the native genius and expose the pessimistic dualism which underlies so much of Indian philosophy. Jainism is a philosophy of the profoundest pessimism. It visualizes the world as a round of endless rebirths, full of sufferings and entirely useless. One shall have to pass through periods of inconsequential pleasures and unbearable pains unless one obtains a release through austerities and self abnegation. In the Jaina Sutras, suicide is called "the incomparable religious death," requiring in some cases a whole life time to cultivate a proper frame of mind for its performance. It is essential that all types of longings including those of death be completely eradicated from one's consciousness. Hence one has to bring about one's extinction in a mood beyond both desire and aversion.

As regards the philosophy of Jainism, it may be said that an eternal and presiding First Cause forms no part of this system, nor do the Jains admit of soul or spirit as distinct from the living principle. They do believe in the independent and eternal existence of spirit and matter, but by spirit they do not mean universal spirit as they have no faith in the Supreme Soul.

The spirits called jivas are eternal but limited and variable because of which they can adjust themselves to the size of the body they happen to inhabit. Their essence is knowledge which is not empirical or sensory. As a matter of fact, perception is a check upon the absolute sight of the soul. In order that the soul may regain its true nature, it is necessary that limitations imposed by the senses be done away with.

The Jains believe in both transmigration and karma. The latter operates by itself. Being a subtle particle of matter, it enters the soul and soils it. Hence no supreme being in the form of God is required to allot rewards and punishments. Mahavira says, "The world is without bounds like a formidable ocean; its cause is action (karma) which is as the seed of the tree. The being (jiva) invested with body, but devoid of judgment, goes like a well sinker ever downwards by the acts it performs, whilst the disembodied being which has attained purity goes ever upwards by its own acts like the builder of a palace. "

Ajiva, the second predicate of existence, comprises objects or properties devoid of consciousness and life. It is regarded as five fold. Out of these, matter is atomic in the final analysis. It possesses the qualities of colour, taste, odour, and touch. All the atoms are supposed to possess souls so that the whole universe seems to be pulsating with life. Time, another ajiva, is eternal. The world has neither an origin nor an end.

As already observed, the karmic particles are mingled with the life monads. It is held that they communicate colours to them which may be white, yellow, flaming red, dove grey, dark blue, or black. These colours are perceived by the Jaina Tirthankaras by virtue of their boundless intuition or omniscience. Ordinarily, black is the characteristic colour of the cruel and the merciless, dark blue that of the greedy and the sensual, dove grey of the reckless and the hot tempered, red of the prudent, yellow of the compassionate and the white of the dispassionate and the impartial.

In the ethics of Mahavira, social life has no place. It is perfect nonactivity in thought, speech, and deed that is recommended. One should be dead to pain and enjoyment and also to all other interests including the intellectual, social, and political to achieve liberation from the bondage of physical existence. Cessation of activity is a stepping stone to the superhuman sphere a sphere which is not only above human beings but also beyond gods.

The doctrine of ahimsa which means renunciation of the will to kill and to damage is an article of faith with the Jains. In the Ayaramgasutta, a Jaina text, it is written, "All saints and Lords... declare thus: One may not kill, nor ill use, nor insult, nor torment, nor persecute any kind of living beings, any kind of creature, any kind of thing having a soul, any kind of beings."

The Jains do not offer bloody sacrifices, do not eat meat, never hunt, and take care that they do not trample on creeping things and insects. The laying down of this commandment is a great thing in the spiritual history of mankind; but it has to be said that the principle is altogether impracticable. It has been assumed that non killing and non harming are possible of fulfilment in this world of ours. Even on purely biological grounds, if on no others, it becomes necessary sometimes to kill as well as to damage both intentionally and unintentionally. "It is more cruel to let domestic animals which one can no longer feed die a painful death by starvation than to give them a quick and painless end by violence. Again and again we see ourselves placed under the necessity of saving one living creature by destroying or damaging another."

Buddhism: As a prince, Buddha's name was Siddhartha and his family name Gautama; his father's name Suddhodana, and his mother's Maya. It is interesting to note that all these navies have meanings from which it is conjectured that Buddha might not have been a historical person. Suddhodana means "he whose food is pure," Maya means "an illusion," Siddhartha means "he by whom the end is accomplished," while Buddha signifies "he by whom all is known." These meanings suggest an allegorical signification, very much in the style of the Pilgrim's Progress. The city of Buddha's birth, Kapilavastu, which has no place in the geography of the Hindus, lends weight to this supposition.

But, in spite of the allegorical interpretation as suggested by the etymology of the names, the historians are pretty well agreed in regarding Buddha as a historical person who lived six centuries before Christ and who was so much disturbed by the transience and miseries of the earthly existence that he renounced his power and wealth and devoted himself to solitary meditation. He engaged himself in sacred study under different Brahmins, but dissatisfied with their teaching he retired into solitude. For six years he practised rigorous austerities. Finding their effect upon the body unfavourable to intellectual energy, he desisted from it and adopted a more genial course of life. At last knowledge dawned upon him, and he was in possession of the object of his search, which he communicated to others.

Buddha had no doubt that the mundane existence is replete with sorrows, afflictions, and tribulations. Not only this; he also believed that the misery of life is unending. All fulfilment of desires is attended by pain. The causes of pain, according to Buddha, are not economical, social, or political. They are rooted in the very nature of human life because of the fact that like everything else it is ephemeral and transitory. Even souls are impermanent and our ignorance on this point is the major reason of our suffering. Everything is in a flux. We deceive ourselves into thinking that there is a permanent base for change. It is the Law of Causality which binds together the. continuous vibration and infinite growth which characterize this world. Buddha did not believe in any ontological reality which is permanent and which endures beneath the shifting appearances of the visible world. He also repudiated the Upanisadic view of a permanent Atman and held that search for a permanent soul inside the body is in vain.

Buddha supposed that the law of karma worked into our very nature and that there was no escape from it, the present and the future being the result of the past. Karma is overcome through nirvana which puts an end to the cycle of births and deaths. Nirvana literally means blowing out; hence it suggests extinction. It is sometimes contended that nirvana is not a negative goal; it has a positive aspect as well. It is not simply extinction but also a state of blessedness or perfection. It is a kind of existence, devoid of egoity and full of peace, calm, and bliss.

To achieve nirvana, Buddha recommended a path of self discipline which is eight fold: right faith, right resolve, right speech, right action, right living, right effort, right thought, and right concentration. The emphasis is on right living which is different in the case of a layman and a monk. The first four are applicable to all, while the remaining four are applicable especially to the priestly class.

The practical part of Buddha's system has the same duality. Five negative injunctions, namely, not to kill, not to steal, not to commit adultery, not to lie, and not to use strong drinks, are binding on all, while not to take repasts at improper times, not to witness dances and plays, not to have costly raiments and perfumes, not to have a large bed or quilt, and not to receive gold or silver, are meant for priests only. Similarly, the virtues of charity, purity, patience, courage, contemplation, and silence have to be cultivated by all, but there are twelve observances binding on recluses only. They have to use clothes made of rags picked up from burning grounds, to have only three such suits all sewn by the wearer's own hand, to have a cloak of yellow wool prepared in the same manner, to live only on food given in charity, to take only one meal daily, never to eat or drink after midday, to live in forests, to have no roof but the foliage of trees, to sit with the back supported by the trunk of a tree, to sleep sitting and not lying, never to change the position of the carpet when it has once been spread, and to go once a month to burning grounds to meditate on the vanity of life on the earth.

Thus, there is a complete distinction between the religion for the masses and the discipline for priesthood. The former is quite human while the latter is cold hearted and unnatural. Ultimate release from transmigration can be attained, in the opinion of Buddha, only after one becomes a monk. The religion of the masses is good for human relationship, but not for the liberation of the soul from the cycle of births and deaths. For Buddha a Brahmin is one who cares not for others, who has no relations, who controls himself, who is firmly fixed in the heart of truth, in whom the fundamental evils are extinguished, and who has thrown hatred away from him. No doubt, one finds here an emphasis on the cultivation of ethical virtues but renunciation and condemnation of worldly ties are also evident. Buddha wants men to be occupied with their own redemption and not with that of their fellow beings.

Buddha attaches no importance to such knowledge as entangles a man in the net of life. There are no doubt practical and theoretical systems of knowledge which enable people to acquire skills and crafts, but ultimately they have no value. Says Buddha, "Such knowledge and opinions, if thoroughly mastered, will lead inevitably to certain ends and produce certain results in one's life. The enlightened one is aware of all these consequences and also of what lies behind them. But he does not attach much importance to this knowledge. For within himself he fosters another knowledge the knowledge of cessation, of the discontinuance of worldly existence, of utter repose by emancipation. He has perfect insight into the manner of the springing into existence of our sensations and feelings and their vanishing again with all their sweetness and bitterness, into the way of escape from them altogether, and into the manner in which by non attachment to them through right knowledge of their character he has himself won the release."

The Philosophical Schools of Buddhism: Religiously, Buddhism is divided into two great schools, the orthodox, known as the Hinayana, and the progressive, known as the Mahayana. The former, representing Buddhism, faithfully believes in the relentless working of the law of karma and refuses to assign any place to God in the scheme of things. The individual has to win his liberation through his own efforts by treading the path of rightness as delineated by Buddha. The responsibility of achieving salvation falls squarely on the shoulders of the individual. Before Buddha breathed his last, he advised his followers to work out their salvation with diligence. Philosophically, the Hinayana Buddhism advocates pure phenomenalism, maintaining the non existence of substances or individuals. What exists is merely passing entities, there being feelings but no feeler, thoughts but no thinker.

The Hinayana school could not satisfy the masses because of its abstract, dry, and arid approach to the problems of life and also because of its denial of God. Its ethics smacked of egoism, since the Hinayana Buddhist was exclusively concerned with his own emancipation, having nothing to do with the moral needs of others. The Mahayana school sought to rectify these mistakes by taking a more realistic view of religion. Instead of the ideal of personal liberation it recommended the "liberation of all sentient beings" as the summun bonum of human life. It also rehabilitated God, by identifying Buddha with a transcendental reality behind the world of phenomena, Gautama being an incarnation of the Buddha. The Hinayana school denied reality to the Self: but the Mahayana school resuscitated the Self too, by holding that it was the little individual self that was false and not the Self of all beings, the one transcendental Self (Mahatman).

The Philosophical Schools of Buddhism: Though Buddha had an abhorrence for metaphysical jargon, his religion being an ethical system with no supernaturalism yet his followers failed to keep themselves away from ontological and epistemological questions of abstruse nature. Consequently, there emerged four schools, two under the Hinayana and two under the Alahavana sect, on the basis of their metaphysical predilections.

The Madhyamika School of Sunyavada: According to this school, everything is void and the universe is totally devoid of reality. In support of their contention they argue that the knower, the known, and knowledge are interdependent and if any one in the series is proved false it will entail the falsity of the other two. It is maintained by the proponents of this theory that cases of illusion demonstrate the falsity of knowledge; consequently, the truth of the other two factors in this epistemological trinity cannot be guaranteed.

The Yogacara School of Subjective Idealism: This school was one with the Madhyamika in dismissing all external reality as illusion, but could not see eye to eye with it in respect of mind. It was urged that if mind was pronounced unreal along with matter, then all reasoning and thinking would be false. It would be as impossible to establish your own position as to demolish the position of your adversary, once mind is dismissed as maya. To this school, mind is the only reality; the external objects exist simply as ideas. No object can be known without consciousness of it; hence the objects cannot be proved to have an existence independent of consciousness.

The Sautrantika School of Representationism: This school believes in the existence of mind and also of the external world. The Sautrantikas maintain that illusions cannot be explained in the absence of external objects. Moreover the objects do not exist as ideas; rather our ideas are copies of objects which exist by their own nature.

The Vaibhasika School: This school recognizes the reality of mind as well as of matter and further holds like the neo realists of the West that unless the object is perceived, there is no means of certifying that the so called copy is a faithful representation of the original. The only plausible position in that case would be subjective idealism of the Yogacara school; and if for some reason the theory of subjective idealism is untenable, then it should be conceded that objects are capable of being perceived directly.

Systems of Indian Philosophy: There are six systems which are recognized as orthodox. Each is called a darsana or a view because it embodies a way of looking at the world. They are generally treated together, in pairs. The first pair includes the Nyaya or the school of Logic founded by Gautama and the Atomic school founded by Kanada. There are, however, reasons to believe that the two systems were organized into one in the fourth/tenth century long after the Muslims had settled down in India and had made their mark on Indian thought and culture. The analysis of the ideas incorporated into the systems after their unification will amply bear this out. Accordingly, these two systems will receive separate treatment after the other systems. The remaining four systems were organized into two pairs before the advent of the Muslims and will be discussed together. While discussing these systems we shall have to ignore such thinkers as were born after the second/eighth century and whose contributions show unmistakable signs of Muslim influence. Their thinking is not purely Indian; it is at least not on conservative lines. There are radical departures both in the understanding of problems and their solutions, and these departures can be accounted for on no other hypothesis than the impact of Muslim thought on the Indian mind.

The first pair to be mentioned will include the Sankhya or Numeral system said to be founded by Kapila and the Yoga or the Mystic system founded by Patanjali; the second pair will include the Purva Mimamsa, the original decider, founded by Jaimini, and the Uttara Mimamsa, the second decider, said to be founded by Vyasa.

The authors of the various schools as given above are generally accepted by the Hindus as real, but there is a great deal of doubt about their authenticity. Rene Guenon writing about Gautama, the author of Nyaya, says, "This name should not be taken as referring to any single individual and it is not accompanied in this case by any biographical details of the vaguest kind... the name denotes what is really an `intellectual aggregate' made up of all those who over a period... devoted themselves to one and the same study.... The same could be said of the proper names that we find associated in a similar way with each of the other darsanas."

Sankhya and Yoga: These two systems are the outer and the inner aspects of a single discipline. In the Bhagavad Gita there is written, "Puerile and unlearned people speak of `enumerating knowledge' (Sankhya) and the `practice of introvert concentration' (Yoga) as distinct from each other, yet anyone firmly established in either gains the fruit of both. The state attained by the followers of the path of enumerating knowledge is attained also through the exercises of introvert concentration. He truly sees who regards as one the intellectual attitude of enumerating knowledge and the practice of concentration." Sankhya is a theoretical system describing the elements of human nature, its bondage and release, while Yoga is a practical discipline to gain the same end through the practice of yogic exercises.

Notes: According to Zimmer, "The main conceptions of this dual system are (i) that the universe is founded on an irresoluble, dichotomy of `life monads' (purusa) and lifeless matter (prakrti), (ii) that `matter,' though fundamentally simple and uncompounded, nevertheless exfoliates, or manifests itself, under three distinctly differentiated aspects (the so called gunas) which are comparable to the three strands of a rope, and (iii) that each one of the `life monads' (purusa) associated with matter is involved in the bondage of an endless `round of transmigration' (samsara)."

Prakrti is a primal entity, out of which the physical universe with all its infinite diversity has evolved. It is all pervasive and complex. Its complexity is due to the fact that it is constituted of three gunas, namely, sattya, rajas, and tamas, which, though different, nevertheless work harmoniously to produce an ordered world. Sattya means what is pure, rajas signifies what is active, while tamas stands for what offers resistance. These three gunas are present in every object since the effect cannot be other than its material cause. This doctrine, according to which nothing new can originate and the effects should be entirely determined. by their antecedent factors, goes by the name of "the doctrine of pre existent effect." The gunas do not combine in the same ratio in every object and that accounts for the multiplicity and the infinite diversity of things.

The first thing to evolve from the prakrti was the intellect, which in turn produced egoism or individuality. From the sattya aspect of egoism there proceeded five sense organs, while from the tamers aspect there emerged five motor organs. Thus, the first to emerge in the course of evolution were those objects which parusa needed. Out of the simple and subtle elements arose gross elements, e.g., space emerged from elemental sound, air from space and elemental tough, fire from these two and elemental colour, so on and so forth.

So far we have naturalism in its most aggressive form, but it is diluted by its recognition of purusa alongside prakrti as an equally important principle in the constitution of the world. Purusa is manifold and simple in contradistinction to prakrti which is single and complex. How can two principles of contradictory attributes come to work together, is a difficult point in this theory.

Purusa is often defined as a pure spirit by virtue of the fact that it is non matter, and yet it has no spirituality about itself. It can be defined only negatively: it is without attributes, without motion "imperishable, inactive, and impassive." After a person acquires full knowledge of the purusa, he becomes indifferent to both the subtle and the gross elements of his material existence. When death comes finally, the subtle and the gross elements dissolve, but the purusa continues to exist having now been released once for all from the clutches of the gunas. This is "final aloofness," or isolation, the summum bonum of yogic practices.

"Yoga consists in the (intentional) stoppage of the spontaneous activities of the life staff." As the mind is in constant commotion, it assumes the shapes of the objects it cognizes. In order to understand its true nature all impulses from within and without have to be stopped. The life monad is so to say in the bondage of life and consciousness; it has to reveal all the processes of the subtle and gross body. In its own nature it is propertyless, without beginning and end, infinite, and all pervading. The only problem with man is to realize his actual freedom by separating the life monad from all distraction and turbulent conditions. To achieve this objective the Sankhya Yoga philosophy prescribes the suppression of right notions arising from correct perceptions, and wrong notions due to misapprehensions, fantasy, sleep, and memory. When this is accomplished, the mind is stilled.

The goal is isolation which becomes possible when the purity of contemplation equals the purity of the life monad. This is explained by a commentator of Patanjali in the words, "When the contemplative power (sattya) of the thinking substance is freed from the defilement of the active power (rajas) and the force of inertia (tamas) and has no further task than that involved in transcending the presented idea of difference between itself (sattya) and the life monad (purusa) and when the interior seeds of hindrances (klesa) have all been burnt, then the contemplative power (sattya) enters into a state of purity equal to that of the life monad. This purity is neither more nor less than the cessation of the false attribution of experience to the life monad. That is the life monad's isolation. Then the purusa having its light within itself becomes undefiled and isolated."

According to the Yoga philosophy, hindrances to the manifestation of the true nature of the purusa are ignorance, I am I, attachment or sympathy, repugnance or hatred, and the will to live. Moreover, the interplay of the gunas is a source of confusion. All these can be eradicated through asceticism, learning, and devotion, or complete surrender to the will of God. Asceticism rids a yogi of passions and spiritual inertia; recitation of holy prayers initiates him in the art of religious detachment; while complete surrender to the will of God develops him spiritually, by making him regard God as the real cause of his achievements. Through this programme, the klesa, i. e., hindrances and impediments, are reduced to nothingness, the rajas and tamas are destroyed, and sattya alone remains to recognize the life monad in its pristine glory. The yogic exercises of starving and torturing the body are calculated to eradicate not only the conscious but also the unconscious tendencies of our biological existence and so to attune the personality to a supersensible type of experience.

Through meditation and self torturing practices one reaches knowledge of the Truth, "Neither I am, nor is aught mine, nor do I exist." Having gained this knowledge the purusa in peace and inaction contemplates nature which is of no interest to him, and at death attains its true life of isolation.

Mimamsa Purva and Uttara: The object of the Purva-Mimasa, also called the Karama Mimamsa, i.e, Action Investigation, is to reach certainty on the subject of dharma or the religious duty of the Hindus, chiefly about the sacrifices and the methods of offering them. In course of time there came into vogue variant opinions and customs for the performance of every kind of ceremony. The Brahmins had laid down very detailed instructions with regard to sacrificial duties but alongside them there had emerged local and family customs and conventions. These two were often hard to reconcile. Hence the problem was to bring the Brahmanic instructions intro harmony with one another and also with the existing family and local customs. A further problem was to discover in these customs a meaning that should satisfy every new generation.

The Purva Mimamsa consists of twelve books, all full of positive and negative injunctions about principal and subordinate rites concerning sacrifices. A cursory perusal of the Mimamsa clearly shows that the work is principally concerned with the interpretation of those Vedic texts as are required for sacrificial purposes and that it raises only incidentally, if at all, genuine metaphysical questions. It does raise the question of the absolute authority of the Vedas together with the doctrine of their eternity, and discusses in this connection the problem of the eternity of sound and the relation between the sound of a word and its meaning.

The Purva Mimamsa is not a treatise on philosophy. Nevertheless, certain metaphysical ideas are implied, or find incidental expression in it. A charge of atheism is often brought against this system. The advocates of the Purva Mimamsa say, "There is no God, or Maker of the world; nor has the world any sustainer or destroyer, for every man obtains a recompense in conformity with his own work. Nor indeed is there any maker of the Vedas, for their words are eternal. Their authoritativeness is self demonstrated; since it has been established from all eternity, how can it be dependent upon anything but itself? " But in Max Muller's view this charge is based upon a misconception. The system does not attribute the fruit of sacrificial acts to any divine agency, nor does it make God responsible for the injustice that seems to prevail in the world. Further, it gives evidence of a firm faith in the operation of the law of cause and effect and, consequently, ascribes the inequalities of the world to the working of good and bad deeds. But all this would not make the system atheistic. It simply proves that the Mimamsa has an unorthodox conception of God. Max Muller's contention seems to conflict with the Mimamsa itself, for the latter says, "Wherefore God ? The world itself suffices for itself."

Uttara Mimamsa or Vedanta: The term Vedanta literally means the end of the Vedas or the doctrines set forth in the closing chapters of the Vedas which are the Upanisads. The Uttara Mimamsa or Later Investigations as against Purva Mimamsa which are Prior Investigations is usually called Vedanta sutras or Brahma sutras. The latter name is given to indicate that Brahman is the spirit embodied in the universe. The work is attributed to Badarayana, but in reality many writers of different times appear to have made their contributions towards its compilation. In five hundred and five sutras which consist mostly of two or three words each, the whole system is developed. The sutras are, however, unintelligible by themselves and leave everything to the interpreters.

The Vedanta sutras discuss the whole theory of the Brahman in four chapters. The first chapter deals with the nature of the Brahman and his relation to the world and the individual souls; the second is polemical; the third deals with the ways and means of attaining Brahman vidya; and the fourth treats of the fruit of Brahman vidya and after life.

Badarayana believes both in the eternity and infallibility of the Vedas. He recognizes two sources of knowledge: sruti and smrti or perception and inference, and maintains that sruti is the basis for smrti. Similarly, he draws a hard and fast line between two realms: one amenable to reason and the other lying beyond it. The area where reason is competent is that of prakrti together with its manifestations, while the realm of Brahman lies beyond the reach of discursive reasoning. Reason can flourish among properties, relations, and characteristics, while Brahman is devoid of all these things and, therefore, cannot be reached through inferential knowledge. The only way to reach the Brahman is to cultivate intuition through meditation and devotion. It will reveal that the Brahman is the basis of reality: the material as well as the final cause of the universe. In creating the world God had no purpose to fulfil; what seems to be His activity is nothing but sport. God is omniscient, formless, and one, in whom the prakrti and the purusaof the Sankhya system combine, both being manifestations or modes of the same Ultimate Reality.

After creating the elements, Brahman entered into them and determined the characteristic manner of their development and production of other things. The Brahman, as it were, transforms Himself into everything that is caused by Him since cause and effect must have similar natures. Two illustrations are given to prove the identity of cause and effect; one is drawn from an inanimate object and the other from an animate object. It is said that when a piece of cloth is rolled up its real nature remains hidden, but when it is spread out it can be known truly. Likewise a person is paralyzed if his breath is held but becomes active the moment his breath is released. In both these cases the qualities of the antecedent are different from those of the consequent although the object is the same, which shows that despite differences the cause and the effect remain identical. Brahman and the world are not disparate in spite of differences. The wooden table is not different from the wood in its essential nature; similarly, Brahman is not different from the multiform objects of the universe.

The world is a sport or lila of the Brahman, which means that it is without purpose and without significance. It is hard to assign any meaning to the universe, since Vedantism declares, "Brahman is true, the world is false, the soul is Brahman and nothing else." And again, "There is nothing worth gaining there is nothing worth enjoying, there is nothing worth knowing but Brahma alone, for he who knows Brahman is Brahman."

In calling the world a sport there is however no implication that God created sufferings for mankind to take pleasure out of them. This would be a very uncharitable view and altogether cynical. Sufferings, woes, and ills of men as well as of other objects, both animate and inanimate, are the result of their own karma a law of moral causation which works inexorably and leaves no scope for the interference of divine or non divine agencies. Likewise all evils and sins are due to karma; they are not caused by Brahman.

The self is concealed within five sheaths, that is to say, five superimposed psycho somatic layers which should be torn away through ethical discipline and self denial. Avidya (nescience) is lack of insight into the nature of reality and is a major hindrance in the path of moksa or release. It is an article of faith with Vedantism that liberation can be obtained through knowledge. Since the Self is with us, though concealed and hidden behind five sheaths, when true knowledge is gained it will be seen that one realizes one's own true nature. This realization can be effected through yogic practices, critical thought, or any other orthodox way. Ethical discipline is also directed to the same end. Its object is to cleanse the soul through rigorous self discipline and impeccable conduct, in a spirit of non attachment.

The highest knowledge is Brahman vidya or vision of God which is attained through the realization of the Self. After an individual soul has reached Brahman there is no return for the liberated soul. This goal is expressed through the oft quoted verse from the Upanisads; "He who realizes Brahman through knowing becomes Brahman."

The Nyaya System: As already observed, because of the singular absence or deficiency of historical data, little is known of Gautama, the author of Nyaya. He is as much a subject of fanciful legend as Kapila, the author of the Sankhya system.

The word nyaya means "propriety" or "fitness." The system undertakes to declare the method of arriving at that knowledge of truth the fruit of which, it promises, is the chief end of man. The name is also used in a more limited application to denominate the proper method of setting forth an argument. This has led to the practice of calling the Nyaya the Hindu logic, which by the way does not adequately describe the scope of the system. According to the author of the system, "Supreme felicity is attained through knowledge about the true nature of the sixteen categories (Padarthas)."

The first work of the Nyaya system consists of sixty aphorisms, and the first sutra gives a list of the subjects to be discussed. These are sixteen in number: (1) pramana or the means by which right knowledge may be gained; (2) prameya or the object of thought; (3) doubt; (4) motive; (5) instance or example; (6) dogma or determinate truth; (7) argument or syllogism; (8) confutation; (9) ascertainment; (10) controversy; (11) jangling; (12) objection or cavilling; (13) fallacy; (14) perversion, (15) futility; (16) conclusion or the confounding of an adversary.

Of the sixteen categories the first two are important; others are only subsidiary indicating the course which a discussion may take from the start to the finish, i.e., from the enunciation of the doubt to the confounding of the doubter.

The first category by the name of pramana signifies proof or evidence, and denotes the legitimate means of knowledge within the rational order. It enumerates four kinds of proofs, namely, perception by the senses (pratyaksa); inference (anumana); comparison (upamana); and verbal authority (sabda)including revelation and tradition. Inference, it says, is of three kinds: from cause to effect, from effect to cause, and by analogy.

The argument which is also called nyaya consists of five constituent members. These are: (1) the proposition to be proved (pratijnia), (2)the reason justifying this proposition (hetu), (3)the example cited in support of the reason (udahrana), (4)the application of the first proposition to the particular case in question (upanaya), and (5) the result (nigamana), which is a statement of the fact that the proposition has been proved.

A typical Indian syllogism would be as follows

1. Yonder mountain has fire.
2. For it has smoke.
3. Whatever has smoke has fire.
4. Yonder mountain has smoke such as is invariably accompanied by fire.
5. Therefore, yonder mountain has fire.

The linguistic form is not considered necessary to syllogism. This is common to all forms of Indian logic.

According to the Nyaya, a notion or a concept can be either right or wrong. In the first case it is obtained through perception or inference or comparison or revelation. A wrong notion is one which is not derived from proof and originates either from doubt or from false premises or from error. A wise man avoids these as well as passions and aversions and is profoundly indifferent to all action.

Blessedness is deliverance from pain. The primary evil is pain. There are twenty one varieties of evil which spring from the organs of sense, from the objects of sense, from mental apprehensions, and even from pleasure. "The soul attains to this deliverance by knowledge, by meditation on itself, by not earning fresh merit or demerit through actions sprung from desire, and by becoming free from passions through knowledge of the evil inherent in objects. It is knowledge... and not virtue which obtains final deliverance from the body."

The Nyaya is predominantly intellectual and analytical. Its value lies in its methodology or the theory of knowledge on which it builds its philosophy. This theory it applies not only to one system but to all systems with modifications here and there. Chatterjee and Datta observe that "the Nyaya theory of pluralistic realism is not so satisfying as its logic. Here we have a common sense view of the world as a system of independent realities.... It does not give us a systematic philosophy of the world in the light of one universal absolute principle.

The Indian syllogism bears a close resemblance to Aristotelian syllogism especially when it is simplified or abridged, consisting either of the last three or the first three terms only. It is, therefore, suggested by a good many historians that either Aristotle or the builders of the Nyaya system drew inspiration from the other. It is also possible that the obligation is mutual.

The Vaisesika System: Vaisesika is derived from visesa which means difference, signifying thereby that multiplicity and not unity lies at the basis of the universe. It is expounded by Kanada in the Vaisesika Sutra which contains about five hundred and fifty aphorisms. Book 1 discusses the five categories substance, quality, action, community or genus, and particularity; Book 2 deals with the substances earth, water, air, ether, space, and time; Book 3 is concerned with the problems of mind and self and also touches the theory of inference; Book 4 is about the atomic theory and discusses the nature of body and the visibility of quality; Book 5 deals with motion; Book 6 contains duties of the four stages of life; Book 7 treats of quality, the atomic theory, the self, and inherence together; Books 8 and 9 deal with perception and inference; while Book 10 is concerned with causality and other related questions.

A fundamental assumption of this system is that objects are independent of the perceiving mind and also of one another. Philosophically, the doctrine may be called pluralistic realism. The entire world of experience can be divided into nine dravya or substances together with their properties and relations: These substances are earth, water, fire, air, akasa, time, space, self, and manas. Besides substances which simply provide a framework for the whole universe there are padartha, or categories, seven in number, namely, guna, karma, visesa, samavaya, samanya, abhava, and dravya, which can be translated as quality, action, individuality, necessary relation, universals, negation, and substance. Qualities depend upon substances, but they can be independently conceived and so exist by their own nature. No distinction is recognized between mental and material qualities or between the primary and secondary qualities. Quite consistent with its pluralistic standpoint, the doctrine holds that the substances reveal their nature through the qualities in which they differ and not in which they agree.

In regarding earth, air, water, and fire as substances, what is implied is that the entire structure of the universe can be interpreted in terms of material causes which are supersensible. The ultimate stuff of which this universe is made is the mass of atoms that are round, extremely minute, invisible, incapable of division, eternal in themselves but not in their aggregate form. Even mind (manas) is regarded as an atom extremely small, because of which only one sensation can be conveyed to the soul at one time.

Vaisesika is basically a dualistic philosophy inasmuch as it recognizes the eternality both of atoms and souls. In fact every Hindu system regards matter as eternal. The only exception is the school of the Vedantists which takes matter as the illusive manifestation of the one Supreme Brahman who is Himself the all.

According to Kanada, the summum bonum for man is nothing but deliverance from pain, which can be achieved through knowledge, resulting in the soul getting into a state of a tranquil, unconscious passivity.

The Influence of Islam on Hinduism-From the account of the six systems of Indian philosophy given above, such writers as were born after the advent of Islam in India have been excluded; not that they were in any way less important than those who saw the light of the day before the first /seventh century, but because their thinking shows unmistakable signs, implicit as well as explicit, of Muslim impact. Details of this impact have been provided in a separate chapter of this volume. Here it will suffice to say that the impact was very deep, firm, and abiding, and left no aspect of Indian thought untouched.

The contact of the Muslims with the Indians began as early as the end of the first/seventh century, and still continues to the advantage of both. Islam was introduced into the Indian sub continent by Arab traders; it was propagated by mystics and saints; and it was established by Muslim rulers of various dynasties who made India their home like several other Muslim immigrants.

The Muslims brought with them their ideology, their philosophy and religion, their beliefs and practices, and, above all, an unconquerable passion to share this wisdom with others. The Sufis who were thinkers of no mean order succeeded by their example and precept in imparting to the natives that ideology and philosophy which the Muslims had expounded from their understanding of the Quran, the hadith, and the Sunnah.

Muhammad bin Qasim is ranked as the first Muslim who entered India as a conqueror in 94/712. His example was followed by a long line of Muslim rulers who wielded the sceptre of authority over the Indian sub continent till 1274/1857, when Indian "mutiny" took place and the Britishers found a splendid excuse to wipe off the last vestige of the Muslim Empire. During a period of one thousand years when the Indian sub continent lay prostrate at the feet of the Muslim emperors, many of whom enjoyed full autocratic powers, it is very unlikely that the culture and philosophy which they cherished and treasured should have left no imprint on the thoughts and beliefs of the native population.

There was, however, no imposition of one culture over another. Culture can never be introduced by the sword, no matter how long and sharp. What happened on the Indian soil was not the replacement of one culture by another but an amalgamation of the two. It was a case of the willing acceptance of the salient features of Muslim culture and making them a part and parcel of the culture of India. What Sankara and Ramanuja did in the sphere of philosophy was done by others in the fields of religion; ethics, and social polity. The result was a great upheaval in the world of Hindu thought. A re evaluation and a re appraisal of old values and thoughts took place on a gigantic scale. Monotheism was stressed and so was universal brotherhood of mankind and a positive approach to life. Casteless society became the goal of social reforms and the Sudras, the accursed and the condemned, were accorded the right to live like others. All this was the product of the impact of Islam on Hinduism.

There is evidence to show that the Nyaya and the Vaiseska were organized into one system after Islam had firmly entrenched itself in India. Not only were the two systems welded into one, they also became monotheistic and advanced for the first time in the history of Hindu thought what are known as the Hindu proofs for the existence of God.

2

PRE-ISLAMIC CHINESE THOUGHT

In the present chapter we shall attempt to survey some of the salient features of Chinese philosophy avoiding any specialized or detailed discussion of the individual schools or of the philosophical technicalities involved. Our purpose is to present, in brief compass, an account of Chinese philosophical thought indicating a number of its peculiar characteristics and its apparent major limitations. This, then, will be a summary of the outstanding peculiarities of Chinese philosophy prior to the arrival of any significant foreign influence.

First, a few words with respect to the period of Chinese philosophy we are covering, that of the Chou Dynasty (1122 ? 256 B.C.). The last centuries of the Chou were marked by political and social turmoil associated with the disintegration of feudalism. The Chinese world was torn by internecine warfare, old political powers were overturned and old values challenged or discarded. During this "time of troubles," to use Toynbee's term China produced a great variety of original schools of philosophical thought, such as Confucianism, Taoism, Mohism, and Legalism as well as a Chinese version of Epicureanism, the so called Logicians, and the Yin Yang school. Because of the creative freshness and richness of the later Chou, it may be regarded as the classical period of Chinese philosophy. Our discussion is, perforce limited to these classical philosophies and their spirit; Chinese medieval and modern philosophies are not delineated, nor is Buddhism in China, nor Chinese Buddhism.

The primary reason for this concentration on the Chou philosophies is that they represent the indigenous Chinese schools of philosophy before they were affected by the advent of other philosophical or religious idea, for example. Buddhism and its attendant Indian metaphysics. Moreover, though some of these schools did not exercise a lasting influence on subsequent Chinese intellectual life, as was the case with Legalism which passed into oblivion with the collapse of the shortlived Ch'in Dynasty (221 207 B.C.), and with Mohism which died out a few centuries after the death of Mo Tzu, its founder, other schools, such as Confucianism, Taoism, and elements of the Yin Yang school, persisted throughout the history of Chinese philosophy. Confucianism, though eclipsed at times, slowly gained a predominant position and became a powerful force in the moulding and direction of Chinese civilization. While these latter schools survived, the others passed into insignificance. For instance, the school of the Logicians never exercised any great influence on the development of later Chinese philosophy. Also, Yang Chu's thought, somewhat similar to the philosophy of Epicurus, was never a threat to the other schools since it consisted more of an attitude toward life than a philosophy of existence. It was too individualistic, too self centred for wide acceptance by the Chinese.

To appreciate adequately the peculiar features of Chinese philosophical thought, it is important that one be cognizant of certain facts of Chinese geography, economics, and sociology with regard to its emergence and development. The distinguished contemporary Chinese philosopher and historian of Chinese philosophy, Fung Yu lan, discusses all three topics at considerable length. From the earliest times the Chinese considered the world and their land, t'ien hsia (all under heaven), to be one and the same. Because of its unique geographical position a vast continental land mass bounded by a great mountain range, desert, and the ocean the early culture of China appears to have developed in comparative isolation from that of other great centres of civilization. At any rate, it seems fairly certain that the Chinese thinkers of the later Chou were not in a position comparable to that of their Greek philosophical contemporaries vis a vis the intellectual, philosophical, religious, and scientific thought of the Egyptian and Mesopotamian civilizations In developing their philosophies, the Greeks were undoubtedly stimulated by other highly civilized peoples. An ancient Greek historian once noted that the Greeks were children compared to the Egyptians. In contrast, in the development of ancient Chinese philosophical thought, there does not seem to have been any significant cross fertilization from other centres of civilization outside the Chou world.

The Greeks and the Chinese differed considerably in their respective economic conditions. The Greeks were a commercial people to a great extent and were, therefore, brought into contact with a wide varietv of ideas, customs, lands and peoples. Their conception of the world recognized the existence of other great civilizations. The Chinese, however, were mainly an agricultural people. None of the Chinese philosophers ventured beyond Chou China. There was, in consequence, a definite insularity attached to Chinese philosophical thought. In addition to this insularity of thought, there was close affinity between the Chinese thinker and the Chinese peasant; both were attached to the land. The Chinese scholar philosopher was usually a landowner, while the peasant cultivated the land. "Hence, throughout Chinese history, social and economic thinking and policy have centred around the utilization and distribution of land."

In a sense, ancient Chinese philosophy may be said to have had an intimate association with, if not absolutely conditioned by, the peasant mentality. The Chinese thinkers' "reactions to the universe and their outlook on life were essentially those of the farmer." With the aid of their learning and genius, the Chinese sages were able "to express what an actual farmer felt but was incapable of expressing himself." Realization of this fact may go long way towards explaining the predominantly practical tone of Chinese philosophical thought. The peculiar problems connected with Chinese economic life tended to limit the spectrum of values in philosophy. Though Confucianism and Taoism are "poles apart from one another, yet they are also the two poles of one and the same axis. They both express, in one way or another, the aspirations and inspirations of the farmer." Confucianism stressed family obligations, while Taoism emphasized the power, beauty, and mystery of nature.

Just as geographical conditions and agricultural life have exerted an influence on the formation and character of Chinese philosophy, so also has done the Chinese social system, particularly the family. A striking feature of Chinese philosophical thought is its preoccupation with problems relating to the ethics of the family and the Chinese social system. The most outstanding example of this preoccupation is to be found in Confucianism. "A great deal of Confucianism," Fung Yu lan asserts, "is the rational justification or theoretical expression of this social system." The mental outlook of the Chinese farmer as well as his values tended to limit the range of philosophical speculation. "The way of life of the farmers is to follow nature. They admire nature and condemn the artificial, and in their primitivity and innocence, they are easily made content. They desire no change, nor can they conceive of any change." Here one may discern the source of strength of much of Chinese classical philosophy as well as its weakness. It reflected the attitudes, interests, prejudices, and values of the Chinese peasant.

A study of classical Chinese philosophy discloses that it possesses at least four highly distinctive features which may be a reflection of the dominance of this peasant mentality: lack of metaphysics, dearth of logical sophistication, preoccupation with ethics, and a regressive theory of history.

We shall comment on the last feature first. The traditional Chinese theory of history is regressive. According to the Chinese, the Golden Age of mankind was in the dim remoteness of the past and all subsequent history has been a tragic degeneration from the ancient ideal age. The Chinese sages sought to find the proper path which would enable mankind to recapture the peace, justice, and harmony of that Golden Age. Associated with this regressive conception of history was the tendency of many of the classical schools to antedate the founder of a rival school of thought. Apparently, in order to make a school or a point of view more attractive and authoritative, it was felt necessary to increase its antiquity. The Confucianists, for example, referred to the mythological rulers, Yao and Shun; the Mohists, in support of their philosophical position, went back beyond Yao and Shun to the legendary Yu; and the Taoists, for their part, went beyond Yu to the mythical Yellow Emperor. The more ancient the beginning of a school, the more was it to be trusted.

The classical Chinese philosophers, for the most part, manifested an aversion to metaphysical speculation. The

Confucianists, Confucius (551 479 B.C.); Mencius (371 289 B.C.), and Hsun Tzu (298 c. 238 B.C.), showed little interest in or even awareness of metaphysical questions. Confucius was not concerned with understanding the character of Ultimate Reality nor with epistemological problems; his concern was with social and political philosophy. Mencius lacks an interest in metaphysics as such, as does Hsun Tzu. At the risk of over simplification, one could say that Confucianism was primarily an educational philosophy. Though Confucius was silent on whether or not human nature was good or evil, and, though Mencius and Hsun Tzu differ greatly on this point the former maintaining that human nature is good, and the latter, that it is evil all three agree on the need and efficacy of education for inculcating or developing ethical conduct. Subtle metaphysical disquisitions are lacking in all three.

Taoism, as set forth in the Tao Te Chingand the works of Chuang Tzu (399 c. 295 B.C.), frequently approaches a metaphysical analysis of reality, but, more characteristically, ends in a hazy mysticism or appears to be fascinated with the enunciation of paradoxes. The Taoist saying that he who knows cannot say and that he who says does not know the Tao (the Way, or Ultimate Reality) is not particularly conducive to metaphysical discourse.

Mo Tzu (c. 479 c. 438 B.C.), founder of Mohism, does not show any interest in metaphysical matters as such. His philosophy stressed an "all-embracing love" based upon utility. He condemned aggressive war and urged an altruism based upon mutual self interest because the results were more pleasant and useful to society. His reasons were practical and devoid of any metaphysical justification.

As for the Logicians, for example, Hui Shih (c. 380 305 B. C.) and Kung sun Lung (380 250 B.C.?), their interest comes nearer to being metaphysical than any other school with the possible exception of the Yin Yang. The Logicians, frequently referred to as the School of Names (Ming Chia), were chiefly concerned with problems relating to the relativity and changeableness of all phenomena, as was Hui Shih, or with the concept of universals the "names" of things which, according to Kung sun Lung, were absolute and unchangeable. Hui Shih contended that concrete things were undergoing constant change and were, therefore, different from one instant to the next. Kung sun Lung insisted that the "names" of things, similar to Platonic ideas, were absolute and unchangeable. In order to substantiate his position, he employed epistemological arguments.

One of his most famous arguments is contained in his discussion concerning "a white horse is not a horse." Many of the Logicians arguments posed paradoxes and logical conundrums and, for this reason, were disparaged by the Confucianists. For example, the great Chinese historian of the Han, Ssu ma T'an, himself a Confucianist described the work of the Logicians as "minute examinations of trifling points in complicated and elaborate statements, which made it impossible for others to refute their ideas." Because of the lack of interest in metaphysical questions peculiar to Chinese classical philosophers in general, the influence of the Logicians was not especially significant in the development of later Chinese thought.

The Legalists, whose most important representative is Han Fei Tzu (died 233 B. C.), were not concerned with problems of metaphysics, logic, or epistemology. Their fundamental concern was political: What happens when a ruler is weak, wicked, or incompetent? How is a State to be unified and governed? For the Legalists, the answer was impersonal law in the place of personal ethics or moral principles. The Legalists, though at odds with the Confucianists, show a similarly overriding interest in the practical aspects of political and social philosophy. Metaphysical speculation is a pastime which neither of these classical schools pursued.

Tsou Yen (305 240 B.C.) of the Yin Yang school probably represents the extent to which the Chinese were willing to pursue metaphysical speculation without the pressure of foreign ideas. Certainly the Taoist and Yin Yang represent indigenous Chinese metaphysical thinking prior to the advent of Buddhism. The Yin Yang school, however, lacks genuine metaphysical profundity and, in essence, appears to be based on a dualistic theory of the interaction of the female and male principles of the universe, the Yin and the Yang respectively. Neither the Yin Yang school nor Taoism possesses a meta physical presentation approaching the works of Plato or Aristotle. One has the feeling that the thinkers of these two schools educed one or two ideas and then used them uncritically and mechanically to explain various phenomena.

In general, Chinese philosophers either ignored metaphysics or showed only a spasmodic interest in understanding, logically and systematically, the nature and character of the Ultimate Reality. Only after the introduction of Buddhism did the Chinese philosophers concern themselves seriously with metaphysics. "Even the basic metaphysical problems, such as God, universals, space and time, matter and spirit, were either not discussed, except in Buddhism, or discussed only occasionally, and then always for the sake of ethics." Chinese thinkers confined themselves to social and political thought; they had always in mind the capability of their respective philosophies for practical implementation. As metaphysics was, in the main, slighted or ignored, so were epistemological problems.

An examination of the history of Chinese philosophy illustrates plentifully that Chinese philosophers occupied themselves with questions of human adjustment to nature or the individual's adjustment to society. The Taoists stressed the former, the Confucianists the latter. The Taoists regarded society as unnatural and unnecessary for Good Life. In this respect it resembles Romanticism. Confucianism maintains that society is natural and necessary for the life of a human being. Society permits a man to satisfy his ethical obligations and also affords him an opportunity to enrich his life with learning, art, music, and moral example. Society is not only a structure of ethical and social relationships but also a product of man's cultural heritage. Man as a member of society is able to appreciate tradition, literature, ceremonies all those things which are not absolutely necessary for physical survival but which are nevertheless the very essence of civilized, cultured existence. As Taoism lauds the state of nature, it is akin to Romanticism; Confucianism is allied to Classicism.

In addition to a lack of metaphysical interest or regard for epistemological problems, Chinese philosophical thought, both classical and medieval, is distinguished by its patent deficiency of logical refinement. Chinese philosophical discourses are usually unsystematic and infrequently based upon rigid logical argumentation. The classical philosopher's approach was simple;

his use of an elaborate philosophical method was almost non existent. The Chinese philosopher was primarily engrossed in questions of ethics and with practical matters relating to the ordering of society according to proper moral principles or, as in the case of Taoism, with the way of nature and naturalness. The arguments employed by the philosophers were eminently practical in the sense that they made no appeal to complicated logical analysis, theory, or hypothesis, but appealed to man's common sense. It would be helpful to illustrate the type of "logical" argumentation frequently encountered in the works of Chinese classical philosophers.

The ancients who wished to illustrate illustrious virtue throughout the kingdom, first ordered well their own states. Wishing to order well their states, they first regulated their families. Wishing to regulate their families, they first cultivated their persons. Wishing to cultivate their persons, they first rectified their hearts. Wishing to rectify their hearts they first sought to be sincere in their thoughts. Wishing to be sincere in their thoughts, they first extended to the utmost their knowledge Such extension of knowledge lay in the investigation of things.

"Things being investigated, knowledge became complete. Their knowledge being complete, their thoughts were sincere. Their thoughts being sincere, their hearts were then rectified. Their hearts being rectified, their persons were cultivated. Their persons being cultivated, their families were regulated. Their families being regulated, their states were rightly governed. Their states being rightly governed, the whole kingdom was made tranquil and happy."

That an over emphasis upon logical analysis may inhibit novel ideas and conceptions of reality, few will deny. Too great a reliance upon logical clarity precision, and consistency may lead to sterile thought. The later medieval period in Europe, which was dominated by Scholastic logic, illustrates sufficiently the perils involved in an over estimation of the power and validity of logical analysis. The Scholastics appear to have regrettably misunderstood the value of logic. The medieval Schoolmen erred in the direction of too much emphasis upon logical acuteness whereas, in contradistinction, the Chinese appear to have been blind to the importance of logical refinement.

Whether through disinterest or because of the intrinsic difficulties involved in their own written language (pictographs and ideographs), Chinese philosophers do not seem to have understood the proper role of logic in the acquisition of new knowledge.

In one of his works, Alfred North Whitehead states succinctly the crucial part logic may play in the advancement of the frontiers of human knowledge. "Logic, properly used," he writes, "does not shackle thought.

It gives freedom, and above all, boldness. Illogical thought hesitates to draw conclusions, because it never knows either what it means, or what it assumes, or how far it trusts its own assumptions, or what will be the effect of any modification of assumptions." Continuing, he remarks, "Also the mind untrained in that part of constructive logic which is relevant to the subject in hand will be ignorant of the sort of conclusions which follow from various sorts of assumptions, and will be correspondingly dull in divining the inductive laws". One can hardly fail to agree with Whitehead's observation when studying Chinese classical philosophy as well as much of the philosophy of the later schools in China.

By confining their attention to the world of everyday affairs and common sense, the Chinese savants felt no need to engage in metaphysical speculation in a systematic manner, nor did they feel any desire to indulge in the luxury of logical subtlety. "Therefore," a well known Japanese philosopher comments, "when their philosophy did not vanish in the mist of vague mysticism, as in the ease of Taoism, it tenaciously clung to the agnosticism of everyday experience...." As we study the Taoist classssic, Tao Te Ching, we can readily understand what is meant by a philosophy losing itself "in the mist of vague mysticism," for example:

The Tao that can be told of

Is not the Absolute Tao;

The Names that can be given

Are not Absolute Names.

The Nameless is the origin of Heaven and Earth;

The Named is the Mother of All Things.

Therefore:

Oftentimes, one strips oneself of passion
In order to see the Secret of Life;
Oftentimes, one regards life with passion,
In order to see its manifest results.
These two (the Secret and its manifestations)
Are (in their nature) the same;
They are given different names
When they become manifest.

They may both be called the Cosmic Mystery:

Reaching from the Mystery into the Deeper Mystery
Is the Gate to the Secret of All Life.

This may be an example of "pure speculation" on the part of a Chinese philosopher. If so, one is inclined again to agree with Whitehead who also observed: "Pure speculation, undisciplined by the scholarship of detailed fact or the scholarship of exact logic, is on the whole more useless than pure scholarship, unrelieved by speculation." The Taoists seem to have engaged in "pure speculation" fairly consistently. For their part, the Confucianists emphasized learning and traditional scholarship and the "business" of social existence and its obligations.

Unfortunately, the excessive engrossment in the realm of the commonplace was as detrimental as the marked tendency to mysticism. Both of these extremes tended to stultify the adventure of thought toward new possibilities of achievement. When Chinese thought did not float away in the clouds, it remained earth bound.

Granted that the confluence of the regressive theory of history, the lack of metaphysical speculation, and a pronounced deficiency of logical refinement are distinctive features of classical Chinese philosophy, in general, probably the most significant characteristic the one which may help explain why metaphysics and logic languished is the dominant concern with ethics, for, indeed, there is little doubt that ethics was the main concern of Chinese philosophers. There were but few exceptions during the classical period and even thereafter. Ethics played a major role in Chinese philosophy. "The moral life," Daisetz Teitaro Suzuki writes, "can be said to have been the only philosophical subject which... has seriously interested the Chinese, and which has been considered worthy of their earnest speculation."

By focussing their attention on ethical problems man and his life in society or in harmony with nature the Chinese seriously restricted the content of philosophy in their culture. The special facts of geography, economics, and sociology exercised a strong influence on the Chinese climate of philosophical opinion and may account, as we have noted, for their almost exclusive concentration on ethic. In the final analysis, the classical Chinese philosopher's ideal was the attainment of the Good Life here and now on earth. Most classical thinkers assented to Confucius observation: "While you do not know life, how can you know about death?" The world of the present requires man's full attention, courage, and ingenuity. To the great majority of Chinese philosophers, righteousness, family, economic security, and a stable social order were the main objects of study. During the later periods of Chinese philosophy, though there were occasional lapses from these objectives, they remained permanent features in the Chinese philosophical tradition.

Tang Chung shu (c. 179 104 ? B. C.) was the thinker who contributed most to the ultimate triumph of Confucianism over all the other schools of the Chou in the Han Dynasty (206 B.C. 200 A.D.). Later, it is true that Confucianism was overshadowed by Buddhism during the period of Division (221 589 A.D.) following the break up of the Han Empire, but, to survive in China as an effective, popular force, Buddhism had to accommodate itself to the peculiarities of the Chinese philosophical temper which we have endeavoured to sketch in the preceding pages. Those schools of Buddhism which tried to preserve their original philosophical purity failed to achieve currency in China and, hence, remained ineffectual in Chinese intellectual life. Chinese Buddhism enjoyed immense support because it was Buddhism a la chinoise.

In short, the cardinal limitation of Chinese philosophy stems from its inordinate attention to what Whitehead calls "practical reason." Chinese thought was too closely associated with practical matters, with social adjustment. It was blinded, so to speak, by the affairs of the present. In concentrating on the "practical reason," it neglected "speculative reason" which is allied with logic and systematic discourse. Here we must stress that flights of fancy or sheer contemplation are not to be construed as speculative reason or speculative philosophy. Speculative philosophy seeks a comprehensive understanding of the nature of reality, of God, of man, and of the universe; it strives for a synoptic vision; while, in contrast, practical reason of practical philosophy is concerned with the empirical approach to concrete problems of living and action.

The speculative philosopher, as here described, often regards his opposite as a victim of spurious knowledge, lost in the hustle and bustle of the marketplace. Though the speculative philosopher may frequently be at odds with the practical philosopher, each needs the other. Unfortunately, the practical thinker may be oblivious of what his counterpart is about and may regard his pursuits as quite extraneous to the business of living.

The speculative thinker does not deny the importance of practical reason; he presupposes it and moves along on a plane above the details of the everyday world. It should be noted that the practical activities of the mind produce data which the speculative thinker may utilize in the formulation of new theoretical possibilities, and these in turn may stimulate the activities of the practical philosopher in his desire to implement them in new social programmes and in new technologies. This interplay between these two types of reason or philosophical endeavour constitutes a kind of creative cultural symbiosis. If a civilization neglects either the practical or the speculative type of reason, it will be affected adversely.

China, until the impact of the modern world was felt, was an example of the harmful effects of a pragmatic, utilitarian philosophical orientation. Though authorities differ on the precise amount of weight to be given to its philosophical orientation as a cause of the somnolence of Chinese society, there appears to be agreement that the stress on practicality and social ethics, especially of Confucianism, played a most important role. Science and technology were retarded; there was no speculative thought to challenge the mind towards new heights of achievement; the scholar class, reared on mundane philosophy, was dominant.

This is not to say that Confucian civilization was not a creative and remarkable civilization in many areas; it is merely an endeavour to point out why a certain type of mind did not flourish. Philosophies which concentrate too completely on social adjustment and utility paralyze, if they do not actually destroy, individual creativity and spontaneity in other avenues of human development. Just as civilizations have cramped the individual by a preponderant religious or materialistic orientation, so the same cramping may occur when social utility is made the absolute measure of value. The case of pre modern Chinese civilization may furnish an example of the great danger attached to continually stressing the "social" or "practical" value of thought. The continued vigour of a culture depends upon how well it is replenished with new insights and challenged by new visions of possibility.

A summary sketch of the philosophical thought of pre Islamic Iran is both a difficult and an easy task difficult in the sense that the texts on which this study must be based are not philosophical in the proper sense of the word, but rather theological or sometimes even mythological, and we have to abstract from them their philosophical gist, translating their ideas into modern philosophical terminology, through a rather personal work of interpretation; easy in the sense that, in this work of reinterpretation, we have to renounce completely a solution of the extremely complicated historical problems put by Iranic philology. An attempt at a philosophical reinterpretation of the Mazdaic outlook can be based, in our opinion, exclusively on the only concrete and systematic form of Mazdaism we know: the late Mazdaism of the Pahlavi books of the Sassanian period and the early times of Islam.

The almost insoluble problems raised by the pre Islamic religion (or, according to others, religions) of Iran depend chiefly on the extreme confusion of different types of religiosity local religion, religion of the elite, etc.

Concerning the sources of Mazdaism the only comparatively sure points are (a) that the Gathas of the Avesta are very old and probably date back to Zarathustra himself (e. 700 600 B.C.); and (b) that the most systematic and the richest Pahlavi texts were written in the third/ninth century, i.e., two centuries after the Islamic conquest of Iran.

An accurate dating of the materials between these two chronological limits (the seventh century B. C. and the ninth century A. D.) seems still impossible and all the learned conclusions of the scholars (who often change their minds from year to year) appear to be no more than conjectures. Moreover, the materials chronologically placed between these two dates are sometimes typologically so incongruous that it is very easy to abstract from them a certain type of religion and attribute it to the founder, making of him, e.g., either on idealistic philosopher or a shaman, and then explain the development of Mazdaism that followed either as the decay or a repaganization of a highly philosophical religion, or as a successive theologization of originally mystical perceptions.

It would be no exaggeration to say that the only comprehensive approach to the enormous and extremely varied religio philosophical materials contained in the corpus of Mazdaic texts is to consider them synchronistically as a whole. Though one may not agree with many details of Professor Corbin's theories, one cannot but agree with him when he writes, "A spiritual morphology that attempts a reconstruction and revaluation of the actually living devotion impels us to consider the canonical Avesta, or at least what we possess of it, its ritual, as preserving at its centre the Psalms (Gathas) of Zarathustra and the middle Iranic (Pahlavi) and Parsi translations and commentaries as a whole. Also in this case, it seems that when the believer recites his Bible or when the Liturgy is celebrated, all objections taking historical stratification as a pretext fail to reach their aim. If we always ask: `Whence does it come?' we practically do nothing more than wander here and there, formulating hypotheses vainly following one another. We should rather ask: `At what does it aim ?' Then the soul would answer, accounting for what has been its purpose."

We shall, therefore, make as the basis of the present chapter the latest form of pre Islamic Iranian religiosity, the form represented by the whole corpus of the Avestic and Pahlavi Scriptures possessed and venerated by the Parsecs (not in the sense, of course, that we shall follow necessarily their interpretation of them). For it is safer for a philosopher to interpret an actual and concrete corpus of religious scriptures, than to interpret the ever changing reinterpretation of them made by the historians.

It will be useful, however, to reproduce, as an introduction, the most widely accepted diachronical explanation of the numerous so called "contradictions" of the present Mazdaic corpus, even though it does not seem to be completely satisfactory. The difficulty is that much of the materials generally considered to be very old are much later or at least they "function" in a much later theological organism.

The branch of the Aryans who in about the eleventh century B. C. detached themselves from their brethren, penetrating afterwards into the jungles of India (a natural place for magic and richest mytho poetical phantasy) and made the yellow and dry plateau of Iran their country, had obviously brought with them their naturalistic religion, clearly delineated in the Vedas and rather similar to that of old Rome and Greece. The sacrifices of animals (e. g., the ox) and the ceremonial libation of the fermented juice of a plant, haoma (Skr. soma), were frequent and taken as sacred rites. At a certain moment, not yet determined with sufficient clearness, though the majority of scholars seem now to fix it at the sixth century B.C., the remarkable personality of a religious reformer, Zarathustra, appeared in the oriental zone of the Iranian plateau.

His name still resists all attempts at etymological interpretation. "The man with the old camels" seems to be the most accepted one. Zarathustra, possibly utilizing a pre existing naturalistic sky god (Varuna), created a new monotheism, so strong that the name of the old gods (devas) came to signify "demons."

This was, up to some time ago, a "classical" theory of the historians of Mazdaism, but now it seems to cede to new hypotheses maintaining that the demonization of the devas was prior to Zarathustra. Henning even asserted that Zarathustra's reform was a "protest against monotheism." The seventeen hymns (Gathas), written in a rather archaic language and forming the central part of the Avesta are generally considered to be the work of Zarathustra himself.

The Gathas uphold veneration for a single supreme God, Ahura Mazdah, the "Wise Lord" (according to some like Pagliaro, "the Thinking Lord"). He is accompanied by a cortege of abstract quasi personified powers or attributes, the six Amesha Spentas (Holy Immortals): Asha (the Cosmic Law or Righteousness), Vohu Manah (Good Thought or Benevolence), Khshathra (Sovereignty), Armaiti (Piety, Docility), Haurvatat (Integrity), Ameretat (Immortality). The Gathas reject rites and sacrifices, especially the ritual killing of cattle and the Haoma cult, preach a very high personal ethic, and enforce wise social laws, foremost of which is the fostering of agriculture against nomadism. In order to explain evil in the world, the idea of the influence of the Evil Spirit (Angra Mainyu) is introduced; in front of it stands Spenta Mainyu (the Holy Spirit), not identical (at least in this oldest stage) with the Wise Lord (Ahura Mazdah).

This monotheism, tendentiously dualistic but, in any case, clearly prophetic and anti naturalistic, "crossed the spiritual sky of Iran as a meteor" (Duchensne Guillemin). The religion which will be now called Mazdaic mazdayasna means "one who worships the Wise (Lord)" reabsorbed in course of time some of the older "heathen" rites and cults, e. g., Haoma's cult, and also accepted the naturalistic gods of the ancient pantheon, some of them like Mithra, the god of sunlight and, then, of the Covenant and Oath being just adopted, while others being inescapably transformed into deva's.

According to some scholars, however, the religion of Mithra existed as a distinct creed in old Iran. At the same time dualism, not so strong and systematized in the beginning, was becoming deeper: it became a cosmologico metaphysical contrast between a good God, Ahura Mazdah, and an evil God, Angra Mainyu, both having their own "creations," the former being accompanied by his Amesha Spentas (ever more clearly personified in course of time) and Yazatas (Venerable Beings, "gods," like Mithra, the goddess Anahita probably introduced from Babylon, etc.), and the latter by the band of the devils and drujs (literally "lies"). Lying seems to have been the worst sin for Zarathustra.

This religion was at a certain moment monopolized by the Magi. Who the Magi were, is another crux of the historians of Mazdaism. Herodotus speaks of the Magi as a tribe of Media and attributes to them a religion rather different from that of the old Persians. Father G. Messina tried to demonstrate that they formed a closed caste with such characteristic features as those of a "tribe." According to him, their name (magavan) means "bearers of the gift" of Zarathustra's doctrine. Their power increased rapidly and it seems that already during the Achaemenid period (558 330 B.C.) the education of the future kings was entrusted to them. They succeeded in spreading among the people certain ethical principles and rites of their founder's religion. But this success was not complete, and this is one of the many possible explanations of the discrepancies between the visible and popular religion of the Persians and the quasi esoteric religion of the Magi.

According to the same view, the Magi became afterwards the "philosophers" of their doctrine, and tried to develop it especially to explain its dualism. Christian sources of the fourth century A.D. (Theodore of Mopsuestia) speak of the birth, in the milieu of the Magi, of the doctrine or heresy called Zurvanism that explained away dualism through the acceptance of a supreme god Zurvan (time) as father of both Ahura Mazdah and Angra Mainyu. But some scholars now speak of Zurvanism as an actually autonomous religion; and others, turning the preceding theory upside down, consider the Magi to be the bearers of the less philosophical, most magical, and punctiliously ritualistic aspect of Zoroastrianism.

In the meanwhile ritual and cult, with complicated precepts of legal purity, were gradually prevailing and when, after a dark period of incubation under the Arsacid Dynasty (250 B. C. 224 A. D.) the caste of the Magi obtained unparalleled power, with the advent of the Sassanians (224 651 A.D.), Mazdaism, now a State religion, became an intolerant faith, persecutor of every form of heresy. Heresy (as it happened first with Manichaeism supported at its beginnings by King Shahpur, 241 272 A. D., and then with communistic Mazdakism, favoured by King Kawat, 488 531) was sometimes a useful pretext for the warrior caste of the kings a caste that seemed to possess its own religious tradition different from that of the priestly caste to escape the excessive power of the Magi. The discontentment hidden under the outwardly uniform orthodoxy, the unbearable poverty of the peasants, never totally imbued with the religion of the elite, and no doubt possessing their own religious customs and traditions practically unknown to us, and the struggle between Throne and Altar, were some of the causes that rendered the conquest of Iran by the Arabs so astonishingly easy.

The Mazdaic religion is commonly defined as "the religion of dualism." A deeper analysis shows that dualism is not the only basic feature of Mazdaism.

The account of Mazdaic philosophy that follows is divided in a rather unorthodox way, necessitated by the fact that Mazdaism is not a philosophy, into the following four sections:

(1) The Concept of Myth,

(2) Mazdaic Angelism,

(3) the Double Dualism,

(4) the Idea of Time.

The Concept of Myth

One of the most interesting features of Mazdaic thought is its being at the same time mythical and theologico philosophical. The Mazdaic texts are very rich in myths, but these are never narrated ex professo; they are rather hinted at in the texts the chief purpose of which is not that of telling myths. Sufficient attention has not been paid to this "style" of Mazdaic Scriptures. This is true not only of the later Pahlavi books but also of Avesta itself. In it myths are inlaid in liturgical hymns or legal and canonical texts in the form of explanations and comments. Avesta shows thus a rather "recent" type of mythtelling. The myth has never in Avesta even in the case of myths having a naturalistic origin the freshness of the Vedic myth; it is always in a phase of rational or theological explanation, and is used as a hint or example in texts that remain fundamentally theological.

We have just mentioned "myths having an ancient naturalistic origin." A sufficiently clear instance of a Mazdaic myth of this type is that of the killed dragon. In the Aban Yasht a hymn to the angel of Waters, Ardvi Sura Anahita, containing a list of all those who in ancient times made sacrifices to that angel goddess, we read among other stories this passage, clearly explaining and confirming the efficacy of prayer and sacrifice to that angel: "To her did Thraetaona, the heir of the valiant

Athwya clan, offer up a sacrifice in the four cornered Varena, with a hundred male horses, a thousand oxen, ten thousand lambs. He begged of her a boon; saying: `Grant me this, O Good, most beneficent Ardvi Sura Anahita! that I may overcome Azhi Dahaka, the three mouthed, the three headed, the six eyed one who has a thousand senses, that most powerful, fiendish Druj, that demon, baleful to the world, the strongest Druj that Angra Mainyu created against the material world, to destroy the world of the good principle; and that I may deliver his two wives, Savanghavach and Erenavach, who are the fairest of body amongst women, and the most wonderful creatures in the world.' Ardi Sura Anahita granted him that boon, as he was offering libations, giving gifts, sacrificing, and entreating that she would grant him that boon."

Comparison with other cultures allows us to reconstruct an ancient myth originally connected with the New Year Feast and with the rites aiming at defeating drought. A divine, Thraetaona (the Faridun of Firdausi's Shahnameh), conquers the fortress of the Dragon and defeats and kills him.

The Waters that were prisoners in his castle are now freed and so are the women held by the monster as slaves in his harem. Now rain falls fertilizing the earth and the young hero liberator celebrates the hieres gamos with the liberated women. But this is simply a reconstruction and the readers or hearers of the Avesta probably had no idea of the original, authentically mythico ritual, meaning of this tale; it probably sounded to them simply as a nice example of pietas towards the angel and of national heroism by Thraetaona.

But there are also other myths, utilized exactly like this and in similar contexts, of a purely theologico symbolical origin. For instance, there is the myth of Vishtaspa who frees the enchained Daena, told always with the same emblematical conciseness in the Farvardin Yasht. This Yasht is chiefly a list of fravashis (see below) or holy men, to whom the believer offers sacrifices. The enterprises of some of these holy men are narrated here in order to encourage the worshipper to offer sacrifice to their respective fravashi. Concerning the fravashi of Vishtaspa, the king who protected Zarathustra, accepted his religion (Daena), and spread it, the hymn says:

"We worship the fravashi of the holy king Vishtaspa; the gallant one, who was the incarnate Word, the mighty speared and lordly one; who, driving the Druj before him, sought wide room for the holy Daena...; who made himself the arm and support of this law of Ahura, the law of Zarathustra. We took her (i. e., the Daena, or Religion) standing bound from the hands of the Hunus, and established her to sit in the middle (of the world), high ruling, never falling back, holy, nourished with plenty of cattle and pastures, blessed with plenty of cattle and pastures."

Here we see, contrary to the former instance, a myth germinating from history. The process of mythicization has reached a very advanced stage, but not so advanced as to render it impossible to recognize the historical materials that lie at the basis of a myth. First of all, a Daena means "Religion," in a quasi personified sense; secondly, the fact myth is connected with the work of the Prophet Zarathustra and that of the holy King Vishtaspa. But it is highly interesting to note that the attributes attached to his name are the same as those of the angel Saraosha of which Vishtaspa is, in a sense, the terrestrial emblem, in the same way as Zarathustra is the terrestrial symbol of Ahura Mazdah.

We notice here an important moment of the passage from history to myth in Mazdaism and also, at the same time, an important aspect of the Mazdaic approach to myth and reality. Mazdaic thought, while denaturalizing and ethicizing naturalistic myths, embodies historical events, in semi mythical persons, and in so doing "angelizes" history. We are in the presence of a "visionary" theology philosophy, in which intellectual entities assume personal forms, moving in an intermediate world of vision (probably a heritage of the mystical experiences of the Founder) so organized as to give a characteristic unitarian savour to the whole Mazdaic thought.

ANGELISM

Once the mythical logic of Mazdaism has been understood, we can proceed to the study of some of the most significant details of the Mazdaic Weltanschauung. The first key to open its shrines is that, in Mazdaic thought, the Absolute is a personal God, the Wise Lord Ahura Mazdah, a God that reminds us of the Biblical and Quranic God. But His attributes are not (be they eternal or created) intelligible concepts; rather they are themselves "persons" or angels." Professor Corbin rightly remarks that the Mazdean, instead of putting to himself the questions: "What is Time ? What is Earth ? What is Water ?", asks: "Who is Time? Who is Earth? Who is Water ?" And so we find in Mazdaic texts that Time is a Youth of fifteen, Earth is the Archangel Spenta Armaiti (the Holy Piety), Water is the beautiful goddess angel Ardvi Sura Anahita The problem lies in rightly interpreting the verb is: in which sense are these images of vision what they represent? Certainly they are not angels in the Biblical and the Quranic sense of mere messengers or servants of God; Corbin compares them rightly with the dii angeli of Proclus.

The Zamyad Yasht, speaking of the six Amesha Spentas, sings thus: "..the Amesha Spentas, the bright ones, whose looks perform their wish, tall, quickly coming to do, strong, and lordly, who are undecaying and holy; who are all seven (their seventh is Ahura Mazdah himself) of one thought; who are all seven of one speech, who are all seven of one deed; whose thought is the same, whose speech is the same, whose father and commander is the same, namely the Maker, Ahura Mazdah; who see one another's soul thinking of good thoughts, thinking of good words, thinking of good deeds, thinking of Garonmana (the supreme paradise, `house of the hymns'), and whose ways are shining as they go down to the libations; who are the makers and governors, the shapers and overseers, the keepers and preservers of these creations of Ahura Mazdah. It is they who shall restore the world, which will thenceforth never grow old and never die, will become never decaying, never rotting, ever living, eves increasing, and master of its wish, when the dead will rise, when life and immortality will come, and the world will be restored at its wish...."

Here it seems that the Amesha Spentas play a role not very dissimilar to that of the "persons" of the Christian Trinity. It is remarkable that they are six, but are called seven, Ahura Mazdah himself being the seventh. This concept of Ahura Mazdah adding himself as the last to every hierarchical series of beings is often found in Mazdaic books. In order to understand it we must remember a sentence in the first chapter of

Bundahishn:"For Ohrmazd is both spiritual and material," or, according to other translations: "For Ohrmazd both creations are celestial"; in other words, everything is, for him, in transcendent, celestial stage. God can descend into all the stages of Being, eternally First and Last of every embodied or disembodied hierarchy, because, sub specie Dei, everything is transcendent and celestial and this descent can in no way "contaminate" Him.

But these six Amesha Spentas are also the archangelic emblem personification of the primordial elements: Earth (Spenta Armaiti), Cattle (Vohu Manah), Fire (Asha), Metals (Khshathra), Water (Haurvatat), Plants (Ameretat).

They are the elements not as allegories of them, but as living personal symbols, as "Lords of the Species." The concept of Ratu, Lord of the Species, is present everywhere in Mazdaic books. The Lord of the Species "Woman" is, for instance, the mythico historical Daena, "'religion"; the Lord of the Species "Bird" is the mythical bird Saena meregha, or in modern Persian simurgh. The theological abstractions that presented themselves to the philosophico ecstatic mind of the Prophet Zarathustra in a period in which a transformation of the mythico theological concepts into pure philosophy was premature, assumed the plastic life of the gods of the former naturalistic pantheon. Holy Piousness, for example, came to be the Earth instead of remaining an abstractly pure intellectual form.

Or, better, it did not come to be in the historical sense of the expression, but was probably already so double faced in the mind of the Prophet, the historical Zarathustra or some other prophet, whose personal mystical experience is fundamental to the understanding of this as of all other concepts. The connection of the Amesha Spentas with their natural kingdoms is already retraceable in the Gathas. In Yt. 31.9Armaiti is seen as specially favouring the earth's tiller. A verse after, the thrifty toiler in the fields is called one "who nourisheth Vohu Manah ("the Good Thought" the Cattle), while in v. 21 Ahura Mazdah will give "the fat of Good Thought (Cattle)" to him who is His friend.

But in the same Gathas we often hear that Ahura Mazdah created the world through Good Thought, which in these contexts seems to have nothing to do with cattle. Whatever the historical origins of these angelico symbolical identifications may have been, the fact remains that they had the highly important function of transfiguring the elements of nature into ethical values. Or, to put it better, there is an exchange of functions: natural elements are coloured with ethos, and ethical values live a cosmic life. This is one of the most typical features of Mazdaism.

The Supreme God of Mazdaism has further interesting aspects that make him rather different from the God of classical monotheisms. He is, for instance, situated in a sort of transcendent Time and Space, Boundless Time and Space Light, or Uncreated Light (but the word for Space, gas, could be also mythologically interpreted as "throne"). There is, in other words, a time tension in God. But the student of Mazdaism becomes even more astonished when he comes to know that Ahura Mazdah has got a soul, or better a fravashi. As the idea of soul is a specially interesting aspect of Mazdaic thought, we shall treat it here as a particular case of Mazdaic "angelism."

In Mazdaic anthropology, according to Bundahishn, man was "fashioned in five parts body (tan), soul (jan), spirit (ruvan), prototype (adhvenak) and fravashi. Body is the material part; soul, that which is connected with the wind the inhaling and exhaling of breath; spirit, that which with consciousness in the body hears, sees, speaks and knows; the prototype is that which is situated in the station of the Sun; the fravashi is that which is in the presence of Ohrmazd, the Lord.

He was created in this fashion because, during the period of the assault of the Aggressor, men die, their bodies rejoin the earth, their souls the wind, their prototypes the Sun, their spirits the fravashi, so that the demons could not destroy the spirit." This is what happens during the period of the "Assault"' or of the Mixture (gumechishn) of the good and evil creations. At the end of this world, however, a real resurrection of the body will take place: the dead will be "reconstructed" (rist virast). The Saviour (born from Zarathustra's miraculously preserved sperm) will perform a sacrifice (yazishn) in which the bull Hatayosh will be killed, and from his fat and the white Haoma the ambrosia (anosh) will be prepared. All men will drink it and become immortal.

A pure concept of the "immortality of the soul," in the Greek sense of the term, seems extraneous to Mazdaic thought. Every (good) man is already an angel, fravashi, eternally in the presense of Ahura Mazdah; resurrection of the body too is not exactly identical with the same idea in Christian and Muslim tradition, for it happens in a moment which is not, properly speaking, a historical moment; but the epoch of frasho kereti (Phl. frashkart) which is no more in Finite Time but in Boundless Time. The metaphysical peculiarity of this epoch is also clearly shown by the immolation of the Bull, otherwise in "normal time, a horrible sin for Mazdaism."

While the first three parts of the human compound do not need any explanation, we have to consider here the two concepts of prototype (adhvenak) and fravashi. The former is the heritage of an older astro biological idea, common also in India, according to which the prototypical soul of the different categories of beings is preserved in the heavenly bodies. The race type of Cattle is preserved, for instance, in the moon (gaochithra, "having the form of Kine," is an Avestic name for the moon), and that of Plants in the stars. Deeper and more easily interpretable in an ethical and philosophical way is the concept of fravashi. This term does not appear in the Gathas (which also ignore adhvenak, Mazdaicized afterwards), but in the so called "more recent" parts of the Avesta it has already become the aspect that will remain fixed in the Pahlavi tradition. It is clearly kept distinct from "soul" in passages like Yt. 26. 7, and it seems that, at least in the beginning, only heroes had been considered to be having a fravashi. Bailey's researches have demonstrated that the idea of fravashi is associated with "the defensive power emanating from a hero, even after his death."

This originally aristocratic idea suffered a process of democratization in the course of time: every (righteous) man thus got his fravashi, whose protective and defensive force is exerted not only in his favour, but in favour of all those who invoke her. The "fravashis of the Righteous" are seen as protectors of specially sacred places, of the mythical lake or sea (Vouru kasha, of the white Haoma, which we saw as an important ingredient of future ambrosia, of Zarathustra's semen from which the future Saviours will be born, etc. In their function as welcomers of the righteous souls after death they remind us of the Germanic Valkyrs. But the fravashis are also something more. In a passage of Avesta we read: "And these we present hereby to the fravashi of Zarathustra Spitama, the saint, for sacrifice, propitiation, and praise, and to those of the people who love Righteousness, with all the holy fravashis of the saints who are dead and who are living, and to those of men who are as yet unborn, and to those of the prophets who will serve us, and will labour to complete the progress and renovation of the world."

Fravashis are, already now, real angelic doublets of the pious and good men, past, present, and future. Also the living seem to have already a fravashi in a sense slightly similar to but not at all identical with the "Guardian Angel" of the Christian tradition. But there is even more: we saw that Zarathustra, the Prophet, the "terrestrial God" as he is called in some parts of Avesta, has his fravashi, and this is obvious. However, it may seem strange to a rationalistic mind that the Archangels and even Ahura Mazdah Himself have their fravashis. In Vendidad 19. 46 48 Zarathustra is invited to invoke the fravashi of Ahura Mazdah. This fascinating idea seems to assume a doublet of God Himself in a further hyper transcendent dimension of Being; but, as is often the case with many original and highly interesting Mazdaic terms and concepts, this idea is mentioned as if by chance and is soon dropped, without any interpretation or comment.

These angelic doublets of the Good are also symbols of Free Choice (see also below). According to a typically Mazdaic myth theologoumenon preserved in Bundahishn, at the beginning of the millennia of the period of "Mixture" (gumechishn), Ahura Mazdah asked the fravashis whether they preferred to remain untouched by and protected from every danger in the invisible, transcendent world or whether they were ready to descend and incarnate themselves in the visible material world in order to struggle with Evil. The fravashis accepted the second alternative. In this way a sort of de doubling happened: now, in this material world the real man is his fravashi, his angelic ego, that is at the same time his destiny and his true transcendental self; the moral responsibility of man is, in a sense, "transcendentalized." Sin becomes equivalent to the treason of an angel.

Metaphysically, every discussion on the existence of soul, etc., is rendered useless by this acceptance of the experienced fact of apriority of angel over man.

We said that the Gathas do not mention the term fravashi. But they contain another idea that certainly contributed to give a new and ethical meaning to the (probably pre Zarathustrian) heroical myth of the Valkyr fravashi. We mean the idea of Daena (Phl. den). This term has been etymologically analyzed in the most discordant ways by philologists, looking for a semantic explanation which may give reason for the double meaning of the word: "religion" and "deep soul," or better angelic personification of human deeds. Here are some interesting Gathic passages containing the term Daena:

> *"He who renders the Saint deceived, for him shall later be destruction: long life shall be his lot in the darkness; foul shall be his foods his speech shall be of the lowest. This is the life, O ye vile! to which your deeds and your Daena will bring you!"*
>
> *"Yea, I will declare the world's two first spirits, of whom the more bountiful thus spake to the harmful: Neither our thoughts, nor our commands, nor our understandings, nor our beliefs, nor our deeds, nor our Da6nas, nor our souls are at one."*
>
> *"But their (of the Evil ones) souls and their daenas will groan when they will approach the Chinvat Bridge ....."*
>
> *"Declare to me, O Ahura, that path of the Good Thought where the Daena of the Saviours, i. e., their good works (ya hukereta), will taste the joys of Righteousness...."*

A later text of Avesta, the Hadekht Nask tells of the righteous soul meeting, after death, his Daena in the form of a beautiful girl of fifteen; here we see again the mytho poetic tendency of Mazdaic thought, making of every intelligible entity an angel.

If we examine the above quoted passages we shall see that in all of them we could freely translate Daena as "religious works," ethical acts metaphysically considered. The fact that these acts "groan" is not at all astonishing, if we remember the easiness with which Mazdeans personify ideas. This explains also how a fravashi has been attributed to Ahura Mazdah himself. Ahura Mazdah has indeed a Daena in the Gathas; in Bundahishun "omniscience and goodness," i. e., supreme religious actions, are called. Ahura Mazdah's den (Daena, "religion"). The primary sense of Daena seems to be ethico religious. It is "religious acting" that (as is the case in quite a different mental environment with the Hindu karma) creates a body, is representable visibly, and for Ahura Mazdah is His light and for man his angel of light. As pointed out by Pagliano, it was this Zarathustric Daena that modified the warrior fravashis (Dumezil) into ethical angels. And it is in our opinion especially the myth of choice that gave also Ahura Mazdah a fravashi. In which sense is Ahura Mazdah so similar to the righteous man as to have Himself a fravashi? Chiefly in the sense that Ahura Mazdah also made a choice. Of the two primordial Spirits say the Gathas-"the most holy Spirit chose the Truth."

This sense of angelic ethos has thus produced one of the deepest ideas of Mazdaism, the image of the "soul angel valkyr religious work."

THE DOUBLE DUALISM

Choice, the central ethical concept of Mazdaism, is a choice between two. This leads us to examine the radical dualism that, according to many, is the basic idea of this religious philosophy. According to a Gathic passage, "the two primordial Spirits that, in deep sleep, were heard as Twins, are the Excellent and the Evil, in thoughts, words, and deeds; and between these two the wise, not the foolish, have made their choice.... And when these two Spirits met, they first established Life and Non Life and (they decided) that, at the end, the worst existence would be that of the followers of Lie, and the best spiritual force (Manah) would be that of the followers of Truth. Between these two Spirits the followers of the Druj chose the acting of the Worst One, but the Most Holy Spirit, who covers himself with the firm stones of heaven as his robes, chose the Truth, and those who desired to satisfy Ahura Mazdah through righteous actions did the same."

Good and evil are thus connected with an ethical choice, even if it seems that in the most ancient parts of Avesta, the

Holy Spirit is not exactly identical with Ahura Mazdah but is probably Ahura Mazdah in His choosing, "acting" aspect. Another point that shows the typical ethicism of Zarathustrian dualism is the name, "Lie," attributed to the evil principle. But in Gathic thought the evil beings and the Evil Spirit are not "fallen creatures" of God, as in the classical monotheism. They are beings of a purely negative and destructive nature, which it would be absurd to think of as having been created by a good God and the final destiny of which seems to be that of being reduced to nothing. Ahriman, in a later Pahlavi catechism (Pandnamak i Zartusht), is if the translation is correct "a being who does not exist, who received nothing in himself," and the same is endowed in Bundahishn with the strange quality pas-bavishnih ("post existence," as opposed to the positive "pre existence" of Ahura Mazdah).

This ethos is, however and here is again the typical feature of Mazdaic thought strongly "cosmicized": Goodness means, above all, promotion of Being, Life, and agriculture. It means "growth" (a word often used in the Mazdaic texts) of good material existence too. "Righteousness, the Bunduhishn says openly, obeys the same rules as (cosmic) Creation." Ethos means also material positivity. The evil people (we often hear, in Mazdaic texts, curses against the nomads, the non producers, and the killers of cattle) are, above at the destroyers of existence.

We can now better understand the second type of dualism, a dualism now not of choice but of transcendence between the invisible (or celestial) menok, and the visible (or terrestrial) getik; for God creates the terrestrial world to protect, foster, or help (adhyarih) the celestial world, which is, in a way, its prototype, its root (bun). This dualism is, however, radically different from the Platonic dualism. A very instructive passage of one of the most philosophical treatises of Mazdaism, the Shikand Gumanik Vichar written in the third/ninth century, will show this difference in a very clear way.

> *"The getik is the fruit (bar) of menok; menok is its root (bun).... The fact that getik is the fruit and menok its root becomes clear when one thinks that every visible and tangible thing passes from invisibility to visibility. It is already well known that man and the other visible and tangible creatures come from the invisible and*

intangible menok; in the same way, the form, the species, and the height and the breadth of a being are the same as those of the being that generated it; the body of man and other creatures, which is now manifested, was hidden and invisible in the semen that came from his parents; the semen itself, that was in the loins of the parents, passed to the stage of manifestation, visibility, and tangibility. We can therefore know by certainty that this visible and tangible getik has been created from an invisible and intangible menok, and there is no doubt that it will come back from visibility and tangibility to the invisibility and intangibility of the same menok".

W e see from this passage that this Mazdaic dualism differs from the Platonic and Gnostic dualism chiefly in the sense that for it matter and the world are in no way an "inferior" stage of Being. On the contrary, Matter is, in a sense, the most mature and perfect aspect (the fruit) of Spirit. It differs, however, also from the views implied by too simple a creationistic monotheism inasmuch as it seems to admit not only "one" personal God and His immediate creation, but various stages of Being.

Regarding the first point we refer the reader to a text in which it is clearly stated that the terrestrial world (getik) is higher in dignity than paradise (vahisht), because it is in this terrestrial, embodied, visible, and tangible world only that the battle against the powers of Evil can be fought and won a struggle that makes it possible for the soul "to strive with his thought (ahang menishn) towards Beatitude." One of the most important miraculous deeds accomplished by the Prophet Zarathustra was that of breaking the bodily forms (shikastan i kalput) of the Devils. Without their bodies the Devils are less perfect and less dangerous in their struggle. And here we find again the fundamentally ethical or rather cosmo ethical function of the getik-menok dualism. Matter is useful in the struggle against Evil.

Regarding the second point, let us remember that in the first chapter of Bundahishn, which contains one of the most detailed accounts of the double creation of the world, the Mazdaic vision seems to involve various stages of creation, the highest of which are prototypical, emblematical. Even from some passages of the Gathas it may appear that God created first the prototypes of things, the Primordial Ox, the Protoanthropos, the Plant, etc.

Coming back to the last sentence of the above quoted passages of Shikand Gumanik Vichar, we see how this life of positive struggle in the material world blossomed forth from the celestial world in a cycle that is at the end destined to be reabsorbed into the celestial and invisible stage, once its ethical task has been fulfilled. Thus it seems that even the first dualism, that between Good and Evil, will become a monism again at the consummation of Time. Here we come to the idea of Time and Cycle as the instrument of a victorious struggle.

TIME AND CYCLE

With regard to the question of Time also the Mazdaic thought shows an originality of conception that distinguishes it both from the Indian outlook assuming "flight from Time" as supreme salvation and beatitude, and from the classical Semitic forms of monotheism by which Time seems to be conceived as an irreversible "line."

In order never to forget the peculiar "angelical" character of Mazdaism, the reader is reminded that in BundahisnTime is an angelic person, a youth of fifteen, "bright, with white eyes, tall and mighty, whose might is from valour, not from robbery and violence." In other words, the Mazdean, in order to understand Time, did not intellectually "discuss" it as we do (that is why European scholars rather anachronistically find so many "contradictions" in the Mazdaic texts referring to Time) but rather experimented with it in vision. And this vision shows them what is told in the first chapter of the same theological book.

"Thus it is revealed in the Good Religion. Ohrmazd was on high in omniscience and goodness: for Infinite Time He was ever in the Light. Omniscience and Light are the robes of Ohrmazd: some call them "religion" (den, see above).... The Time of the robes is infinite like Ohrmazd, and Goodness and Religion, during all the time of Ohrmazd, were, are and will be Ahriman, slow in knowledge, whose will is to smite, was deep down in the darkness: (he was) and is, yet will not be.

The will to smite is his robe, and darkness is his place: some call it the Endless Darkness."

The cosmic drama unfolds itself in a Time and in a Space, but Ahrimanic time is composed of only two moments, past and present. Time and Space have also a transcendent aspect. Transcendent Time is the so called "Boundless Time" (zaman i akanarak) or "Time of the Long Dominion" (zaman i derang khvatai). Time (not of course our "serial" time) exists even in the heart of the Absolute. There is not, in Mazdaic thought, too simple a contrast between Time and Eternity. But let us continue our reading and see the "aim" of our serial time. Ohrmazd creates first a purely transcendent prototypical creation.

Ahriman rises from the depths, sees it, and rushes forward to smite and destroy it. When Ohrmazd sees that struggle is unavoidable, He says to Himself: "If I do not fix a time for battle against him, then Ahriman could do to my creation even as he threatened, and the struggle and the mixture will be ever lasting; and Ahriman could settle in the mixed state of creation and take it to himself.

And "Ohrmazd said to the Destructive Spirit: `Fix a time, so that by this pace we may extend the battle for nine thousand years.' For He knows that by fixing a time in this way the Destructive Spirit would be made powerless. Then the Destructive Spirit, not seeing the end, agreed to that treaty, just as two men who fight a duel fix a term saying: `Let us on such a day do battle till night falls.' This too did Ohrmazd know in His omniscience that within these nine thousand years, three thousand would pass entirely according to the will of Ohrmazd, three thousand years in mixture would pass according to the will of both Ohrmazd and Ahriman, and that in the last battle the Destructive Spirit would be made powerless and that He Himself would save creation from aggression."

Limited time, i. e., serial time (during 9,000 years), is then conceived in an ethical light, just like the material world in which it is manifested. Serial time is something like a great detour, an ample digression from Infinite Time, but a substantially positive detour, because its aim is to render the battle against Evil possible and successful. Hence come some important consequences.

Destiny: If Time is a "youth" and if, as it is said in another text, "the creator Ohrmazd dyed Time with colour," Time cannot be an a priori form in the Kantian sense. Time is objectively coloured; it can be practically identified with "destiny" (bakht, assigned lot).

Some Mazdaic texts as, for example, the beautiful myth of the choice of the fravashis already mentioned, seem favourable to free will, some others seem in favour of predestination. Apart from the problems connected with the historical formation of these ideas, we must say that Mazdaic theology solves the problem in a rather consequential way. Pahlavi Vendidad (5. 9. 33) maintains that "in the material world every thing happens according to destiny (pat bakht), whereas in the celestial world everything is according to free action (pat kunishn).

This solution of the problem of time is indeed a consequence of the angelic, emblematical outlook of Mazdaism. Destiny is no more than the visible, terrestrial, getik aspect of its truer transcendent, invisible, naenok prototype, which is freedom. More over, in all this a part is also played by the Ohrmazd Ahriman dualism, in the sense that Ahriman, through the creation of the seven accursed planets (these are for Mazdaism evil entities, while the fixed stars, and especially the Zodiacal signs are good, and called "the generals of Ohrmazd"), inserts himself into the play, trying to change the temporal destinies of men and of the world.

In this he succeeds, however, only temporarily. And there is still another interesting concept, that of bagho bakht or portion allotted by the gods (divine destiny), a "supplement," as it were, of destiny, added to that initially established (or, to put it better, added to the terrestrial emblem of transcendent human freedom) in order to recompense specially meritorious actions.

"But the gods, we read in the above mentioned texts, rarely concede that supplement of destiny, and they manifest it only in the celestial world," in order to avoid a possible destruction of it by Ahrimanic forces, if it is manifested visibly in the getik. We must never forget that transcendent entities can struggle, and win and lose, only through their incarnation in the visible world.

It is, however, obvious that such an approach to the problem of destiny and free will results in a fatalism even more radical than that reproached by some in the classical monotheistic religions. This is true especially when we think that some theological schools of Mazdaism, e. g., Zurvanism, maintain that both gods, Ohrmazd and Ahriman, are subject to Time's power of destiny. Time (Zurvan) is regarded as supreme God; and even Ohrmazd is taken to have created the world "with the approval of Infinite Time" (pat afrin-i zaman-i akanark).

The Apocatastasis: When we consider limited Time to be a detour, a digression from transcendent Infinite Time, we are able to understand better the idea of the "cosmic cycle" typical of Mazdaism. Reading theological Mazdaic texts one is impressed by a tendency to connect the facts and happenings of the proto history with those of the end of the world.

The Heroes who will contribute to the creation of the "Future Body" (tan i pasen) are the same Heroes as, at the dawn of existence, were the protagonists of the myth of the Beginning. The Saviour, or, better, the three eschatological Saviours are sons of the first Revealer of the Faith, Zarathustra. They are practically Zarathustra himself. To justify the enormous distance in time, there is the myth of Zarathustra's sperm miraculously preserved in a lake, protected by the fravashis.

The beginning is the end. There is, in the limited, serial time, a circle leading it fatally towards Infinite Time. Gayomart, the first Man, the Protoanthrope, will also be the first Resurrected man; the ancient hero Yamshet (Mod. Pers. Jamshid) has already prepared, at the beginnings of history, the mythical Ark (var) to save men from the terrible trials of the End. Past and Future seem united in an eternal Present, if seen sub specie menok.

The Apocatastasis is, transcendentally (menokiha), happening already (and sometimes, we find in these theological texts future events told by verbs in the past). Serial time is like an immense "delay" from metaphysical Time, but there is in it a positive curving towards the Origin. All events of this period of "delay" are eschatologically justified. The ancient victory of Sahm, the Hero, on certain demonic monsters is explained as necessary, because, without it, "it would have been impossible to fulfil Resurrection and Future Life." It is, however, interesting to remark that the tan i pasen, the "Future Body" or Future Life, is, though in a transcendent form, a real body and at least judging by some texts the renewed world will not be a mere re identification with the first stage of the prototypical menok creation, when it was "without thought, without touch, without movement in a moist stage like semen."

On the contrary, the idea of the positivity of time, and that of the presence of an "Infinite Time" even in Eternity, seems to confer a colour of novelty and true Life to the new world, prepared by the struggling experience of the embodied creatures. It would be, however, too risky to proceed in these considerations further; for, as mentioned before, the Mazdaic texts too often leave the reader in the expectation of something that never comes. A really theological and philosophical development of their highly suggestive and interesting intuitions is absent.

Ethics: We have not to fix our ideas on the chivalrous ethics of the struggle situated in Time. This struggle, like that of "two men who fight a duel," is a free one, one in which man can always succumb; but just because Time is also an angel, the struggle is coloured with a metaphysical, supreme, "engagement."

It transcends everyday's secular ethics. The metaphysico-ethical responsibility of the Mazdean is such that he can pray in the words of the Gatha: "May we be such as those who will bring about the Transfiguration of the World." At the same time, however, and for the same reasons, Mazdaic ethics, rooted as it is in an objective Time, is a heavily heteronomous one. This causes it to be different not only from our modern autonomous ethics; but also from the purely theo-nomous ethics of the classical forms of monotheism.

Mazdaic ethics is still strictly connected with semi mythical realities and with a moral dualism always in danger of transforming itself into a cosmological dualism. In other words, Good and Evil mean to the Mazdean something more than what they mean to us.

There is an entire series of situations and objects (Time is dyed with colour) intrinsically evil, Ahrimanic. We deduce from various passages in Mazdaic Scriptures that not only the nomad is naturally evil, but also the non Iranian (aneran) is something objectively evil in comparison with the Iranian; insects and snakes are evil and so on.

The idea that the natural essence (gohr) of certain given beings is radically and metaphysically diabolical is very clear from the texts, and even some characters of history, such as Alexander the Greek and Frasiyak the Turanian are no more than devilish creatures of Ahriman. The problem of how much did Evil permeate the creation of Ahura Mazdah during the period of "Mixture" has been solved by Mazdeans in a rather heavy, objective, classificatory way.

There have been, however, acute minds that started to meditate on the origin of that Evil which the traditional Mazdaic texts gave as an unexplained presupposition, or rather considered it a fact not needing any explanation. So was born Zurvanism, a theologico philosophical school, that is considered by some European Orientalists to be a real autonomous religion. To solve the problem of the origin of Evil, Mazdaic mind again created a myth: that of the primordial "doubt" of the Time God (Zurvan), a doubt from which Ahriman was born, as a wicked "twin" of Ohrmazd.

This school seems also to have shown a tendency, at least according to recent studies, to unify and symmetrize the two dualisms already mentioned, in the sense that the material world, the realm of the flesh, begins to be identified with the Ahrimanic creation.

This remained only a very vague tendency in Zurvanism, but the identification, quite in the spirit of Gnosticism, was totally accomplished by Manichaeism, in the Iranian texts in which Zurvan is the name of the Supreme God, while Ohrmazd passes to the stage of Protoanthropos. But such an identification completely breaks the frame and organism of Mazdaic thought, that has always considered Manichaeism to be the most dangerous and most Ahrimanic heresy.

CONCLUSION

We have studied in too rapid and perhaps too unphilosophical a way, the mythical logic, the dualistic and angelical metaphysics, the chivalrous and fatalistic ethics of

Mazdaism. It is now necessary to say a word on the importance of this thought for the development of the subsequent phases of the philosophical history of Iran and Islam. Those who know the strange and highly interesting world of Muslim "heresies" cannot deny that some features of their theological systems strongly remind us of the Mazdaic Weltanschauung.

We mean, above all, their curious angelical approach to metaphysics, their tendency to recreate a purely "mental" mythology, identifying, e. g., the first intellect or Logos with this or that historical person, or telling, as the Nusairis do, that `Ali is the Ma'na (Supreme Meaning) and Muhammad is the Ism (Transcendent Name), etc.

Professor Corbin demonstrated in his remarkable essays the influence of pre Islamic Iranian thought on Muslim thinkers like Suhrawardi Maqtul and on Isma'ilism, but his contempt of history and historical method seems rather exaggerated. It is indeed very difficult to identify the historical channels through which these influences may have penetrated Islam.

Many seem, however, to forget that the most important Pahlavi theological texts were written in Muslim Persia in the most flourishing period of Islam and that discussions among Muslims, Christians, Manichaeans, and Mazdeans are documented in the third/ninth century at the Court of the Caliph al Mamun. The influences seem to have been mutual, for it has been shown that some Pahlavi texts constant quotations from the Quran and mention contemporary Muslim currents of thought such as that of the Mu'tazilah.

But apart from this direct influence, we could more surely admit another kind of indirect convergence. The late systematic Mazdaic thought was no doubt influenced by late Hellenism and Gnosticism, in the same way as the first Islamic thought was influenced by Hellenism, Sabaeanism, and Gnosticism during the second and third/eighth and ninth centuries. Hence there resulted, in both the spiritual worlds, a similar functioning that can give the illusion of direct influence, especially when similar languages, Pahlavi and modern Persian, are used.

If these considerations may seem to discourage the exaggerated enthusiasm of some pan Iranianists (it is sufficiently known that even ancient Iran had been rather strongly "semitized" by Babylonian and old Syrian influences) they also point to the fact that the organic thought of Mazdaism assumed its truer and deeper historical value just because it did not remain the heritage of a single race or a single people, but, being in itself historically a composite product, synthesized itself with the seeds of the extremely original and rich philosophico theological value, Islam, that was destined in its turn to spread them in their most mature form throughout the entire civilized world.

Note The quotations from Avesta and Pahlavic texts are given, modifying here and there some rather contradictory European versions, after comparing them with the original texts. The writer is fully aware of the fact that some of them remain personal and rather conjectural interpretations.

3

PRE ISLAMIC ARABIAN THOUGHT

In the present chapter, we are concerned only with the people of Arabia who lived in the age immediately preceding the rise of Islam. The ancient civilized inhabitants of southern Arabia, the Sabaeans and Himyarites, have been left out of account, not only because the relevant materials at our disposal are scanty and fragmentary, but also because they are far removed from the Islamic times, with which the present volume is primarily and directly concerned.

We cannot hope to understand properly the religious or philosophical ideas of a people without comprehending their economic and social background. A few words about the social structure of pre Islamic Arabs should, therefore Form a suitable and helpful prelude to a description of their religious outlook.

The land of Arabia is mainly a sandy plain, which is partly steppe land and partly desert. Except in the oases which are few and far between, the land is bare and monotonous, unfit for cultivation and unable to support settled communities. From times immemorial, its inhabitants have been of necessity nomadic, living on the produce of their camels and sheep.

The majority of the ancient Arabs were, therefore, pastoralists who were constantly on the move in search of grass and water for their herds and flocks. Restless and rootless, with no permanent habitations, they stood at a low level of culture and were innocent of those arts and sciences which are associated in our minds with civilized life. The art of reading and writing was confined only to a few individuals in certain commercial centres, while illiteracy was almost universal among the sons of the desert. Their mental horizon was narrow, and the struggle for existence in their inhospitable environment was so severe that their energies were exhausted in satisfying the practical and material needs of daily life, and they had little time or inclination for religious or philosophic speculation. Their religion was a vague polytheism and their philosophy was summed up in a number of pithy sayings.

Although the ancient Arabs had no written literature, they possessed a language which was distinguished for its extraordinary rich vocabulary. In the absence of painting and sculpture, they had cultivated their language as a fine art and were justly proud of its enormous power of expression. Accordingly, the poets and orators who could make an effective and aesthetic use of its wonderful resources were held in especially high esteem among them.

Judging by the evidence furnished by the pre Islamic poets, polemical passages in the Quran and the later Islamic literature, idolatry based on polytheism prevailed throughout ancient Arabia. Almost every tribe had its own god, which was the centre of its religious life and the immediate object of its devotion. The ancient Arabs, however, at the same time believed in the existence of a Supreme God, whom they called Allah. But this belief was rather vague and their faith in Him was correspondingly weak. They might invoke Allah in time of danger, but as soon as the danger was over they forgot all about Him. They also recognized and worshipped a large number of other subordinate gods along with Him, or at least thought that they would intercede for them with Him. Three deities in particular, viz., al 'Uzza, al Manat, and al Lat, were accorded special veneration as the daughters of Allah. It was this association of subordinate deities with Allah which is technically known as shirk (association of gods with Allah) and which was condemned by the Prophet as an unpardonable sin. Shirk was held in special abhorrence, as it obscured belief in the oneness of God.

The innumerable deities, which the pagan Arabs worshipped, form a long series and are the subject of a monograph, written by ibn al Kalbi, who flourished in the second century of the Islamic era and is counted among the leading authorities on Arabian antiquity. A few of them have been incidentally mentioned in the Quran also.

These Arabian deities, which were of diverse nature, fell into different Categories. Some of them were personifications of abstract ideas, such as jadd (luck), sa'd (fortunate, auspicious), rida' (good will, favour), wadd (friendship, affection), and manaf (height, high place). Though originally abstract in character, they were conceived in a thoroughly concrete fashion. Some deities derived their names from the places where they were venerated. Dhu al-Khalasah and Dhu al Shara may be cited as examples of this kind.

The heavenly bodies and other powers of nature, venerated as deities, occupied an important place in the Arabian pantheon. The sun (shams, regarded as feminine) was worshipped by several Arab tribes, and was honoured with a sanctuary and an idol. The name `Abd Shams, "Servant of the Sun," was found in many parts of the country. The sun was referred to by descriptive titles also, such as shariq, "the brilliant one." The constellation of the Pleiades (al Thurayya), which was believed to bestow rain, also appears as a deity in the name `Abd al Thurayya. The planet Venus, which shines with remarkable brilliance in the clear skies of Arabia, was revered as a great goddess under the name of al `Uzza, which may be translated as "the Most Mighty." It had a sanctuary at Nakhlah near Mecca. The name `Abd al `Uzza was very common among the pre Islamic Arabs. The Arabian cult of the planet Venus has been mentioned by several classical and Syriac authors.

There were certain Arabian deities whose titles in themselves indicate that they occupied a position of supreme importance in the eyes of their votaries. Such deities were: al Malik, "the King" (compare the personal name, 'Abd al Malik); and Ba'l or Ba'al, "the Lord" which was very common among the northern Semites.

The deities of heathen Arabia were represented by idols, sacred stones, and other objects of worship. Sacred stones served at the same time as altars; the blood of the victims was poured over them or smeared over them. At the period with which we are dealing, the Arabs sacrificed camels, sheep, goats, and, less often, kine. The flesh of the sacrifice was usually eaten by the worshippers, the god contenting himself with the blood alone. Originally, every sacrifice was regarded as food to be consumed by the god concerned or at least as a means of pacifying him. The sacrifice was, thus, believed to bring the worshipper into close connection with the deity. Hence the Arabic terms, qurba and qurban (derived from the root, QRB, to be near), which are used for a sacrifice.

The Arabs, like the Hebrews, were in the habit of sacrificing the firstlings of their flocks and herds (fara'). Soon after the birth of an infant, his head a shaven and a sheep was sacrificed on his behalf. This practice has survived among the Arabs and other Muslim peoples to the present day under the name of `aqiqah. Perhaps, this was originally a ransom, offered as a substitute for the child himself.

The gods of heathen Arabia were represented not only by rude blocks of stone (nusub, pl. ansab), but also by statues, made with more or less skill. The usual word for a divine statue, whether of stone or wood, was sanam. The other word used for this purpose was wathan, which seems primarily to mean nothing more than a stone.

Examples of tree worship are also found among the ancient Arabs. The tree known as dhat al anwat, "that on which things are hung," received divine honours; weapons and other objects were suspended from it. At Nakhlah, the goddess `Uzza is said to have been worshipped in the form of three trees.

The gods of the heathen Arabs were mostly represented by idols, which were placed in temples. These temples served as places of worship, where offerings and sacrifices were made by their votaries. The temples were by no means imposing buildings like those of the Egyptians or the Greeks. They were simple structures, sometimes mere walls or enclosures marked by stones. Not only the temples were venerated as holy places, but sometimes the surrounding areas were also treated as sacred and inviolable (hima), and were supposed to be under the special protection of their respective gods.

In connection with several temples, we read of priests who served as their custodians (sadin, pl. sadana). They received the worshippers and gave them admission to the shrine. The office was generally hereditary, since we read of priestly families which were attached to particular temples. Another word used for a priest was kahin, a term which was employed for a soothsayer as well. The priests were believed to be under the influence of the gods and to possess the power of foretelling future events and of performing other superhuman feats. In this way, their pronouncements resembled the ancient Greek oracles and were likewise vague and equivocal. In course of time, the priest who was in the beginning simply the custodian of the temple developed the character of a soothsayer as well, and thus the term kahin came to acquire the sense of a soothsayer and seer.

There were female soothsayers as well. Arabic literature has preserved many stories about kahin and many utterances are attributed to them. These utterances were usually made in rhymed prose, and are interesting not only in respect of their content but also with regard to their style. Their pronouncements consisted of a few concise sentences, which ended in words having the same rhyme. This mode of expression was known as saj`. The same style is found in the earliest revelations received by the Prophet which now constitute the last chapters of the Quran. It is, therefore, not surprising that the contemporaries of the Prophet called him a kahin, a position which he firmly repudiated. While in the beginning, the Quran adopted the style peculiar to saj', it raised the conception to a level far beyond the imagination of the soothsayers. There is another point of similarity which should be noted here. The utterances of the kahins were prefaced by oaths, swearing by the earth and sky, the sun, moon, and stars, light and darkness, and plants and animals of all kinds. These oaths offer an interesting point of comparison with the oaths used in the Quran.

The temples of the heathen Arabs were for them not only places of worship but also places of pilgrimage. They assembled there periodically at certain times of the year, when these assemblies assumed the character of fairs and festivals.

An important sanctuary of this kind was located at Mecca, a town in western Arabia, which was situated at a distance of about fifty miles inland from the Red Sea. The town lay on the trade route which led along the sea from the Yemen to Syria, and its situation may have been partly determined by the presence of a well, called Zamzam, which has a considerable and fairly constant supply of water. The sanctuary consisted of a simple stone structure of cube like appearance, which was called the Ka'bah by the Arabs. One of the walls contained a black stone (al hajar al aswad). Inside the Ka'bah was the statue of the god, Hubal. At its feet, there was a small pit in which offerings to the temple were deposited. Besides Hubal, al Lat, al `Uzza, and al Manat were also worshipped at Mecca and are mentioned in the Quran. At the rise of Islam, the temple is said to have contained as many as three hundred and sixty idols. It seems that in course of time the various Arab tribes had brought in their gods and placed them in the Ka'bah, which had consequently acquired the character of the national pantheon for the whole of Arabia.

From times immemorial, the Ka'bah at Mecca had been the centre of a great pilgrimage, in which the most diverse tribes from all over Arabia took part. But this was possible only when peace reigned in the land. For this purpose, the month of Dhu al Hijjah in which the rites and ceremonies connected with the pilgrimage were performed and the preceding and succeeding months of Dhu al Qa'dah and Muharram altogether three consecutive months were regarded as sacred months, during which tribal warfare was prohibited. This period was sufficiently long to enable the tribes from the remotest corners of Arabia to visit the Ka'bah and return to their homes in peace. The territory around Mecca was also treated as sacred (haram); and the pilgrims laid aside their weapons when they reached this holy territory. The pilgrimage was called hajj.

During the pilgrimage, the pilgrims had to perform a number of rites and ceremonies, which lasted for several days and which can be described here only with the utmost brevity.

As soon as the pilgrims entered the sacred territory, the haram, they had to practise self denial by observing a number of prohibitions: they had to abstain from hunting, fighting, sexual intercourse, and certain other things. They circumambulated the Ka'bah, and also kissed the Black Stone which was fixed in one of its walls. An essential rite of the hajj was a visit to the hill of `Arafat on the ninth of Dhu al Hijjah, when the pilgrims assembled in the adjoining plain and stayed there till sunset for the prescribed wuquf (the stays or halts).

The hill of 'Arafat is said to have borne another name, Ilal, which may have been the name of the shrine or rather of the deity worshipped there in ancient times. The pilgrims then went to Muzdalifah, which was consecrated to Quzah, the thunder god. Here they spent the night, when a fire was kindled on the sacred hill. At sunrise the pilgrims left for Mina, an open plain, where they sacrificed the animals, camels, goats, and sheep, which they had brought with them for the purpose. The animals meant for sacrifice were distinguished by special coverings or other marks. During their stay at Mina, the pilgrims also used to throw stones at three prescribed sites as a part of the pilgrimage ceremonial. After staying at Mina for three days, the pilgrims left for their homes. Women took part in the pilgrimage along with men.

The hajj as described above was retained by the Prophet as a major religious institution of Islam, with certain modifications of its ceremonials which were intended to break the link with their pagan associations. While the position of the Ka'bah was emphasized as the house built by the Patriarch Abraham for the service of Allah, the halts (wuquf)at 'Arafat (along with the one at Muzdalifah) was retained as an essential feature of the Islamic hajj.

In addition to the innumerable gods, the heathen Arabs also believed in the existence of demons, shadowy beings, which they called the jinn (variant: jann). The word probably means covered or hidden. Hence the jinn meant beings invisible to the eye. They were regarded as crafty and mischievous, almost malevolent, and were consequently held in fear. They were supposed to haunt places dreaded either for their loneliness or for their unhealthy climate. The fear of the jinn, therefore, gave rise to various stories, in which they are said to have killed or carried off human beings. Like many other primitive peoples, the heathen Arabs believed in demoniacal possession. The jinn were supposed to enter human beings and even animals, rendering them "possessed" or mad. According to the testimony of the Quran, the Meccans believed that there was a kinship between Allah and the jinn, and that they were His partners. Accordingly they made offerings to them and sought aid from them. In spite of the bewildering multiplicity of the subordinate gods whom. The pre Islamic Arabs venerated, they believed in the existence of a Supreme God whom they called Allah. The word Allah is found in the inscriptions of northern Arabia and also enters into the composition of the numerous personal names among them. There are a large number of passages in the poetry of the heathen Arabs in which Allah is mentioned as a great deity. Allah also occurs in many idiomatic phrases which ere in constant use among them. The Quran itself testifies that the heathens themselves regarded Allah as the Supreme Being. Their sin, however, consisted in the fact that they worshipped other gods besides Him. It was against this shirk that the Prophet waged an unrelenting war. In any case, it is important to note that the Quranic monotheism did not find it necessary to introduce an altogether new name for the Supreme Being and, therefore, adopted Allah, the name already in use.

Even before the advent of Islam, old polytheism was losing its force in Arabia, since the Arabs notion of their gods had always been vague. With the decline of old paganism, a number of men had appeared in various parts of the country who had become convinced of the folly of idolatry, and were seeking another more satisfying faith. They were fairly numerous and were called Hanifs. The Quran uses this term in the sense of a monotheist, and describes Abraham the Patriarch as the first Hanif. But none of these Hanifs had the vision and force of conviction and the proselytizing zeal which distinguished the mission of Muhammad.

The ancient Arabs believed that the human soul was an ethereal or air like substance quite distinct from the human body. As such, they considered it identical with breath. This identification was so complete in their view that the word for breath, nafs, came to mean human personality itself. They were confirmed in this belief by their experience that death resulted when a human being ceased to breathe. At the time of death, breath along with life itself escaped through its natural passage, the mouth or the nostrils. When a person passed away on his death bed, his soul was said to escape through his nostrils (mata hatfa anfihi), and in the case of a violent death, e. g., on a battle field, through the gaping wound.

When a person was murdered, he was supposed to long for vengeance and to thirst for the blood of the murderer. If the vengeance was not taken, the soul of the murdered man was believed to appear above his grave in the shape of an owl continually crying out, "Give me to drink" (isquni), until the murder was avenged. The restless soul in the form of a screeching owl was supposed to escape from the skull, the skull being the most characteristic part of the dead body. Certain rites of burial, prevalent among the pre Islamic Arabs, show that they believed in some sort of future existence of the soul. In order to show honour to a dead chief, for instance, a camel which had been previously hamstrung was tethered near the grave and was left to starve. This usage can be explained only on the hypothesis that the animal was to be at the service of the dead man. The custom of slaughtering animals at the graves of elders has been kept up in Arabia to the present day. Ancient poets often express the wish that the graves of those whom they love may be refreshed with abundant rain. Similarly, their sometimes address greetings to the dead. It may be that expressions of this kind are not merely rhetorical figures of speech; they probably indicate their belief in the survival of those who have departed from this world.

Although there are indications that the ancient Arabs hard some notion, however hazy, of the survival of the human soul after death, they had no clear notion of life after death. As stated in the Quran, they could not understand how a human being, after his bones had been reduced to dust, could be called to life once again. Since life after death was something beyond their comprehension, the question of retribution for human deeds did not arise in their minds.

The Quran uses the word ruh (spirit) as well as nafs for the human soul. Accordingly, the Muslim theologians do not make any distinction between the two terms in designating the soul. The ancient Arabs were generally fatalists. They believed that events in the lives of human beings were preordained by fate, and, therefore, inevitable. However hard they might try, they could not escape the destiny, that was in store for them. The course of events was believed to be determined by dahr or time, so that suruf al dahr (the changes wrought by time) was a most frequent expression used by the Arabs and their poets for the vicissitudes of human life. The same feeling is expressed in several of their proverbs and maxims. This view was probably born of their practical experience of life. In no part of the world is human life quite secure against the sudden changes of fortune, but in the peculiar milieu of Arabia man seems to be a helpless victim to the caprice of nature to an unusual degree. The sudden attack of a hostile neighbouring tribe or a murrain in his herds and flocks may reduce a rich man to dire poverty almost overnight; or in the case of a prolonged drought, he may be brought face to face with fearful famine and death. The peculiar circumstances of desert life, thus, seem to have encouraged the growth of fatalistic tendencies among the Arabs. Bearing in mind the existence of these tendencies among the ancient Arabs, it is not surprising to find that similar views prevailed in the first centuries of Islam and that the dogma of predestination was almost universally accepted among the Muslim masses. Predetermination was, however, divorced from dahr.

The feeling of utter helplessness in the face of inexorable fate has probably given rise to another idea among the Arabs; the idea of resignation as a commendable virtue. Possibly, it has a survival value for those who adopt a submissive attitude towards the hardships and adversities of human life. Instead of fretting and fuming and hurling oneself in violent revolt against the decree of fate and thus running the risk of complete disintegration, there seem comparative safety and the possibility of ultimate survival in accepting calmly and patiently the dictates of fate. The inculcation of resignation as a virtue, thus, seems to be a natural corollary to the dogma of predestination.

Although religion had little influence on the lives of pre Islamic Arabs, we must not suppose them to be an all together lawless people. The pagan society of ancient Arabia was built on certain moral ideas, which may be briefly described here. They had no written code, religious or legal, except the compelling force of traditional custom which was enforced by public opinion; but their moral and social ideals have been faithfully preserved in their poetry, which is the only form of literature which has come down to us from those old days.

The virtues most highly prized by the ancient Arabs were bravery in battle, patience in misfortune, loyalty to one's fellow tribesmen, generosity to the needy and the poor, hospitality to the guest and the wayfarer, and persistence in revenge. Courage in battle and fortitude in warfare were particularly required in a land where might was generally right and tribes were constantly engaged in attacking one another. It is, therefore, not a mere chance that in the famous anthology of Arabian verse, called the Hamasah, poems relating to inter tribal warfare occupy more than half of the book. These poems applaud the virtues most highly prized by the Arabs bravery in battle, patience in hardship, defiance of the strong, and persistence in revenge.

The tribal organization of the Arabs was then, as now, based on the principle of kinship or common blood, which served as the bond of union and social solidarity. To defend the family and the tribe, individually and collectively, was, therefore, regarded as a sacred duty; and honour required that a man should stand by his people through thick and thin. If kinsmen sought help, it was to be given promptly, without considering the merits of the case. Chivalrous devotion and disinterested self-sacrifice on behalf of their kinsmen and friends were, therefore, held up as a high ideal of life.

Generosity and hospitality were other virtues which were greatly extolled by the Arab poets. They were personified in Hatim of the tribe of Tayy, of whom many anecdotes are told to this day. Generosity was specialty called into play in the frequent famines, with which Arabia. is often afflicted through lack of rain. The Arabian sense of honour also called blood for blood. Vengeance for the slain was an obligation which lay heavy on the conscience of the pagan Arabs. It was taken upon the murderer or upon one of his fellow tribesmen. Usually this ended the matter, but sometimes it led to a regular blood feud, which lasted for a long period and in which many persons lost their lives. The fear of retribution had a salutary effect in restraining the lawless instincts of the Bedouin; but the vendetta in some cases was carried to extreme limits and involved a great loss of human life.

In the century before Muhammad, Arabia was not wholly abandoned to paganism. Both Judaism and Christianity claimed a considerable following among its inhabitants. Almost every calamity that befell the land of Palestine sent a fresh wave of Jewish refugees into Arabia, sometimes as far as the Yemen. They had probably taken refuge there after the conquest of

Palestine by Titus in 70 A. D. Jewish colonists flourished in Medina and several other towns of northern Hijaz. In the time of the Prophet, three large Jewish tribes, viz., Nadir, Quraizah, and Qainuqa, dwelt in the outskirts of Medina, and the fact that the Prophet made an offensive and defensive alliance with them for the safety of the town shows that they were an important factor in the political life of those times. These colonies had their own teachers and centres of religious study. Judging by the few extant specimens of their poetry, these refugees, through contact with a people nearly akin to themselves, had become fully Arabicized both in language and sentiment. They, however, remained Jews in the most vital particular, religion, and it is probable that they exerted a strong influence over the Arabs in favour of monotheism.

Another religious factor which was strongly opposed to Arabian paganism was the Christian faith. How early and from what direction Christianity first entered Arabia is a question which it is difficult to answer with certainty; but there is no doubt that Christianity was widely diffused in the southern and nothern parts of Arabia at the time of the Prophet. Christianity is said to have been introduced in the valley of Najran in northern Yemen from Syria, and it remained entrenched in spite of the terrible persecution it suffered at the hands of the Himyarite king, Dhu Nawas, who had adopted the Jewish faith. The Prophet received at Medina a deputation of the Christians of Najran and held discussions with them on religious questions.

Christianity in the south west of Arabia received a fresh stimulus by the invasion of the Christian Abyssinians, who put an end to the rule of Dhu Nawas. There were Christians in Mecca itself; Waraqah ibn Naufal, a cousin of Khadijah, the first wife of the Prophet, was one of them. Christianity was also found among certain tribes of the Euphrates and the Ghassan who lived on the borders of Syria. Their conversion was due to their contact with the Christian population of the Byzantine Empire. The Ghassanids, who were Monophysites, not only defended their Church against its rivals but also fought against the Muslims as the allies of the Byzantine emperors. The Christians were also found at Hirah, a town in the north east of Arabia, where Arab princes of the house of Lakhm ruled under the suzerainty of the Persian kings. These Christians, who were called `Ibad or the "Servants of the Lord," belonged to the Nestorian Church, and contributed to the diffusion of Christian ideas among the Arabs of the Peninsula.

By the sixth century, Judaism and Christianity had made considerable head way in Arabia, and were extending their sphere of influence, leavening the pagan masses, and thus gradually preparing the way for Islam.

PHILOSOPHICAL TEACHINGS OF THE QURAN

The Quran Although the Scriptures revealed to the earlier prophets, especially those of the Christians and the Jews, are regarded by the Muslims as holy, yet the Book (al Quran) revealed to the last Prophet, Muhammad, is their chief sacred Book. The doctrine propounded by the Quran is not a new doctrine, for it is similar to the Scriptures of the earlier apostles. It lays down the same way of faith as was enjoined on Noah and Abraham. It confirms in the Arabic tongue what went before it, the Book of Moses and the Gospel of Jesus in being a guide to mankind, admonishing the unjust and giving glad tidings to the righteous. God never abrogates or causes to be forgotten any of His revelations, but according to the needs and exigencies of the times, He confirms them or substitutes for them something similar or better.

The Quran is a book essentially religious, not philosophical, but it deals with all those problems which religion and philosophy have in common. Both have to say something about problems related to the significance of such expressions as God, the world, the individual soul, and the inter relations of these; good and evil, free will, and life after death. While dealing with these problems it also throws light on such conceptions as appearance and reality, existence and attributes, human origin and destiny, truth and error, space and time, permanence and change, eternity and immortality. The Quran claims to give an exposition of universal truths with regard to these problems an exposition couched in a language (and a terminology) which the people immediately addressed, the Arabs, with the intellectual background they had at the time of its revelation, could easily understand, and which the people of other lands, and other times, speaking other languages, with their own intellectual background could easily interpret. It makes free use of similitude to give a workable idea of what is incomprehensible in its essence. It is a book of wisdom, parts of which relate to its basic principles, (umm al kitab) and explain and illustrate them in detail, others relate to matters explained allegorically. It would be a folly to ignore the fundamentals and wrangle about the allegorical, for none knows their hidden meanings, except God. In what follows, a brief account is given of the Quranic teaching with regard to the religio philosophical problems mentioned above.

Ultimate Beauty: God and His Attributes The Ultimate Being or Reality is God. God, as described by the Quran for the understanding of man, is the sole self subsisting, all pervading, eternal, and Absolute Reality. He is the first and the last, the seen and the unseen. He is transcendent in the sense that He in His full glory cannot be known or experienced by us finite beings beings that can know only what can be experienced through the senses or otherwise and what is inherent in the nature of thought or is implied by it. No vision can grasp Him. He is above all comprehension. He is transcendent also because He is beyond the limitations of time, space, and sense content. He was before time, space, and the world of sense came into existence. He is also immanent both in the souls (anfus) and the spatio temporal order (afaq). Of the exact nature of God we can know nothing. But, in order that we may apprehend what we cannot comprehend, He uses similitudes from our experience.

He "is the light of the heavens and the earth. The parable of His light is as if there were a niche and within it a lamp, the lamp enclosed in glass; the glass as if it were a brilliant star lit from a blessed tree, an olive, neither of the east nor of the west, whose oil is well nigh luminous, though fire scarce touched it: light upon light !" Likewise for our understanding, He describes through revelation His attributes by similitude from what is loftiest in the heavens and the earth and in our own experience (our highest ideals). This He does in a language and an idiom which the people addressed to may easily understand. These attributes are many and are connoted by His names, but they can all be summarized under a few essential heads: Life, Eternity, Unity, Power, Truth, Beauty, Justice,

Love, and Goodness. As compared to the essence of God, these attributes are only finite approaches, symbols or pointers to Reality and serve as the ultimate human ideals, but though signs and symbols, they are not arbitrary symbols. God has Himself implanted them in our being. For that reason they must, in some sense, be faithful representations of the divine essence. They must at least be in tune with it, so that in pursuing them we human beings are truly in pursuit of what is at least in harmony with the essence of God, for they are grounded in that essence.

God is, thus; a living, self subsisting, eternal, and absolutely free creative reality which is one, all powerful, all knowing, all beauty, most just, most loving, and all good.

As a living reality God desires intercourse with His creatures and makes it possible for them to enter into fellowship with Him through prayer, contemplation, and mystic gnosis, and lights with His light the houses of those who do not divert from His remembrance, nor from prayer, nor from the practice of regular charity. His life expresses itself also through His eternal activity and creativeness. God is one and there is no god but He. He is the only one and there is none like Him. He is too high to have any partners. If there were other gods besides Him, some of them would have lorded over others. He is the One and not one in a trinity. Those who attribute sons and daughters to Him and those who say Christ is the son of God and is himself God only blaspheme God.

He has begotten neither sons nor daughters nor is He Himself begotten. And how could He be said to have sons and daughters when He has no consort ? And yet the unbelievers have taken besides Him gods that create nothing, but are themselves created, who have no power to hurt or do good to themselves and can control neither death, nor life, nor resurrection. Therefore no god should be associated with God. Setting up of gods is nothing but anthropomorphism. The gods that people set up are nothing but names of conjectures and what their own souls desire. They do blaspheme who say, "God is Christ the son of Mary"; for said Christ, "O children of Israel, worship God my Lord and your Lord." They regard the angels as females, as if they had witnessed their creation.

God and the World God is omnipotent. To Him is due the primal origin of everything. It is He, the Creator, who began the process of creation and adds to creation as He pleases. To begin with He created the heavens and the earth, joined them together as one unit of smoky or nebulous substance, and then clove them asunder. The heavens and the earth, as separate existents with ail their produce; were created by Him in six days (six great epochs of evolution).

Serially considered, a divine day signifies a very long period, say, one thousand years of our reckoning or even fifty thousand years. Non serially considered, His decisions are executed in the twinkling of an eye or even quicker, for there is nothing to oppose His will. When he says, "Be," behold' it is. His decree is absolute; no one can change it. He draws the night as a veil over the day, each seeking the other in rapid succession. He created the sun, the moon, and the stars, all governed by the laws ordained by Him and under His command. Every creature in the heavens and the earth willingly submits to His laws. The sun runs its course for a determined period; so does the moon. The growth of a seed into a plant bearing flowers and fruit, the constellations in the sky, the succession of day and night these and all other things show proportion, measure, order, and law. He it is who is the creator, evolver, and restorer of all forms. He it is who sends down water from the sky in due measure, causes it to soak in the soil, raises to life the land that is dead, and then drains it off with ease.

God is the Lord of all the worlds, and of all mysteries. He has power over all things, and to Him belong all forces of the heavens and the earth. He is the Lord of the Throne of Honour and the Throne of Glory Supreme, the Lord of the dawn and all the ways of ascent. It is He who spreads out the earth like a carpet, sends down water from the sky in due measure to revive it with fruit, corn, and plants, and has created pairs of plants, each separate from the others, and pairs of all other things. He gives the heavens' canopy its order and perfection and night its darkness and splendour, the expanse of the earth its moisture, pastures, and mountains; springs, streams, and seas ships and cattle; pearls and coral; sun and shadow; wind and rain; night and day; and things we humans do not know. It is He who gives life to dead land and slakes the thirst of His creatures and causes the trees to grow into orchards full of beauty and delight.

To God belong the dominions of the heavens and the earth and everything between them. To Him belong the east and the west. Withersoever you turn, there is His presence, for He is all pervading. Neither slumber can seize Him, nor sleep. His Throne extends over the heavens and the earth, and He feels no fatigue in guarding and preserving His creatures, for He is the most high and supreme in glory, exalted in might; and wise.

It is He who gives life and death and has power over all things.

God is not only the creator, but also the cherisher, sustainer, protector, helper, guide, and reliever of distress and suffering of all His creatures, and is most merciful, most kind, and most forgiving.

God has not created the world for idle sport. It is created with a purpose, for an appointed term, and according to a plan, however hidden these may be from us humans. "God is the best of planners." He it is who ordains laws and grants guidance, creates everything and ordains for it a proportion and measure, and gives it guidance. There is not a thing but with Him are the treasures of it, but He sends them down in a known measure.

The world is not without a purpose or a goal; it is throughout teleological and to this universal teleology human beings are no exception. To everyone of them there is a goal and that goal is God Himself.

God is all knowledge. He is the Truth. With Him are the keys of the unseen, the treasures that none knows but He. He witnesses all things, for every single thing is before His sight in due proportion. Verily, nothing on the earth or in the heavens is hidden from Him, not even as much as the weight of an atom. Neither the smallest nor the greatest of things are but recorded in a clear record.

On the earth and in the sea not even a leaf does fall without His knowildge. Should not He that created everything know His own handiwork? He is full of wisdom. He understands the finest of mysteries. He knows what enters the earth and what comes forth out of it; what comes down from heaven and all that ascends to it. He knows every word spoken. No secrets of the heart are hidden from Him, for He has full knowledge of all things, open or secret. He knows and would call us to account for what is in our minds, whether we reveal it or conceal it. Two other attributes of God and our basic values are always mentioned together in the Quran. These are justice and love, the latter including among other attributes the attributes of munificence, mercy, and forgiveness.

God is the best to judge and is never unjust, He does not deal unjustly with man; it is man that wrongs his own soul. On the Day of Judgment, He will set up the scales of justice and even the smallest action will be taken into account. He is swift in taking account, and punishes with exemplary punishment. He commands people to be just and loves those who are just.

For those who refrain from wrong and do what is right there is great reward, and God suffers no reward to be lost. People's good deeds are inscribed to their credit so that they may be requited with the best possible award.

Divine punishment is equal to the evil done. It may be less, for, besides being most just, God is most loving, most merciful, and forgiver of all sins, but it is never more. Such is not, however, the case with His reward. He is most munificent and bountiful and, therefore, multiplies rewards for good deeds manifold. These rewards are both of this life and the life hereafter.

Islam, no less than Christianity, lays emphasis on the basic value of love. Whenever the Quran speaks of good Christians, it recalls their love and mercy. God is loving, and He exercises His love in creating, sustaining, nourishing, sheltering, helping, and guiding His creatures; in attending to their needs, in showing them grace, kindness, compassion, mercy, and forgiveness, when having done some wrong, they turn to Him for that; and in extending the benefits of His unlimited bounty to the sinners no less than to the virtuous. It is, therefore, befitting for man to be overflowing in his love for God and be thankful to Him for His loving care.

God is all good, free from all evil (quddus). He is also the source of all good and worthy of all praise.

The Quran uses synonymous words for beauty and goodness (husn wa khair).The word radiance or light (nur) is also used to signify beauty. God is the beauty (nur) of the heavens and the earth and His names (attributes) are also most beautiful (asma al husna). He is the creator possessed of the highest excellence. He creates all forms and evolves them stage by stage (al bari al musawwir).

Everything created by Him is harmonious and of great beauty. Notice the beauty of trees and fields and the starry, heaven. He is the best bestower of divine colour to man who has been made in the best of moulds and has been given the most beautiful shape. How lovable is the beauty of animals whom you take out for grazing at dawn and bring home at eventime. Throughout history God has sent messages of great excellence, and given the best of explanations in His revealed books. Therefore, people must follow the best revealed book (ahsan al kitab). How beautiful is the story of Joseph given in the Scripture.

God's judgment is of the highest excellence, and belief in the Day of Judgment of extreme beauty. Of great excellence is the speech of the righteous that call to God, for they invite people to Him by beautiful preaching and say only those things which are of supreme excellence.

The Quran lays the greatest stress on the beauty of action. It exhorts mankind to do the deeds of high value, for God loves those who do excellent deeds. It wants men to return greetings with greetings of great excellence and repel evil with what is best, for in so doing they enhance the excellence of their own souls.

Notes: Patience is graceful (sabr i jamil) and so is forgiveness. Excellence of conduct shall not be wasted. Those whose deeds are beautiful shall be given the highest reward in this world and better still in the next. They shall be given in paradise the most beautiful abodes and places for repose, and excellent provisions shall be made for them.

GOD'S RELATION TO MAN

God created man's spirit out of nothing and created mankind from this single spirit. He created his mate of the same kind and from the twain produced men and women in large numbers. From the point of view of personal history and perhaps also from the point of view of the evolutionary process, man is created for an appointed term as a being growing gradually from the earth, from an extract of certain elements of the earth, then by receiving nourishment from the objects of sustenance, and being endowed with life, like all other living beings, taking the form of water or watery clay or adhesive mud moulded into shape in due proportions as a life germ, a leech like Clot of congealed blood, growing into a lump of flesh, further developing into bones clothed with flesh, and finally emerging as a new creation, a human being in two sexes, gifted with hearing and sight, intelligence, and affection, destined to become God's vicegerent on earth, decreed to die one day, and destined to be raised again on the Day of Resurrection.

The form in which he will be raised again he does not know. The whole of mankind is one family, because it is the progeny of a single pair.

In reality, man is the highest of all that is created, for God has created him in the most beautiful of moulds. He is born with the divine spirit breathed into him, even as for the Hindu, Greek, and Christian sages he is made in the image of God. Human perfection, therefore, consists in being dyed in divine colour in the fullest achievement and assimilation of divine attributes, for God desires nothing but the perfection of His light, the perfection of these attributes in man.

The sole aim of man, therefore, is a progressive achievement of all divine attributes all intrinsic values. God encompasses and cherishes mankind. He is always near man nearer than his jugular vein. He is with him wheresoever he may be and sees all that he does. Whithersoever he turns, there is the presence of God, for He is all pervading. He listens to the prayer of every suppliant when he calls on Him.

Soul The soul of man is of divine origin, for God has breathed a bit of His own spirit into him. It is an unfathomable mystery, a command of God, of the knowledge of which only a little has been communicated to man. The conscious self or mind is of three degrees. In the first degree it is the impulsive mind (nafs ammarah) which man shares with animals; in the second degree it is the conscientious or morally conscious mind (nafs lawwamah) struggling between good and evil and repenting for the evil done; in the third degree it is the mind perfectly in tune with the divine will, the mind in peace (nafs mutma'innah).

Theory of Knowledge Man alone has been given the capacity to use names for things and so has been given the knowledge which even the angels do not possess. Among men those who are granted wisdom are indeed granted great good.

Understanding raises a man's dignity. Those who do not use the intellect are like a herd of goats, deaf, dumb, and blind no better than the lowest of beasts. The ideal of the intellect is to know truth from error. As an ideal or basic value for man wisdom means the knowledge of facts, ideals, and values.

There are three degrees of knowledge in the ascending scale of certitude (i) knowledge by inference (`ilm al yaqin), (ii)knowledge by perception and reported perception or observation (`ain al yaqin), and (iii) knowledge by personal experience or intuition (haqq al yaqan) a distinction which may be exemplified by my certitude of (1) fire always burns, (2) it has burnt John's fingers, and (3) it has burnt my fingers. Likewise, there are three types of errors: (i) the errors of reasoning, (ii) the errors of observation, and (iii) the errors of intuition.

The first type of knowledge depends either on the truth of its presupposition as in deduction, or it is only probable as in induction. There is greater certitude about our knowledge based on actual experience (observation or experiment) of phenomena.

The second type of knowledge is either scientific knowledge based on experience (observation and experiment) or historical knowledge based on reports and descriptions of actual experiences. Not all reports are trustworthy. Therefore, special attention should be paid to the character of the reporter. If he is a man of shady character, his report should be carefully checked.

Scientific knowledge comes from the study of natural phenomena. These natural phenomena are the signs of God symbols of the Ultimate Reality or expressions of the Truth, as human behaviour is the expression of the human mind.

Natural laws are the set ways of God in which there is no change. The study of nature, of the heavens and the earth, is enlightening for the men of understanding.

The alternation of day and night enables them to measure serial time. They can know the ways of God, the laws of nature, by observing all things of varying colours mountains, rivers, fields of corn, or other forms of vegetation, gardens of olives, date palms, grapes, and fruit of all kinds, though watered with the same water, yet varying in quahty; by studying the birds poised under the sky and thinking how they are so held up and likewise by observing the clouds and wondering how they are made.

Those who think can know God and can conquer all that is in the heavens and the earth night and day, and the sun the moon, and the stars. Knowledge of the phenomenal world which the senses yield is not an illusion, but a blessing for which we must be thankful.

No less important for individuals and nations is the study of history. There is a measure and law in human society as much as in the whole cosmos. The life of every nation as a collective body moves in time and passes through rises and falls, successes and reverses, till its appointed period comes to an end.

For every living nation there are lessons in the history of the peoples that have lived in the past. It should, therefore, study the "days of God," the momentous periods of history, the periods of divine favour and punishment, the periods of nations glory and decline. People should traverse the earth to see what had been the end of those who neglected the laws of nature, the signs of God. Those who do not guide others with truth and so do not act rightly, even though their days are lengthened, are gradually brought down by such means as they do not know.

God never changes the condition of a people until they change it themselves, but once He wills it, there can be no turning it back. Therefore, it is all the more important to take lessons from the past. In the stories about the past there are instructions for men of understanding. Even the bare outlines of the rise and fall of nations, of great events of history, and their consequences provide object lessons for their guidance and warning.

Let them remember momentous events of the lives of such peoples and societies as the Israelites, the Magians, the Sabians, the Romans, the Christians, the people of Saba, the people of Madyan, of `Ad, of Thamud, of Lot, Companions of the Cave, the Seven Sleepers, the Companions of al Rass, the Companions of the Rocky Tract, and those of the Inscription, and Gog and Magog; prophets like Noah, Abraham, Isma`il, Isaac, Jacob, David, Solomon, Joseph, Moses, Aaron, Elisha, Jonah, Jesus; and other personages great for their piety, power or wisdom, e.g., Mary, the Queen of Saba, Dhu al Qarnain (probably Cyrus of Iran), and the Pharaoh (Thothmes I of Egypt), and Aesop.

So much importance has been given to history that fifteen chapters of the Quran have been given the titles bearing historical significance. Nor indeed has the study of contemporary history been ignored. The Quran refers to contemporaneous events such as the battle of Badr, the battle of Tabuk, the trade and commerce of the Quraish, the hypocrisy of those who were enemies pretending to have embraced Islam, and the animosity of persons like abu Lahab and his wife.

God reveals His signs not only in the experience of the outer world (afaq) and its historical vistas, but also through the inner experience of minds (anfus).

Thus, the inner or personal experience is the third source of knowledge. Experience from this source gives the highest degree of certitude. Divine guidance comes to His creatures in the first instance from this source. The forms of knowledge that come through this source are:

(1) divinely determined movement movement determined by natural causes, as in the earth, and the heavens,

(2) instinct, e.g., in the bee to build its cell,

(3) intuition or knowledge by the heart,

(4) inspiration as in the case of Moses mother when she cast her tenderly suckled child into the river, and

(5) revelation as in the case of all true prophets, God's messengers.

Man's Power God has subjected for the use of man, His vicegerent on the earth, everything in the heavens and the earth, the sun and the moon; day and night; winds and rain; the rivers and the seas and the ships that sail; pearls and corals; springs and streams, mountains, moisture, and pastures; and animals to ride and grain and fruit to eat.

FREE WILL

God has given man the will to choose, decide, and resolve to do good or evil. He has endowed him with reason and various impulses so that by his own efforts he may strive and explore possibilities. He has also given him a just bias, a natural bias towards good.

Besides this He has given him guidance through revelation and inspiration, and has advised him to return evil with good, to repel it with what is best (ahsan). Hence if a man chooses to do good, it is because in giving him these benefits God has willed him to do so. He never changes the gracious benefits which He has bestowed on a people until they change themselves.

Therefore, whatever good come from man or to man is ultimately from God. On the other hand, his nature has a bias against evil, his reason is opposed to it, and he has been given a warning against it through the revealed books; therefore, whatever evil comes from him or to him is from his own soul.

If God had willed He would have destroyed evil or would not have allowed it to exist, and if it were His will, the whole of mankind would have had faith, but that is not His plan? His plan envisages man's free use of the divine attribute of power or freedom to choose and take all judicious and precautionary measures to suit different situations. In the providential scheme man's role is not that of a blind, deaf, dumb and driven herd of goats. So even his free choice of evil is a part of the scheme of things and no one will choose a way unto God, unless it fits into that scheme or is willed by God.

There is no compulsion in faith. God's guidance is open to all who have the will to profit by it. Whosoever wills, let him take the straight path to his Lord. Truth is from God, then whosoever wills, let him believe it; and whosoever wills, let him reject it. The prophets are sent to every nation for guiding the whole of mankind. Their duty is to preach, guide, and inspire by persuasion and not to drive or force people to anything, nor to watch over their doings or dispose of their affairs. They cannot compel mankind against their will to believe.

Death Death of the body has been decreed by God to be the common lot of mankind. Wherever a man is, death will overtake him even if he is in a tower strong and high. No soul can die except by God's leave, the term being fixed as if by writing, but every soul shall be given a taste of death and in the end brought back to God and duly judged on the Day of Judgment, and only he who is saved from fire will be admitted to paradise; it is then that he will have attained the goal of his life. As compared to that life, the life of this world is only a life of vainglory.

Life after Death There are some who think revival after death is far from their understanding and ask how they shall be raised up after they have been reduced to bones and dust.

Let them recall to mind that they were created out of nothing; first as dust, then a sperm, then a leech like clot, then a piece of flesh, partly formed and partly unformed, kept in a womb for an appointed term, then brought out as babes and then fostered so that they reached an age of full strength; and further, let them ponder over the fact that the earth is first barren and lifeless but when God pours down rain, it is stirred to life, it swells, and puts forth every kind of beautiful growth in pairs. Let them understand that He who created the heavens and the earth is able to give life to the dead, for He has power over all things.

God created man from the earth, into it shall he return and from it shall he be brought out again. For everyone after death there shall be an interval (Barzakh)lasting till the Day of Resurrection.On that day all the dead shall be raised up again. Even as God produced the first creation, so shall He produce this new one. We do not know in what form we shall be raised, but as a parable the Quran describes the Day of Resurrection as follows

On that day there shall be a dreadful commotion. The heaven shall be rent asunder and melted like molten brass. The sun folded up and the moon darkened shall be joined together, and the stars shall fall, losing their lustre. In terrible repeated convulsions, the earth shall be shaken to its depths and pounded into powder. The mountains shall crumble to atoms flying hither and thither like wool, the oceans shall boil over, there shall be a deafening noise, and the graves shall be turned upside down.

A trumpet shall be blown, no more than a single mighty blast, and there shall come forth every individual soul and rush forth to the Lord the sinners as blackened, blinded, terror smitten with eyes cast down and hearts come right up to their throats to choke; and the virtuous, happy and rejoicing. Then all except such as it will please God to exempt shall fall into a swoon. Then a second trumpet shall be sounded, when, behold! they will all be standing and looking on. The earth will shine with the glory, of the Lord and the record of deeds shall be opened.

All shall fully remember their past deeds. Anyone who will have done an atom of good shall see it and anyone who will have done an atom of evil shall see it. They shall also recognize one another, though each will have too much concern of his own to be able to be of help to others.

They will have neither a protector, nor an intercessor except God or those whom permission is granted by Him and whose word is acceptable to Him. They shall all now meet their Lord. The scale of justice shall be set up, and not a soul shall be dealt with unjustly in the least; and if there be no more than the weight of a mustard seed, it will be brought to account, and all shall be repaid for their past deeds.

There will be a sorting out of the sinners and the righteous. The sinners will meet a grievous penalty but it shall not be more than the retribution of the evil they will have wrought. All in proportion to their respective deeds and for a period longer and shorter shall go through a state of pain and remorse, designated in the Quran as hell, and the righteous saved from hell shall enter a state of perpetual peace, designated as paradise. Paradise has been described in the Quran by similitude in terms of what average human beings value most: dignity, honour, virtue, beauty, luxury, sensuous pleasures, and social discourse and hell in terms of what they all detest.

People shall be sorted out into three classes.

(1) Those who will be foremost and nearest to God, with whom God is well pleased and who are well pleased with God. They shall have no fear, no grief, no toil, no fatigue, no sense of injury, no vanity, and no untruth. They shall enjoy honour and dignity, and, dressed in fine silks and brocade and adorned with bracelets of gold and pearls, shall live for ever in carpeted places. They will recline on thrones encrusted with gold and jewels facing one another for discourse. They will be served by youths of perpetual freshness, handsome as pearls, with goblets, beakers, and cups filled out of clear fountains of crystal white and delicious drinks free from intoxication and after aches, which they will exchange with one another free of frivolity and evil taint. They shall be given fruit and flesh of their own choice in dishes of gold to eat, and shall get more than all they desire. Their faces shall be beaming with the brightness of bliss. They shall have as companions chaste women, their wives, beautiful like pearls and corals. Those who believe and whose families follow them in faith, to them God shall join their families, their ancestors, their spouses, and their offsprings. Rest, satisfaction, and peace will reign all round. This will be their great salvation; but their greatest reward, their supreme felicity, will consist in being in the presence of God.

(2) Companions of the right hand who shall have their abode in another garden. They will sit on thrones on high in the midst of trees, having flowers, pile upon pile, in cool, long extending shades by the side of constantly flowing water. They will recline on rich cushions and carpets of beauty, and so will their pretty and chaste companions, belonging to a special creation, pure and undefiled. They will greet one another with peace. They will also have all kinds of fruits, the supply of which will not be limited to seasons. These are parables of what the righteous shall receive.

(3) Companions of the left hand who shall be in the midst of a fierce blast of fire with distorted faces and roasted skin, neither alive nor dead, under the shadows of black

> smoke. They shall have only boiling and fetid water to drink and distasteful plants (zaqqum) to eat. Nothing shall be there to refresh or to please.

The fire of hell shall, however, touch nobody except those most unfortunate ones who give the lie to truth.

But for these similitudes, we cannot conceive the eternal, bliss and perpetual peace that awaits the righteous in the life hereafter, nor can we conceive the agony which the unrighteous will go through. They will, however, remain in their respective states only so long as it is the will of God and is in accordance with His plans.

Neither is the bliss of paradise the final stage for the righteous, nor is the agony of hell the final stage for the unrighteous. Just as we experience the glowing sunset, then evening, and then the full moon at night one after another, even so shall everyone progress whether in paradise or in hell stage by stage towards his Lord, and thus shall be redeemed in the end.

4

ETHICAL TEACHINGS OF THE QURAN

VALUES

As it has been explained in the preceding chapter, the real goal of man, according to the Quran, is the assimilation of divine attributes. These attributes, as also shown in the same chapter, can be summarized as life, eternity, unity, power, truth, beauty, justice, love, and goodness.

Life God is the living one Himself and gives life to others. The moral laws enunciated in the Quran are life giving and life enriching and, therefore, by living in this world in accordance with these laws man is able to realize one of God's attributes. If anyone saved a life, it would be as if he saved the life of the whole people. On the social plane, the importance of life on this earth is duly emphasized. The ideal of the Quran is to develop a healthy social organization which traverses the middle path of rectitude avoiding all forms of extreme. People are to partake of the good things of the world and wear beautiful apparel, to eat and drink without going to excess, and for this reason monasticism which implies denial of life on this earth is condemned as being incompatible with human nature. Man is advised not to forget his portion in the life of this world. Wealth and property are good things to be enjoyed and appreciated and are blessings of God which make life smooth and comfortable.

The life of the present world is no doubt significant and purposive, but it's purposes are directed towards the good of future life, for the real abode of life is in the hereafter. God created life and death to test which of the people are best in point of deed. The present world is a place of sojourn and a place of departure; its enjoyments are short and comforts are few, while as compared with these the life in the hereafter is better and more enduring. It is best for the righteous and will last for ever. The present life and the future life, however, are to be viewed as a unity, for man's creation here and his resurrection later on are events related to an individual soul. In fact, life on this earth is a preparation for the life hereafter. The good works that we do here in this life will run before us to illumine our path in the hereafter where we shall have full opportunity to develop our spiritual light to ever greater perfection.

Eternity This attribute in its fullness is exclusively God's and man is created within time for a stated term; yet he has within himself a deep craving for eternity and for a kingdom that never fails or ends. Though finite and temporal, man does not and cannot rest content with that. The way is open for the finite and temporal man to attain life everlasting.

Unity The greatest emphasis in the Quran is on the unity of God which implies belief in the divine causality and the presence of moral order in the universe where people are judged according to the merit of their deeds and not arbitrarily. This moral order works without any favour not only in the case of individuals but also in the case of societies and peoples. God has entered into covenant with men within the limits of this moral order with men as such and not with particular nations or races.

Unity, as one of the ideals of man, implies unity in the internal life of man, a co ordination of reason, will, and action. It requires complete control of one's passions and lust. It also stands for the unity of profession and practice. Faith in God is the necessary prerequisite of moral life, but it should not be mere verbal acceptance; it must be accompanied by good deeds, implying an attitude of mind which is motivated by a complete submission to God's will. Poets generally say what they do not practise, and hypocrites say with their tongues what is not in their hearts, but all believing men and women are truthful in their words and deeds.

Externally, the ideal of unity demands that men should develop a healthy social organization which traverses the middle path of rectitude avoiding all forms of extreme. The righteous are advised to get together and strive, so that tumult, oppression, and mischief are removed from the face of the earth. This ideal of unity also implies peace and harmony among members of a family. A woman is a mate for man so that both may dwell in tranquillity with an attitude of mutual love and kindness; each is like a garment for the other for mutual support, mutual comfort, and mutual protection. It is the duty of man to live with woman on a footing of kindness and equity. Unity also implies that members of a national or ideological group should develop ties of intimate relationship among themselves so that the ideal of an organic whole may be realized in a broader context. The Quran says that all Muslims are brothers and have great love and affection among themselves. No excuse should be allowed to stand in the way of doing good or making peace between different persons. Every effort should be made to bring about conciliation between men, yet we should co operate in righteousness and piety, not in sin and rancour. We should be kind to those in need, to neighbours, and to the wayfarers.

This attitude, of kindness and fairness is to be maintained and upheld even in the case of enemies and opponents. We should try to forgive those who plot against us and overlook their deeds, cover evil with pardon, and turn off evil with good.

This attitude of toleration is to be cultivated in our relation to people of other faiths. The Quran aims at establishing a peaceful social atmosphere where people belonging to other faiths can enjoy freedom of conscience and worship for which purpose the believers are urged to rise and fight against the oppressors so that monasteries, churches, synagogues, and mosques in which the name of God is commemorated in abundant measure may not be pulled down. It unreservedly praises some of the people of the Book for their faith. It is as a consequence of this attitude of tolerance that according to the Quran all those who believe in God and the Last Day and practise righteousness, whether they are Muslims, Jews, Christians, or Sabaeans, shall get their reward from their Lord. The Quran gives an open invitation to the people of the Book to come together and work conjointly for the establishment of peace and social harmony based on the idea of the unity of God.

Above all, this ideal of unity leads to the conception of unity of the whole of humanity. Mankind was created from a single pair of a male and a female and from a single breath of life. All people are equal members of the human community; the only distinction recognized by the Quran is based on the degree of righteousness possessed by people.

Power Power as a human ideal implies that man has the potentiality of assuming responsibility undertaken by him of his own accord. God breathed His Spirit into him and, therefore, made him His vicegerent on the earth. Everything in the universe was created subservient to him even the angels were ordered to bow down to him. He was given a position of great honour in the universe and was elevated far above most of God's creations. He has all the faculties that are necessary for his physical and spiritual development and can pass beyond the limits of the heavens and the earth with the power given to him by God. He is given the power to distinguish between good and evil and, therefore, he alone is responsible for what he does. He is endowed with freedom of action, but his freedom is limited by the free causality of God. His responsibility is proportionate to his powers; he has been shown the path of righteousness and it is up to him to accept its lead or reject it.

Being created after the pattern of God's nature man is capable of developing from one stage to the next higher stage. But this development involves struggle against the immoral forces of the external world which he is able to meet successfully with the co operation and help of God. This effort of man is, however, viewed not in any exclusive spirit of otherworldliness. It is the primary duty of the believers to participate actively in the struggle for the establishment of asocial order based on peace, harmony, and justice in which everybody is equal beforre the law, and people in authority work out their policies after ascertaining the views of the people.

In this endeavour to realize the moral law in his individual and social life, man has often to contend against evil forces represented in the person of Satan. But it is within his power to resist and overcome them. Though man is always prone to weakness and susceptible to seduction by the forces of evil, yet his weakness is rectifiable under the guidance of revelation, and such men as follow the law of righteousness shall be immune from these lapses. They shall never be afraid of anything or be cowardly in their behaviour.

The ideal of power demands that in order to establish a State on the basis of peace, freedom of thought, worship, belief, and expression, the morally orientated individuals will have to strive hard. Jihad or utmost striving with might and main with wealth and their person, as they ought to strive, becomes their foremost duty so that tumult, oppression, and mischief should be totally eliminated from the world and there should be left no possibility for the aggressors to kindle the fire of war, to hinder men from the path of God, and to oppress people for professing a faith different from their own.

This struggle against the forces of evil and oppression demands that its participants must be characterized by perseverance, courage, fearlessness, and trust in God the moral qualities which are described by the Quran as characteristic of the righteous in the social context. Those who patiently persevere in the path of righteousness will be in possession of a determining factor in all the affairs of this life and will be above trivial weaknesses. Those who are firm and steadfast will never lose heart, nor weaken in will, nor give in before the enemy. A small band of steadfastly persevering people often vanquish a big force. Similarly, trust in God is the moral quality of all believers. This quality does not involve any negation of planning in advance as is evident from the attitude of Jacob while advising his sons who were going to Egypt. After you have taken all possibilities into consideration and taken a decision, put your trust in God.

TRUTH OR WISDOM

Wisdom as a human ideal stands for man's search for knowledge or truth. It is something which is distinguished from conjecture or imperfect knowledge and mere fancy. Different stories are related in the Quran, several similitudes and signs pointing to reality are detailed and explained, so that people may reflect and ponder over things. It is the characteristic of the righteous that they not only celebrate the praises of God, standing, sitting, and lying down on their sides, but also contemplate and ponder over the different phenomena of nature. The people are, therefore, advised repeatedly to look at and observe the phenomena of nature, pondering over everything in creation to arrive at the truth.

None can grasp the message of revelation except men of understanding and those firmly grounded in knowledge. Lack of true knowledge leads people to revile the true God, invent lies against Him, and worship other gods besides Him. The only safety lies in following the revelation which is replete with the knowledge of God. Whosoever has been given knowledge has indeed been given abundant good. Those who dispute wrongly about God are the ones who are without knowledge, without guidance, and without a book of enlightenment. Only those people will be promoted to suitable ranks and degrees who have faith and are possessed of knowledge, and only those who have knowledge really fear God and tread the path of righteousness.

When Solomon asked the people of his Court who would be able to bring the throne of the Queen of Sheba, it was only the one possessed of knowledge who offered himself to bring it and later actually did baring it.

The Quran advises the Holy Prophet to pray for advance in knowledge. The mysterious teacher of Moses who tried to help him have a glimpse of the working of the unseen had knowledge proceeding from God, i.e., `ilm al ladunni. Saul (Jalut) was appointed king of the Israelities because he was gifted by God abundantly with knowledge and bodily prowess. Noah, David, and Solomon possessed knowledge and judgment. Jacob had a lot of knowledge and experience; Joseph possessed abundant power and knowledge, and so also was Moses given wisdom and knowledge. It was through knowledge and reflection on the phenomena of nature, the heaven and the earth, that Abraham was able to arrive at the ultimate truth. It was through his personal experience and knowledge that Joseph refused to follow the path of the unbelievers and adopted the path of Abraham.

JUSTICE

Justice is a divine attribute and the Quran emphasizes that we should adopt it as a moral ideal. God commands people to be just towards one another and, in judging between man and man, to judge justly, for He loves those who judge equitably.

All believers stand firmly for justice even if it goes against themselves, their parents, their kith and kin, without any distinction of rich and poor. God's Revelation itself is an embodiment of truth and justice; it is revealed with the Balance (of right and wrong) so that people may stand forth for justice. The value of justice is absolute and morally binding and the believers are, therefore, warned that they should not let the hatred of some people lead them to transgress the limits of justice or make them depart from the ideal of justice, for justice is very near to piety and righteousness.

Justice demands that people should be true in word and deed, faithfully observe the contracts which they have made and fulfil all obligations. When Muslims enter into treaties with people of other faiths, they must fulfil their engagements to the end and be true to them, for that is the demand of righteousness. They are also advised to establish the system of weights with justice and not to skimp in the balance and cause thereby a loss to others by fraud, and unjustly withhold from others what is due to them, for that would lead to the spread of evil and mischief on the earth.

LOVE

Love as a human ideal demands that man should love God as the complete embodiment of all moral values above everything else. It demands that man should be kind and loving to parents, especially to the mother who bore him in pain and gave birth to him in travail. This obligation of loving kindness is further broadened to include kindred, orphans, those in need, neighbours who are near and neighbours who are strangers, and the wayfarers.

Righteousness is to spend a part of our substance out of love for God, for kin, for orphans, for the needy, for the wayfarer, and for the indigent. The Holy Prophet who is a mercy to believers and mercy to all creatures always dealt gently with people. Moses was advised by God to speak to Pharaoh mildly and gently. It is one of the characteristics of the believers that they are compassionate and loving to one another; they walk on the earth in humility, and hold to forgiveness; they are friendly to others, and forgive and overlook their faults, even though they are in anger.

GOODNESS

Goodness is an attribute of God and, therefore, it becomes the duty of every person to obey his own impulse to good. He should do good as God has been good to all and love those who do good. Believers hasten in every good work. As all prophets were quick in emulating good works, so all people are advised to strive together (as in a race) towards all that is good and virtuous. Truly did Solomon love the love of good with a view to glorifying the Lord. All good things are for the believers; goodly reward in the hereafter and highest grace of God awaits those who are foremost in good deeds. Believers are advised to repel evil with what is better, for thereby enmity will change into warm friendship.

Beauty-God possesses most beautiful names and highest excellence, and creates everything of great beauty. Man is created in the best of moulds and is given a most beautiful shape.

God has revealed the most beautiful message in the form of a book and given the best of explanations in the revealed books. We are, therefore, advised to follow the best of revelations from God. The Quran relates most beautiful stories. The association of believers, prophets, sincere lovers of truth, witnesses (to the truths of religion in word and deed), and the righteous is a beautiful fellowship.

Who is better in speech than those who invite people to the ways of the good with wisdom and beautiful preaching and argue with them in ways that are best and most gracious and say only those things that are of supreme excellence ? The Quran exhorts people to adopt ways of the highest value, for God loves those who perform deeds of excellence, good will, and conciliation.

It advises people to return greetings with greetings of greater excellence and repel evil with that which is best, for thereby they will be adding to the beauty of their own sculs. Patience is graceful and so are forgiveness and overlooking others faults. Those who perform beautiful deeds shall have the highest rewards in this world and their reward in the hereafter shall be still better when they shall enjoy the fairest of places for repose and be provided with excellent provisions.

DISVALUES

Corresponding to these values there are some disvalues which are symbolized in the Quran as Satan or Iblis..He is described as a persistent rebe who is constantly engaged in deceiving people and misleading them from the path of righteousness. He sows the seeds of enmity and hatred, creates false desires, commands what is shameful and wrong, and defaces the fair nature created by God. He is in short an enemy of mankind; and believers are, therefore, advised that they should beware of his machinations.

Destruction of Life Opposed to the value of life is weakness of man to make mischief in the earth and shed blood symbolized by the first unlawful and unjustified murder in the history of mankind by the first issue of Adam. All life being sacred, it is forbidden to commit suicide or to kill anybody without a just cause. It is equally sinful to murder one's children for fear of want or poverty. Killing a person without reason, in the view of the Quran, is tantamount to slaying the human race. Fight for the cause of righteousness is permitted only because tumult and oppression, which necessitate resort to armed resistance, are worse than killing.

All those tendencies which weaken a man's hold on life are condemned in the Quran. People are warned of falling into fear, grief, and despair or of being unmindful of the ultimate mercy of God. But any unjust clinging to life which involves sacrifice of other values is to be avoided at all cost. It does not become a man to be cowardly in the face of difficulties or to turn back and run away for life from the battle field. Similarly, covetousness, niggardiiness, and the hoarding of wealth are condemned, for they betray man's unjustified clinging to values as means, as if they were ends in themselves.

There are certain disvalues which imply disrespect of life in oneself as well as in others. Begging importunately from all and sundry, which leads to killing one's self respect, is looked upon by the Quran as unbecoming a true believer. It forbids slandering, throwing fault or sin on somebody who is innocent of it, and swelling one's cheek out of pride at men.

Scandal mongering and backbiting are hateful deeds. The Quran advises men and women not to laugh at, defame, be sarcastic to one another or call one another by offensive nicknames, and not to be suspicious, not to spy on others or speak ill of them behind their backs. It deprecates the man who is ready with oaths, is a slanderer going about with calumnies, is a transgressor beyond bounds, or is deep in sin, violence, and cruelty.

Things Momentary: Opposed to his natural urge for eternity, man sometimes through ignorance seems to be enamoured of the life of the moment, which tends to vanish and is mere play and amusement. It is no good to be pleased and remain satisfied with the transitory things of this world and the fleeting and temporal life that has a span of but an hour of a day. The true goal of man is eternity which is the home of peace, satisfaction, security, and supreme achievement for which man must, according to his nature, ever toil and struggle.

Lack of Unity: Against the value of unity there is the disvalue of the denial of the unity of the Ultimate Reality (kufr) and the association of partners with God (shirk) and likewise the disvalues of disunity, discord, and disharmony in the life of the individual and society.

Those who turn back and disobey God and His Apostle deny God's creative power, His purpose, and design, follow a part of the revealed book and disregard the rest, accept some prophets and deny others, are all deniers of the true unity of God. Hair splitting in religious matters, failure to judge by the light of divine revelation, indulgence in magic in order to sow seeds of disunity among people, are all acts which tantamount to disbelief in God.

God's unity implies that He alone deserves worship, a worship which demands exclusive submission to His will, tinged and informed with the highest emotional attachment.

Association of partners with God does not mean that, people deny God's power of creation and control of world's affairs; where they err is the belief that these partners may bring them nearer to God, wrongly and foolishly ascribe to them a share in bestowing gifts, as for example, the gifts of a goodly child, thus leading to lack of consistency in their moral conduct and lack of exclusive loyalty towards the highest ideal, which indeed is a form of most heinous sin and the highest wrong doing

A form of associating partners with God is ancestor worship. If people are invited to the path of righteousness, they refuse by saying: "Nay! we shall follow the way of our fathers," even if their fathers were devoid of knowledge and guidance. Sometimes people succumb to their personal ambitions and self importance which signifies their lack of faith in the ultimate causality of God; implied in the belief in the unity of God. When some trouble or affliction comes to man he turns to God, but when it is removed he forgets that he ever turned to him, and ascribes its removal to others besides, sets up rivals unto Him a great blasphemy and sometimes thinks that it was his own skill and knowledge which helped him in removing his difficulties.

The disvalues of discord and disunity are the result of the denial of the unity of God. The unbelievers and those who associate partners with God are always subject to fear and lack a sense of unity and harmony. It is the devil that incites people to discord and, therefore, the Quran very forcefully forbids people to be divided among themselves, and looks upon disunity as the result of lack of wisdom. It denounces divisions and splits in religion and disagreements among different sects and schisms through insolent envy. Similarly, all those acts which tend to spread mischief and tumult after there have been peace and order are condemned because they tend to create disorder, disunity, and disharmony in life.

Inertia: Opposed to power, weakness is a disvalue. It is wrong to show weakness in face of difficulties, to lose heart, to be weak in will, to be weary and faint hearted, to despair or boast, to be impatient and fretful. It is forbidden to be afraid of men or of Satan and his votaries.

There are certain disvalues which arise out of misuse of power. Warning is given to those people who oppress men with wrong doing and insolently transgress beyond bounds through the land, defying right and justice. It is forbidden to indulge in vain talk, to exhibit fierceness, to be arrogant against God, for arrogance blinds people to the truth, to swell one's cheek with pride, or walk in insolence through the earth, for one cannot rend the earth asunder or reach the mountains in height. Arrogant and obstinate transgressors, vainglorious people, those fond of self glory, people rebellious and wicked, and vying with one another in pomp and gross rivalry, are held out as examples of those who misuse their power. Satan is condemned to everlasting punishment for abusing power and becoming haughty. Moses was sent to Pharaoh because the latter had become proud and arrogant. The people of 'Ad were punished because they behaved arrogantly and thought themselves very powerful. The Israelites slew their apostles because of pride. The hypocrites turn away from truth out of arroganee. The Christians are described as nearest in love to the Muslims because they are not arrogant.

Some people try to cover their misuse of power under the cloak of determinism, but the Quran repudiates this stand as totally unrealistic. Man has the power to shape his destiny in the light of the truth of revelation.

Error: Opposed to truth or wisdom, error, conjecture, and fancy are all disvalueas which the Quran at several places denounces as equivalent to untruth or lies and which do not lend support to an individual in his moral life. Fancy and conjecture can avail nobody against truth. It is forbidden to accept a report without ascertaining its truth, to utter slander, intentionally forging falsehood and to throw fault or sin on somebody who is innocent of it; for these are all against the value of truth. Indulgence in disputation, vain discourses; and susceptibility to superstitions are disvalues opposed to wisdom. Those who do not try to save themselves from these are liable to be always afraid of others, to be unable to distinguish truth from falsehood, and right from wrong; their hearts always turn away from the light of truth and wisdom towards depths of darkness. Such are the people who have hearts wherewith they understand not, eyes wherewith they see not, and ears wherewith they hear not; in short, like cattle they lack truth and wisdom.

Hypocrisy is another disvalue. A hypocrite is one who says with his tongue what is not in his heart, who is distracted in mind, being sincerely neither for one group nor for another. Hypocrites are liars. They expect people to praise them for what they never do, compete with one another in sin and rancour, and hold secret counsels among themselves for iniquity, hostility, and disobedience. Hypocrites men and women enjoin evil and forbid what is just, and if by chance they come into possession of a position of authority, they make mischief in the land, break ties of kinship, and yet claim to be peace makers.

Showing off (riya') is also a disvalue. God does not love those who give away even money in order to be seen doing so by others, for such men have no faith in God and the Last Day. Such showing off cancels the spirit of their charity. It is like sowing seeds on a hard, barren rock on which there is little soil, and where heavy rain has left nothing but a bare stone.

Injustice: Opposed to the value of justice is the disvalue of injustice and violation of the principle of the mean. It is forbidden by the Quran to be influenced by people's vain desires and to deviate from the truth while judging between them. It is also forbidden to distort justice or decline to dc justice or to withhold justice from people merely because they are your enemies. It would be perfectly unjust to oneself and to others to pile up wealth, to bury gold and silver, and not to spend them in the cause of God and righteousness. The Quran equally forbids as violation of the principle of justice the squandering of wealth like a spendthrift and recommends the middle way of prudence which is neither extravagance nor niggardhness. It advises one neither to make one's hand tied to one's neck nor stretch it forth to its utmost reach so that one becomes blameworthy and destitute. One should eat and drink but not waste by exeess for that would be violating the principle of justice. Excess in any form is forbidden whether in food or in religion.

Usury is forbidden, for it means devouring other people's substance wrongfully and involves injustice on both sides.

Hatred and Unkindness: Against the value of love is the disvalue of hatred, harshness, or unkindness to others. People are advised not to speak any word of contempt to their parents, to orphans, and to beggars. Believers are not to revile even those whore the unbelievers call upon besides God. The Holy Prophet is described as safe from severity and hard heartedness towards others.

Vice: Against goodness the Quran denounces the disvalue of vice, i. e., doing wrong and shameful deeds. It is Satan who commands people to do what is evil and shameful. People are forbidden to come near adultery, for it is a shameful deed and an evil, opening the road to other evils. Similarly, wine and gambling involve great sin, for they are the work of Satan. The Quran forbids all shameful and evil deeds and uses a very comprehensive term zulm to cover them all. Hypocrites and unbelievers enjoin and plot evil and hold secret counsels for iniquity, evil, and rebellion and wrongfully eat up other people's property. The believers are advised, therefore, not to help one another in sin and rancour.

The Quran refers to several Satanic tendencies in man, such as ungratefulness, hastiness, impatience, despair, and unbelief in times of adversity, and pride and conceit in times of prosperity; quarrelsomeness, arrogance, greed of ever more and yet more, niggardliness, transgression of the bounds of propriety, and false sense of self sufficiency. These tendencies often lead to different forms of wrong doing and, therefore, must be counteracted by all right thinking people.

Moral Discipline: Toproduce the attitude of moral righteousness (taqwa), the discipline of prayer, fasting, zakat, and pilgrimage is enforced. People are commanded to guard strictly their habit of prayers and stand before God in a devout frame of mind, pay the zakat, spend in charity secretly and openly a beautiful loan to God a bargain that will never fail, involving a glad tidings for the believers and a cause of prosperity and spiritual joy. Those people who follow these principles are on the right path under the true guidance of the Lord. They remove the stain of evil from the people and help them refrain from shameful and unjust deeds. It is the duty of all Muslims, as witnesses for mankind in general, to hold fast to God. It is the practice of all believing people that when God grants them power in the land, they enjoin the right and forbid the wrong. All Muslims ought to follow these disciplinary principles. Those who neglect them are bound to fall into the snares of their passions.

Similarly, fasting is recommended as a discipline during the month of Ramadan in which the Quran was revealed as a guide to mankind and as an embodiment of guidance and judgment between right and wrong. It involves observance of certain limits and rules by all those who may wish to become righteous (acquire taqwa). Performance of hajj is symptomatic of a righteous life in which there should be no obscenity, nor wickedness, nor wrangling, and the best provision for which is right conduct, i. e., taqwa.

Repentance: Though man is by nature after the pattern of God's nature and, therefore, capable of approximating to the ideal embodied in the most beautiful names, yet being prone to different weaknesses he is often led to wrong his soul in spite of his best efforts to follow moral discipline. Adam disobeyed God and thus was about to run into harm and aggression, but as soon as he realized his mistake, he repented and God accepted his repentance and promised that whoever follows His guidance shall be free from grief and sorrow.

The Lord accepts repentance from His servants and forgives the sins of those who do evil in ignorance but repent soon afterwards and are never obstinate in persisting in the wrong intentionally. Even the thieves and those who had waged wars against God are covered by the universal mercy and loving kindness of God provided they repent and amend their conduct, earnestly bring God to mind, hold fast to God, purify their religion solely for God, and openly declare the Truth. There is no scope, for pessimism and despair arising from the natural weaknesses of men in doing wrong to their souls, for God turns to them that they might repent. Turning to God in repentance and seeking of forgiveness from Him lead to the grant by God to man of good and true enjoyment and abounding grace in this life. He will rain bounties from the sky and add to people's strength. To turn continually to God in repentance is the sign of the true believer; and this attitude of mind is strengthened by remembrance of God (dhikr), for it enables a man in most difficult and odd situations to keep firm and steadfast and find in it a source of deep satisfaction and mental equipoise.

Taqwa: It is the whole pursuit of value and avoidance of disvalue in general that is designated by the Quran as righteousness (taqwa). It is dependent on and is the result of faith in God and adoration of Him. The Quran is revealed solely to produce this attitude of taqwa among people. It is the presence of this moral attitude which saves people from destruction and it is this which helps them maintain God's commands in their conjugal life, in sacrifice, in different aspects of social life, and in fulfilling faithfully their social obligations.

The motive which prompts people to adopt this moral attitude of taqwa is the desire to win the pleasure of God, to gain nearness to Him, and to seek His face or countenance implying that their motive is not self interest but the seeking of good for the sake of good, which benefits their own souls and which they seek even at the sacrifice of life. The aim of such people is mainly a desire for increase in self purification without any idea of winning favour from anyone or expecting any reward whatsoever. They will get a reward of the highest value and attain complete satisfaction and prosperity the final attainment of the Eternal Home, well pleasing unto God. These people resemble a garden high and fertile, heavy rain falls on it and makes it yield a double increase of harvest, and if it receives not heavy rain, light moisture suffices it. For such people are the gardens in nearness to their Lord, a result of the pleasure of God.

To be righteous (muttaqi) is to believe in God, and the Last Day, and the angels, and the Books, and the messengers; to spend out of one's substance, out of love for God, for kin, for orphans, for the needy, for the wayfarer, for those who ask, for the ransom of slaves; to be steadfast in prayers, and to pay the zakat; to fulfil the contracts which have been made; and to be firm and patient in pain (or suffering), adversity, and periods of danger. Such people as follow these are possessed of true taqwa, i.e., righteousness. And of the servants of God the most gracious are those who walk on the earth in humility, and when the ignorant address them, they say, "Peace"; those who spend the night in adoration of their Lord prostrating and standing; those who, when they spend, are not extravagant nor niggardly, but hold a just balance between these two extremes; those who invoke not, with God, any other god, nor slay such life as God has made sacred, except for just cause, nor commit fornication; those who witness no falsehood, and, if they pass by futility, they pass by it with honourable avoidance; those who, when they are admonished with the signs of their Lord, do not show indifference to them like the deaf or the blind; and those who pray, "Our Lord! give us the grace to lead the righteous."

The better and more lasting reward of the Lord is for those who believe and put their trust in Him; those who avoid the greater crimes and shameful deeds, and, even when they are angry, they forgive; those who hearken to their Lord, and establish regular prayer; who conduct their affairs by mutual consultation; who spend out of what God bestows on them for sustenance; who, when an oppressive wrong is inflicted on them, (are not cowed but) help and defend themselves; and those who recompense injury with injury in degree equal thereto and, better still, forgive and make reconciliation. But indeed if any do help and defend themselves after a wrong is done to them, against such there is no cause of blame. The blame is only against those who oppress men with wrong doing and insolently transgress beyond bounds through the land, defying right and justice; for such there will be a grievous penalty. But indeed showing patience and forgiveness is an exercise of courageous will and resolution in the conduct of affairs.

There is yet a higher stage of moral achievement described as ihsan which signifies performance of moral action in conformity with the moral ideal with the added sense of deep loyalty to the cause of God, done in the most graceful way that is motivated by a unique love for God. Performance of righteous actions accompanied by a true faith is only a stage in the moral life of man which, after several stages, gradually matures into ihsan. God is with those who perform good deeds and perform them with added grace and beauty. Those who sacrifice animals with a spirit of dedication have piety (taqwa) no doubt, but those who thereby glorify God for His guidance, acknowledging fully the extent of His bounties provided in abundance, are the people who are characterized by ihsan. In the life hereafter the morally upright will be in the midst of gardens and springs wherein they will take spiritual enjoyment in the things which their Lord gives as a reward for leading a life of graceful righteousness.

The sincerely devoted people (muhsinin) are those who willingly suffer thirst, fatigue, or hunger in the cause of God, or tread paths which may raise the ire of the unbelievers, or receive injury from an enemy; who despite all that do not conduct themselves in life as to cause mischief on the earth but call on Him with fear and longing; who spend of their substance in the cause of God, refrain from evil, and are engaged in doing truly good deeds; who spend freely whether in prosperity or in adversity; who restrain anger and pardon all men; who are steadfast in patience and exercise restraint; who establish regular prayer and pay the zakat and have in their hearts the assurance of the hereafter; and who are always ready to forgive people and overlook their misdeeds. Almost all the prophets are included in this category which signifies that the muhsinin are those who are not only on the right path themselves, but in addition by their good example and magnetic personality lead others to the way of righteousness and help in establishing a social order based on peace, harmony, and security.

Complete power, wisdom and knowledge, true guidance from the Lord, prosperity, rise in worldly position, power, and knowledge are the by products of their life of graceful righteousness (ihsan). Their reward shall never be lost, for God is always with them and loves them and will bestow on them the rank of friendship as He did on Abraham. He who submits his whole self to the will of God and moreover does it gracefully and with a spirit of dedication (muhsin) has grasped indeed the most trustworthy handhold, and enjoys the most beautiful position in religion for he is following Abraham who was true in faith. He will get his reward from his Lord and shall experience neither fear nor grief. God is well pleased with those who followed in the footsteps of the vanguard of Islam the first of those who forsook their houses and of those who gave them aid in a spirit of devotion and graceful loyalty as well as those who followed them, as they are all with Him. For them God has prepared the garden of paradise, as their eternal home of supreme felicity.

5

ECONOMIC AND POLITICAL TEACHINGS OF THE QURAN

ECONOMIC TEACHINGS

The first economic principle emphasized by the Quran with repeated stress is that all natural means of production, and resources which subscribe to man's living, have been created by God. It is He who made them as they are and set them to follow the laws of nature that make them useful for man. It is He who allowed man to exploit them and placed them at his disposal.

On the basis of the aforesaid truth the Quran lays down the principle that an individual has neither the right to be free in acquiring and exploiting these resources according to his own sweet will, nor is he entitled to draw a line independently to decide between the lawful and the unlawful. It is for God to draw this line; for none else. The Quran condemns the Midians, an Arabian tribe of old, because its people claimed to possess a right to acquire and expend wealth in any way they liked without restriction of any kind.

It calls it a "lie" if a man describes a certain thing as lawful and another unlawful on his own account. The right to pronounce this rests with God and (as God's deputy) His Prophet.

Under the, sovereign command of God and within the limits imposed by Him, the Quran recognizes the right of holding private property as implied in several verses.

The economic scheme presented in the Quran is based entirely on the idea of individual ownership in every field. There is nothing in it to suggest that a distinction is to be made between consumption goods and production goods (or means of production) and that only the former may be held in private ownership, while the latter must be nationalized. Nor is there anything in the Quran suggesting or implying that the above mentioned scheme is of a temporary nature to be replaced later by a permanent arrangement in which collectivization of all means of production may be desired to be made the rule. Had that been the ultimate object of the Quran, it would have certainly stated it unequivocally and given us instructions with regard to that future permanent order. The mere fact that it mentions in one place that "the earth belongs to God" is not enough to conclude that it either denies or forbids private ownership of land and sanctions nationalization. Elsewhere it says, "Whatever is in the heavens and the earth belongs to God," but nobody has ever concluded from this verse that none of the things in the heavens or the earth can be held in individual possession or that all these things should be State property. If, a thing which belongs to God ceases to belong to human beings, certainly it ceases to belong to individuals and States alike.

It is equally erroneous to draw from verse xli, 10 the inference that the Quran desires to distribute all the means of livelihood in the earth equally among all men, and conclude that since this can be achieved only under nationalization, the Quran advocates or favours the introduction of that system. For the purpose of this interpretation the verse is wrongly rendered to mean that "God has put in the earth its means of sustenance proportionately in four days, alike for those who seek." But even this wrong translation does not serve the purpose. It would be incorrect to apply the words "alike for those who seek" to human beings alone. All kinds of animals, too, are among "those who seek," and there is little doubt that their means of sustenance have also been placed by God in the earth. If this verse, then, denotes an equal share to all who seek, there is no justification for restricting this equality of share to members of the human species alone.

Similarly, it would be wrong to stretch those verses of the Quran which emphasize providing for the weak or the have nots to extract from them the theory of nationalization. It should be seen that wherever it stresses this need of providing for the poor, it also prescribes the only way of meeting it, namely, that the rich and the well to do of a society should spend their wealth generously for the welfare of their poor kin, the orphans, and the needy for the pleasure of God; in addition to this, the State should collect a fixed portion of it and spend it for the same purpose. There is no hint in the Quran of any other scheme proposed to be put in practice to meet this end.

No doubt, there is nothing in the Quran to prevent a certain thing from being taken over from individual control and placed under collective control, if necessary; but to deny individual ownership altogether and adopt nationalization as an economic system does not go with the Quranic approach to man's economic problems.

The fact that, as in other things, all men do not enjoy equality in sustenance and means of earning, is described in the Quran as a feature of God's providence. Extravagant disparities devised by various social systems aside, natural inequality, as it goes, is described as the outcome of His wise apportionment, issuing from His own dispensation. The idea that this inequality is to be levelled up and substituted by dead equality is alien to the Book of God.

The Quran advises people not to covet that by which Allah has made some of you excel others; men shall have the benefit of what they earn and women shall have the benefit of what they earn, and ask Allah of His grace.

It is sometimes tried to conclude from verses xvi, 71 and xxx, 28 that the Quran desires equality of provision for everybody. But both the words and the context of these verses tell that they do not attempt to disparage inequality and urge equality to take its place, but press this fact (of inequality among men) as an argument against taking some of God's creatures as His partners. They argue that when men are not prepared to share their wealth (given by God) with their slaves as equal partners, what on earth leads them to think that God will share His powers with His servants and have partners with Him from amongst His creation?

The Quran also asserts with full and repeated emphasis that God has created His bounties for men so that they use them for their benefit. It is not His intent that men should have nothing to do with them and live a life of renunciation. However, He desires that they should distinguish between things pure and impure, lawful and unlawful. They should use and exploit only what is pure and lawful, and there too should observe moderation.

To achieve this end the Quran ordains that wealth should be acquired by lawful means only and that unlawful ways and means should be discarded altogether: "O you who believe, take not your wealth among yourselves in wrongful ways, but let there be trade among you by mutual agreement...."

These "wrongful ways" have been detailed at length by the Holy Prophet and the great jurists of Islam have elucidated them in books of law. Some of them, however, have been described in the Quran as under:

(a) "And do not eat one another's property among yourselves in wrongful ways, nor seek by it to gain the nearness of the judges that you may sinfully consume a portion of other men's goods and that knowingly."

(b) "If one of you deposits a thing on trust with another, let him who is trusted (faithfully) deliver his trust, and let him fear God, his Lord."

(c) "He who misappropriates (the public money) will come on the Day of Judgment with what he has misappropriated; then shall everyone be given in full what he earned."

(d) "The thief, male or female, cut off his or her hands."

(e) "Those who devour the property of orphans unjustly, devour fire in their bellies, and will soon endure a blazing fire."

(f) "Woe to the defrauders who, when they take the measure from men, exact full measure, but when they measure or weigh for them, give less than is due."

(g) "Those who love that indecent things should spread among the believers, for them is a painful chastisement, in the life of this world and the hereafter.

(h) "Force not your slave girls to prostitution that you may enjoy (some) gain of the present life, if they desire to live in chastity." "And approach not fornication, surely it is a shameful deed and an evil Way." "The adulterer and the adulteress, flog each of them with a hundred stripes."

(i) "O ye believers, wine and gambling and idols and divining arrows are an abomination of Satan's handiwork; so avoid them that you may prosper."

(j) "God has permitted trade and forbidden usury." "O ye believers, fear God and give up what remains (due to you) of usury if you are believers (indeed). If you do not do so, take notice of war from God and His Messenger. But if you repent you shall have your principal. Neither you wrong, nor shall you be wronged. If the debtor is in straintened circumstances, give him time till it is easy (for him to pay), and that you remit (the debt), by way of charity, that is the best thing for you, if you only knew."

Thus we see that the Quran has prohibited the following ways of acquiring wealth:

(i) Taking another's property without, his consent or remuneration or with consent and with or without remuneration in such a way that the consent is forced or obtained by guile.

(ii) Bribes.

(iii) Forcible acquisitions.

(iv) Fraud, whether with private or public wealth.

(v) Theft.

(vi) Misappropriation of orphans' property.

(vii) Taking or giving wrong measure

(viii) Businesses which help to spread indecency.

(ix) Prostitution and its earnings.

(x) Manufacture, buying and selling, and carriage of wines.

(xi) Gambling, including all such ways in which the transfer of wealth from one person to another depends on mere chance.

(xii) Manufacture, buying, and selling of idols, and service of temples where idols are kept or worshipped.

(xiii) Earnings from businesses like astrology, foretelling of fate, divination, etc.

(xiv) Usury.

After prohibiting these wrong ways of acquiring wealth the Quran also strongly condemns the amassing of wealth in a covetous and niggardly way. Along with this we are warned that love of wealth or a hankering after riches and pride of fortune hae always been among the causes that have led men astray and ultimately sent them to ruin.

On the other hand, the Quran condemns it in equally strong terms that one should squander one's properly acquired wealth in wasteful pursuits, spend it for one's own lust or luxury, and put it to no use save raising one's own standard of living. The proper course for man, according to the Quran, is to spend moderately on his own needs and those of his family. He and his dependants have rights to his wealth which must be granted without stint, but he cannot be allowed to squander everything on himself and his family, for there are other obligations, too, which must be recognized.

After he has satisfied his own needs with moderation, a man should spend what is left over of his well earned wealth in the following ways:

> *"They ask you what they should spend (in charity). Say: `Whatever exceeds your needs."'*

> *"It is not piety that you turn your faces towards east or west. Piety is that a man should believe in God and the Last Day and the angels and the Book and the Prophets, and give his wealth for the love of God to his kinsfolk and the orphans and the needy and the traveller and to those who ask, and for setting the slaves free."*

> *"You will never attain piety until you spend what you love (of your wealth). And whatever you spend, God knows it well."*

> *"Serve God, and associate no partner with Him, and be kind to parents and kinsmen and orphans and the needy, and the neighbour who is of kin, and the neighbour who is a stranger, and the companion by your side, and the traveller, and the slaves that your right hands own. Surely God does not love the proud and the boastful."*

> *"(Charity is) for those poor people who are so restrained in the way of God that they cannot travel in the land*

to earn their living. The ignorant man regards them as wealthy because of their self possession. You shall know them by their mark, they do not beg of men importunately. What ever (wealth) you spend (on them) God surely knows it."

"They (the righteous) feed the needy, the orphan, and the captive, for the love of God, saying: `We feed you for the sake of God alone. We desire no reward from you nor any thanks.'"

"(Excepted from the fire of hell are) those in whose wealth there is a fixed portion for the beggar and the destitute."

The Quran not only tells that this kind of spending is the essence of piety but also warns that its absence in a society must mean its decay and ruination:

"Expend in the way of God, and cast not yourself with your own hands into ruin."

Besides this general and voluntary spending in the way of God the Quran enjoins expending of wealth as expiation of omissions and sins. For instance, if a man takes an oath and then forswears it, "the expiation for it is to feed ten poor persons with the average of food which you serve to your own folk, or to clothe them, or to give a slave his freedom; or if anyone does not find (the wherewithal to do so) let him fast three days."

Similarly, if anyone makes his wife unlawful for him by declaring her to be his mother or sister by zihar and later seeks to retract and take her again, it is ordained that "he should free a slave before the two touch each other, and he who has not (the wherewithal for that) should fast for two months consecutively... and he who is unable to do so let him feed sixty poor persons."

Like expiations have also been ordained to make up for omissions in the performance of piilgrimage and proper observance of the month of fasting.

But all such expense will count as expense in God's way only if it is really free from selfishness, guile, and display, and there is no attempt to hurt or lay anyone under obligation. One must also make no attempt to sort out the worse of one's goods to disburse in charity. One must give the choice of them, and bear nothing in mind except the love and pleasure of God.

This expending of wealth which the Quran variously terms as "spending in God's way" or charity or zakat, is not a mere act of piety, an almsgiving; rather it is the third among the five pillars of Islam, viz., (1) the witness of faith (iman), (2) prayer (salat), (3) charity (zakat), (4) fasting (saum) and (5) pilgrimage (hajj). It has been mentioned constantly with prayer (salat) some thirty seven times in the Quran and both of them have been described with full emphasis as essentials of Islam, without which there can be no salvation. Zakat, it says, has been a pillar of true religion preached by all the prophets of God.

And so this zakat is a pillar of Islam now in the religion of the last Prophet of God. It is as essential for one who joins the fold of Islam as bearing witness to the truth of faith (iman) or prayer (salat).

Zakat is not only for the good of society; it is also necessary for the moral development and edification of the giver himself. It is for his own purification and salvation. It is not only a tax, but also an act of worship just like prayer. It is an essential part of that programme which the Quran prescribes for the amelioration of man's soul.

But the Quran was not content to infuse a general spirit of voluntary benevolence and philanthropy among people. It instructed the Prophet as the Head of the Islamic State to fix an obligatory minimum for it, and arrange for its regular receipt and disbursement.

"Take a charity from their wealth."

The words "a charity" pointed out that a certain fixed measure determined by the Prophet was to be enjoined on people, besides the usual charity they practised of their own accord. Accordingly, the Prophet fixed a maximum allowable limit in respect of different kinds of wealth, and the following rates were fixed for the holdings that stood above that limit

(1) On gold, silver, and cash hoardings -2 1/2 % annually

(2) On agricultural produce from unirrigated land-10 % annually

(3) On agricultural produce from artificially irrigated land-5 % annually

(4) On livestock kept for breeding and trade the rates are different for sheep, goats, cows, camels, etc.

(5) On mines in private ownership and treasure troves-20 % annually.

The Prophet of God imposed these rates of zakat as a duty on Muslims like the five daily prayers. As duties, and in being incumbent, there is no difference between the two. According to the Quran, it is one of the basic objects of an Islamic State that it should institute prayer (salat) and manage regular receipt and distribution of zakat.

It should be noted that although, as seen above, the collection and disbursement of zakat is a duty of an Islamic State, the believers will not be absolved from paying it (privately), just as they are not absolved from prayer, in case the Islamic State ceases to exist or is neglectful of its duty.

To the funds collected under zakat the Quran adds another item a part of the spoils of war. The rule prescribed by the Book is that the soldiers fighting in a battle should not loot the spoils which fall into their hands after a victory, but bring everything before the commander who should distribute four fifth of the whole booty amongst soldiers who participated in the engagement and hand over the remaining fifth to the State for the following purposes:

> *"Know that whatever booty you take, the fifth of it is for God and the Prophet and the kinsmen and the orphans and the needy and the traveller."*

The income from these two sources, according to the Quran, is not a part of the general exchequer maintained to furnish comforts and provide for essential services for all including those who contribute to the zakat fund. On the contrary, it is reserved for use on the following items:

> *Alms are meant for the poor and the needy and those who work on them (i. e., collect, disburse, and manage them) and those whose hearts are to be reconciled, for the ransoming of slaves and those in debt, and the cause of God and the traveller a duty from God."*

The Quranic rule with regard to the property which a person leaves behind him after his or her death is that it should be distributed among his parents, children, and wife (or husband, as the case may be) according to a specified ratio. If he leaves neither parents nor children, his brothers and sisters (real, step, or uterine) should divide it. Detailed instructions relating to this may be seen in chapter iv of the Quran. We omit to reproduce them here to avoid prolixity.

The guiding principle here is that property accumulated by a person during his life time should not remain accumulated there after his death but scatter among his kinsfolk. This is opposed to the principle underlying primogeniture, the joint family, and other like systems which aim at keeping accumulated wealth accumulated even after the death of its holder.

The Quran also rejects the system of adopting children to make them heirs, and lays down that inheritance should go to those who are actually related, not to those fictitiously adopted as sons and daughters to pass on property.

However, after ensuring blood relations their rights, the Quran advises them to be generous to the other relations who are not going to inherit but are present on the occasion of the division of property. They also may be given something out of kindness.

In prescribing the law of inheritance the Quran allows a person's right to make a will before he dies in respect of the property he is leaving behind him.

This ordinance instructs a man who is passing away to urge his offspring to be kind to his parents the young being often inclined to neglect the proper care of their aged grand parents; and to bequeath some of his property to those of his kinsfolk who deserve help but are not entitled to inherit anything under the law. Besides this if a person is leaving much wealth he may bequeath a part of it for charitable purposes or works of social welfare, for the above quoted verse does not ask him to restrict his will to his parents and relatives alone.

It is evident from these laws of inheritance that the rule in respect of the heritage of private property is that two thirds of it must be divided among legal heirs and the remaining one third left to the discretion of the dying person to dispose it of as he wills, provided, however, the purpose for which he means to bequeath it is just and lawful, and no one is robbed of his right.

As for those people who cannot husband their property well on account of idiocy or want of intelligence and are wasting it away or, it is genuinely feared, are likely to do so, the instruction is that they may not be allowed to hold it in their care. Such property should lie in the care of their guardians or responsible judicial officers and may be restored to them only when there is satisfaction that they are able to manage their affairs properly. An important point described in this verse about private possessions is that although they are the property of their owners according to law, yet they do not wholly belong to them, because the interest of society is also involved in them. That is why the Quran calls them "your property" instead of "their property."

That is also why, where unintelligent use of private property is causing, or is likely to cause, harm to the collective interest of society, it allows guardians or magistrates to take it over in their own hands, without, however, disturbing the owner's right of owning it or benefiting by it.

The Quranic direction in respect of properties, wealth, and incomes that belong to the State is that they should not be used for the welfare of rich classes only but of all alike and particularly the poor whose interest deserves more looking after than that of any other class.

> *"Whatever God has bestowed on His Messenger, (taking it) from the people of these towns, is for God and the Messenger and the kinsfolk and the orphans and the needy and the traveller, in order that it may not circulate among the rich of you (only).... (It is also) for the poor emigrants who have been expelled from their homes and possessions."*

In the matter of levying taxes the Quran teaches the principle that their incidence should lie on those who possess more than they need, and on that part of their wealth which is surplus after all legitimate needs have been met.

> *"They ask you what they should spend. Say: 'What is spare after meeting your needs."*

The characteristic features and basic principles of the economic scheme drawn by the Quran for man and described in the above twenty one paragraphs may be summed up as follows:

i. It works a happy co ordination between economic and moral values. Instead of being treated as distinctly separate things, the two are drawn together into a harmonious blend. The economic problem has been tackled not from the purely "economic" point of view; it has been solved after being appropriately placed in the overall scheme of life based on ethical concepts of Islam. (paras 1, 2, 4, 5.)

ii. All resources and means of living are regarded as God's magnanimous gift to mankind; this implies that all kinds of monopolization, individual, collective, or national, should be discouraged and all men should be provided with free opportunities of earning on God's earth to the maximum limit possible. (para 5.)

iii. It allows individual right of ownership but not to an unlimited extant. Besides putting restrictions on it in the interest of other individuals and society as a whole, it admits on a person's property the rights of his relatives, neighbours, friends, the needy, the unfortunate, and, so to speak; of all members of society. Some of these are made enforceable by law; as for others, arrangement has been made to educate people morally and intellectually enabling them to understand these rights and prepare themselves to honour them of their own free will. (paras 3, 5, 7 14, 16, 18, 19.)

iv. The natural way for the economic system to operate according to this scheme is that individuals should work it and try to improve it with free endeavour. However, they are not left to do as they may without checks and restraints of any kind. For their own cultural and economic welfare and for that of their society this freedom has been curtailed within limits. (paras 6, 14, 21.)

v. Man and woman are alike declared owners of the wealth they earn, inherit, or acquire by other lawful means, and allowed to derive benefit from their possessions. (paras 3, 4, 17.)

vi. To preserve economic balance people have been urged to give up miserlyness and renunciation, and take to putting the gifts of God to good use. But at the same time they have been strongly warned not to indulge in extravagance of any kind. (paras 5, 7, 8.)

vii. To secure economic justice it has been assured that unjust means are not employed to force the flow of wealth in particular channels. Nor should wealth acquired by just means remain stored at a place and fall out of circulation. Arrangement is also made to ensure that wealth remains in constant use and circulation, particularly for the benefit of those classes which are deprived of their due and reasonable share for one reason or another. (paras 6 8, 10, 11, 14, 16 18, 20.)

viii. The scheme does not depend much upon the interference of law or the State to ensure economic justice. After declaring a few unavoidable things to be the responsibility of the State for this purpose, it seeks to enforce the other items in its plan through the intellectual and moral uplift of the individuals comprising a society and its general amelioration. Economic justice is thus secured in perfect concord with the principle of allowing the exercise of individual freedom in the economic field. (paras 5 21.)

ix. Instead of producing class conflict it puts an end to the causes of such conflicts and produces a spirit of co operation and comradeship among the different classes of society. (paras 4, 6 10, 12, 14 16, 20, 21.)

When these principles were worked out and put into practice in governmental and social spheres during the time of the Holy Prophet and his "Guided Successors," many more injunctions and precedents came into existence. But our present study precludes that discussion. Books of history, biography, traditions, and jurisprudence abound in such matters and may be consulted for details.

POLITICAL TEACHINGS

The political philosophy of the Quran is essentially based on its fundamental concept of the universe which should be clearly kept in mind for its proper appreciation and right appraisal. If we study this concept of the universe from the political point of view, the following four points vividly come into prominence

(a) That God is the creator of the whole of this universe including man and all those things which he exploits and harnesses into his service.

(b) That God Himself is the sole master, ruler, director, and administrator of His creation.

(c) That sovereignty in this universe does not and cannot vest in anyone except God. Nor has anyone else any right to share this sovereignty with Him.

(d) That all attributes and powers of sovereignty are solely His prerogatives. He is living, self existent, self sufficient, eternal, omniscient, omnipotent, and exalted above all flaw, defect, or weakness. His is the supreme authority; everything submits to Him willingly or unwillingly; to Him belong all powers. He can dictate whatever He likes and none has the power to interfere in or review His commandments. No one can intercede with Him save by His leave. Nobody has the power to harm those whom He intends to benefit and none can protect whom He intends to harm. He is accountable to none; everyone else is accountable to Him. He is the guardian of one and all. He can protect against all, but none can give quarters against Him. His are the powers of inflicting punishment or granting forgiveness. He is the supreme Lord over all other rulers. He grants an opportunity to rule on His earth to whomsoever He desires and withdraws this privilege whenever He so wills.

These essential powers and attributes of a sovereign being vest solely in God.

On the basis of this concept of the universe the Quran asserts that the real sovereign of mankind too is the same as the sovereign of the whole universe. His is the only rightful authority in human affairs just as in all other affairs of creation. No one else, be he human or non human, has any right to give orders or decide matters independently.

There is, however, one vital difference.

In the physical sphere of the universe the sovereignty of God is established by itself regardless of whether one willingly submits to it or not. In that sector of his life even man has no option to do otherwise. He too finds himself totally regulated by the inexorable laws of nature like any other object from the tiniest speck of an atom to the magnificent galaxies in space. But in the volitional sphere of his life man has been allowed a certain amount of free will and God has not coerced him to an unwilling submission. Herein He has chosen only to invite and persuade mankind through His revealed Books (the last of which is the Holy Quran) to surrender themselves before His Lordship and acknowledge His sovereignty with deliberate willingness. The Quran has discussed the different aspects of this subject at great length. For instance:

(a) The Lord of the universe is indeed the Lord of man, and this position must be fully recognized by him.

(b) God alone has the right to decide and order. Mankind should submit to none save Him. This is the only right course.

(c) The right to rule belongs to God alone because He is the creator.

(d) The right to order and decide belongs to God because He is the ruler of the universe.

(e) His rule is right and just, because He alone comprehends reality and none else is in a position to give unerring guidance.

On these grounds the Quran lays down that an unadulterated obedience is the due of God alone; that it is His Law that should rule supreme; and that to obey others or to follow one's own wishes against the Law of God, is not the right way.

The Quran also asserts that no one has the right to transgress the limits that have been laid down by God for the regulation of human affairs.

It also points out that all orders and decisions in contravention of the Law of God are not only wrong and unlawful but also unjust and blasphemous. It condemns all such orders as anti Islamic and the attempt to abide by them as negation of faith.

Then the Quran says that prophets are the only source of our knowing the Law of God. They alone are the bearers of revelation and are in a position to convey to mankind the commandments and directions of their Lord. They again are the persons divinely authorized to explain those commandments by their word and deed. Thus, the prophets are embodiments of the legal sovereignty of God. That is why obedience to them has been considered to be obedience to God Himself and faith in them has been made a necessary condition for demarcating belief from disbelief.

According to the Quran, the commandments of God and the Prophet of Islam constitute the Supreme Law and the Muslims as such cannot adopt any attitude other than that of complete submission to it. A Muslim is not allowed to follow his own independent decisions in matters which have been finally and unequivocally decided by God and His Apostle. To do that is a negation of faith.

The right form of government for mankind according to the Quran is one in which the State relinquishes its claim to sovereignty in favour of God and, after recognizing the legal supremacy of God and His Apostle, accepts the position of Caliphate (vicegerency) under the suzerainty of the Rightful Ruler. In this capacity all the legislative, executive, and judicial powers of the State will necessarily be circumscribed by the limits which have been described in paras 3, 4, and 5 above.

The conception of Caliphate as it has been put forth by the Quran, can be summed up in the following terms

(a) All the powers that man possesses in this world are in fact not his own, but have been endowed to him by God Almighty. The Lord Himself has assigned to man the position in which he may exercise these delegated powers within the limits prescribed by Him. Man is thus not an independent master but a vicegerent of the real Sovereign.

(b) Every nation that acquires the power and authority to rule over any part of the world is in reality a vicegerent of God in its domain.

(c) This vicegerency, however, cannot be right and lawful unless it is subservient to the commandments of the real Sovereign. Any State independent of Him and not subservient to His commands is not a vicegerency. It is really a revolt against the Lord.

The powers of a true Caliphate do not vest in any individual nor in any clan, class or community, but in those who believe and do good. The text of xxiv, 55 that "God has promised to those of you who believe and do good that He will most certainly make them His vicegerents on the earth..." is quite clear on this point. According to this verse, every good Muslim is fit to hold the position of a Caliph. It is this aspect of Islamic Caliphate that distinguishes it from a kingship, an oligarchy, and a theocracy. It is different even from modern democracy. There is a basic difference between the two. The edifice of democracy is raised on the principle of popular sovereignty; while in Islamic Caliphate the people themselves surrender their independence to the sovereignty of God and of their own accord limit their powers within the four corners of the divine Law and the promise of vicegerency has been held out to them only if they are morally good.

The government of a State established with a view to running an Islamic Caliphate cannot claim an absolute or unlimited obedience from the people. They are bound to obey it only so far as it exercises its powers in accordance with the divine Law revealed in nature and the Sacred Book. There can be neither obedience nor co operation in sin and aggression.

In all affairs of the State, right from its constitution to the election of its Head and members of its parliament, and the matters of legislation and administration, the Muslims should make it a rule to take counsel among themselves.

The following qualifications must be kept in view in choosing the people responsible to run the State:

(a) They must have faith in the principles according to which they have to manage the affairs of the Caliphate. Evidently, an ideological system cannot work in the hands of those who do not subscribe to its principles.

(b) They should not be unjust, licentious, forgetful of God, or transgressors of divine limits. They should be, on the other hand, honest, trustworthy, Godfearing, and virtuous.

(c) They should not be unwise and ignorant. They must be rather educated, wise, intelligent, and both bodily and intellectually fit to pilot the State.

(d) They should be men of integrity so that they may be safely entrusted with public responsibilities.

The constitution of such a State shall be based on the following principles:

(a) "O ye who believe! obey Allah, and obey the Apostle and those of you vho are in authority; and if you have a dispute concerning any matter, refer it to Allah and the Apostle if ye are (in truth) believers in Allah and the Last Day. That is better and more seemly in the end."

This verse elucidates five constitutional points:

(i) That obedience to God and His Apostle must be given priority to every other obedience.

(ii) That obedience to those who are in authority is subject to the obedience to God and His Apostle.

(iii) That the Head of the State must be from amongst the believers.

(iv) That it is possible for the people to differ with the government and its rulers.

(v) That in case of dispute the final authority to decide between them is the Law of God and His Apostle.

(b) The Quran does not give us any hard and fast rules about the method of election and consultation. It lays down only broad based principles and leaves the problem of their practical implementation to be decided in accordance with the exigencies of time and the requirements of society.

(c) In those matters about which clear injunctions have been given or definite principles laid down or limits prescribed by God and His Apostle, the legislature has only the right to interpret them, or to frame bye laws and rules of procedure to bring them into practice. As for those matters about which the Supreme Law is silent, the legislature is allowed to legislate for all purposes and needs of the society keeping in view the spirit and the general principles of Islam. The very fact that no clear injunction exists about them in the Quran and Sunnah is sufficient to show that the Lawgiver has Himself left it to the good sense of the believers.

(d) The judiciary must be free from every pressure and influence to adjudicate impartially without being carried away by the public or the people in authority. Its foremost duty is to give verdict strictly in accordance with the law and requirements of justice without being swayed either by the passions or prejudices of its own members or those of others.

This State comes into being for two main purposes. First, that justice and equity should be established in human affairs, and, secondly, that, the powers and resources of the State should be harnessed for the welfare of the people, i. e., for promotion, for them, of all that is good and eradication of all that is evil. All citizens of the State, whether Muslims or non Muslims, must be guaranteed the following fundamental rights, and it is the bounden duty of the State to safeguard them against all types of encroachment:

(a) Security of person.

(b) Security of property.

(c) Protection of honour.

(d) Right of privacy.

(e) The right to protest against injustice.

(f) The right to enjoin what is good and forbid what is evil. This includes the right of criticism.

(g) Freedom of association, provided it is used for good ends and does not become an instrument for spreading dissensions and creating fundamental differences in the society.

(h) Freedom of faith and conscience.

(i) Protection against wrongfully hurting one's religious susceptibilities. The Quran has clearly laid down in this connection that in matters of religious differences an academic discussion can be held, but it must be conducted in a fair and decent manner.

(j) Limiting the responsibility of every person only to his or her own deeds.

(k) Security from action being taken against anyone on false reports about his or her crime.

(l) The right of the destitute and the needy to be provided with basic necessities of life by the State.

(m) Equal treatment of all its subjects by the State without discrimination.

An Islamic State has the following rights against its citizens:

(a) That they must submit to its authority.

(b) That they must be law abiding and should not disturb the public order and tranquillity.

(c) They must give unstinted support to the State in its rightful activities.

(d) They must be prepared to sacrifice their life and property for the defence of the State.

The Quran gives the following important directions about the foreign policy of the Islamic State:

(a) Sanctity of treaties and pledges.

(b) Honesty and integrity in all transactions.

(c) International justice.

(d) Respect for the rights of neutrals in war.

(e) Love of peace.

(f) Non participation in the efforts directed to self aggrandizement and oppression in the world.

(g) Friendly treatment to all non hostile powers.

(h) Fair deal with all those who are good and honest in their dealings.

(i) Retaliation in proportion to the high handedness of others and no more.

The salient features of the State envisaged in these sixteen points laid down by the Holy Quran are as follows:

(i) This State is brought into existence by a conscious resolve on the part of a politically free nation to renounce all claims to sovereignty in favour of God Almighty, to surrender its autonomy accepting the position of vicegerency under Him, and to work according to precepts and directions given by the Book of God and the Sunnah of His Apostle.

(ii) It is theocratic in so far as it is based on the doctrine of sovereignty of God but, in actual and practical realization of this doctrine, it is vitally different from theocracy. Instead of delegating the vicegerency of God to a particular order of priests and vesting them with the full powers to rule, it vests the believers whose deeds are good with the right of Caliphate.

(iii) It is democratic in the sense that the formation of government, change in its administrative set up, and its working wholly depend upon the general will. But the rights of the people in this system are not so unlimited that they may change the law of the State, its ideology, its internal and external policy, and its resources according to their own sweet will. On the other hand, the Supreme Law of God and His Apostle with its legal and moral code provides a permanent and inviolable check which always keeps the life of the community on the right keel and on a broad pattern which can be changed neither by the executive, nor by the legislature, nor by the judiciary, nor even by the whole nation unless it decides to renounce the religion of God and break its pledge with Him.

(iv) It is an ideological State which must be run only by those who accept its basic ideology and principles wholeheartedly. As for those who do not subscribe to its ideology but live within its territorial bounds, the State guarantees them the same civil rights as are enjoyed by the other inhabitants provided they pledge to behave as law abiding citizens.

(v) It is a State which makes no discrimination whatsoever on grounds of race or colour and is not bound by any linguistic or geographical barriers. It is a purely ideological State. All peoples, no matter to whatever race, nation, or country they belong, can accept this ideology and become equal partners in all the affairs of the State. Such an ideological

State bids fair to become a world State. But even if more than one such States are established in different parts of the world, all of them will be equally Islamic. And instead of there being any nationalistic conflicts among them, they will extend fraternal support and co operation to one another. Not only that, there is every possibility of their joining together in a world confederation of their own.

(vi) The real spirit of this State lies in subordinating politics to morality and conducting affairs conscientiously and God fearingly. Honour and eminence must come through moral excellence alone. Paramount importance should be given to character besides ability in selecting men of authority. Honesty, fairness, and justice are to prevail in every sphere of domestic administration. And the whole foreign policy is to devolve upon truth, faithfulness, love of peace, fair dealing, and international justice.

(vii) Policing is not the only function of this State. It does not come into existence merely to maintain law and order and to defend its territory against external attacks. It is a State with a purpose and a mission. It must positively strive for the achievement of social justice, promotion of good, and eradication of evil.

(viii) Equality of rights, status and opportunities, supremacy of Law, co-operation in virtue and non co operation in vice, sense of accountability to God Almighty, sense of duties more than that of rights, unity of purpose between the individuals, society, and the State, guarantee of the basic necessities of life to everyone in need, are the fundamental values of this State.

(ix) The relations between State and individual are so balanced in this system that neither the State has been vested with absolute authority reducing individuals to virtual slavery, nor has individual freedom been allowed to turn itself into licence threatening the interest of society. On the one hand, by guaranteeing fundamental rights to its citizens and by making the State authority subject to the Supreme Law of God and the democratic process of shura, it provides ample opportunities for the development of individual personality and protection from undue interference by others. And, on the other hand, it binds the individual to a definite code of morality, makes it obligatory for him faithfully to obey the orders of the State working in accordance with the Law of God, to co operate wholeheartedly with it in the cause of virtue, to avoid disturbing its tranquillity, and to sacrifice even his life and property in its defence.

MU'TAZALISM

Mu'tazilism by Mir Valiuddin, M.A Ph.D., Professor of Philosophy, Osmania University, Hyderabad Deccan (India)

THE GENERAL MU'TAZILITE POSITION

Subsequent to the times of the Companions of the Prophet of Islam, the Mu'tazilah creed made its appearance. It had its inception nearly two centuries after the migration (Hijrah) of the Holy Prophet to Madinah. The Mu'tazilites were thorough going ratiorialists. They believed that the arbiter of whatever is revealed has to be theoretical reason. Let us, for a moment, consider why the Mu'tazilites were so named. The story goes that one day Imam al Hasan al Basri was imparting instruction to his pupils in a mosque. Before the lessons were finished someone turned up and addressed him thus:

> *"Now, in our own times a sect of people has made its appearance, the members of which regard the perpetrator of a grave sin as an unbeliever and consider him outside the fold of Islam. Yet another group of people have appeared who give hope of salvation to the perpetrator of a grave sin. They lay down that such a sin cb an do no harm to a true believer. They do not in the least regard action as a part of faith and hold that as worship is of no use to one who is an unbeliever, so also sin can do no harm to one who is a believer in God. What, in your opinion, is the truth and what creed should we adopt?"*

Imam al Hasan al Basri was on the point of giving a reply to this query when a long necked pupil of his got up and said: "The perpetrator of grave sins is neither a complete unbeliever nor a perfect believer; he is placed midway between unbelief and faith an intermediate state (manzilah bain al manzilatain)."

Having spoken he strode to another corner of the mosque and began to explain this belief of his to others. This man was Wasil ibn `Ata. The Imam shot a swift glance at him and said, "I'tazala `anna," i. e.,"He has withdrawn from us." From that very day Wasil and his followers were called al Mu'tazilah, the Withdrawers or Secessionists.

Ibn Munabbih says that the title of al Mu'tazilah came into vogue after the death of al Hasan al Basri. According to his statement, when al-Hasan passed away, Qatadah succeeded him and continued his work. `Amr ibn `Ubaid and his followers avoided the company of Qatadah; therefore, they were given the name of al Mu'tazilah. In brief, the word i'tizal means to withdraw or secede, and the Mu'tazilites are the people who in some of their beliefs were diametrically opposed to the unanimous consent of the early theologians or the People of the Approved Way (ahl al sunnah). The leader of all of them was Wasil b. `Ata who was born in 80/699 at Madinah and died in 131/748.

Muslims generally speak of Wasil's party as the Mu'tazilites, but the latter call themselves People of Unity and Justice (ahl al tauhid wal `adl). By justice they imply that it is incumbent on God to requite the obedient for their good deeds and punish the sinners for their misdeeds. By unity they imply the denial of the divine attributes. Undoubtedly, they admit that God is knowing, powerful, and seeing, but their intellect does not allow them to admit that these divine attributes are separate and different from the divine essence. The reason for this view of theirs is that if the attributes of God are not considered to be identical with the essence of God, "plurality of eternals" would necessarily result and the belief in unity would have to be given up. This, in their opinion, is clear unbelief (kufr). Unity and justice are the basic principles of the beliefs of the Mu'tazilites and this is the reason why they call themselves "People of Unity and Justice."

Now, from the basic beliefs of unity and justice a few more beliefs necessarily follow as corollaries God Almighty's justice necessitates that man should be the author of his own acts; then alone can he be said to be free and responsible for his deeds. The same was claimed by the Qadarites. The Mu'tazilites accepted totally the theory of indeterminism and became true successors of the Qadarites. If man is not the author of his own acts and if these acts are the creation of God, how can he be held responsible for his acts and deserve punishment for his sins? Would it not be injustice on the part of God that, after creating a man helpless, He should call him to account for his sins and send him to hell? Thus, all the Mu'tazilites agree in the matter of man's being the creator of his volitional acts. He creates some acts by way of mubasharah and some by way of taulid. By the term taulid is implied the necessary occurrence of another act from an act of the doer, e.g., the movement of Zaid's finger necessitates the movement of his ring. Although he does not intend to move the ring, yet he alone will be regarded as the mover. Of course, to perform this act the medium of another act is necessary. Man creates guidance or misguidance for himself by way of mubasharah and his success or failure resulting from this is created by way of taulid. God is not in the least concerned in creating it, nor has God's will anything to do with it. In other words, if a man is regarded as the author of his own acts, it would mean that it is in his power either to accept Islam and be obedient to God, or become an unbeliever and commit sins, and that God's will has nothing to do with these acts of his. God, on the other hand, wills that all created beings of His should embrace Islam and be obedient to Him. He orders the same to take place and prohibits people from committing sins.

Since man is the author of his own acts, it is necessary for God to reward him for his good deeds and this can be justly claimed by him. As al Shahrastani puts it: "The Mu'tazilites unanimously maintain, that man decides upon and creates his acts, both good and evil; that he deserves reward or punishment in the next world for what he does. In this way the Lord is safeguarded from association with any evil or wrong or any act of unbelief or transgression. For if He created the wrong, He would be wrong, and if He created justice, He would be just."

It is the creed of most of the Mu'tazilites that one possesses "ability" before the accomplishment of the act, but some Mu'tazilites (e. g., Muhammad b. `Isa and abu `Isa Warraq) like the Sunnites are of the view that one has ability to act besides the act.

The justice of God makes it incumbent upon Him not to do anything contrary to justice and equity. It is the unanimous verdict of the Mu'tazilites that the wise can only do what is salutary (al salah) and good, and that God's wisdom always keeps in view what is salutary for His servants; therefore, He cannot be cruel to them. He cannot bring into effect evil deeds. He cannot renounce that which is salutary. He cannot ask His servants to do that which is impossible. Further, reason also suggests that God does not place a burden on any creature greater than it can bear.

According to the Mu'tazilites, things are not good or evil because God declares them to be so. No, God makes the distinction between good and evil on account of their being good and evil. Goodness or evil are innate in the essence of things themselves. This very goodness or evil of things is the cause of the commands and prohibitions of the Law.

The human intellect is capable of perceiving the goodness and evil of a few things and no laws are required to express their goodness and evil, e. g., it is commendable to speak the truth and despicable to commit oneself to untruth. This shows that the evil and goodness of things are obvious and require no proof from the Shari`ah. Shameful and unjust deeds are evil in themselves; therefore, God has banned indulgence in them. It does not imply that His putting a ban on them made them shameful and unjust deeds. The thoroughgoing rationalism of the Mu'tazilites is thus expressed by al Shahrastani in these words: "The adherents of justice say: All objects of knowledge fall under the supervision of reason and receive their obligatory power from rational insight. Consequently, obligatory gratitude for divine bounty precedes the orders given by (divine) Law; and beauty and ugliness are qualities belonging intrinsically to what is beautiful and ugly."

From the second principle of the Mu'tazilites, the unity of God, the following beliefs necessarily result as corollaries:

1. Denial of the beatific vision. The Mu'tazilites hold that vision is not possible without place and direction. As God is exempt from place and direction, therefore, a vision of Him is possible neither in this world nor in the hereafter.
2. Belief that the Quran is a created speech of Allah. It was held by them that the Quran is an originated work of God and it came into existence together with the prophethood of the Prophet of Islam.
3. God's pleasure and anger, not attributes, but states. According to the Mu'tazilites, God's pleasure and anger should not be regarded as His attributes, because anger and pleasure are states and states are mutable the essence of God is immutable. They should be taken as heaven and hell.

The following is the summary of some more beliefs of the Mu'tazilites:

1. Denial of punishment and reward meted out to the dead in the grave and the questioning by the angels Munkar and Nakir.
2. Denial of the indications of the Day of Judgment, of Gog and Magog (Yajuj and Majuj), and of the appearance of the Antichrist (al Dajjal).
3. Some Mu'tazilites believe in the concrete reality of the Balance (al Mizan) for weighing actions on the Day of Judgment. Some say that it is impossible for it to be a reality and think that the mention made in the Quran of weight and balance means only this much that full justice will be done on the Day of Judgment. It is clearly impossible to elicit the meanings of the words weight and balance literally, for deeds, which have been said to be weighed, are accidents and it is not possible to weigh accidents. Theoretical reason is incapable of comprehending this. Substances alone can possess weight. Further, when nothing is hidden from God, what is the use of weighing the deeds? It has been mentioned in the Quran that the books of bad or good deeds will be handed over to us. This too is merely a

metaphor. It means only our being gifted with knowledge.

4. The Mu'tazilites also deny the existence of the Recording Angels (Kiraman Katibin). The reason they give for this is that God is well aware of all the deeds done by His servants. The presence of the Recording Angels would have been indispensable if God were not acquainted directly with the doings of His servants.
5. The Mu'tazilites also deny the physical existence of the "Tank" (al Haud), and the "Bridge" (al sirat). Further, they do not admit that heaven and hell exist now, but believe that they will come into existence on the Day of Judgment.
6. They deny the Covenant (al Mithaq). It is their firm belief that God neither spoke to any prophet, angel, or supporter of the Divine Throne, nor will He cast a glance towards them.
7. For the Mu'tazilites, deeds together with verification (tasdiq) are included in faith. They hold that a great sinner will always stay in hell.
8. They deny the miracles (al karamat) of saints (walis), for, if admitted, they would be mixed up with the evidentiary miracles of the prophets and cause confusion. The same was the belief of the Jahmites too.
9. The Mu'tazilites also deny the Ascension (al Mi'raj) of the Prophet of Islam, because its proof is based on the testimony of individual traditions, which necessitates neither act nor belief; but they do not deny the Holy Prophet's journey as far as Jerusalem.
10. According to them, the one who prays is alone entitled to reap the reward of a prayer; whatever its form, its benefit goes to no one else.
11. As the divine decree cannot be altered, prayers serve no purpose at all. One gains nothing by them, because if the object, for which prayers are offered, is in conformity with destiny, it is needless to ask for it, and if the object conflicts with destiny, it is impossible to secure it.

12. They generally lay down that the angels who are message bearers of God to prophets are superior in rank to the human messengers of God to mankind, i. e., the prophets themselves.
13. According to them, reason demands that an Imam should necessarily be appointed over the ummah (Muslim community).
14. For them, the mujtahid (the authorized interpreter of the religious Law) can never be wrong in his view, as against the opinion of the Ash`arite scholastics that "the mujtahid sometimes errs and sometimes hits the mark."

The Mu'tazilites and the Sunnites differ mostly from one another in five important matters:

(1) The problem of attributes.
(2) The problem of the beatific vision.
(3) The problem of promise and threat.
(4) The problem of creation of the actions of man.
(5) The problem of the will of God.

Ibn Hazm says in his Milal wal Nihal that whosoever believes

(1) that the Quran is uncreated,
(2) that all the actions of man are due to divine decree, and
(3) that man will be blessed with the vision of God on the Day of Judgment, and
(4) admits the divine attributes mentioned in the Quran and the Tradition, and
(5) does not regard the perpetrator of a grave sin as an unbeliever, will not be styled as one of the Mu'tazilites, though in all other matters he may agree with them.

This statement of ibn Hazm shows that the Mu'tazilites were a group of rationalists who judged all Islamic beliefs by theoretical reason and renounced those that relate to all that lies beyond the reach of reason. They hardly realized the fact that reason, like any other faculty with which man is gifted, has its limitations and cannot be expected to comprehend reality in all its details. The point does not need elaboration. As Shakespeare puts it, "There are more things in heaven and earth, Horatio, than are dreamt of in your philosophy." Some modern thinkers have recognized that there is a place for intuition in the field of comprehension and, as a corollary to this, have admitted the claim of revelation or wahi as a source of knowledge. That is why Iqbal exclaimed

"At the dawn of Life the Angel said to me

`Do not make thy heart a mere slave to reason."'

And probably on a similar ground Iqbal's guide, Rumi, offered the following meaningful advice

"Surrender thy intellect to the Prophet!

God sufficeth. Say, He sufficeth.

Beware of wilful reasoning,

And boldly welcome madness!

He alone is mad who madness scoffs,

And heeds not the agent of Law!"

SOME LEADING MU'TAZILITES

In presenting a bird's eye view of the beliefs of the Mu'tazilites in the above paragraphs, it has not been suggested that these views were in their totality shared by all the leading Mu'tazilites. There were differences of opinion within themselves. For instance, abu al Hudhail al `Allaf differed from his companions in respect of ten problems; Ibrahim ibn Sayyar al Nazzam in thirteen; Bishr ibn al Mu'tamir in six; Mu'ammar ibn Khayyat `Abbad al Sulami in four; and `Amr ibn Bahr al Jahiz, in five. Abu al Husain and his followers are called the "Mu'tazilites of Baghdad" and abu al Jubba'i, his son abu Hashim, and their followers were known as the "Mu'tazilites of Basrah." Below is given a brief account of the lives and ideas of some of the leading Mu'tazilites.

Wasil ibn Ata

Wasil was born at Madinah in 80/699 and was brought up in Basrah. "Suq i Ghazzal," a bazaar in Basrah, used to be his familiar haunt and on that account people associated its name with him. He died in 131/748. Wasil had a very long neck. Amr ibn `Ubaid, who was a celebrated Mu'tazilite, on looking at him once remarked: "There will be no good in a man who has such a neck." Wasil was althagh, i.e., he could not pronounce the letter r correctly, but he was a very fluent and accomplished speaker and in his talk totally avoided this letter. He never allowed it to escape his lips, despite the great difficulty in avoiding it in conversation. He compiled a voluminous treatise in which not a single r is to be found. He would often maintain silence which led people to believe that he was mute.

Wasil was a pupil of abu Hashim `Abd Allah ibn Muhammad ibn al Hanafiyyah, but in the matter of Imamate, as in some other matters, he opposed his master. Before becoming a Mu'tazilite he used to live in the company of Imam Hasan al Basri.

His works are: Kitab al Manzilah bain al Manzilatain, Kitab al Futya, and Kitab al Tauhid. The first books on the science of al Kalam were written by him. Ibn Khallikan has recounted a number of his works.

In his illustrious work al Milal wal Nihal, al Shahrastani says that the essential teachings of Wasil consisted of the following:

(1) Denial of the attributes of God.

(2) Man's possession of free will to choose good deeds.

(3) The belief that one who commits a grave sin is neither a believer nor an unbeliever but occupies an intermediate position, and that one who commits a grave sin goes to hell.

(4) The belief that out of the opposing parties that fought in the battle of the Camel and from among the assassinators of `Uthman and his allies one party was in error, though it cannot be established which.

Denial of Attributes: Wasil denies that knowledge, power, will, and life belong to the essence of God. According to him, if any attribute is admitteed as eternal, it would necessitate "plurality of eternals" and the belief in the unity of God will thus become false. But this idea of Wasil was not readily accepted. Generally, the Mu'tazilites first reduced all the divine attributes to two knowledge and power and called them the "essential attributes." Afterwards they reduced both of these to one attribute unity.

Belief in Free Will: In this problem Wasil adopted the creed of Ma'bad al Juhani and Ghailan al Dimashqi and said that since God is wise and just, evil and injustice cannot be attributed to him. How is it justifiable for Him that He should will contrary to what He commands His servants to do ? Consequently, good and evil, belief and unbelief, obedience and sin are the acts of His servant himself, i.e, the servant alone is their author or creator and is to be rewarded or punished for his deeds. It is impossible that the servant may be ordered to "do" a thing which he is not able to do. Man is ordered to do an act because he has the power to do that act. Whosoever denies this power and authority rejects a self evident datum of consciousness.

As ibn Hazm frankly said, the excellent work of the Mu'tazilites can be seen in the doctrine of free will and that of promise and threat. If man were to be regarded as absolutely determined in his actions, the whole edifice of Shari'ah and ethics would tumble down.

Intermediary Position of the Grave Sinners: On account of his belief that one who commits a grave sin is neither a believer nor an unbeliever but occupies an intermediate position, Wasil withdrew himself from the company of Imam Hasan al Basri and earned the title Mu'tazilite. Wasil thought that the expression "true believer" is one which means praise. The person who commits grave sins can never deserve praise; therefore, he cannot be called a true believer.

Such a person has, nevertheless, belief in the Islamic faith and admits that God alone is worthy of being worshipped; therefore, he cannot be regarded as an unbeliever either. If such a person dies without penitence, he will ever stay in hell, but as he is right in his belief, the punishment meted out to him will be moderate.

As Imam al Ghazali has pointed out in his Ihya' `Ulum al Din misinterpretation of the following verses of the Quran was the cause of the Mu'tazilites' misunderstanding:

> *"By (the token of) Time (through the ages), verily mankind is in loss, except such as have faith and do righteous deeds and (join together) in the mutual teaching of truth, patience, and constancy."*

"For any that disobey God and His Apostle for them is hell; they shall dwell therein for ever: "

In the light of these and similar other verses, the Mu'tazilites argue that all the perpetrators of grave sins will always stay in hell, but they do not think over the fact that God also says:

"But, without doubt, I am (also) He that forgiveth again and again those who repent, believe, and do right, who, in fine, are ready to receive true guidance:"

"God forgiveth not that equals should be set up with Him; but He forgiveth anything else, to whom He pleaseth."

The last quoted verse shows that in the case of all sins, except polytheism, God will act according to His pleasure. In support of this the clear saying of the Holy Prophet of Islam can be cited, viz., "that person too will finally come out of hell who has even an iota of faith in his heart." Further, some words of God, e.g., "Verily We shall not suffer to perish the reward of anyone who does a (single) righteous deed," and "Verily God will not suffer the reward of the righteous to perish," clearly show that for the commission of one sin, He will not ignore a man's basic faith and deprive him of all the reward for his good deeds. Therefore, the general belief is that as the perpetrator of grave sins is by all means a true believer, even if he dies without repentance, after being punished for his sins in hell and thereby purified of them, he will eventually enter heaven.

Unestablished Errors: Wasil had firm conviction that out of those who fought in "the battle of the Camel" and "the battle of Siffin" and the killers of `Uthman, the third Caliph, and his allies, one party was definitely in error, though it cannot be established which.

Abu al Hudhail `Allaf

`Allaf was born in 131/748 and died in c. 226/840. He received instruction from `Uthman bin Khalid Tawil, a pupil of Wasil. He was a fluent speaker and vigorous in his arguments. He often made use of dialectical arguments in his discussions. He had a keen insight in philosophy. He wrote about sixty books on the science of Kalam but all of them have long been extinct.

`Allaf was an accomplished dialectician. The story goes that by his dialectics three thousand persons embraced Islam at his hand. We shall here speak of two of his debates. In those days there lived a Magian Salih by name who believed that the ultimate principles of the universe are two realities, Light and Darkness, that both of these are opposed to each other, and that the universe is created by the mixture of these two. This belief led to a discussion between Salih, the Magian, and Allaf. Allaf inquired of him whether the mixture was distinct and different from Light and Darkness or identical with them. Salih replied that it was one and the same thing. `Allaf then said, "How could two things mix together which are opposed to each other? There ought to be someone who got them mixed, and the mixer alone is the Necessary Existent or God." On another occasion, while Salih was engaged in a discussion with `Allaf, the latter said, "What do you now desire?" Salih replied, "I asked a blessing of God and still stick to the belief that there are two Gods." `Allaf then asked, "Of which God did you ask a blessing ? The God of whom you asked for it would not have suggested the name of the other God (who is His rival)."

Wasil was not able to clarify the problem of divine attributes. In this respect his ideas were still crude. `Allaf is opposed to the view that the essence of God has no quality and is absolutely one and by no means plural. The divine qualities are none other than the divine essence and cannot be separated from it. `Allaf accepts such attribute as are one with the essence of God, or one may say, accepts such an essence as is identical with the attributes. He does not differentiate between the two, but regards both as one. When one says that God is the knower, one cannot mean that knowledge is found in the essence of God, but that knowledge is His essence. In brief, God is knowing, powerful, and living with such knowledge, power, and life as are His very essence (essential nature).

Al Shahrastani has interpreted the identity of divine essence and attributes thus: God knows with His knowledge and knowledge is His very essence. In the same way, He is powerful with His power and power is His very essence; and lives with His life and life is His very essence. Another interpretation of divine knowledge is that God knows with His essence and not with His knowledge, i.e., He knows through His essence only and not through knowledge. The difference in these two positions is that, in the latter, the attributes are denied altogether, while in the former, which `Allaf accepts, they are admitted but are identified with God's essence.

This conforms to the statements of the philosophers who hold that the essence of God, without quality and quantity, is absolutely one, and by no means admits of plurality, and that the divine attributes are none other than the essence of God. Whatever qualities of Him may be established, they are either "negation" or "essentials."

Those things are termed "negation" which, without the relation of negation, cannot be attributed to God, as, for instance, body, substance, and accidents. When the relation of negation is turned towards them and its sign, i.e., the word of negation, is applied, these can become the attributes of God, e. g., it would be said that God is neither a body, nor a substance, nor an accident. What is meant by "essential" is that the existence of the Necessary Existent is Its very essence and thus Its unity is real.

`Allaf did not admit the attributes of God as separate from His essence in any sense. For he sensed the danger that, by doing so, attributes, too, like essence, would have to be taken as eternal, and by their plurality the "plurality of eternals" or "the plurality of the necessary existents" would become inevitable, and thus the doctrine of unity would be completely nullified. It was for this reason that the Christians who developed the theory of the Trinity of Godhead had to forsake the doctrine of unity.

Among the "heresies" of `Allaf was his view that after the discontinuation of the movement of the inmates of heaven and hell, a state of lethargy would supervene. During this period calm pleasure for the inmates of heaven and pain and misery for the inmates of hell will begin, and this is what is really meant by eternal pleasure and perpetual pain. Since the same was the religious belief of Jahm, according to whom heaven and hell would be annihilated, the Mu'tazilites used to call `Allaf a Jahmite in his belief in the hereafter.

Allaf has termed justice, unity, promise, threat, and the middle position as the "Five Principles" of the Mu'tazilites.

Al Nazzam

Abu Istiaq Ibrahim ibn Sayyar, called al Nazzam, was younger than `Allaf and it is generally known that he was `Allaf's pupil. He lived during the reign of Caliphs al Mamun and al Mu'tasim and died in 231/845. He was a peerless litterateur and poet. He studied Greek philosophy well and made full use of it in his works. His main ideas are as follows.

Denial of God's Power over Evil: God has no power at all over sin and evil. Other Mu'tazilites do not deny the power of God over evil, but deny the act of His creating evil. In their opinion, God has power over evil, but He does not use it for the creation of evil. Al Nazzam, in opposition to them, says that when evil or sin is the attribute or essence of a thing, then the possibility of the occurrence of evil or the power to create it will itself be evil. Therefore, it cannot be attributed to God who is the doer of justice and good. Similarly, al Nazzam holds that in the life hereafter too, God can neither mitigate nor add to the punishment and reward of the inmates of heaven and hell; nor indeed can He expel them from heaven or hell. As to the accusation that the denial of God's power over evil necessitates the affirmation that He is impotent against evil, al Nazzam replies that this equally follows from the denial of divine action to create evil. He says: "You, too, deny Him the wrong act, so there is no fundamental difference between the two positions."

God, who is Absolute Good and Absolute Justice, carnot be the author of evil. Besides, if God has power over evil, it will necessarily follow that He is ignorant and indigent. But this is impossible; therefore, its necessary consequence is also impossible. The sequence of the argument may be explained thus:

If God has power over evil, then the occurrence of evil is possible, and as the supposition of the occurrence of a possible thing entails no impossibility, let us suppose that evil did occur. Now, God might or might not have had knowledge of the evil which occurred. If we say that He did not have the knowledge of it, it would necessarily follow that He was ignorant; and if we say that He did have it, it would necessarily follow that He was in need of this evil; for had He not been in need of it, He would not have created it. When a person is not in need of a thing and knows its inherent evils, he will have nothing to do with it, if he is wise. It is definitely true that God is all wise; so when any evil is caused by Him, it necessarily follows that He needed it, otherwise He would have never produced it.

But since it is impossible to think that God needs evil, it is impossible to think that He creates it.

Denial of the Will of God: Apart from the power of action and action, al Nazzam does not admit that God has will, which has priority over both power and action. He holds that when we attribute will to God we only mean that God creates things according to His knowledge. His willing is identical with His acting, and when it is said that God wills the actions of men, what is meant is that He enjoins them to act in a certain way.

Why does al Nazzam deny the will of God? He does so, because, according to him, will implies want. He who wills lacks or needs the thing which he wills, and since God is altogether independent of His creatures, He does not lack or need anything. Consequently, will cannot be ascribed to Him. Therefore, the will of God really connotes His acts or His commands that are conveyed to man.

Divisibility of Every Particle ad Infinitum: Al Nazzam believes in the divisibility of every particle ad infinitum. By this he means that each body is composed of such particles as are divisible to an unlimited extent, i. e., every half of a half goes on becoming half of the other half. During the process of divisions, we never reach a limit after which we may be able to say that it cannot be further divided into halves.

Now, to traverse a distance, which is composed of infinite points, an infinite period of time would necessarily be required. Is, then, the traversing of a distance impossible? Does it not necessitate the denial of the existence of the movement itself? Among the Greek philosophers, Parmenides and Zeno had denied movement itself. They could not declare untrue the movement which is observable and is a fact, so they claimed that perception cannot reveal reality. They maintained that senses are not the instruments of real knowledge and are deceptive; and the phenomenal world is illusory; a mirage. The real world is the rational world, the knowledge of which is gained by reason alone in which there is neither plurality nor multiplicity, neither movement nor change. It is an immutable and immovable reality. But they could not explain how this illusory and deceptive world was born out of the real world. Thus their system of philosophy, in spite of their claiming it to be monism, ended in dualism.

Al Nazzam did not accept the solution of these Greek philosophers, but to tide over this difficulty he offered the theory of tafrah. The word tafrahmeans to leap; it means that the moving thing traverses from one point of distance to another in such a manner that between these two points a number of points are traversed. Obviously, it happens when the moving thing does not cross all the points of a distance, but leaps over them. This indeed is an anticipation of the present day doctrine of the "quantum jump."

Latency and Manifestation (Kumun wa Buruz): According to al Nazzam, creation is to be regarded as a single act of God by which all things were brought into being simultaneously and kept in a state of latency (kumun). It was from their original state of latency that all existing things: minerals, plants, animals, and men, have evolved in the process of time. This also implies that the whole of mankind was potentially in Adam. Whatever priority or posteriority there may be, it is not in birth but in appearance. All things came into existence at the same time, but were kept hidden till the time of their becoming operative arrived, and when it did arrive, they were brought from the state of latency to the state of manifestation. This doctrine stands in direct opposition to the Ash'arite view that God is creating things at all moments of time.

Materialism of al Nazzam: For al Nazzam, as for many before and after him, the real being of man is the soul, and body is merely its instrument. But the soul is, according to him, a rarefied body permeating the physical body, the same way as fragrance permeates flowers, butter milk, or oil sesame. Abu Mansfir `Abd al Qahir ibn Tahir, in his work al Farq bain al Firaq, has discussed this theory critically and has attempted to refute it.

Besides these philosophical ideas, there are what the orthodox called the "heresies" of al Nazzam. For example, he did not believe in miracles, was not convinced of the inimitability of the Quran, considered a statute necessary for the determination of an Imam, and thought that the statute establishing the Imamate of `Ali was concealed by `Umar, that the salat al tarawih was unauthorized, that the actual vision of the jinn was a physical impossibility, and that belated performance of missed prayers was unnecessary.

Among al Nazzam's followers, the following are well known: Muhammad ibn Shabib, abu Shumar, Yunus ibn 'Imran, Ahmad ibn Hayat, Bishr ibn Mu`tamir, and Thamamah ibn Ashras. Ahmad ibn Hayat who lived in the company of al Nazzam held that there are two deities: one, the creator and eternal deity, and the other, the created one which is Jesus Christ son of Mary. He regarded Christ as the Son of God. On account of this belief he was considered to have renounced Islam. According to his faith, Christ in the hereafter will ask the created beings to account for their deeds in this world, and in support of his claim Ahmad ibn Hayat quoted the verse: "Will they wait until God comes to them in canopies of clouds?" There is a tradition that, looking towards the moon on the fourteenth day of the lunar month, the Holy Prophet of Islam said, "Ye will behold your Lord just as ye behold this moon." Ahmad ibn Hayat twisted the meaning of this tradition and said that the word Lord referred to Jesus Christ. He also believed in incarnation for, according to him, the spirit of God is incarnated into the bodies of the Imams.

Fadl al Hadathi, who was another pupil of al Nazzam, had faith similar to that of ibn Hayat. He and his followers believed in transmigration. According to them, in another world God created animals mature and wise, bestowed on them innumerable blessings, and conferred on them many sciences too. God then desired to put them to a test and so commanded them to offer thanks to Him for His gifts. Some obeyed His command and some did not. He rewarded His thankful creatures by giving them heaven and condemned the ungrateful ones to hell. There were some among them who had partly obeyed the divine command and partly not obeyed it. They were sent to the world, were given filthy bodies, and, according to the magnitude of their sins, sorrow and pain, joy and pleasure. Those who had not sinned much and had obeyed most of God's commands were given lovely faces and mild punishment. But those who did only a few good deeds and committed a large number of sins were given ugly faces, and were subjected to severe tribulations. So long as an animal is not purified of all its sins, it will be always changing its forms.

Bishr ibn al Mu'tamir

One of the celebrated personalities of al Nazzam's circle is Bishr ibn al Mu'tamir. The exact date of his birth is not known, but his date of death is 210/825.

Bishr made the "Theory of Generated Acts" (taulid) current among the Mu'tazilites. The Mu`tazilites believe in free will. They admit that man is the author of his voluntary actions. Some actions arise by way of mubasharah, i. e., they are created directly by man, but some actions arise by way of taulid, i.e., they necessarily result from the acts done by way of mubasharah. Throwing of a stone in water, for example, necessitates the appearance of ripples. Even if the movement of the ripples is not intended by the stonethrower, yet he is rightly regarded as its agent. Similarly, man is the creator of his deeds and misdeeds by way of mubusharah, and all the consequential actions necessarily result by way of taulid. Neither type of actions is due to divine activity.

Bishr regards the will of God as His grace and divides it into two attributes: the attribute of essence and the attribute of action. Through the attribute of essence He wills all His actions as well as men's good deeds. He is absolutely wise, and in consequence His will is necessarily concerned with that which is suitable and salutary. The attribute of action also is of two kinds. If actions are concerned with God, they would imply creation, and if concerned with men, they would mean command.

According to Bishhr, God could have made a different world, better than the present one, in which all might have attained salvation. But in opposition to the common Mu'tazilite belief, Bishr held that God was not bound to create such a world. All that was necessary for God to do was that He should have bestowed upon man free will and choice, and after that it was sufficient to bestow reason for his guidance to discover divine revelation and the laws of nature, and combining reason with choice, attain salvation. Mu'tamir's pupil abu Musa Isa bin Sabih, nicknamed Mizdar, was a very pious man and was given the title of the hermit of the Mu'tazilites. He held some very peculiar views. God, he thought, could act tyrannically and lie, and this would not make His lordship imperfect. The style of the Quran is not inimitable; a work like it or even better than it can be produced. A person who admits that God can be seen by the eye, though without form, is an unbeliever, and he who is doubtful about the unbelief of such a person is also an unbeliever.

Mu'ammar

Mu'ammar's full name was Mu'ammar ibn `Abbad al Sulami. Neither the date of his birth nor that of his death can be determined precisely. According to some, he died in 228/842.

To a great extent Mu`ammar's ideas tally with those of the other Mu'tazilites, but he resorts to great exaggeration in the denial of the divine attributes and in the Theory of Predestination.

The following is the gist of his ideas.

Denial of Divine Knowledge: Mu'ammar maintains that the essence of God is free from every aspect of plurality. He is of the view that if we believe in the attributes of God, then God's essence becomes plural; therefore, he denies all the attributes, and in this denial he is so vehement that he says that God knows neither Himself nor anyone else, for knowing (or knowledge) is something either within or without God. In the first case, it necessarily follows that the knower and the known are one and the same, which is impossible, for it is necessary that the known should be other than and distinct from the knower. If knowledge is not something within God, and the known is separate from the knower, it means that God's essence is dual. Further, it follows also that God's knowledge is dependent on and is in need of an "other." Consequently, His absoluteness is entirely denied.

By Mu'ammar's times, more and more people were taking interest in philosophy and Neo Platonism was gaining ground. In denying the attributes Mu'ammar was following in the footsteps of Plotinus. According to the basic assumptigns of Plotinus, the essence of God is one and absolute. God is so transcendent that whatever we say of Him merely limits Him. Hence we cannot attribute to Him beauty, goodness, thought, or will, for all such attributes are limitations and imperfections. We cannot say what He is, but only what He is not. As a poet has said, He is

"The One whom the reason does not know,

The Eternal, the Absolute whom neither senses know nor fancy.

He is such a One, who cannot be counted He is such a Pure Being!"

It is universally believed in Islam that human reason, understanding, senses, or fancy cannot fathom the essence of God or the reality of His attributes or His origin. Says `Attar

"Why exert to probe the essence of God?

Why strain thyself by stretching thy limitations ?

When thou canst not catch even the essence of an atom,

How canst thou claim to know the essence of God Himself?"

To reflect on the essence of God has been regarded as "illegitimate thinking." The Prophet of Islam is reported to have said: "We are all fools in the matter of the gnosis of the essence of God." Therefore, he has warned the thinkers thus: "Don't indulge in speculating on the nature of God lest ye may be destroyed." He has said about himself: "I have not known Thee to the extent that Thy knowledge demands !" Hafiz has expressed the same idea in his own words thus

"Take off thy net; thou canst not catch 'anqa

For that is like attempting to catch the air!"

Denial of Divine Will: Mu'ammar says that, like knowledge, will too cannot be attributed to the essence of God. Nor can His will be regarded as eternal, because eternity expresses temporal priority and sequence and God transcends time. When we say that the will of God is eternal, we mean only that the aspects of the essence of God, like His essence, transcend time.

God as the Creator of Substances and not of Accidents: According to Mu'ammar, God is the creator of the world, but

He did not create anything except bodies. Accidents are the innovations of bodies created either (i) by nature, e. g., burning from fire, heat from the sun, or (ii) by free choice, such as the actions of men and animals. In brief, God creates matter and then keeps Himself aloof from it. Afterwards He is not concerned at all with the changes that are produced through matter, whether they may be natural or voluntary. God is the creator of bodies, not of accidents which flow out of the bodies as their effects.

Mu'ammar regards man as something other than the sensible body. Man is living, knowing, able to act, and possesses free will. It is not man himself who moves or keeps quiet, or is coloured, or sees, or touches, or changes from place to place; nor does one place contain him to the exclusion of another, because he has neither length nor breadth, neither weight nor depth; in short, he is something other than the body.

Thamamah

Thamamah ibn Ashras al Numahi lived during the reign of Caliphs Haran al Rashid and al Mamun. He was in those days the leader of the Qadarites. Harun al Rashid imprisoned him on the charge of heresy, but he was in the good books of al Mamun and was released by him. He died in 213/828. The following is the substance of his ideas.

(1) As good and evil are necessarily known through the intellect and God is good, the gnosis of God is an intellectual necessity. Had there been no Shari'ah, that is, had we not acquired the gnosis of God through the prophets, even then it would have been necessitated by the intellect.

(2) The world being necessitated by the nature of God, it has, like God, existed from eternity and will last till eternity. Following in the footsteps of Aristotle, he thinks that the world is eternal (qadim) and not originated (hadith) and regards God as creating things by the necessity of His nature and not by will and choice.

(3) Bishr ibn al Mu'tamir, who had put into usage the theory of generated acts among the Mu'tazilites, was wrong in thinking that men are not directly but only indirectly the authors of such acts. Neither God nor

man is the author of generated acts; they just happen without any author. Man is not their author, for otherwise when a deed has been generated after a man's death, he, as a dead man, will have to be taken as its author. God cannot be regarded as the author of these acts, for some generated acts are evil and evil cannot be attributed to God.

(4) Christians, Jews, and Magians, after they are dead, will all become dust. They will neither go to heaven nor to hell. Lower animals and children also will be treated in the same manner. The unbeliever, who does not possess and is not keen to possess the gnosis of his Creator, is not under the obligation to know Him. He is quite helpless and resembles the lower animals.

Al Jahiz

`Amr ibn Bahr al Jahiz, a contemporary of Mu'ammar, was a pupil of al-Nazzam and was himself one of the Imams of the Mu'tazilites. Both the master and the disciple, it was held, were almost of one mind. Al Jahiz had drunk deep of Greek philosophy. He had a keen sense of humour and was a good anecdotist. He usually lived in the company of the Caliphs of Baghdad. His permanent residence was the palace of ibn Zayyat, the Prime Minister of the Caliph Mutawakkil. When ibn Zayyat was put to death by the orders of the Caliph, Jahiz too was imprisoned. He was released after some time. He was the ugliest of men; his eyes protruded out, and children were frightened at his very sight. In his last years he had a stroke of paralysis. He died in his ninetieth year at Basrah in 255/869. During his illness he would often recite the following couplets

"Dost thou hope in old age To look like what you were in youth?

Thy heart belieth thee: an old garment never turns into a new one."

He was the author of a number of books out of which the following are noteworthy: Kitab al Bayan, Kitab al Hayawan, and Kitab al Ghilman. He also wrote a book dealing with Muslim sects.

It was the belief of al Jahiz that all knowledge comes by nature, and it is an activity of man in which he has no choice. He was a scientist philosopher. In the introduction to his Kitab al Hayawan, he writes that he is inspired by the philosophical spirit which consists in deriving knowledge from sense experience and reason. It employs observation, comparison, and experiment as methods of investigation. He experimented on different species of animals, sometimes by cutting their organs, sometimes even by poisoning them, in order to see what effects were thus produced on animal organism. In this respect he was the precursor of Bacon whom he anticipated seven and a half centuries earlier. Al Jahiz did not, however, base knowledge on sense-experience alone. Since sense experience is sometimes likely to give false reports, it needs the help of reason. In fact, in knowledge reason has to play the decisive role. He Says, "You should not accept whatever your eyes tell you; follow the lead of reason. Every fact is determined by two factors: one apparent, and that is sensory; the other hidden, and that is reason; and in reality reason is the final determinant."

According to al Jahiz, the will is not an attribute of man, for attributes are continually subject to change, but the will is non changing and non temporal.

He holds that the sinners will not be condemned to hell permanently but will naturally turn into fire. God will not send anybody to hell, but the fire of hell by its very nature will draw the sinners towards itself. Al Jahiz denies that God can commit a mistake or that an error can be imputed to Him. Al Jahiz, also denies the vision of God.

Al Jubba'i

Abu 'Ali al Jubba'i was born in 235/849 at Jubba, a town in Khuzistan. His patronymic name is abu `Ali and his descent is traced to Hamran, a slave of `Uthman. Al Jubba'i belonged to the later Mu`tazilites. He was the teacher of abu al Hasan al Aah`ari and a pupil of abu Ya'qub bin `Abd Allah al Shahham who was the leader of the Mu'tazilites in Basrah.

Once there was a discussion between him and Imam al Ashari in respect of the Theory of the Salutary to which reference has already been made in the foregoing pages. The story goes that one day he asked Imam al Ash'ari: "What do you mean by obedience ?" The Imam replied, "Assent to a command," and then asked for al Jubba'is own opinion in this matter. Al Jubba'i said, "The essence of obedience, according to me, is agreement to the will, and whoever fulfils the will of another obeys him." The Imam answered, "According to this, one must conclude that God is obedient to His servant if He fulfils his will." Al Jubba'i granted this. The Imam said, "You differ from the community of Muslims and you blaspheme the Lord of the worlds. For if God is obedient to His servant, then He must be subject to him, but God is above this."

Al Jubba'i further claimed that the names of God are subject to the regular rules of grammar. He, therefore, considered it possible to derive a name for Him from every deed which He performs. On this Imam al Ash`ari said that, according to this view, God should be named "the producer of pregnancy among women," because he creates pregnancy in them. Al Jubba'i could not escape this conclusion. The Imam added: "This heresy of yours is worse than that of the Christians in calling God the father of Jesus, although even they do not hold that He produced pregnancy in Mary." The following are other notable views of al Jubba'i.

(1) Like other Mu'tazilites, he denies the divine attributes. He holds that the very essence of God is knowing; no attribute of knowledge can be attributed to Him so as to subsist besides His essence. Nor is there any "state" which enables Him to acquire the "state of knowing." Unlike al Jubba'i, his son abu Hashim did believe in "states." To say that God is all hearing and all seeing really means that God is alive and there is no defect of any kind in Him. The attributes of hearing and seeing in God originate at the time of the origination of what is seen and what is heard.

(2) Al Jubba'i and the other Mu'tazilites regard the world as originated and the will of God as the cause of its being originated; they also think that the will of God too is something originated, for if the temporal will is regarded as subsisting in God, He will have to be regarded as the "locus of temporal events." This view he held against the Karramites who claimed that the will subsists in God Himself, is eternal and instrumental

in creating the world which is originated, and, therefore, not eternal.

Against al Jubba'i it has been held that independent subsistence of the will is entirely incomprehensible, for it tantamounts to saying that an attribute exists without its subject or an accident exists without some substance. Besides, it means that God who has the will is devoid of it, i.e., does not have it a clear contradiction.

(3) For al Jubba'i the speech of God is compounded of letters and sound: and God creates it in somebody. The speaker is He Himself and not the body in which it subsists. Such speech will necessarily be a thing originated. Therefore, the speech of God is a thing originated and not eternal.

(4) Like other Mu'tazilities, al Jubba'i denies the physical vision of God in the hereafter, for that, according to him, is impossible. It is impossible because whatever is not physical cannot fulfil the conditions of vision.

(5) He equally agrees with other Mu'tazilites regarding the gnosis of God, the knowledge of good and evil, and the destiny of those who commit grave sins. With them he holds that man is the author of his own actions and that it lies in his power to produce good or evil or commit sins and wrongs, and that it is compulsory for God to punish the sinner and reward the obedient.

(6) In the matter of Imamate, al Jubba'i supports the belief of the Sunnites, viz., the appointment of an Imam is to be founded on catholic consent.

Abu Hashim

Al Jubba'is son, abu Hashim `Abd al Salam, was born in Basrah in 247/861 and died in 321/933. In literature he eclipsed al Jubba'i. Both of them undertook new researches in the problems of Kalam. In general, abu Hashim agreed with his father, but in the matter of divine attributes he widely differed from him. Many Muslim thinkers of the time believed that the attributes of God are eternal and inherent in His essence. Contrary to this belief, the Shi'ites and the followers of the Greek philosophers held that it is by virtue of His essence that God has knowledge. He does not know by virtue of His knowledge. The divine essence, which is without quality and quantity, is one and in no way does it admit of plurality. According to the Mu'tazilites, attributes constitute the essence of God, i.e., God posses knowledge due to the attribute of knowledge, but this attribute is identical with His essence. God knows by virtue of His knowledge and knowledge is His essence; similarly, He is omnipotent by virtue of His power, etc. Al Jubba'is theory is that though God knows according to His essence, yet knowing is neither an attribute nor a state, owing to which God may be called a knower.

As a solution to this problem, abu Hashim presents the conception of "state." He says that we know essence and know it in different states. The states go on changing, but the essence remains the same. These states are in themselves inconceivable; they are known through their relation to essence. They are different from the essence, but are not found apart from the essence. To quote his own words, "A state in itself is neither existent nor non existent, neither unknown nor known, neither eternal nor contingent; it cannot be known separately, but only together with the essence."

Abu Hashim supports his conception of states by this argument: Reason evidently distinguishes between knowing a thing absolutely and knowing it together with some attribute. When we know an essence, we do not know, that it is knowing also. Similarly, when we know a substance, we do not know whether it is bounded or whether the accidents subsist in it. Certainly, man perceives the common qualities of things in one thing and the differentiating qualities in another, and necessarily gains knowledge of the fact that the quality which is common is different from the quauty which is not common. These are rational propositions that no sane man would deny. Their locus is essence and not an accident, for otherwise it would necessarily follow that an accident subsists in another accident. In this way, states are necessarily determined. Therefore, to be a knower of the world refers to a state, which is an attribute besides the essence and has not the same sense as the essence. In like manner abu Hashim proves the states for God; these states are not found apart but with the essence.

Al Jubba'i and the other deniers of states refute this theory of abu Hashim. Al Jubba'i says that these states are really mental aspects that are not contained in the divine essence but are found in the percipient, i. e., in the perceiver of the essence. In other words, they are such generalizations or relations as do not exist externally but are found only in the percipient's mind. Ibn Taimiyyah also denies states. In this respect one of his couplets has gained much fame

"Abu Hashim believes in State, al Ash'ari in

Acquisition and al Nazzam

in Leap.

These three things have verbal

and no real existence."

After a little hesitation, Imam Baqilani supported abu Hashim's views. Imam al Ash'ari and the majority of his followers disputed them and Imam al Haramain first supported but later opposed them.

ASH'ARISM

AL ASHARI'S LIFE AND WORK

Asharism is the name of a philosophico religious school of thought in Islam that developed during the fourth and fifth/ tenth and eleventh centuries. This movement was "an attempt not only to purge Islam of all non Islamic elements which had quietly crept into it but also to harmonize the religious consciousness with the religious thought of Islam." It laid the foundation of an orthodox Islamic theology or orthodox Kalam, as opposed to the rationalist Kalam of the Mu'tazilites; and in opposition to the extreme orthodox class, it made use of the dialectical method for the defence of the authority of divine revelation as applied to theological subjects.

The position at the end of the third/ninth century was such that the development of such a movement as orthodox Kalamwas inevitable. The rationalization of faith, which developed, at the beginning of the second century of the Hijrah as a systematic movement of thought, in the name of rationalism in Islam or Mu'tazilite movement, was, in its original stage, simply an attempt to put Islam and its basic principles on a rational foundation, by giving a consistent rational interpretation to the different dogmas and doctrines of Islam. But when the

Mu'tazilite rationalists began to study the Arabic translations of the works of Greek physicists and philosophers made available to them by the early 'Abbasid Caliphs, particularly by al Mansur and al Mamun, they began to apply the Greek philosophical methods and ideas to the interpretation of the basic principles of Islam as well.

Some of the early 'Abbasid Caliphs, particularly al Mamun, began to patronize the rationalism of the Mu'tazilites in public. The Mu'tazilite speculation, in the hands of the later Mu'tazilites, those of the second and third generations, under the influence of Greek philosophy and with the active support and patronage of the Caliphs, tended to be purely speculative and "absolutely unfettered, and in some cases led to a merely negative attitude of thought." They made reason the sole basis of truth and reality and thus identified the sphere of philosophy with that of religion. They tried to interpret faith in terms of pure thought. They ignored the fact that the basic principles of religion are, by their very nature, incapable of logical demonstration or rational proof. The basic principles of Islam deal with supersensible realities and, as such, they must first be accepted on the authority of revelation.

The Mu'tazilites, in their zeal to judge everything by reason alone, destroyed the personality of God and reduced Him to a bare indefinable universality or to an abstract unity. This idea of an abstract, impersonal, absolute God could not appeal to the ordinary Muslims. The orthodox section of the people reacted strongly against the Mu'tazilite rationalism and began to consider the Mu'tazilites to be heretics. The extreme rationalistic attitude of the later Mu'tazilites was followed by powerful reaction from the orthodox section of the people. This reaction was greatly aggravated by the unfortunate attempt of the Caliph al Mamun to force Mu'tazilism (rationalist Kalam) on his subjects by introducing mihnah (a compulsory test of faith) in the Mu'tazilite doctrines, particularly in their doctrine of the createdness of the Quran. The whole of the third/ninth century was a time of reaction.

The orthodox Muslims (and among them were the Traditionists [the Muhaddithin]), the Zahirites (the followers of Dawud ibn `Ali), and the Muslim jurists (fuqaha') adhered strictly to Tradition and literal interpretation of the Quran and the Sunnah, and refused to admit any "innovation" (bid'ah) in the Shari'ah (the Islamic Code). Any theological discussion was considered an "innovation" and was as such a cause of displeasure to them. The reactionary influence of Imam Ahmad bin Hanbal and his Zahirite followers was very strong at that period and the orthodox Muslims kept themselves safely aloof from the Mu'tazilites and the philosophers. The reaction against the rationalist Kalamwent to such an extreme that even the anthropomorphic verses of the Quran were interpreted by them in a purely literal sense. Malik bin Anas said: "God's settling Himself firmly upon His Throne is known, the how of it is unknown; belief in it is obligatory; and questioning about it is an innovation." Any speculation about sacred things was considered an innovation. Every dogma was to be befieved in without raising the question how or why (bila kaifa).

But such an attitude of blind faith could not be maintained for any length of time. Islam, as a universal religion and as a living force, had to adapt itself to new thoughts and to new surroundings. So, as time went on, there arose gradually a party, from amongst the orthodox section of the Muslims, who realized the necessity of putting Islam on a solid ground by advancing "reasons" for the traditional beliefs, of defending these beliefs against all sorts of attacks internal and external, and thus purging their faith of all the non Islamic elements that had crept into it. They founded the orthodox theology of Islam by using Kalamor the philosophical method in order to meet the dialectical reasoning of the Mu'tazilites. These theologians who employed Kalamfor the defence of their faith were, therefore, known as the Mutakallimun (orthodox theologians).

But, although these thinkers used philosophical method in their discussions, they obtained the primary materials from revelation. They developed a rival science of reasoning to meet the Mu'tazilites on their own ground. In the beginning this new orthodox theological movement developed privately and secretly. It was at first a gradual unconscious drift. It could not come to the open for fear of public criticism. Al Junaid, for instance, had to discuss the unity of God behind closed doors. Al Shafi'i held that some trained people might defend and purify the faith but that should not be done in public. Al Muhasibi and other contemporaries of Imam Ahmad ibn Hanbal incurred his displeasure for defending the faith with arguments or reason. But gradually the movement gathered strength and began to be openly preached almost at the same time in different places of the Muslim world in Mesopotamia by abu al Hasan `Ali bin Isma`il al Ashari (d. 330 or 334/941 or 945), in Egypt by al Tahawi (d. 331/942), and in Samarqand by abu Mansnr al Maturidi (d. 333/ 944). But of these three, al Ash'ari became the most popular hero, before whom the Mu'tazilite system (the rationalist Kalam) went down, and he came to be known as the founder of the orthodox philosophical theology, and the school founded by him was named after him as Ash`arism.

Al Ash'ari was born at Basrah. Regarding his date of birth there is difference of opinion. Ibn Khallikan, in his discussion of the life of al Ash'ari, mentions that he was born in 260 or 270/873 or 883 and died at Baghdad in 330/941 or some time after that. According to Shibli Nu'mani and ibn `Asakir (the author of Tabyin Kidhb al Muftari, on the life and teachings of al Ash'ari), he was born in 270/873 and died in 330/941. He was buried between Karkh and Bab al Basrah (the gate of Basrah). He was a descendant of abu Musa al Ash'ari, one, of the famous Companions of the Prophet. Al Ash'ari, in his early youth, came under the care of the great Mu'tazilite scholar of the Basrite school, abu 'Ali Muhammad bin `Abd al Wahhab al Jubba'i, and, as a disciple of his, became an adherent of the Mu'tazilite school and continued to support its doctrines up to the age of forty.

After that there happened a sudden change in his mind and one day he went to the Mosque of Basrah and declared: "He who knows me, knows who I am, and he who does not know me, let him know that I am abu al Hasan 'Ali al Ash'ari, that I used to maintain that the Quran is created, that eyes of men shall not see God, and that the creatures create their actions. Lo! I repent that I have been a Mu'tazilite. I renounce these opinions and I take the engagement to refute the Mu'tazilites and expose their infamy and turpitude." What brought about this sudden change in al Aah'ari is not definitely known to us. Shibli in his `Ilm al Kalam says that "the change came to him due to some directions which he had obtained in a dream.." Ibn Khallikan mentions in this connection the story of a public discussion in which al Ashari met his old Mu'tazilite teacher, al Jubba'i, on the problem of salah un aslah, i. e., the problem whether God's actions are to be based on rational consideration and whether He is bound to do what is best for His creatures. Al Ash'ari came to al Jubba'i and presented the case of three brothers, one being God fearing, another godless, and a third having died as a child, and asked him as to what would be their positions in the next world. Al Jubba'i could not give a satisfactory and consistent reply to that question and, on his having failed to justify rationally the Mu'tazilite doctrine of salah wa aflah, al Ash'ari abandoned the Mu'tazilite camp. But whatever might have been the cause of this change, when he changed he was terribly in earnest.

After the change he wrote a number of books and ibn Furak says that the number amounted to three hundred. Ibn `Asakir Dimashqi has given the titles of ninety three of them, but only a few have been preserved and are enumerated by Brockelmann. His work al Ibanah `an Usul al Diyanah was printed at Hyderabad, Deccan (India), in 1321/1903 and a small treatise Risalah fi Istihsan al Khaud fi al Kalam was printed in 1323/1905 and reprinted at Hyderabad in 1344/1925. Al Ash'ari's other famous works are al Maqalat al Islamiyyin (published in Istanbul in 1348/1929), Kitab al Sharh wal Tafsil, Luma`, Mu'jaz, I`adah al Burhan, and Tab'in. Of these books the Maqalat al Islamiyyin wa Ikhtilaf al Musalliyyin is the most authentic book on the views of different schools about religious dogmas and doctrines.

Al Maqalat was written much earlier than the other books on the same subject, such as Shahrastani's Kitab al Milal wal Nihal, or ibn Hazm's al Fasl fi al Milal wal Ahwa' wal Nihal. Ibn Taimiyyah said in his Minhaj al-Sunnah that the most comprehensive of the books he went through on the views of different people on the basic principles of Islam was al Ash'ari's al Maqalat al Islamiyyin and that he (al Ash'ari) discussed many of such views in details as were not even mentioned by others. Ibn al Qayyim also spoke very highly of this work. In his Hadi al Arwah and Ijtima` al Juyush al Islamiyyah, he said, "Shahrastani, `Abd al Qahir Baghdadi, and other later writers on the subject simply copied from al Ash'ari's book and did not discuss the views in details." Al Ash'ari's other famous book al

Ibanah 'an Usul al Diyanah seems to have been written by him just after his abandoning the Mu'tazilite views. In this book we find he is almost a Zahirite.

The reaction against the Mu'tazilite speculation might have been very strong in his mind at that period. Al Maqalat seems to be a later work. The Risalah fi Istihsan al Khaud deals with the objections raised by the extremely orthodox against the use of Kalam, and the replies given by al Ash'ari, justifying its use in matters of faith. Al Ash'ari's theology has been discussed mainly in these books. He had a good number of pupils who passed as famous theologians and who spread and developed his doctrines and dogmas. Some of those older Ash'arites were abu Sahl Saluqi, abu Quffal, abu Zaid Maruzi, Zahir bin Ahmad, Hafiz abu Bakr Jurjani, Shaikh abu Muhammad Tabari, and abu al Hasan Bahili. Some of the pupils of these older Ash'arites became still more famous and the best known among them are Qadi abu Bakr Baqillani, abu Bakr bin Furak, abu al Qasim al Qushairi and abu Ishaq Isfra'ini and his pupil abu al Ma'ali al Juwaini, known as Imam al Haramain.

ASH'ARITE THEOLOGY

Al Ash'ari maintaines an intermediary position between the two diametrically opposed schools of thought prevailing at the time. He had to fight against both the opposing parties. At the one extreme were the Mu'tazilites who made reason in preference to revelation the sole criterion of truth and reality and, thus, passed slowly into comparatively innocuous heretics. At the other extreme were the orthodox groups, particularly the Zahirites, the Mujassimites (anthropomorphists), the Muhaddithin (Traditionists), and the Jurists, all of which were wholly opposed to the use of reason or Kalamin defending or explaining religious dogmas and condemned any discussion about them as innovation. Al Ash'ari wrote his Istihsan al Khaud mainly to meet the objections raised by the orthodox school against the use of reason in matters of faith. In that treatise he says: "A section of the people (i.e., the Zahirites and other orthodox people) made capital out of their own ignorance; discussions and rational thinking about matters of faith became a heavy burden for them, and, therefore, they became inclined to blind faith and blind following (taqlid). They condemned those who tried to rationalize the principles of religion as `innovators.'

They considered discussion about motion, rest, body, accident, colour, space, atom, the leaping of atoms, and attributes of God, to be an innovation and a sin. They said that had such discussions been the right thing, the Prophet and his Companions would have definitely done so; they further pointed out that the Prophet, before his death, discussed and fully explained all those matters which were necessary from the religious point of view, leaving none of them to be discussed by his followers; and since he did not discuss the problems mentioned above, it was evident that to discuss them must be regarded as an innovation."

They further contended that these so called theological problems were either known to the Prophet and his Companions and yet they kept silent and did not discuss them or they were not known to them. If they knew them and yet did not discuss them, we are also to follow them in keeping silent, and if they could remain unaware of them we can also do so. In both cases discussion about them would be an "innovation." These were, in brief, their objections against the use of Kalamin matters of faith.

Al Ash'ari, then, proceeds to justify theological discussions about matters of faith. He tries to meet these objections in three ways. First, by turning the objections of the orthodox against themselves by pointing out to them that the Prophet had not said that those who would discuss these problems were to be condemned and charged as innovators. Hence, their charging or condemning others as innovators was itself an innovation, for it amounted to discussion about matters which the Prophet did not discuss, and condemn the action of those whom the Prophet did not condemn.

Secondly, "the Prophet was not unaware of all these problems of body, accident, motion, rest, atoms, etc., though he did not discuss each of them separately. The general principles (usul) underlying these problems are present in general, not in details, in the Quran and the Sunnah." Al Ash'ari then proceeds to prove his contention by citing verses from the Quran and the sayings of the Prophet, and thereby showing that the principles underlying the problems of harkah, sukun, tauhid, etc., are, as a matter of fact, present in the Quran and the Sunnah.

Thirdly, "the Prophet was not unaware of these matters and knew them in detail, but as problems about them did not arise during his life time, there was no question of his discussing or not discussing them." The Companions of the Prophet discussed and argued about many religious matters which appeared during their life time, although there was no direct and explicit "saying" of the Prophet about them, ánd because of the absence of any explicit injunction from the Prophet they differed in their judgments about them. Had the question, for instance, of the creation of the Quran, or of atoms or substance, been raised in so many words in the life of the Prophet, he would have definitely discussed and explained it as he did in the case of all those problems which were then raised. "There is no direct verdict (nass) from the Prophet, for instance, as to whether the Quran is created or uncreated. If to call the Quran created is an `innovation,' then, on the same ground, to call it uncreated must also be an `innovation."' Al Ash'ari then concludes that Islam is not opposed to the use of reason; on the other hand, rationalization of faith is a necessity in Islam.

Al Ash'ari discussed the main theological problems in his Maqalat al Islamiyyin and al Ibanah `an Usul al Diyanah.In these books al Ashari selects a few principles which distinguish the Ash'arites from the Mu'tazilite school of thought. Later on al Ghazali put them in a consolidated form in his Ihya as the "Principles of Faith" or Qawa'id al `Aqa'id, and Imam Fakhr al Din al Razi explained them more elaborately. The main problems about which the Ash'arites differed from the Mu'tazilites are:

(1) The conception of God and the nature of His attributes.

(2) Freedom of the human will.

(3) The criterion of truth and the standard of good and evil.

(4) The vision (ruyah) of God.

(5) Createdness of the Quran.

(6) Possibility of burdening the creatures with impossible tasks.

(7) Promise of reward and threat of punishment.

(8) The rational or non rational basis of God's actions.

(9) Whether God is bound to do what is best for His creatures.

The problems discussed by the Ash'arites in their system may be broadly classified into two categories: (i) theological, and (ii) metaphysical.

FUNDAMENTAL PRINCIPLES OF THE ASH'ARITE THEOLOGY

Conception o f God and the Nature of His Attributes: According to the Ash'arites, God is one, unique, eternal, existent Being; He is not a substance, not a body, not an accident, not limited to any direction, and not in any space. He possesses attributes such as knowledge, power, life, will; He is hearing and seeing and has speech.

About the nature of divine attributes two extreme views were held before the Ash'arites. On the one hand, there were the extreme Attributists (Sifatis), the Anthropomorphists (Mujassimin), and the Comparers (Mushabbihin), who maintained that God possesses all the attributes mentioned in the Quran and that all such attributes as God's having hands, legs, ears, eyes, and His sitting firmly (istiwa) on His Throne must be taken in their literal sense. Such a view of the attributes of God is pure anthropomorphism, implying God's bodily existence. On the other hand, there were the Mu'tazilites who held that God is one, eternal, unique, absolute Being, having no touch of dualism in Him. His essence is self contained. He does not possess any attributes apart from His essence. His essence is, for instance, knowing, powerful, seeing, willing, etc. They denied the attributes of God as anything other than and addition to His essence.

The Ash'arites maintained a view which was, so to say, a reconciliation between the two extreme views. In agreement with the Sifatis and in opposition to the Mu'tazilites and the "philosophers" (those who were under Greek influence), the Ash'arites held that God possesses attributes in general. They classified the attributes of God into two main groups: (i) sifat i salbiyyah, or negative attributes, and (ii) sifat i wujudiyyah or existential or positive attributes. According to them, the sifat i wujudiyyah, which they also called sifat i `aqliyyah or rational attributes; were seven: knowledge, power, will, life, hearing, seeing, and speech.

The extreme Sifatis asserted that even those attributes of God which imply His bodily existence are also to be taken in their true literal sense. As against them, the Ash'arites maintained that God possesses the apparently anthropomorphic attributes no doubt, but these should be understood not in their literal sense. They are to be believed in bila kaifa, without asking "how," and bila tashbih, without drawing any comparison.

The Ash'arites here introduced a principle that the attributes of God are unique and fundamentally different from those of the created beings and as such should not be compared to them. This is known as the doctrine of mukhalafah, or absolute difference. This doctrine signifies that if any quality or term is applied to God, it must be understood in a unique sense and never taken in the sense in which it is normally used when applied to created beings. Because of the doctrine of mukhulafah, the Ash'arites held that we are not allowed to ascribe any attribute to God unless it is expressly so applied in the Quran. God's attributes differ from those of the creatures, not in degree but in kind, i. e., in their whole nature.

The Ash'arites, as against the Mu'tazilites, held that "God has attributes which inhere eternally in Him and are in addition to His essence." These attributes are eternal, but they are neither identical with His essence, nor are they quite different from or other than His essence. God is knowing, for instance, means that God possesses knowledge as an attribute, which is inherent in God, and although it is not exactly the same as His essence, yet it is not something quite different from and other than His essence. The Ash'arites, here, maintained a very difficult position. They were between the two horns of a dilemma. They could neither assert the eternal attributes of God to be identical with nor wholly different from the essence of God.

They could not agree to the Mu'tazilite view and assert the identity of the attributes with the essence of God, because that would be a virtual denial of the attributes. They could not also assert that these eternal attributes are something absolutely different, or other than and separate, from God, as that would lead to multiplicity of eternals, and go against divine unity.

They, therefore, maintained that these attributes are, in one sense, included in and, in another sense, excluded from, the essence of God. It is common knowledge that the Asharites contended that essence (mahiyyah), and attributes (sifat) are two different things and they cannot be otherwise in the case of God, the Supreme Being. The Ash'arites made a distinction between the meaning or connotation (mafhum) of a thing and its reality (haqiqah). So far as their meaning is concerned, the attributes and the essence of God are not the same and as such the attributes are in addition to the essence of God, i.e., they have different meanings. The meaning of dhat (essence) is different from the meanings of different attributes. God's essence, for instance, is not knowing or powerful or wise, but so far as their ultimate haqiqah (reality or application) is concerned, the attributes are inherent in the divine essence, and hence are not something quite different from or other than the essence of God.

In support of the above view of theirs, the Ash'arites advanced the following arguments.

The analogical argument of the Ash'arites of the older generation: God's actions prove that He is knowing, powerful, and willing; so they also prove that He possesses knowledge, power, will, etc., because the ground of inference cannot differ in different things. What is true in the case of a created being must also be true in the case of the Divine Being. In the case of a human being, by "knowing" we mean one who possesses knowledge and even common sense and draws a line of demarcation between an essence and its attributes. On the same analogy, distinction must be drawn between the essence of God and His attributes. The essence and the attributes should not be supposed to be blended in the Divine Being. Hence the attributes of God cannot be identical with His essence, as the Mu'tazilites held. But this analogical reasoning is very weak, for what is true of a finite being need not necessarily be true of an infinite being. But, according to the doctrine of mukhalafah, God's knowledge or power or will and, as a matter of fact, all His rational attributes signify quite different meanings when applied to created beings.

Secondly, they argued that if all the attributes of God are identical with His essence, the divine essence must be a homogeneous combination of contradictory qualities. For instance, God is merciful (rahim) and also revengeful (qahhar); both the contradictory attributes would constitute the essence of God, which is one, unique, and indivisible (ahad), and that is absurd.

Further, if the attributes are identical with God's essence, and if, for instance, His being knowing, powerful, and living is His essence itself, no useful purpose will be served by ascribing them to Him, for that would ultimately be the virtual application of His essence to itself, which is useless. Hence the divine attributes cannot be identical with the divine essence.

Thirdly, if the attributes of God are not distinct from His essence, the meanings of the different attributes will be exactly the same, for God's essence is a simple and indivisible unity. The meanings of knowing, willing, and living, for instance, will be exactly the same, and thus knowledge will mean power, or power will mean life, and so on. This also is an absurdity. These different attributes imply different meanings and hence they cannot be identical with God's essence. His essence is one and He possesses many attributes which eternally inhere in Him and, though not identical with His essence, yet they are not absolutely different from His essence.

Free will: On the question of free will or on the ability of man to choose and produce actions, the Ash'arites took up again an intermediary position between the libertarian and fatalistic views, held by the Mu'tazilites and the Jabrites respectively. The orthodox people and the Jabrites maintained a pure fatalistic view. They held that human actions are predetermined. and predestined by God. Man has no power to produce any action. "Everything," they contended, "is from God." God has absolute power over everything including human will and human actions. The Mu'tazilites and the Qadarites, on the other hand, held that man has full power to produce an action and has complete freedom in his choice, though the power was created in him by God.

The Ash'arites struck a middle path. They made a distinction between creation (khalq) and acquisition (kasb) of an action. God, according to the Ash'arites, is the creator (khaliq) of human actions and man is the acquisitor (muktasib). "Actions of human beings are created (makhluq) by God, the creatures are not capable of creating any action." "There is no creator except God and the actions of man are, therefore, His creation." Power (qudrah), according to them, is either (i) original (qadamah) or (ii) derived (hadithah).

The original power alone is effective. Derived power can create nothing. The power possessed by man is given by God and as such it is derived. Al Ash'ari said, "The true meaning of acquisition is the occurrence of a thing or event due to derived power, and it is an acquisition for the person by whose derived power it takes place." God is, thus, the creator of human actions and man is the acquisitor. Man cannot create anything; he cannot initiate work. God alone can create, because absolute creation is His prerogative.

God creates in man the power and the ability to perform an act. He also creates in him the power to make a free choice (ikhtiyar) between two alternatives between right and wrong. This free choice of man is not effective in producing the action. It is the habit or nature of God to create the action corresponding to the choice and power created by Himself in man. Thus, the action of man is created by God, both as to initiative and as to production or completion. Man is free only in making the choice between alternatives and also in intending to do the particular action freely chosen: Man, in making this choice and intending to do the act, acquires (iktisab) either the merit of appreciation and reward from God if he makes the right choice, or the demerit of condemnation and punishment if he makes the wrong choice.

The Ash`arites, thus, in order to avoid the fatalistic position, introduced the doctrine of acquisition by which, they thought, they could account for man's free will and lay responsibility upon him. Man has no free will in the Mu'tazilite sense; he has no real and effective power, but has some derived power by which he acquires a share in the production of the act: In the case of voluntary actions of human beings, there are, so to say, two causes. The action is the combined effect of the real cause, God, and the choice and intention of man, the acquisitor, the possessor of ineffective power because of its being derived power.

God creates in two ways: either with a locus (mahall) or without a locus. Human actions are His creation with a locus. "God creates, in man, the power, ability, choice, and will to perform an act, and man, endowed with this derived power, chooses freely one of the alternatives and intends or wills to do the action, and, corresponding to this intention, God creates and completes the action." It is this intention on the part of man which makes him responsible for his deeds. Man cannot take the initiative in any matter, nor can he originate any action. But the completion of the act is partially due to his intention: He, thus, acquires the merit or demerit of the action because of his intending to do a good or bad action. Man's free choice is, so to say, an occasion for God's causing the action corresponding to that choice. In this the Ash`arites come very close to the occasionalism of Malebranche which was expounded in Europe eight centuries and a half later. This correspondence and harmony between the choice of man and God's creation, according to the Ash'arites, is not due to a harmony established by God previously, but because of His habit or nature to create the harmony whenever human action is done.

This, in short, is the solution of the problem of free will offered by the Ash'arites. The Ashh'arite view on this problem is not free from logical and ethical difficulties. It was really very difficult for them to reconcile the absolute determination of all events by God with man's accountability and responsibility for his deeds. Some, of the later Ash'arites, particularly Imam Fakhr al Din al Razi, discarded the veil of acquisition in order to escape the charge of fatalism, and advocated naked determinism.

The Problem of Reason and Revelation and the Criterion of Good and Evil: The Ash`arites differ from the Mu'tazilites on the question whether reason or revelation should be the basis or source of truth and reality: Both the schools admit the necessity of reason for the rational understanding of faith, but they differ with regard to the question whether revelation or reason is more fundamental and, in case of a conflict, whether reason or revelation is to get preference. The Mu'tazilites held that reason is more fundamental than revelation and is to be preferred to revelation. Revelation merely confirms what is accepted by reason and, if there be a conflict between the two, reason is to be preferred and revelation must be so interpreted as to be in conformity with the dictates of reason.

The Ash`arites, on the other hand, held that revelation is more fundamental as the source of ultimate truth and reality, and reason should merely confirm what is given by revelation. The Ash`arites prefer revelation to reason in case of a conflict between the two. As a matter of fact, this is one of the fundamental principles in which the rational Kalam of the Mu'tazilites differs from the orthodox Kalam of the Ash'arites. If pure reason is made the sole basis or source of truth and reality, including the truth and reality of the most fundamental principles or concepts on which Islam is based, it would be a pure speculative philosophy or at best a rational theology in general and not a doctrinal theology of a particular historic religion, i. e., that of Islam in particular. Islam is based on certain fundamental principles or concepts which, being suprasensible in nature, are incapable of rational proof. These principles, first, must be believed in on the basis of revelation. Revelation, thus, is the real basis of the truth and reality of these basic doctrines of Islam. This faith, based on revelation, must be rationalized. Islam as a religion, no doubt, admits the necessity of rationalizing its faith.

But to admit the necessity of rationalizing faith is not to admit pure reason or analytic thought to be the sole source or basis of Islam as a religion. Reason, no doubt, has the right to judge Islam and its basic principles, but what is to be judged is of such a nature that it cannot submit to the judgment of reason except on its own terms. Reason must, therefore, be subordinated to revelation. Its function is to rationalize faith in the basic principles of Islam and not to question the validity or truth of the principles established on the basis of revelation as embodied in the Quran and the Sunnah. The problem of the criterion of good and evil follows as a corollary to the problem of reason and revelation. The problem of good and evil is one of the most controversial problems of Islamic theology. The Mu'tazilites held that reason, and not revelation, is the criterion or standard of moral judgment, i.e., of the goodness and badness of an action. The truth and moral value of things and human actions must be determined by reason. They contended that moral qualities of good and evil are objective; they are inherent in the very nature of things or actions and as such can be known by reason and decided to be good or bad.

The Ash'arites, as against the Mu'tazilites, held that revelation and not reason is the real authority or criterion to determine what is good and what is bad. Goodness and badness of actions (husn wa qubh) are not qualities inhering in them; these are mere accidents (a'rad). Actions in themselves are neither good nor bad. Divine Law makes them good or bad.

In order to make the ground of controversy between the Mu'tazilites and the Ash'arites clearer, we may explain here the three different senses in which these two terms, good and evil, are used.

(i) Good and evil are sometimes used in the sense of perfection and defect respectively. When we say that a certain thing or action is good or bad (for instance, knowledge is good and ignorance is bad), we mean that it is a quality which makes its possessor perfect or implies a defect in him.

(ii) These terms are also used in a utilitarian sense meaning gain and loss in worldly affairs. Whatever is useful or has utility in our experience is good, and the opposite of it is bad. So whatever is neither useful nor harmful is neither good nor bad.

Both the Ash'arites and the Mu'tazilites agree that in the two senses, mentioned above, reason is the criterion or standard of good and evil. There is no difference of opinion in the above two senses. But good and bad in the second sense may vary from time to time, from individual to individual, and from place to place. In this sense there will be nothing permanently or universally good or bad; what is good to one may be bad to others and vice versa. This implies that good and evil are subjective and not objective and real. Hence actions are neither good nor bad, but experience or workability would make them so and, therefore, they can be known by reason without the help of revelation.

(iii) Good and evil are also used in a third sense of commendable and praiseworthy or condemnable in this world and rewardable or punishable, as the case may be, in the other world.

The Ash'arites maintained that good and evil in their third sense must be known through revelation, not by reason as the Mu'tazilites had held. According to the Ash'arites, revelation alone decides whether an action is good or bad. What is commanded by Shar' is good, and what is prohibited is bad. Shar` can convert previously declared good into bad and vice versa. As actions by themselves are neither good nor bad, there is nothing in them which would make them rewardable (good) or punishable (bad). They are made rewardable or punishable by revelation or Shar'. As there is no quality of good or evil seated in the verypature of an act, there can be no question of knowing it by reason.

The Problem of the Eternity of the Quran: There was a great controversy over the question whether the Quran is created or unereated and eternal. This question is bound up with another question whether speech is one of God's attributes or not. The orthodox section of the Muslims, including the Ash'arites, held that God has it as one of His seven rational attributes, and as His attributes are eternal, divine speech, i.e., the Quran, is also eternal.

As regards the eternity of the Quran, the Ash'arites adopted again an intermediary position between the extreme views of the Zahirites and the Mu'tazilites. The Hanbalites and other Zahirites (extreme orthodox schools) held that the speech of God, i. e., the Quran, is composed of letters, words, and sounds which inhere in the essence of God and is, therefore, eternal. Some of the Hanbalites went to the extreme and asserted that even the cover and the binding of the Quran are eternal. The Mu'tazilites and a section of the Rafidites went to the other extreme and maintained that the Quran was created. They denied all attributes of God, including the attribute of speech, on the ground that if it be an eternal attribute of God, there would be multiplicity of eternals, to believe which is polytheism and contrary to the basic principles of Islam. They further argued that "the Quran is composed of parts, successively arranged parts, and whatever is composed of such parts must be temporal."

Hence the Quran must be created. The Ash'arites maintained that the Quran is composed of words and sounds, but these do not inhere in the essence of God. They made a distinction between the outward and concrete expression of the Quran in language, and the real, self subsistent meaning of it, and held that the Quran, as expressed in words and sounds, is, no doubt, temporal (hadath); but against the Mu'tazilites they asserted that the Quran in its meanings is uncreated and eternal. The "self subsisting meaning" eternally inheres in the essence of God. These meanings are expressed; their expression in language is temporal and created. It is so because the same meaning, while remaining the same, might be expressed differently at different times, in different places by different persons or nations. They further maintained that this meaning is an attribute other than knowledge and will and, as such, inheres eternally in the essence of God and is, therefore, eternal.

In support of this contention the Ash`arites advanced the following arguments:

(i) The Quran is "knowledge from God"; it is, therefore, inseparable from God's attribute of knowledge which is eternal and uncreated. Hence it is also eternal and uncreated.

(ii) God created everything by His word kun (be) and this word, which is in the Quran, could not have been a created one, otherwise a created word would be a creator, which is absurd. Hence God's word is uncreated, i. e.. eternal.

(iii) The Quran makes a distinction between creation (khalq) and command (amr) when It says, "Are not the creation and command His alone?" Hence God's Command, His word or Kalam, which is definitely something other than created things (makhluq), must be unereated and eternal.

(iv) Further, God says to Moses, "I have chosen thee over mankind with My apostolate and My word." This verse signifies that God has speech. Again, Moses is addressed by God with the words: "Lo, I am thy Lord." Now, if the word which addresses Moses is a created thing, it would mean that a created thing asserts that it is Moses Lord

(God), which is absurd. God's word, therefore, must be eternal. The Ash'arites further pointed out that all the different arguments advanced by the Mu'tazilites (and in Sharh i Mawaqif as many as eight such arguments have been mentioned), in support of their view that the Quran is created, would apply only to the expressed Quran and not to the real Quran, the latter being the "meanings of the Quran."

The Problem of the Beatific Vision: On the question of the beatific vision, the Ash`arites, true to their attitude of reconciliation, again tried to adopt a course lying midway between the extreme anthropomorphic view of the Zahirites and other orthodox Muslims on the one hand and the view of the Mu'tazilites and the "philosophers" on the other. The extreme orthodox Muslims and the Zahirites, in particular, held that it is possible to see God and the righteous persons would actually have His vision as the chief reward for their good actions. They further held that God is settled firmly on His Throne, He exists in different directions, and is capable of being pointed out.

The Mu'tazilites and the "philosophers" denied the possibility of seeing God with eyes, as that would imply His bodily existence, which is absurd. The Ash'arites, as against the Mu'tazilites and the "philosophers," and in agreement with the orthodox class, held that it is possible to see God; but they could not agree to their view that God is extended and can be shown by pointing out. They accepted the philosophical principle that whatever is extended or spatial must be contingent and temporal, and God is not an extended and temporal being. This admission landed them into a difficulty, for if God is not extended and only extended things can be seen, God cannot be seen; but this conclusion conflicts with their position that beatific vision is possible. So, in order to get out of this difficulty, they asserted the possibility of seeing an object even if it is not present before the perceiver. This was a very peculiar and untenable position, for it repudiated all the principles of optics.

It is possible to see God even though our sense of vision does not receive the corresponding "impression" of the object on it. Besides, it is possible for God to create in human beings the capacity to see Him without the necessary conditions of vision, such as the presence, in concrete form, of the object itself in space and time, normal condition of the appropriate sense organ, absence of hindrance or obstruction to perception, and so on; and though God is unextended and does not exist in space and time, "yet He may make Himself visible to His creature like the fall moon." They further contended that the vision of God is possible without any impression on our sense organ for another reason. There is practically no difference between a "sensation" and an "after image" except that the sensation possesses an additional quality over and above the common qualities present in both, and this additional quality, i.e, impression on the sense organ produced by the external object, does not make any difference in the perception of an object. Hence, though this impression is missing in the case of seeing God, it may still be called "seeing." The weakness of this argument is apparent to any student of psychology, because an after image is possible only when it is preceded by an actual impression of the object on the sense organ. The actual impression of the object is, therefore, a precondition of an after image in the case of beatific vision too.

The Ash'arites were faced with another difficulty. The Mu'tazilites had pointed out that if seeing of God is possible, it must be possible under all circumstances and at all times, for this possibility is due either to His essence or to an inseparable attribute in Him. In either case, it should be possible at all times. And if it is possible at all times, it must be possible now; and if it is possible to see Him now, we must see Him now, for when all the conditions of "vision" are present, the actual seeing must take place. The Ash'arites met this objection in a very naive manner by saying, "We do not admit the necessity of actual seeing taking place, even when all its eight conditions are present."

The Ash'arites supported their views on the basis of revelation. According to the Quran, Moses asked of God, "O, my Lord, show Thyself to me so that I can see Thee." Had seeing been impossible, Moses would not have said so, for, otherwise, it must be assumed that either he knew its impossibility or did not, and both the alternatives are absurd, because an intelligent person like him could not have been ignorant of this impossibility and could not have asked for what he knew was impossible.

Again, according to the Quran, God said to Moses, "If the mountain remains fixed in its place, you can see Me," and if the antecedent is possible the consequent must be possible. Here, evidently, the antecedent, fixity of the mountain, is in itself a possible thing. Therefore, the consequent, the vision of God, must also be possible. Some other verses also support the conclusion.

There are a few more controversial problems of secondary importance, in which the Ash`arites differed from the Mu'tazilites. These are, for example, promise of reward and threat of punishment by God; whether God can make His creatures responsible for the actions for which they have no ability; whether God's actions are bound to be based on rational considerations and on purpose; whether He is bound to do what is best for His creatures; and whether the knowledge of God or recognition of His existence is based on reason or revelation.

These theological problems of secondary importance are more or less the corollaries of the main principles in which the Ash'arites and Mu'tazilites differed.

The Ash'arites held that God is the only real cause of everything; He alone possesses real and effective power and this power is unlimited; His will is absolutely free not determined by anything. Whatever power human beings apparently possess is given by God. Man does not possess any real and effective power. God, being absolutely free in His action, is not bound to act on rational purpose. He does not act teleologically for, otherwise, His actions would be determined by something external to and other than Himself and He would not remain absolutely free. External purpose would put a limit to God's omnipotence. Like Spinoza, al Ash'ari held that there is no purpose in the mind of God which would determine His activity. From thus anti teleological view it follows that as God's action is not teleological, He is not bound to do what is best for His creatures. He does whatever He wills. But as He is an absolutely intelligent and just being, His actions, as a matter of fact, are all full of wisdom.

As against the Mu'tazilites, the Ash'arites held that God can make us responsible for the actions which we have no power to do. The Mu'tazilites held that God cannot do so, because that would be an irrational and unjust act on His part. It is admitted by all schools of thought in Islam that power or ability of men to do a thing is given by God. But opinions differ on the question whether this power or ability is really effective in producing any action. The Mu`tazilites and the Qadarites held that man's power is fully effective and can produce an action. But the Ash'arites maintained that, being derivative, it can have no effective force. Similar are their respective positions with regard to the ability to act. This ability is no doubt given by God as an accident, but the Mu'tazilites, particularly abu al Hudhail `Allaf, held that this ability is given to man simultaneously with the performance of the act. But the Ash'arites maintained that it is given before the actual performance of the act; but being a mere accident in man, it has only a momentary existence and is of no practical use to man in performing the act. As a matter of fact, it ceases to exist when the actual action takes place. Man, therefore, does the act, practically without having the power and the ability to do so. He is held responsible for his actions because of his choosing freely one of the two alternative actions and intending to do the action so chosen. But neither his choice nor his intention can produce the action. It is God who creates the action and is thus its effective and real cause.

There is an almost similar controversy over the question of God's promise of reward to the virtuous and His threat of punishment to the wrong doer. This was one of the five main problems with which the Mu'tazilite movement started. The Mu'tazilites held that God is bound to fulfil His promises of reward and punishment. Every action, good or bad, must take its own course and be followed by its logical and normal consequence. A right action, therefore, must be followed by its reward and a wrong one by punishment. God has made promises in the Quran and He, being a just being, cannot do otherwise, i.e., He cannot punish the virtuous and forgive the wrong doer.

On the other hand, the Ash'arites maintained that, being all powerful and absolutely free in His will, God can punish His creatures even if they have not committed any sins or reward His creatures even though they have done no virtuous deeds. There is nothing binding on God; His will is not subject to teleological considerations. It is by the inner necessity of His own nature that He fulfils His promises of reward to the virtuous and does not do otherwise. And it is in His infinite mercy that He may forgive any wrongdoer or vicious person, in spite of the threats of punishment for his vicious acts. This act of forgiveness will also be in accordance with His nature as the most generous and gracious being.

ASH'ARITE METAPHYSICS

Al Ash'ari's interest was purely theological and his discussions did not contain much metaphysics. But the subsequent Ash'arites found it impossible to achieve their main object of defending the faith and harmonizing reason with revelation without making reference to the ultimate nature of reality. Al Ash'ari's theological system was, thus, considered to be incomplete without a support from metaphysics. The system was fully developed by the later Ash'arites, particularly by Qadi abu Bakr Muhammad bin Tayyyib al Baqillani who was one of the greatest among them. He was a Basrite, but he made Baghdad his permanent residence and died there in 403/1013. He was a great original thinker and wrote many valuable books on theology and various other subjects. He made use of some purely metaphysical propositions in his theological investigations, such as substance is an individual unity, accident has only a momentary existence and cannot exist in quality, and perfect vacuum is possible, and thus gave the school a metaphysical foundation. About him a Western scholar has remarked: "It is his glory to have contributed most important elements to, and put into fixed form what is, perhaps, the most daring metaphysical scheme, and almost certainly the most thorough theological scheme, ever thought out. On the one hand, the Lucretian atoms raining down through the empty void, the self developing monads and pre-established harmony of Leibniz; and all the Kantian "things in themselves" are lame and impotent in their consistency beside the parallel Ash'arite doctrines; and, on the other, not even the rigours of Calvin; as developed in Dutch confessions, can compete with the unflinching exactitude of the Muslim conclusions.

The Ash'arites, being primarily interested in theological problems, kept their philosophical discussions mainly confined only to those questions which they thought had a direct or indirect bearing on these problems. Willingly or unwillingly, they had to philosophize "in order to meet the contemporary philosophers on their own ground." But when they began philosophizing, they were very earnest and became great metaphysicians.

In dealing with the most important basic principles of Islam: (i) the existence of God, as the creator of the universe, and His unity and oneness, and (ii) the belief in the prophethood of Muhammad, they had to use certain proofs which necessitated some metaphysical and epistemological discussions. Hence they had to develop a theory of knowledge and a theory of reality, which were peculiarly their own. God, the ultimate principle, is, according to the Ash'arites, a necessary existent; His existence is identical with His essence. In proving God's existence the Ash'arites used three arguments. Their argument from the contingent nature of motion is not of much importance to our discussion. The other two are

(i) All bodies, they argued, are ultimately one in so far as their essence is concerned. But, in spite of this basic unity, their characteristics are different. Hence there must be an ultimate cause for these divergent characteristic, and that ultimate cause is God.

(ii) The world is contingent. Every contingent thing must have a cause; therefore, the world must have a cause, and as no contingent thing can be the cause, that cause must be God. The major premise (i.e., every event must have a cause) does not require a proof. The minor premise the world is contingent they proved in the following manner: Everything that exists in the world is either a substance or a quality. The contingent character of a quality is evident, and the contingence of substance follows from the fact that no substance could exist apart from qualities. The contingence of quality necessitates the contingence of substance; otherwise, the eternity of substance would necessitate the eternity of quality.

The Ash'arites believed in miracles which were considered to be the basis of the proof of prophethood and, in order to defend this view, they had to deny the laws of nature. They also denied causality in nature and made God the only cause of everything. Now, in order to explain the full implication of the above arguments, it was necessary for them to develop a theory of knowledge and a metaphysics.

The world consists of things. Now, the question arises: What is meant by a thing, what is its nature, and how far do we know it?

Al Baqillani defined knowledge as the cognition of a thing as it is in itself. A thing is defined by the Ash'arites as "that which is existent." Everything is an existent and every existent is a thing. So, according to the Ash'arites, existence, whether necessary or contingent, is the thing or the essence of the thing in itself and not a quality in addition to it, as the Mu'tazilites held.

Al Jahiz, al Jubba'i, and some other Mu'tazilites of the Basrite school defined a "thing" as that which is known, and held that existence is a quality of it, added to its essence. The Ash'arites, as against these Mu'tazilites, contended that if existence is an additional quality, the essence in itself would be a nonexistent and hence a non entity and the subsequent addition of the quality of "existence" to it would involve a clear contradiction in so far as it would make the non existent existent. This is an absurdity.

The thing in itself which is the object of knowledge according to the Ash'arites, is, therefore, an existent thing or a body. Everything that exists in the world has a contingent existence and is either substance or quality. In this sense God is not a thing.

The Aristotelian categories of thought were subjected by the Ash'arites to a searching criticism. Only two of those categories, substance and quality, were retained by them. The other categories, quality, place, time, etc., are nothing but relative characteristics (i'tibarat) that exist subjectively in the mind of the knower, having no corresponding objective reality.

Like Berkeley, the Irish philosopher, they also did not make any distinction between the primary and secondary qualities of objects. The world, therefore, consists of substance, on which the mind reflects, and qualities, which are not in the thing in itself but only in the mind of the knower.

The qualities are mere accidents which are fleeting, transitory, and subjective relations, having only a momentary existence. A quality or accident cannot exist in another accident but only in a substance. No substance could ever exist apart from a quality.

The substance, being inseparable from its accidents, must also be transitory, having only a moment's duration, just as the accidents are. Everything that exists, therefore, consists of mere transitory units (subjective), having only a moment's duration. The Ash'arites, thus, rejected the Aristotelian view of matter as "a permanent potentiality (hayula) of suffering the impress of form (surah)," because a possibility is neither an entity nor a non entity but purely a subjectivity. With inert matter, the active form and all causes must also go. They, too, are mere subjectivities. This led them straight to the atomists and, as a matter of fact, they did become atomists after their own fashion.

In this connection we may observe that the object of the Ash'arites was, like that of Kant, to fix the relation of knowledge to the thing in itself; and they showed here a great originality in their thought. On this question they not only anticipated Kant but, in reaching the thing in itself, they were much more thorough than Kant.

"In his examination of human knowledge regarded as a product and not merely a process, Kant stopped at the idea of 'Ding an sich' [thing in itself], but the Ash'arite endeavoured to penetrate further, and maintained, against the contemporary Agnostic Realism, that the so called underlying essence existed only so far as it was brought in relation to the knowing subject."

Ash'arite Atomism: The substances perceived by us are atoms which come into existence from vacuity and drop out of existence again. The world is made up of such atoms. The Ash'arite atoms are fundamentally different from those of Democritus and Lucretius.

The Ash`arite atoms are not material; they are not permanent; they have only a momentary existence; they are not eternal but every moment brought into being, and then allowed to go out of existence by the Supreme Being, God, the only cause of everything in the universe. These atoms are not only of space but of time also.

They are-nonmaterial or ideal in character. They resemble the monads of Leibniz. But the Ash'arite monads differ from those of Leibniz in having no possibility of self development along certain lines. Each monad has certain qualities but has extension neither in space nor in time. They have simply position, not bulk, and are isolated from and independent of one another.

There is absolute void between any two monads. Space and time are subjective. All changes in the world are produced by their entering into existence and dropping out again, but not by any change in themselves.

The Ash'arite ontology necessitated the existence of God. Their monads must have a cause, without which they could not have come into being, nor could there be any harmony or connection between them. This cause must be a cause sui; otherwise there would be an infinite regress of the causal nexus. The Ash'arites found this cause in the free will of God. It creates and annihilates the atoms and their qualities and, thus, brings to pass all motion and change in the world.

The Ash'arites were, thus, thoroughgoing metaphysicians. Being was all important in their ontology. The will of that Being or God must, therefore, be the ground of all things. Hence they did not find any difficulty, as Leibniz did, in explaining the harmony and coherence among the isolated, windowless, and independent monads, constituting the one orderly world. Leibniz had to bring in, in his monadology, a Monad of monads or God, and fall back upon the Theory of Pre established Harmony to bring his monads into harmonious and orderly relations with one another, and this he could do only at the cost of his monadology, and by abandoning his pluralistic,and individualistic metaphysics.

But the Ash'arites, consistently with their ontology, fell straight back upon God, and found in His will the ground of orderliness and harmony in the universe. They were, thus, more thorough and consistent than Leibniz in their theory of monads. The Ash'arite atomism approaches that of Lotze's, who in spite of his desire to save external reality, ended in its

Complete reduction to ideality. But, like Lotze, they could not believe their atoms to be the inner working of the infinite Primal Being.

The necessary consequence of their analysis is a thorough going idealism like that of Berkeley. Their theory of knowledge reduced the universe to a mere show of ordered subjectivities which, as they maintained like Berkeley, found their ultimate explanation in the will of God. Their interest, as we have already pointed out, was mainly theological. Interest in pure monotheism was very strong with them. Their metaphysical and epistemological discussions were actuated by a pious desire to defend the idea of divine creations, to drive men back to God and His revelation and compel them to see in Him the one grand fact of the universe.

The Ash'arites are here more consistent than Berkeley. God, according to them, is the only cause in the true sense of the term. No created thing, having created power, could be the cause of anything.

The attitude of the Ash'arites towards the law of causation was sceptical. They denied objective validity of causality in nature. No created thing or being can be the cause of anything. Things or beings in nature do not possess any power or quality which could produce any effect.

The so called power which men and objects of nature seem to possess is not an effective power, for it is a derived power, not an original power which alone can produce effect. Whatever power the creatures might possess must have been given by God, who alone possesses all real power. Being (God) is the only Ultimate Reality.

The things of the world are composed of indivisible units monads which, every moment, are created and annihilated; and it is God who creates and annihilates them and their qualities, thereby bringing about all the motion and change in the world. There is, thus, no such thing as a law of nature and the world is sustained by a constant, ever repeated activity of God. There is no such thing as a secondary cause; when there is the appearance of such a cause, it is only illusionary. God produces the appearance of the effect as well as the effect. Things of the world do not possess any permanent nature. Fire, for instance, does not possess the nature or quality of burning; it does not burn. God creates in a substance "a being burned" when fire touches it.

The Ash'arites thus denied power in the cause as well as the necessary connection between the so called cause and effect. Shibli mentions that the Ash'arites rejected the idea of causation with a view to defending the possibility of miracles on the manifestation of which, according to them, prophethood depended.

The orthodox school believed in miracles as well as in the universal law of causation; but they also maintained that, at the time of manifesting a miracle, God suspends the operation of this law and thus brings about an exception. Asha`ari, however, maintained that a cause must have always the same effect (i.e., the effect of one and the cause cause could not be different at different times).

Having accepted this principle as formulated by their leader, the Ash'arites could not agree to the orthodox view and, therefore, to prove the possibility of miracles they rejected the law of causation altogether, According to them, there is no power in the antecedent to produce the consequent. "We know nothing but floating impressions, the phenomenal order of which is determined by God."

Objection might be raised against the Ash'arite metaphysics that it establishes in effect a relationship between God and the atoms, but relationships, according to the Ash'arites, are subjective illusions.

In reply to this objection it may be pointed out that all relationship applies only to contingent beings or things perceived by the senses. It would not hold in the case of the Necessary Being, God, who is suprasensible. And according to their principle of mukhalafah, nothing which is applied to created things or beings can be applied to God in the same sense. God is not a natural cause but a free cause.

This is the Ash'arite system as completed by Qadi abu Bakr al Baqillani. It faced a strong opposition from the orthodox, particularly from the followers of Abmad bin Hanbal. Al Ashari's opinions did not get much recognition outside the Shafi'ite group to which he belonged. The Hanafites preferred the doctrines of his contemporary al Maturidi who differed from al Ash'ari in certain minor controversial. points. Shibli has mentioned nine such points. In Spain, ibn Hazm (d. 456/1063) opposed the Ash'arite doctrines.

The Saljuq Sultan Tughril Beg, who was an adherent of the Hanbalite school, treated the Ash'arites very badly, but his successor Sultan Alp Arsalan and especially his famous vizier, Nizam al Mulk supported the Ash`arites and put an end to the persecution to which they had been exposed. Nizam al Mulk founded the Nizamite Academy at Baghdad in 459/1066 for the defence of Ash'arite doctrines. It is under his patronage that abu al Ma'ali `Abd al Malik al Juwaini got the chance of preaching the Ash'arite doctrine freely.

The Ash'arite system could not obtain widespread acceptance until it was popularized by al Juwaini and al Ghazali in the East and by ibn Tumart in the West. It was al Juwaini who could legitimately claim the credit of making the Ash'arites' doctrines popular. His vast learning and erudite scholarship brought him the title of Dia' al Din(the light of religion). Al Juwaini received his early education from his father, Shaikh abu Muhammad `Abd Allah, and after the death of his father, he got further education from his teacher, abu Ishaq al Isfara'ini, a great Ash'arite scholar.

Al Juwaini, in course of time, was recognized by the scholars of the time to be Shaikh al Islam (the chief leader of Islam) and Imam al Haramain (the religious leader of Makkah and Madinah). For thirty years, he continued teaching and preaching the Ash'arite doctrines.

Al Juwaini was the teacher of al Ghazali. He wrote many books on various subjects. Some of these are: al Shamil, on the principles of religion; al Burhan, on the principles of jurisprudence; al `Aqidat al Nizamiyyah; and Irshad, on theology. He was born in 419/1028 and died at Nishapur in 478/1085.53 Being the Shaikh al Islam and the Imam of Makkah and Madinah, al Juwaini's Fatawa (judgments on religious matters) used to be respected by people in general throughout the Muslim world; and for this reason, his writings got the widest circulation and, through these writings, Ash'arite doctrines became known everywhere.

One great theological result of the Ash'arite system was that it checked the growth of free thought which tended to dissolve the solidarity of the Islamic Shari'ah. The Ash`arite mode of thought had its intellectual results also.

It led to an independent criticism of Greek philosophy and prepared the ground for philosophies propounded by men like al Ghazali and Fakhr al Din al Razi. Al Ghazali is generally included among the Ash'arites and it is he who maybe said to have completed the Ash'arite metaphysics. It was he who, by giving a systematic refutation of Greek philosophy in his famous work, Tahafut al Falasifah, completely annihilated the dread of intellectualism which had characterized the minds of the orthodox. It was chiefly through his influence that people began to study dogma and metaphysics together. Strictly speaking, al Ghazali was not an Ash'arite, though he admitted that the Ash'arite mode of thought was excellent for the masses. "He held that the secret of faith could not be revealed to the masses; for this reason he encouraged exposition of the Ash`arite theology, and took care in persuading his disciples not to publish the results of his private reflection."

Al-Ghazali made the Ash'arite theology so popular that it became practically the theology of the Muslim community in general and has continued to remain so up to the present time.

6

TAHAWISM

TAHAWI'S LIFE AND WORKS

Abu Ja'far Ahmad b. Muhammad b. Salamah al Azdi, al Hajri, al Tahawi, was born at Taha, a village in upper Egypt. His forefathers came from the Yemen to Egypt and settled there after it had come under the Muslim rule. There is a considerable difference of opinion as to the year of his birth. The years 229/843, 230/ 844, 238/852 and 239/853 are mentioned by different biographers. Al Sam'ani asserts that he was born in 229/843 and this is correct. He died in Egypt in 321/933.

Al Tahawi was mainly interested in Hadith and Fiqh, and was regarded as one of the greatest Muhaddithin and fuqaha' of his time. According to abu Ishaq al Shirazi, he was the last leader of Hanafi Fiqh in Egypt. He began to study Shafi'i Law under his maternal uncle abu Ibrahim Ismail al Muzani (d. 264/878), the most celebrated pupil of Imam al Shafi'i, and then leaving his school he took up the study of Hanafi Law under al Shaikh abu Jafar Ahmad b. abi,`Imran (d. 285/898), who became the Chief Qadi of Egypt in 270/883. Different versions are given by his biographers of his conversion to Hanafi school, but the most probable reason seems to be that the system of Imam abu Hanifah appealed to his critical insight more than that of Imam Shafi`i.

Al Tahawi went to Syria in 268/882 for further studies in Hanafi Law and became a pupil of Qadi abu Khazim `Abd al Hamid b. Ja'far, the then Chief Justice of Syria. He learnt hadith from a large number of Shaikhs especially from those who visited Egypt at his time, and had also many pupils of distinction. He is a distinguished author of many important works of which the following may be mentioned here: 1. Sharh Ma'ani al Athar, 2. Mushkil al Athar, 3. Ahkam al Quran, 4. Ikhtilaf al Ulama', 5. al Nawadir al Fiqhiyyah, 6. Kitab al Shurut al Kabir, 7. al Shurut al Ausat, 8. Sharh al Jami` al Saghir, 9. Sharh al Jami' al Kabir, 10. al Mukhtasar, 11. Manaqib Abi Hanifah, 12. Tarikh al Kabir, 13. al Radd `ala Kitab al Mudallisin, 14. al Radd `ala Abi `Ubaid, 15. al Radd `ala `Isa b. Abban, 16. Hukm `Aradi Makkah, etc.

His original contribution to Hadith literature, so far as we can estimate is that he introduced a new system of collecting legal traditions, developed a new method of interpreting and harmonizing the conflicting traditions, and adopted a new criterion for criticizing them. His predecessors and contemporaries, the authors of al sihah al Sittah (the Six Canonical Compilations) collecting traditions according to their own standards and principles, left out a large number of genuine traditions. Al Tahawi made a strenuous effort to collect all the genuine legal traditions of the Prophet, narrated by different authorities on a particular subject, together with the opinions of the Companions of the Prophet, their Successors and the distinguished jurisprudents. He then scrutinized traditions (ahadith)and showed by evidence which of them were authentic, strong, weak, unknown, or such as might be supposed to have been repealed. Thus, his collection provided for the scholars an unprecedented opportunity to judge for themselves the merits or demerits of a particular tradition. The criterion for judging the genuineness of a tradition, according to the Traditionists in general, was the isnad (chain of the narrators), and so they paid greater attention to the scrutiny of the isnad than to the scrutiny of the text (matn)of a tradition. But al Tahawi, while scrutinizing a tradition, took into consideration the matn as well as the isnad of the tradition. He also aimed at a harmonizing interpretation in case of conflicting traditions.

Al Tahawi, like al Maturidi, was a follower of Imam abu Hanifah (d. 150/ 767) in jurisprudence as well as in theology. He wrote a little treatise on theology named Bayan al Sunnah w al Jama'ah, generally known as al`Aqidat al Tahawiyyah. In the introduction to this treatise he says he will give therein an account of the beliefs of the ahl al sunnah w al jama'ah according to the views of imam abu Hanifah, abu Yusuf, and Muhammad al Shaibani the well known jurisprudents of the community. So the importance of his creed lies in the fact that it corroborates the views of Imam abu Hanifah, the founder of the school, that have come down to us from different sources. Al Tahawi made no attempt to explain the views of the Imam or to solve the old theological problems by advancing any new arguments. His sole aim was to give a summary of the views of the Imam and to show indirectly that they were in conformity with the traditional views of the orthodox school.

The difference between him and al Maturidi the two celebrated authorities on the views of the Imam is quite evident. Al Maturidi was a thorough dialectician and his main endeavour was to find out a philosophical basis for the views of the leader and to support these views by scholastic reasoning, and thereby bring them closer to the views of the rationalists. Al Tahawi, as a true traditionist, did not favour, as will be seen, any rational discussion or speculative thinking on the articles of faith, but preferred to believe and accept them without questioning. There is no reference in his creed to the critical examination of the method, sources, and means of knowledge, or the foundation on which his theological system is built. So his system may be termed as dogmatic, while that of al Maturidi as critical. The critical method followed by al Tahawi in Hadith is quite lacking in theology. Thus, though both of them belong to the same school and uphold faithfully the doctrines of their master, they differ from each other in temperament, attitude, and trends of thought.

In order to indicate the characteristics of the system of al Tahawi and to make an estimate of his contributions to theology, we propose to give in the following pages an outline of the views of Imam abu Hanifah along with the views of both al Tahawi and al Maturidi on some of the most important theological problems that arose in Muslim theology.

Imam abu Hanifah directed his movement against the Kharijites, Qadarites, Mu'tazilites, Shiites, Jabrites, the extreme Murji'ites, and the Hashwiyyah, the last being a group of the orthodox people who under the influence of the converted Jews, Christians, and Magians fell into gross anthropomorphism, and ascribed to God all the characteristics of a created being. He was the first theologian among the fuqaha' who adopted the principles and method of reasoning and applied them to a critical examination of the articles of faith and the laws of the Shariah. That is why he and his followers were called by the Traditionists the People of Reason and Opinion (ashab al ra'i w al qiyas). This rational spirit and philosophical attitude were more consistently maintained by al Maturidi than by al Tahawi. Their views on the nature of faith, attributes of God, beatific vision, divine decree, and human freedom may be mentioned here to indicate the distinctive features of their methods.

NATURE OF FAITH

Faith, according to the well known view of Imam abu Hanifah, consists of three elements: knowledge, belief, and confession; knowledge alone or confession alone is not faith. Al Maturidi holds the same view and lays emphasis on knowledge (ma'rifah)and belief (tasdiq). But, according to his explanation, knowledge is the basis of faith and confession is not in reality an integral part of faith but only an indication (`alamah)of faith, a condition for enforcement of Islamic laws and enjoyment of the rights and privileges of the Muslim community. So the belief based on the knowledge of God is the basis of faith. Al Tahawi excludes knowledge from his definition of faith and holds that it consists in believing by heart and confessing by tongue.

As regards the relation between faith and action Imam abu Hanifah maintains that Islam demands from its followers two things: belief and practice, and both are essential for a perfect Muslim. The two are very closely related like back and belly, but they are not identical. Practice is distinct from faith and faith is distinct from practice, but both are essential elements of Islam. "Allah has ordained practice for the faithful, faith for the infidel, and sincerity for the hypocrite." The term al din (religion) includes both faith and action. Faith, according to him, is a living conviction of the heart an absolute and indelible entity having its own existence independent of action. From this definition of faith he arrived at the following conclusions: (a) Faith is not liable to increase or decrease. (b) Faith is impaired by doubt. (c) The faithful are equal in faith but different in degree of superiority regarding practice. (d) No Muslim should be declared devoid of faith on account of any sin, if he does not declare it to be lawful. One may be a man of faith with bad behaviour, but not an infidel. (e) A believer who dies unrepentant, even though guilty of mortal sins, will not remain in hell for ever. Allah may grant him forgiveness or punish him in accordance with his sins.

Pointing out the differences between himself and the Murji'ites, Imam abu Hanifah says: "We do not say that sins do not harm the faithful, nor do we say that he will not enter hell, nor do we say that he will remain there for ever, although he should be a man of evil practice (fasiq), after having departed from this world as a man of faith. And we do not say that our good actions are accepted and our sins are forgiven, as the Murji'ites say. But we say that no one who performs a good action, fulfilling all its conditions and keeping it free of all defects, without nullifying it by infidelity, apostasy, or bad conduct during any part of his life, shall be neglected by God. God may punish in hell or grant complete forgiveness to a person who commits an evil deed (polytheism and infidelity excluded) and dies without repenting.

The Kharijites and Mu'tazilites laid so much emphasis on the doctrine of threats (wa`id) that they led the believers to despair and take a depressing view of life; while the Murji'tes emphasized the doctrine of promise (wa'd) so much that they quite endangered the ethical basis of Islam. Imam abu Hanifah endeavoured to strike a middle course between these two extremes. Sins, according to him, are not without consequences; a sinner is always liable to blame or punishment, but to drive him out from the fold of Islam, to declare him an infidel, or to condemn him to eternal punishment is quite inconsistent with divine justice. His broad outlook and tolerant attitude were consistently continued by al-Maturidi and al Tahawi. The latter has summarized the views of his master on these questions in the following words:

> *"We do not declare anyone of the people of qiblah an infidel on account of a sin, so long as he does not deem it lawful. And we do not say that sin with faith does no harm to him who commits it. We entertain hope for the righteous among the faithful, but we have no certainty about them, and we do not certify that they will be in paradise. We ask forgiveness for their evil actions and*

we have fear for them, but we do not drive them into despair. Sense of security and despair both turn a man away from religion. The true way for the people of qiblah lies midway between these two. A faithful servant does not go out of the field of faith except by renouncing what had brought him into it."

Al Tahawi substituted the phrase ahl al qiblah for mu'min and Muslim, evidently to avoid the theological controversies regarding their identification, and to make the circle of the believers wider and at the same tune to give the question a practical bias. He also avoided the theoretical definition of a Muslim or mu'min, and instead described how one could be regarded as such. He says: "We give those who follow our qiblah the name Muslim or mu'min, so long as they acknowledge what the Prophet brought with him and believe in what he said and what he narrated."

Knowledge of God and belief in Him may save those who are guilty of mortal sins from eternal punishment, and they may entertain hope of deliverance from hell through divine mercy and the intercession of the righteous. "Those who are guilty of grievous sins will not remain eternally in hell, if they died as unitarians, even if they were not repentant. They are left to God's will and judgment; if He wills He will forgive them out of His kindness, as He has said: `Surely Allah will not forgive the setting up of other gods with Himself; other sins He may forgive if He pleases; ' and if He wills He will punish them in hell in proportion to their sins as demanded by His justice. Then He will bring them out of it through His mercy and the intercession of His obedient people, and finally He will send them to paradise. This is because Allah is the Lord of those who know Him well, and He has not destined them in either world to be like those who denied Him, went astray from His guidance, and did not obtain His help and favour."

It may be noticed here that, although al Tahawi did not include knowledge in his definition of faith, he was fully conscious of the cognitive aspect of it.

As regards intercession, Imam abu Hanifah seems to restrict it to the prophets in general and particularly to Prophet Muhammad, but al Tahawi extends this privilege to the righteous and the pious among the faithful. As regards the independent character of faith and equality of the faithful, al Tahawi says: "Faith is one and the faithful are equal; their comparative eminence lies in fear (of Allah), in righteousness, in disobeying lust, and in pursuing what is best. All the believers are friends of the Merciful. The most honourable among them before God are those who are the most obedient and the best followers of the Holy Quran."

On the question whether it is obligatory for a man to know God before the advent of His messenger, and whether to follow precedence (taqlid) is allowed in matters of faith, al Tahawi does not express his opinion explicitly, though his master was quite outspoken on these questions. These questions pertain to the Mu'tazilites doctrine of promise and threat (al wa'd w al wa'id), which gave rise to the discussion of the nature and value of reason and revelation. They held that as God has endowed men with reason and they can easily perceive by proper use of this faculty that the world has a creator, it is obligatory on their part to know God even if the call of the Prophet does not reach them. But they were divided as to whether knowledge of God is acquired and a posteriori (kasabi)or necessary and a priori (daruri). Imam abu Hanifah agreed with the Mu'tazilites on the original question and maintained that "no one can have any excuse for ignorance about his creator, as he sees the creation of the heaven and the earth of his own as well as of others. So even if Allah should not have sent any messenger to the people, it was obligatory on them to know Him by means of their intellect."

GOD'S ESSENCE AND ATTRIBUTES

As to the relation between God's essence and attributes Imam abn Hanifah is stated to have advised his pupils not to enter into discussion on this question, but to be content with ascribing to God the qualities which He Himself ascribed to Himself. He even once declined to discuss this problem with Jahm. In order to avoid the difficulties involved in affirming attributes, he simply declared that "they are neither He, nor other than He" (la huwa wa la ghairuhu). According to the explanation of al Maturidi, this phrase means that the attributes of God are neither identical with nor separate from His essence.

Al Tahawi made no reference to the philosophical problem of the relation between God and His essence, nor did he make a clear distinction between the attributes of essence and those of actions. But he emphatically asserts the eternity of the attributes and says: "Allah has eternally been with His attributes before He created the world and nothing has been added to His qualities after the creation, and as He has been from eternity with His qualities, He will remain with these to eternity...."

Expressing his vigorous attitude against the Antbropomorphists he declared "Whosoever attributes to Allah any of the human senses (ma'ani), he becomes an infidel." The true path lies, he asserts, between tashbih and ta'til. "He who does not guard against denial (of attributes) and assimilation slips and does not attain tanzih. Verily our Lord the High and Exalted has been attributed with the attribute of oneness and has been qualified with the quality of uniqueness. No one of the creation possesses His qualities. Allah is most high and praise be to Him. He is without limits, ends, elements, limbs, and instruments. The six directions do not encompass Him as they do the created things."

It may be inferred from the above statement and the similar one in the `Aqidah, that al Tahawi is against the literal interpretations of the anthropomorphic expressions of the Quran, such as the face of Allah, His eyes and hands, etc. But he does not indicate what these terms signify. Abu Hanifah clearly states that these terms denote His qualities. Even then he also is not in favour of giving any rational interpretation of them, as he fears that this may lead to the denial of His qualities. He says: "He has hand, face, and soul as mentioned in the Quran, and whatever Allah mentioned in the Quran as face, hand, or soul is unquestionably His quality. It should not be said with the Qadarites and the Mu'tazilites that by His hand is meant His power or His bounty, because this leads to the rejection of certain attributes. Nay. His hand is His attribute without description."

The Imam had also adopted the principle of leaving the judgment to God (tafwid) regarding the interpretation of the ambiguous verses of the Quran; al Tahawi stuck to this principle very consistently. He says: "The foot of Islam does not stand firm but on the back of submission and surrender. Whosoever wishes to attain that knowledge which was forbidden for him and whose intelligence does not remain content with submission, his desire certainly hinders him from access to pure concept of unity (tauhid), clear knowledge, and correct faith, and he then wavers between faith and infidelity, belief and disbelief, confession and denial as a sceptic, distracted, eccentric, and fugitive person without being a faithful believer or a faithless disbeliever."

The attitude of al Maturidi on this question is more rational and liberal than that of al Tahawi. According to the former, leaving judgment to God and passing an interpretative judgment for oneself are both allowed; and he is in favour of interpreting them in the light of explicit verses of the Quran.

Throne of Allah Regarding the Throne of Allah ('arsh) as mentioned in the Quran, abu Hanifah maintains that the expression should not be taken in the literal sense to mean a particular place. God being the creator of place cannot be thought of to be limited by place. He is where He has been before the creation of place. Abu Muti` al Balkhi, one of the disciples of the Imam, asked him, "What will you say if anyone asks: `Where is Allah the Exalted?'" He replied: "He should be told that Allah has been existing while there was no place before He created the universe; He has been existing while there was no `where (aina), no created being, nor anything else. He is the creator of everything." Refuting the idea of the Anthropomorphists that God is in a particular place, he declared: " We confess that Allah has seated Himself on the Throne without any necessity on His part, and without being fixed on it. If He had been under any necessity, He would not have been able to create the world and would have governed it like the created beings; and if He should feel any necessity to sit down and remain seated, where then was He before the creation of the Throne? God is exalted and high far above such ideas."

It is evident that, according to abu Hanifah, God, being eternal and incorporeal, cannot be conceived as being encompassed by direction and place. Al Tahawi, as has been quoted above, firmly holds this view. "God is without limits, ends, elements, limbs, and instruments. The six directions do not encompass Him as they encompass the created things." Referring to the Throne and the Chair, he states: "The Throne and the Chair are realities as Allah described them in His honoured Book. But He is not in need of the Throne nor of what is besides the Throne. He encompasses everything and is above everything.

Al Maturidi went a step further to allow rational interpretation of those verses, the apparent sense of which created an impression of His being in a place. He refuted the view of those who thought that the Throne was a particular place and God was on it, in it, or encompassed by it, as well as the views of those who thought that He was in every place. According to him, God being eternal, infinite, and incorporeal is free of time and space which imply rest, change, motion, and movement. Explaining the verses which were interpreted to prove His being in a particular place or in every place by the champions of these views, he asserts that these verses refer to His creative function, controlling power, absolute authority, sovereignty, eternity, and infinitude and indirectly prove that He is above the limitations of time and space.

Beatific Vision: This question was discussed with much fervour by the Companions of the Prophet. Besides their intense love of God and an ardent desire to enjoy the happiness of seeing their Lord in the next world, the accounts of Ascension (mi'raj), and the prayer of Moses to have a vision of his Lord as referred to in the Quran, aroused in them fervent zeal for a discussion of this topic. It seems quite certain that as a result of this discussion they arrived at the following conclusions: (a) God is invisible in this world; no human being saw Him or will ever see Him in this world except the Prophet Muhammad who, according to some of them, saw Him on the night of mi'raj; (b) God will be seen by the faithful in paradise. The eager inquiries of the Companions of the Prophet whether he saw his Lord or whether believers will see Him in the next world and the vehement opposition of a group of leading Companions, including `A'ishah, to the common belief that the Prophet saw his Lord, all clearly indicate that the Companions were fully conscious of the difficulties involved in answering these questions. Their standpoint on this question, like that on the problem of essence and attributes was just to believe and refrain from a detailed discussion of such matters as cannot be comprehended by human reason. The seeing of God in paradise was regarded by them as the highest blessing and happiness for the believers and the summum bonum of their life. They believed in it without description (wasf) or rational explanation. (ta'wil).

The Anthropomorphists, in the subsequent period, found in this belief a strong basis for their gross and crude anthropomorphic conception of God. As God will be seen in paradise He must have body and form and may be seen in this world, nay, He may even assume the form of a beautiful man.

It was Jahm who, in order to oppose tashbih, laid great emphasis on tanzih and quite consistently with his idea of abstract God denied for the first time, according to our present information, the vision of God in paradise. The Mu'tazilites adopted this view and interpreted the beatific vision allegorically. Imam abu Hanifah upheld the view of the Companions and discarded both anthropomorphic and allegorical interpretation of "seeing God." God will be seen by the faithful in paradise, he maintains, with their bodily eyes, but without any idea of place, direction, distance, comparison, or modality and without any description. Al Tahawi maintains the same position and emphasizes that beatific vision is an article of faith and it must be accepted without any doubt, without any rational interpretation, and without any idea of anthropomorphism. Any attempt to interpret it by reason will amount, according to him, to the denial of this tenet. Al Maturidi also supported this orthodox view and opposed tashbih and ta'wil and showed by elaborate discussion that the verses of the Quran and the traditions of the Prophet on this question do not allow any allegorical interpretation. His main argument, as we have already seen, is that the conditions of seeing a physical object in this world should not be applied to seeing God who has no body and no form and is not limited by time and space, and that too in the next world where nature of things and state of affairs would be quite different from what prevails here.

Speech of God and the Quran: Speech (kalam), according to abu Hanifah, is an attribute of God pertaining to His essence and is eternal like all other divine attributes, and God speaks by virtue of this eternal speech. As regards the relation between kalam of Allah and the Quran, he says: "We confess that the

Quran is the uncreated speech of Allah; inspiration or revelation from Him is neither He nor other than He, but His quality in reality, written in the copies, recited by the tongues, and preserved in the breasts. The ink, the paper, the writing are created, for they are works of men. The speech of Allah, on the other hand, is uncreated; the writings, the letters, the words, and the verses are signs (dalalat) of the Quran for the sake of human needs. The speech of Allah is self existing and its meaning is understood by means of these symbols. Whosoever says that the speech of Allah is created, he is an infidel: His speech, though recited, written, and retained in the hearts, is yet never dissociated from Him."

Abu Hanifah thus refutes the ideas of the Mu'tazilah who denied the attribute of speech being identical with divine essence and declared the Quran to have been created, as well as the ideas of those Mushabbihah and Hashwiyyah (extreme orthodox) who thought that divine speech, like human speech, consists of words and sounds and that the script in which the Quran was written was as eternal as the Quran itself. Kalam of Allah, according to him, is not identical with His Being, for this will make His Being complex and lead to the plurality of Godhead; nor can it be something other than Himself, for this will mean that He acquired a new quality and became what He was not before. This also implies imperfection and change in the divine nature; hence absurd. Divine speech, therefore, must be eternal, and as the Quran is universally accepted to be the speech of Allah, it is necessarily uncreated.

Al Tahawi treated this subject with great caution and condemned controversies about the Quran and practically declined to enter into a philosophical discussion on the nature of divine speech. He says: "Verily the Quran the kalam of Allah originated (bada`)from Him as words without description (bila kaifiyyah)and He sent it down to His Prophet as revelation; and the faithful believed it to be truly as such, and they knew for certain that it was in reality the kalam of Allah, the Exalted, not created like the speech of the created beings. So whoever supposes it to be human speech is an infidel."

The main point of controversy, it may be mentioned here, between the Jahmiyyah and Mu'tazilah, on the one hand, and the orthodox, on the other, was on the nature of the divine word and its relation to the Quran, after they had all agreed that the Quran was the revealed book of Allah. So al Tahawi, in fact, bypassed the main point at issue. He also made no reference to the relation of the speeches of created beings or that of Allah's word addressed to them such as to the Prophet Moses, as mentioned in the Quran, with the eternal speech a problem, which evidently bewildered the minds of Ja'd, Jahm, and their followers. Abu Hanifah sought to remove this doubt with reference to the eternal divine attributes of knowing and creating. "Allah had indeed been speaking before He spoke to Moses, as Allah had indeed been creating from eternity before creating any creatures. So, when He spoke to Moses, He spoke to him with His speech which is one of His eternal attributes." Similarly, "whatever Allah mentions in the Quran, quoting from Moses and other prophets and from Pharaoh and Iblis, is the eternal speech of Allah about them. The speech of Allah is uncreated, but the speech of Moses and other created beings is created. The Quran is the speech of Allah and not their speech; therefore, it is eternal."

Divine Will and Human Freedom: The all pervading will of God, His eternal decree (qadar) and infinite power, on the one hand, and freedom of the human will and action, on the other, are equally stressed in the Quran. According to the Quran, divine will, decree, and power are not inconsistent with human freedom. These problems were discussed by the Prophet and his Companions. Belief in qadar was declared by the Prophet as an article of faith, but at the same time he asserted that qadar does not deprive a man of his freedom in his limited sphere.

Thus, according to the Quran and the Tradition, God is the creator of all things including their nature, and nothing can go against this nature. He is the creator of the human soul and its nature and He has created in it freewill and bestowed upon it the faculty of knowing, thinking, and distinguishing and the power of judging, choosing, and selecting. God, being the omniscient creator, knows from eternity what His creatures will do in future this is the "writing of the destiny" and "the eternal divine decree."

That the Prophet laid stress both on qadar and human freedom and on the possibility of human action side by side with divine action, is also evident from his famous saving on natural religion (din al fitrah): "Every child at birth is born in the fitrah, then it is his parents who make of him a Jew, a Christian, or a Magian." This is testified by the Quranic verse, "The fitrah of Allah in which He hath created mankind, there is no change." The sayings of the Prophet that divine decree comprises all human care and precautions for life, that prayer can change destiny, and that God has provided remedy for every disease, and similar other traditions also clearly indicate that the divine decree is not despotic or tyrannical in its nature and that it does not imply any compulsion, nor is it inconsistent with freedom and responsibility.

The Companions of the Prophet also believed both in qadar and human freedom and emphatically denied the idea of compulsion (jabr). Some prominent Companions explained qadar as foreknowledge. Abu Musa al Ash`ari said: "God decreed as He knew." `Abd Allah b. `Amr (d. 63/682) used to say: "The Pen has dried up according to the knowledge of God." `Ali (d. 40/661) gave a clear exposition of his view on the problem and said: "Perhaps you think that the judgment (qada') is binding and the decree (qadar) is final. Had it been so, then reward and punishment would be meaningless and the promise and threat null and void, and no reproach then should have come from Allah against a sinner and no promise for a righteous person. This is the view of the brethren of Satan.... Verily Allah has enjoined discretion, issued prohibitions, and given warnings. He has not burdened (men) with compulsion, nor has He sent the prophets in vain...."

Imam abu Hanifah made, a bold attempt to harmonize the contradictory views of the self determinists and the predeterminists by explaining the nature of divine power, will, and decree and enunciating the doctrines of natural religion (din al itrah), divine help, and guidance (taufiq), abandoning (khadhlan) and acquisition (kasb). God had knowledge concerning things before they existed from eternity, and His will, decree, decision, and writing on the Preserved Tablet are in accordance with this foreknowledge. So the eternal decree is of a descriptive nature and not of a decisive nature. God created men with natural dispositions (fitrah), endowed them with intellect, then addressed them and commanded them through His messenger to believe and abstain from unbelief. Thereupon some people deviated from this natural religion, disavowed truth, and turned to unbelief.

This unbelief is their own act, their own acquisition, preferred by their free will, which God created in them, and is not due to any compulsion from Him, but due to His leaving them to themselves. Those who clung to their nature received divine help and guidance. "Allah did not compel any of His creatures to be infidel or faithful, and He did not create them either as faithful or infidel, but He created them as individuals, and faith and unbelief are acts of men.... All the acts of man, his moving as well as his resting, are truly his own acquisition, but Allah creates them and they are caused by His will, His knowledge, His decision, and His decree." But while good actions are according to His desire, pleasure, judgment, command, and guidance, evil actions are not in accordance with these.

Al Maturidi, as we have already noticed, explained this view quite elaborately and laid emphasis on the freedom of acquisition and choice. Al Tahawi discourages all speculative thought on the subtle and mysterious question of predestination (taqdir), because this may lead one to despair and disobedience. But he asserts that all human actions are creations in relation, to God and acquisition an relation to men, and God is never unjust to them so as to burden them beyond their power and capacity.

7

ZAHIRISM

BACKGROUND

Since the second/eighth century, an interminable dispute dragged on for a long time between those who upheld the authority of Tradition (ahl al hadith)in all matters of theology and jurisprudence, and those who advocated opinion (ashab al ra'i).

It was expected, as pointed out by ibn Khaldun in his Muqaddimah (p. 805)that the people of the Hijaz, particularly those of Madinah, should be versed in the science of Tradition (the sayings and doings of the Prophet Muhammad). With the rise of the `Abbasid Caliphate and the shifting of the political power and the religious leadership completely to Iraq, where the people had had less access to the sayings of the Prophet, and where the aspects of life, the agrarian problems, for instance, were more diverse and complicated through the intermingling of the successive civilizations since times immemorial a new school, that of opinion, made its inevitable appearance.

The upholders of opinion, however, did not neglect Tradition, but they found it necessary to supplement Tradition with additions drawn from older codes and prevalent usages or framed by considerations of the actual situation in their new environment.

At the same time an esoteric movement also began among the Shiites under a variety of names, the most current of which was the Batiniyyah (seekers after the inner or spiritual interpretation of revelation). The forming of this sect is attributed to a certain Maimun of whose descent we are completely in the dark.

The Batiniyyah movement took its name from the belief of its followers that every zahir (apparent state of things) has a batin (an inner, allegorical. hidden, or secret meaning), especially in connection with revelation. Since this movement adopted some aspects of Greek philosophy, such as emanationism, its followers were considered by Sunni authors to be heretics and outside the pale of faith. During the Caliphate of al Mamun (198/813 281/833) the Batiniyyah movement was quite strong; some half a century later it was widely spread in Iraq, Persia, Sind (western India), and Oman (south east Arabia), as well as in North Africa, but it did not enjoy an enduring influence. It is to be remarked, however, that while a number of individuals in Muslim Spain had shared ideas with the Batiniyyah, no sectarian or heretical doctrine ever struck roots or succeeded in winning over communities of any dimensions there.

So, the second/eighth century had witnessed a heavy atmosphere of esoterism weighing on some fundamentals of Islam such as the essence of God, the under standing of the Quran, and the attitude towards the Caliphate. Added to this there was a trend of upholding opinion as a valid source of jurisprudence at the same level with the Quran and the sayings of the Prophet. At the same time there was also the Mu'tazilite school which assumed reason as a more deciding factor than revelation in all matters of religion.

Since all these movements had chosen Iraq as their principal battle field, another school, contrary to all of them and as extremist as any of them appeared in Iraq itself and insisted on the verbal understanding of the Quran and of the sayings of the Prophet Mubammad as the sole guiding line to their real meanings clothed in the words of God and of His Apostle. This school was founded by a jurist Dawud ibn 'Ali, and it received its name the Literalists' (Zahiriyyah) school from the clinging of its followers to the wording of the revelation and not to the interpretation of it.

DAWUD IBN 'ALI, HIS DOCTRINE AND HIS SCHOOL

The family of Dawud ibn 'Ali belonged to Kashan, a town in the neighbourhood of Isfahan. His father was a secretary (katib)to `Abd Allah ibn Khalid, judge of Isfahan, in the days of the Caliph al Mamun. Dawud himself a was born in Kufah in 202/817. His family moved later to Baghdad where he was brought up, educated, and afterwards laid the foundation of his school of jurisprudence which bore his name al madhhab al Dawudi, but which was better known as the Zahirite school (al madhhab al zahiri).

In Baghdad, Dawud ibn 'Ali attended the lectures of many eminent jurists, the most prominent of whom was abu Thaur (d. 246/860); a friend and follower of Shafi'i. The trend of education he received from them made him shift from the Hanafite rite to that to which his father belonged, the Shafi'ite, apparently because most of his professors (shuyukh)were more inclined to the Traditionists (ahl al hadith)school to which Shafi'is belonged than to the school of the upholders of opinion (ashab al ra'i)who were the followers of abn Hanifah par excellence. Dawud perfected his education by an academic trip to Nishapur to meet Ishaq ibn Rahawaih (d. 237/851 or 238/ 852), who also was a friend and follower of Shafi`i. Afterwards, he returned to Baghdad where he wrote his books.

Perhaps it is not very strange that a close and profound study of the Shafi'ite school of jurisprudence led Dawud ibn 'Ali finally to be dissatisfied with it. He forsook it and founded a new school, the Zahirite school, which recognized the Quran and the Hadith as the only sources of jurisprudence. He accepted, at any rate, consensus (ijma`)of the Companions of the Prophet, but he rejected analogy (qiyas), opinion (ra'i), personal approval (istihsan), and decisions on the authority of older generations (taqlid)altogether.

Dawud ibn 'Ali was accomplished, trustworthy, learned, God fearing, pious, and ascetic; he was also versed in logic and proficient in the art of disputation. It was said that he believed that the Quran was created and not eternal, but it seems that this was only an accusation. He died in 270/884 in Baghdad.

Dawud ibn 'Ali was a prolific writer. Ibn al Nadim enumerates about one hundred and fifty titles from him. It seems that many of these titles were only chapters of some of his books. But there are also titles which represent bulky works of two thousand, three thousand, and even four thousand folios each. A few of these books touched the fundamentals of religion, e. g., "On the Usul," "On the Caliphate," "Consensus and the

Refutation of Qiyas," and "On the Refutation of Taqlid." Most of his other books treated of branches (furu`)or minor aspects of Fiqh concerning worship and legal transactions Unfortunately, no book has reached us from him. Ibn Hazm, nevertheless refers to him frequently. Muhammad al Shatti (d. Damascus 1307/1889) made a collection of Dawud's Fiqh gleaned from the various works of his followers.'

It was related that Dawud ibn 'Ali admitted analogy where the cases in question were obvious, but it is more probable that he rejected analogy wholly, whether the cases were ambiguous or obvious. As for consensus (ijma'), his position was totally different: he admitted the ijma` of the Companions of the Prophet only, on the ground that these Companions were in constant contact with the Prophet and fully aware of his intentions.

In his theology in particular he maintains, for example, that God is hearing, seeing, etc. But he says: "I do not say that He is seeing with the agency of sight ..."

Dawud ibn 'Ali re examined all aspects of Fiqh on the basis of his Zahirite attitude. The following are three examples illustrating his trend of thought and argumentation in this respect.

Prayer on a Journey: God has said in the Quran: "And when you journey in the earth, there is no blame on you if you shorten the prayer."

This led the Muslims to reduce prayer on a journey from four rak`ahs to only two. Muslim jurists generally assert that this verse envisages cutting the prayer short on a journey of some duration. Dawud, on the other hand, maintained that since there is no mention of the duration of the journey in the Quran, prayer should be cut short on any journey whatever, even though it is a journey from one encampment to another.

Fasting on a Journey: Muslims fast in Ramadan, the ninth month of the lunar year. In this connection we read in the Quran: "But he among you who shall be sick, or on a journey, shall (not observe the days on which he travels but he shall) fast the same number of other days (when he returns home)." It is agreed upon by all Sunni jurists that a Muslim may not observe Ramadan fasts on a journey which involves certain hardship, either on account of its long duration or its difficult nature, on hot days for example. Dawud and his followers assert that a Muslim should not observe fasts on a journey because the wording of the verse does not stipulate any condition. If a Muslim, according to Dawud, did observe fasts for some days on a journey, even then he should keep fast for the same number of days when he returns home, for his fasting while journeying was not valid.

The Question of Usury (Riba): Usury is forbidden in Islam. But a difficulty arose from a tradition concerning it. It is related that the Prophet Muhammad said: "(You may barter) gold for gold, silver for silver, wheat for wheat, barley for barley, dates for dates, and salt for salt, only in equivalent quantities and on the spot. In all other commodities you may deal as you like, provided (the barter is transacted) on the spot." Early Muslim jurists concluded from this tradition that a quantity of any commodity should not be bartered for a larger quantity of the same commodity; otherwise, the surplus taken would be usury (riba).

But if, for instance, a quantity of wrought gold was bartered for a larger quantity of unwrought gold, the surplus would be a gain or, better, a wage for craftsmanship. Furthermore, they considered the six commodities named by the Prophet to be examples only; thus bartering copper, coffee, leather, apples, or wool for a larger quantity of these commodities respectively is also regarded by analogy as a form of usury. Dawud ibn `Ali, on the other hand, believed that the Prophet Muhammad had named these commodities on purpose. Had he intended to prolong the list, nothing would have prevented him from doing so. Accordingly, if a man bartered a quantity, say of iron, maize, apples, or pepper for a larger quantity of the same commodity, the surplus would not be usury but gain.

The jurists contemporary with Dawud ibn 'Ali took a very critical attitude regarding him and his school. The Shafi'ites in general criticized him severely and considered the Zahirite school to be worthless. Al Isfara'ini (d. 418/1027) maintained that no account should be taken of the Zahirites. Since they rejected analogy (qiyas), he asserted, they could not have been able to exercise judgment and, therefore, no one of them should be elevated to the position of a judge. Some others presumed that Dawud ibn `Ali was ignorant; others considered him to be a disbeliever. Abmad ibn Hanbal (d. 241/855), the famous founder of the Hanbalite school, did not hold him in estimation. Abu `Abd Allah Muhammad ibn Zaid al Wasiti (d. 306/918 919), an eminent Mu'tazilite of Baghdad, looked down upon the Zahirite school as ridiculous. The followers of Dawud ibn `Ali, nevertheless, were not only numerous but some of them were also prominent.

Dawud ibn `Ali was succeeded, as the head of the Zahirite school, by his son, abu Bakr Muhammad ibn Dawud (c. 255/869 297/910). But the latter was more of a poet, litterateur, and historian than an enthusiastic scholar of jurisprudence. At any rate, he propagated the tenets of his father's school and bestowed on it so much prestige that the Zahirite rite was in his own days the fourth of the four rites prevailing in the East, the other three being the Shafi'i, Maliki, and Hanafi rites.

Abu Bakr Muhammad ibn Dawud owes his real fame, however, to an anthology of love poetry known as Kitab al Zahrah The first and only extant half of this anthology was edited by A.R. Nykl and Ibrahim Tukan. Abu Bakr Mubammad ibn Dawud had some inclination towards philosophy, but philosophy did not constitute a component part of Zahirism before ibn Hazm.

In the fourth/tenth century the Zahirite school had enjoyed its widest expansion and the climax of its prestige. The `Abbasid poet ibn al Rumi (d. 283/896) praised abu Bakr Muhammad ibn Dawud in a poem which opens with the words: "O son of Dawud! O jurist of Iraq!" The famous historian, Tabari (d. 310/923), though not a Zahirite, paid close attention to Zahiri jurisprudence and studied it with Dawud ibn `Ali himself. The foremost jurist of the Zahirite school in the fourth/tenth century was Abd Allah ibn Ahmad ibn al Mughallis (d. 324/936), through whom the Fiqh of Dawud ibn `Ali became popular in the Muslim world.

In the following century the Zahirite school was already losing ground in the East; and before the middle of the century, in the days of the Hanbalite judge abu Ya'la (d. 459,/1066), the Hanbalite rite took its place. The Zahirite school, at any rate, continued to enjoy in Syria some prestige until 788/1386. In

Egypt the school lived longer and had deeper roots. Al Maqrizi (d. 845/ 1442), the famous historian of the Mamluk age in Egypt, was not a follower of the Zahirite school, but he had a favourable attitude towards Zahirism.

THE ZAHIRITE SCHOOL IN MUSLIM SPAIN

Al Balluti

The first representative of Zahirism in Spain was Mudhir ibn Said al Balluti who was born at al Nashsharin, a suburb of Cordova, in 273/886. After completing his studies at Cordova, he travelled to Egypt and the Hijaz for a little over three years. On his return, he was appointed as judge (Qadi) in the city of Merida, then transferred to the Northern Frontiers and finally made the Chief Justice of Cordova, which post he held until his death towards the end of 355/965. He upheld Dawud's doctrines and defended his views, though, in practice, he administered justice according to the established law of the country based on the Malikite school of jurisprudence. He was also a man of letters, poet, theologian, physiographer, and eloquent speaker. In fact, he was the real forerunner of ibn Hazm.

Ibn Hazm

Life and Works Ibn Hazm was the real founder of the Zahirite school in Muslim Spain and the most famous and prominent of the Zahiri jurists. With him the school reached its zenith, and with his death it died away. In reality, the Zahirite rite never recruited a community in Muslim Spain. It came on the stage as a philosophy supported by a single man who failed to use his genius in the right way.

Ibn Hazm was the descendant of a non Arab, an Iberian in all probability, but he preferred to link his genealogy with a Persian freedman of Yazid ibn Sufyan, a brother of Mu'awiyah, the founder of the Umayyad Caliphate in the East.

The family did not attain any fame before Ahmad ibn Said, the father of ibn Hazm, who became a minister to the Hajib al Mansur ibn abi Amir, the Prime Minister of Hisham II, in 381/991. Ibn Hazm, who was born in 384/994 during the long ministerial term of his father, was brought up in luxurious environment. He was fortunate enough to have been given a good education. The teacher who had the greatest influence on him was ibn Muflit (d.426/1035), a Zahirite and a follower of Dawud ibn 'Ali; he chose to be eclectic in matters of worship and jurisprudence and did not agree that one should confine oneself to a particular school.

Ibn Hazm did not continue to enjoy prosperity and peace for long. With the outburst of the disturbances in 400/1009 and the death of his father only two years later, misfortunes began to overcome him and his family; and when he preferred, on this account, to withdraw from public life, his life became very obscure. A few years later, however, he decided to enter public life again. As a result, he experienced all ups and downs of life, from forming the cabinet to frequent imprisonments.

Six years after the fall of the Umayyad Caliphate in Cordova (422/1031) and the assassination of the fugitive Hisham III, life became unbearable for ibn Hazm in the whole peninsula, not only because he was a client and partisan of the falling dynasty, but because he entertained also a religious doctrine which the rulers and the ruled in the peninsula did not share.

The only respite which ibn Hazm had was during his stay on the island of Majorca, from 430/1039 to 440/1049. The local Governor of Majorca was abu al `Abbas Ahmad ibn Rashiq, an able statesman and a man of letters. For reasons inexplicable, he invited ibn Hazm for a sojourn on the island. Ibn Hazm took refuge there and began, as soon as he could breathe freely, to propagate Zahirism. Since he was supported by the Governor, some Majorcans followed him perhaps out of conviction, perhaps out of political tact but it seems certain that the majority of the islanders were not in favour of the intruding doctrine. In 439/1047, the famous Maliki jurist, abu al Walid al Baji (403/1013-474/1081) returned from a journey in the East. He held debates with ibn Hazm and caused his disgrace. In the following year, ibn Hazm was obliged to leave the island and go back on the mainland, but he was chased out of every town and village in which he tried to secure a footing. Finally, after fifteen years of complete oblivion, he found asylm on the estate of his own family in Manta Lisham where he passed away in 456/1063.

Ibn Hazm was a very prolific writer on different subjects ranging from genealogical tables to epistemology. It is believed that his books were four hundred comprising 80,000 folios of some twenty million words. The most important of these books are Tauq al Hamamah (the Dove's Neck Ring on confidence and confidents), Al-Milal w al Nihal (Religions and Sects), Al-Ihkam fi Uul al Ahkam (Precision Concerning the Principles of Religious Matters) and Al-Muhalla bi al Athar (the Gilded or Ornamented with Revelation and Tradition). This last is a comprehensive book on the aspects of worship and jurisprudence in Islam. Ibn Hazm was also a man of letters, poet, and statesman, but he is more famous as a rationalist and theologian.

Ibn Hazm's Rationalism In his book Al-Milal w al Nihal, ibn Hazm appears to be a rationalist. The problems of a priori, of time and space which confronted Kant (d. 1804) so often in his Critique of Pure Reason, had busied ibn Hazm in the same way It is really astonishing that the Muslim theologian had tackled these problems in the same spirit of objectivity seven and a half centuries before the German philosopher. Let us take up the theory of knowledge as discussed by ibn Hazm. Knowledge arises, according to him, from the following

(a) Sensory perception (shahadat al hawas), that is, observation or sensory evidence.
(b) Primary reason (badihat al `aql or awwal al `aql), that is, a priori reason without the use of the five senses.
(c) Proof (burhan), which goes back, either closely or remotely, to the evidence of the senses or to primary reason.

Ibn Hazm holds definitely that man has six senses, and that the soul grasps perceptible objects (material objects) by the five senses; thus a pleasant odour is accepted by reason... thus also the soul is aware that red is different from green, yellow, etc., or that there is a distinction between rough and smooth, hot and cold, etc.

The sixth sense, ibn Hazm holds, is the soul's knowledge of primary things; that is, there are some things which man can know through his reason as being axiomatic, without requiring any proof for them. "Such is the soul's knowledge that the part is less than the whole; thus the young child, who is only just able to discriminate, cries when he is given only two dates, but is satisfied when you give him another. This is because the whole is greater than a part, even though the child cannot define the limits of his knowledge.... The same sense gives the child the knowledge that two things cannot occupy the same spot; you will see him fight for a place where he wants to sit, knowing that that place is not big enough for another person, and that so long as another person occupies the place there is no room for him also ...

"This is a form of primary intelligence which is common to all except those whose reason is distorted ... or whose bodies are diseased or impotent in certain respects.... These truths of primary reason are truly axiomatic; they are beyond doubt and stand in no need of proof except to a madman... or to a scornful sophist." Ibn Hazm's argument for the view that these things require no proof is this: "To demand proof of anything requires time; primary reason cannot possibly avoid that fact.... Yet between the soul's first learning to discriminate phenomena and its knowing the complete truth of all that we have mentioned, there is not a single minute, nor can there be." But ibn Hazm did not deny absolutely the necessity of proof to these things; rather, he held that such proof is a matter for personal acquisition which one may achieve, while another may not, and that it may carry weight only for such as have reached a high level of intellectual training.

Other means of acquiring knowledge, according to ibn Hazm, are God's naming of things and men's convention as represented by the languages of the different nations. These two means, however, belong to theology and are discussed under that topic.

Philosophy and Science Like all Muslim thinkers prior to his days, ibn Hazm had no access to Greek originals. He had a predisposition towards argumentation, and was versed in the science of dialectics (Kalam). He claimed to have read (evidently through translations) the works of the Milesian and Eleatic schools, of Euclid and Ptolemy, of Plato and Aristotle, and of Alexander of Aphrodisias, and to have had a general knowledge of astronomy, astrology, and medicine. He also stated that he was well versed in mathematics in general and geometry in particular.

Ibn Hazm does not agree with Heraclitus that the world is in constant flow nor with the Eleatics that motion is non existent. On Being and NonBeing, he agrees with the Eleatics: Non Being is not. In keeping with his general trend of thought, he affirms that space and time are limited and that they are, like all other things, created by God. In the same way he maintains that atoms are divisible because it is in the power of God to do everything, and to this power of His, infinite divisibility of an atom is no exception.

In physiography, he holds that the world is limited and the earth is spherical and that the sun is larger than the earth, but he agrees with Anaximenes that the sky is like a vault over the earth. He disagrees, however, with Pythagoras that there is a sister earth which helps the earth keep itself in the correct position. The world, at any rate, is created, but it has existed for a very long time.

In ethics, he touches lightly on Greek philosophy and maintains with Prodicus of Ceos that death has no pain and that it should not be feared. He also holds with Epicurus and his contemporaries that the desire for pleasure and the repulsion from care are the criteria of happiness. But building up and improvement of character cannot be achieved by philosophy alone; the help of the prophets is necessary.

In his theory of knowledge, ibn Hazm emphasizes, in addition to sensory perception and primary reason, three means of acquiring religious knowledge which are particularly fundamental in Islam. These are: the literal sense of the Quran, the sayings and doings of the Prophet Mubammad, and consensus (ijma).

The first and foremost source of knowledge is the literal sense of the text of the Quran. This must follow from the context of the fifty ninth verse of the fourth Surah, "O ye who believe! obey Allah and obey the Messenger and those of you who are in authority, and if ye have a dispute concerning any matter refer it to Allah and to the Messenger...." The text of the Quran must be understood literally unless the words in question are used metaphorically and in a way current among the early Arabs. No divergence is allowed from the text of the Quran except where one verse is modified or abrogated by another. A total dependence on the Quran is made possible by the fact that every aspect of life and every need of men, material or spiritual, is treated in the Quran or provided for in it. God says, "We have neglected nothing in the Book." This implicit meaning was reiterated explicitly in this verse: "This day have I perfected for you your religion and completed My favour to you and chosen for you Islam as a religion."

The second source of knowledge is the Tradition, the sayings and actions of the Prophet Muhammad. Ibn Hazm accepts the true hadith or the Sunnah when related in a sure way and by reliable men in a connected chain which reaches the Prophet Muhammad. The Prophet is certainly trustworthy, and ibn Hazm quotes in this connection from the Quran: "Nor does he speak out of desire. It is naught but revelation that is revealed."

Ibn Hazm accepts, as a third source of knowledge, consensus (ijma`) or general agreement of the Companions of the Prophet but on a further condition that all of them should have been aware of the matter agreed upon and that no one of them should have shown any disagreement or hesitation about it. In contradistinction to the other schools of jurisprudence in Islam, the Hanafite school in particular, ibn Hazm rejects all other sources of jurisprudence such as intuition (ilham), hearsay (khabar), interpretation (tawil), deduction (istinbat), personal approval (istihsan), refraining from the unseemly (ihtiyat), legitimating a matter passed over in silence (dalil al khitab), looking for a reason in matters other than, mentioned in the Quran (ta'lil), and holding a belief on the ground that it has been held by one's predecessors or some prominent contemporaries (taqlid). Only the Prophet Muhammad must be taken as a model in all matters of belief and behaviour. He equally rejected, and more forcibly, analogy (qiyas) and opinion (ra'i) or that which a man conceives as true butt without a proof, or that which a man chooses out of mere desire. The Muslims should not abide by the beliefs and laws preached by prophets prior to Muhammad unless they are accepted by Islam as well.

Ibn Hazm's views about God, His essence and His attributes, are: God is one and unique; He is incorporeal; so nothing resembles Him nor does He take the shape of anything He has created. He is the creator of everything, of time, of space, and even of His own Throne. He is eternal, all powerful and all knowing. His power and knowledge as well as all His other names are eternal. God cannot be conceived of as ruled by space and time, since He existed before there were space and time, for these were also created by Him. The verses in which God says of Himself: "The God of mercy sitteth on His Throne" and "Then He directed Himself to the heaven," ibn Hazm affirms with the Asharites that God's sitting or settling Himself on the Throne is known; but how it is done is unknown.

God has no attributes which modify His essence: His qualities are names and not adjectives, nor are they derived from adjectives. He says of Himself: "God's are the fairest names. Invoke Him by them." Thus, only these names, ninety nine in number, by which God has named Himself, may be said to be His; we are not allowed to call Him by names which He has not mentioned as His, for example, the happy, the healthy, the beloved, the noble, or the brave, although these titles are, in themselves, true of Him and cherished by us.

We are also not allowed to call Him by names, derived from the verbs with which He predicated Himself. God says: "And when they (the disbelievers) meet the faithful they say, `We believe'; but when they are apart with their satans (comrades), they say, `Verily we hold with you and at them we only mock.' God shall mock at them." God says further: "And they (the Jews) plotted, and God plotted: but of those who plot, God is the best." He also says: "And the heaven with our hands have We built it up." In spite of all that, says ibn Hazm, we cannot call God the mocker, plotter, or builder, simply because He did not call Himself by these name. Moreover, we do not interpret His names to know how or why He is called thus: He called Himself, for instance, the hearer, the One who sees, but we cannot say that He has the sense of hearing or of sight.

Furthermore, God speaks in the Quran of His (one) hand, of His two hand, and of His hands; so we may ascribe to Him one hand, two hands, or many hands. In the Quran He speaks also of His eye and of His eyes, but not of two eyes of His. According to ibn Hazm, we may ascribe to God either one eye or ascribe to Him eyes, but not two eyes. When we speak of God's eye hand, or face, we do not mean, at any rate, that He has members similar to ours. On the contrary, the words: face, eye, and hand are used as free metaphors to mean simply God.

And though God is incorporeal, ibn Hazm asserts that the Muslims would see Him on the Day of Judgment. They cannot see Him, for certain, with the power of sight in their eyes but perhaps with the power which is called by some thinkers "the sixth sense."

Regarding our knowledge of God, ibn Hazm says, we do not maintain that we come to know Him by primary reason, for we do not want to run the risk of being refuted by somebody asserting that his primary reason does not lead him to the knowledge of God. Nor may we allow that the knowledge of God can be acquired by the art of reasoning, by argumentation or proof; since the masses are not capable of such dialecticism. Failing to attain knowledge of God through these channels, some come to the conclusion that He does not exist. Nor may we allow authority or hearsay to be the criteria of the knowledge of God, because these cannot lead to real conviction. We know God only through revelation to the Prophet who is trustworthy and whose word should be accepted on its face value.

Ibn Hazm does not believe in the absolute free will of man. Predestination, according to him, is nothing but the command of God that a thing should follow a definite course. Allah has created in man aptitudes, and every man behaves in compliance with his aptitudes. Accordingly, we. may say that all actions of men, good and bad, are ultimately created by God.

Ibn Hazm was a polemist by nature, and often right in his contentions. As Hitti says, "In this work [Al-Milal w al Nihal] he pointed out difficulties in the biblical narratives which disturbed no other minds till the rise of higher criticism in the sixteenth century." Yet he is to blame for the harsh language he used in his attacks on all religions and sects indiscriminately. On some occasions he attacked even some of those who shared with him the same doctrine.

Faith and Islam, says ibn Hazm, are one and the same thing. Islam had abrogated all anterior religions. Therefore, no religion precedent to Islam should be followed, because every religion except Islam is obsolete and, consequently, annulled. Muhammad is the Prophet to all nations; he preached religion according to the prescription of God to him; and when he died revelation ceased. Islam was made complete; it is impossible either to add anything to it, or deduct anything from it, or make any change in it in any way.

The best people are the messengers of God; next are the prophets not entrusted with any mission to any people. After them are the Companions of the Prophet Muhammad. These last differ in their prestige in accordance with their efforts in the service of Islam and their personal character and behaviour, determined by the truth and ideals established by the Quran and the sayings and actions of the Prophet Muhammad.

ZAHIRISM AFTER IBN HAZM

For a certain period Zahirism constituted in the East a school of jurisprudence, but in Muslim Spain it never grew beyond a persecuted philosophy. Even as a philosophy it began to decline there after the death of ibn Hazm. It is true that ibn Hazm built a Zahirite system of dogma and revised Muslim law from that standpoint, but his views enjoyed only a restricted acceptance in the Muslim West. In the East they found practically no echo. This. is due to the uncompromising attitude he had taken in all matters of creed, worship, and legal transactions as well as to the harsh language he used while speaking of all those who did not share with him the views he entertained. The Zahirites in the East, and the Hanbalites too, have always preferred to follow Dawud ibn 'Ali, though very little Fiqh has reached us from him. The few attempts to introduce Zahirism into North Africa were due largely to political considerations. On the Andalusian soil Zahirism found support or acceptance with individuals here and there. Ibn `Abd al Barr (368 463/978 1071), the famous traditionist and biographer, had some leaning towards it.

A young contemporary of ibn Hazm and of ibn `Abd al Barr, al Humaidi was a historian and biographer of established fame. He was a declared Zahirite. When the persecution of the followers of the Zahirite school reached a high pitch in Muslim Spain, he left his native land, went to the East, and settled down in Baghdad where he died forty years later. Al Humaidi was the first man to introduce ibn Hazm's works into the East, but there they made no impression.

One would expect, despite all persecution, that Zahirism should have had numerous followers for a certain period at least, as has been the case with most other movements. Ibn al Athir says: "There was in the Muslim West a multitude of them (of the Zahirites) called the Hazmiyyah or followers of ibn Hazm." Asin Palacios tried to draw a complete list of them. Some of these were, to be sure, Zahirites or with Zahirite leanings. But a number of those who were considered by him to be such were certainly not. That al Ghazali was antagnostic to the Batinites and was one who advocated a strict religious behaviour and showed a dislike for all innovations, as we see clearly in all his works, does not make him a Zahirite, and less so a follower of ibn Hazm, as Asin Palacias tried to ahow. Nor can we agree with Asin Palacios that ibn Rushd (Averroes) wars a Zahirite on the mere fact that he quoted ibn Hazm three times in his Tahafut al Tahafut. Ibn Rushd mentioned also the Zahirites once with disdaine and twice with indifference. Moreover, his theme in his two small but worthy epistles, Fasl al Maqal and Manahij al Adillah, is that the masses cannot rise or be raised above the literal meaning of the Law, while the thinkers are called upon to ponder on the intentions of religion.

With the advance of the sixth/twelfth century, Zahirism became a problem in the Muslim West, in Spain, and in North Africa: while the masses behaved on the narrowest Zahirite lines, Zahirism itself was being fought on every side. Philosophy was equally combated. The rationalist thinker ibn Tufail furnishes us with a very clear picture of the situation there; a few enlightened individuals were living in the midst of a multitude of common people unwilling and incapable of thinking for themselves.

8

IKHWAN AL-SAFA

INTRODUCTION

The name Ikhwan al Safa was assumed by a group of libres penseum who cultivated science and philosophy not for the sake of science and philosophy, but in the hope of forming a kind of an ethico spiritual community in which the elites of the heterogeneous Muslim Empire could find a refuge from the struggle that was raging among religious congregations, national societies, and Muslim sects themselves.

External evidence concerning the Ikhwan al Safa is so scanty that no clear historical picture of them is in any way possible. Were it not for abu Hayyan al Tauhidi (d. after 400/1009), a famous author and a friend of some members of the group, no facts about them would have come down to us.

The group of the Ikhwan al Safa originated in Basrah. In about 373/983, the group was already famous and its "Epistles," which contain its spiritual doctrines and philosophical system, were in wide circulation. The complete name of the group was Ikhwan al Safa wa Khullan al Wafa wa Ahl al Hamd wa Abna' al Majd a name which was suggested to them by the chapter of the "Ring Necked Dove" in Kalilah wa Dimnah, a book which they very highly esteemed.

The Ikhwan al Safa succeeded in keeping complete secrecy about their names. But when abu Hayyan was asked in about 373/983, about them, he named, perhaps at random, five of them: abu Sulaiman Muhammad b. Ma'shar ad Busti, known as al Muqaddisi, abu al Hasan 'Ali b. Harun al Zanjani, abu Ahmad Muhammad al Mihrajani, a certain al 'Aufi, and the famous Zaid b. Rifa'ah.

The Ikhwan al Safa produced numerous works the most famous and important of which is the encyclopedic compilation entitled Rasa'il Ikhwan al Safa (Epistles of the Ikhwan al Safa), which will henceforth be referred to as Rasa'il or "Epistles." These "Epistles" are definitely the result of a collaboration of various writers many of whom may not have been members of the group. The compilation must have dragged over a long period, but by 373/983 the "Epistles" must have been already complete in the first recension at least. It is, moreover, practically certain that the Ikhwan al Safa embarked upon the compilation of the "Epistles" with the number fifty in their mind. The current edition, however, have fifty three epistles.

Closely connected with the "Epistles" is al Risalat al Jami'ah (the Comprehensive Epistle) which was a summarium and summa of the original "Epistles." It was also intended for private circulation among the more advanced members of the group. The Jami'ah discards much of the scientific information originally the backbone of the "Epistles," and expounds more fully and frankly the ideas which the Ikhwan al Safa intended to inoculate into their followers.

The Jami'ah was further summarized in Risalat al Jami'at al Jami'ah au al Zubdah min Rasa'il Ikhwan al Safa (the Condensation of the Comprehensive Epistle or the Cream of the Epistles of Ikhwan al Safa), called also al Risalat al Jami'ah. The scientific information as well as chapters of the "Epistles" are eliminated, while the symbolic and esoteric interpretation of the verses of the Quran are brought out vigorously.

The Ikhwan al Safa made arrangements for holding meetings everywhere they had followers. In these meetings, which were held once every twelve days and were restricted to the members and followers of the group, subjects of metaphysical and esoteric nature were discussed. There were also occasional meetings for the initiation of young people. Apparently, some of the followers were given, during these meetings, to singing, drinking, and other indulgences for which the Ikhwan al Safa rebuked them indirectly.

The Ikhwan al Safa were a secret group. They were recruited through personal and confidential contacts. The emissaries were advised to work among the youth, as old people are usually rigid and unfit for any movement. The group had four grades in which its members were placed generally according to their age.

The first and most inferior grade was that of those who had attained their fifteenth year; the second of those between thirty and forty years of age; the third of those between forty and fifty. The fourth, last and highest grade, was that of those who were already fifty years of age.

The Ikhwan al Safa were Muslims. But they had a special interpretation of religion in general, and of Islam in particular. The Shi`ite colouring, which is very conspicuous in their missionary work, is only dramatic because it helped them to play cleverly upon the emotions of the masses. In the strict historical sense, the Ikhwan al Safa did not belong to any sect. In fact, they sought, with the aid of Islam and Greek philosophy, to work out a spiritual doctrine which would take the place of the historical religions and which would, at the same time, suit everyone and insult nobody.

As far as we can gather from the "Epistles," the Ikhwan al Safa had no political programme. It seems, however, that some of their followers had pressed for political action to take the reins of government into their hands.

The Ikhwan al Safa themselves, the magnates among them, were not of this opinion; they reiterated in this connection that their sole aim was to uphold the faith and attain the bliss in the hereafter. In the meantime they tried to acquire knowledge and be versed in theoretical sciences. They declared, further, that they intended to build up a spiritual city, a Utopia, which was not of this world, neither on the continent; nor on the high seas, nor in the air.

The sections, in the "Epistles," referring to daulatu ahl al khairi and daulatu ahl al sharri (literally, the State of the people of good and the State of the people of evil) contain only a brief and general discussion on, the terms of governments or dynasties and on their succession.

The Ikhwan al Safa referred once to the coming of daulatu ahl al khairi; but they meant simply "the time when the adherents to their group would form the bulk of the nation."

SYSTEM AND THEORIES

Classification of the Sciences

Sciences may be classified in different ways. The Ikhwan al Safa mentioned a few classifications and adopted that which divided all branches of knowledge roughly into three major classes: mathematics, physics, and metaphysics, a classification which was current since Aristotle's days. Mathematics included, in the "Epistle," the theory of numbers, geometry, astronomy, geography, music, theoretical and practical arts, ethics, and logic. Physics included matter, form, motion, time, space, the sky, generation, corruption, minerals, the essence of nature, plants, animals, the human body, the senses, life and death, microcosm, pleasure, pain. and language. Metaphysics was subdivided, as should be expected, into psycho rationalism and theology. The first subdivision included psychics, rationalistics, being, macrocosm, mind, great years, love, resurrection, and causality. Theology included the beliefs of the Ikhwan al Safa, friendship, faith, divine Law, prophethood, call unto God, the incorporeals, polities, the structure of the world, and magic.

Theory of Knowledge

The Ikhwan al Safa were very much interested in epistemology or the theory of knowledge. General knowledge, they said; may be acquired in three ways:

(1) The way of the five senses is the natural and the most common way of acquiring knowledge. But through our senses we acquire only the material changes immediately apprehended by us and occurring in space and time.

(2) Man acquires knowledge also by means of primary reason, by pure or mere thinking. But reason, if unaided by sound senses, cannot acquire knowledge. Moreover, concepts having no connection with our senses, like those of God and the First Matter, cannot be acquired thus. Akin to the two previous ways is the way of proof, the way of the trained dialecticians.

(3) The way of acquiring knowledge which agrees best with the esoteric doctrine of the Ikhwan al Safa is the way of initiation and authority, i.e., receiving knowledge personally from an authorized elder, a teacher in the

broadest and deepest sense. This teacher receives his knowledge from the Imam (religious leader) who, in turn, receives it, through other Imams, from the Prophet whose ultimate source of knowledge is God.

Philosophy, wisdom or philosophical wisdom, according to the Ikhwan al Safa, is to behave Godlike as best as a human being can. A more detailed definition would be "love for science added to knowledge of the essence of all beings, gained" as best as one can, together with profession and public behaviour in harmony with that." In the "Epistles" of the Ikhwan al Safa metaphysics proper is quite meagre.

Metaphysics

If metaphysics did not include theology, it would have interested them very little.

Form and Matter: The views of the Ikhwan al Safa regarding form and matter are Aristotelian: every body consists of matter and form which are insepararable, since pure forms are only concepts like the soul and the intellect. Matter and form are both simple essences. The form is more important, since bodies are different because of their forms, their matter being in many cases the same; but matter is theoretically older. In keeping with their disposition towards compilation, they show some leaning to Plato when they say that the images, figures, frames, and characteristics which we see in the world of (sublunary) bodies and in the essences of the heavenly bodies are examples, likenesses, and colourings of those forms which are in the world of spirits.

Space and Time: As regards space and time, their view was that both are not realities; space is more objective, since it is related to bodies which have dimensions: it is the vessel which holds the contained.

Time has no independent existence. It cannot be conceived of except in connection with moving bodies. Note, if space is the outer surface of the world and time is the reckoning of the rotations of the spheres, space and time would be unthinkable prior to the spheres themselves. These views led some to think that they believed in the eternity of the world. They were aware of this accusation and tried to defend themselves against it.

Motion: There are six general kinds of motion grouped in three pairs: generation and corruption, increase and decrease, change and displacement. The particular kinds are numerous. The continuous and perfect motion is spherical; the straight motion is also continuous but not perfect. The arrow when passing through the air forms, from the bowstring to its falling place, one continuous course. Here they disagree, in the example of the arrow, with Zeno of Elea (d. 430 B.C.) who argued that if a line was made up of points, there must be always space among these points. And so, an arrow in any given moment of its flight must be at rest in some particular point.

Causality: In the field of causality the Ikhwan al Safa depended on Aristotle. `Ilal (pl. of `illah,, fem.) or major causes are four: the hayulaniyyah (material, the matter or substance of which a thing is made), suriyyah (formal, the form which is given to a certain substance to produce that thing), fa'iliyyah (active, the agent which gives that substance its form) and tamamiyyah (fulfilling, the end which that produced thing serves).

The answer to a question concerning any of the causes, and especially the fourth cause, is always difficult because it is a question about the essence of things. These four causes should act together, otherwise the intended thing would not come into existence, and they should hold on, so that the produced thing might persist. It is needless to say that God is the ultimate cause of all beings.

Number: Numbers are the vehicle of the doctrine of the Ikhwan al Safa. The Pythagorean theory of numbers (their properties: proportion, progression, etc.) and their linking mystically to the life and after life of man captured their imagination.

The Ikhwan al Safa divided the numbers into two classes: a factor which is the "one" and a "series from two ad infinitum." The one is an absolute unity, indivisible, undiminishable, and unincreasable. All the numbers originate from the one: the two by the repetition of the "one" twice; the other numbers by adding the "one"; whence its character as a factor to every subsequent number. This dexterous acrobatism was necessary to arrive at the following, half theological and half metaphysical statement: Just as "the one is of a different nature from the numbers which originate from it, so the One (God) is unlike all the beings emanating from Him."

Being and Emanation: This leads us to Being and Emanation, the coming of the universe into existence, or its creation.

The universe is not eternal but created by God through emanation. Emanation was a compromise between the strict religious notion of creation and the Aristotelian view of the eternity of the world. Theoretically, creation was accomplished in two steps: first, God willed, in one thought, that the universe should come into existence ex nihilo; then, immediately emanation began and proceeded gradually, until the universe took its present shape. The order and character of emanation were as follows:

(i) Al Bari (The Maker, Creator, or God). Al Bari is the First and only Eternal Being, the One, Unique, and One in every respect. He has no partner and no peer. No anthropomorphic attribute or action should be ascribed to Him. Only the will to create pertains to Him.

(ii) Al `Aql (Intellect or Gr. Nous). Al `aql was the first being to emanate from al Bari. God created it directly, necessarily, without break, and with no need for movement or effort. From God's eternity it acquires its own eternity; and through His perpetuance it receives its continuity and perfection. It is one in number as God Himself is One. But since God does not condescend to deal with material bodies, He created in the intellect all the forms of subsequent beings and instituted in it the office of re emanation: from it emanated the world soul and the first matter. It is clear, then, that the office attributed usually to God belongs, in the opinion of the Ikhwan al Safa, to the intellect, a counterpart, duplicate, or image of God.

(iii) Al Nafs al Kulliyyah (The Absolute Soul, the World Soul) The worldsoul is the soul of the whole universe, a simple essence which emanated from the intellect. It receives its energy from the intellect. It manifests itself in the sun through which it animates the whole sublunary (material) world. What we call creation, in our world, pertains actually to the world soul.

(iv) Al Hayula (Arabicized from Gr. hyle: substance, matter, stuff), First Matter First matter is a simple and spiritual essence already substance without bulk, and yet without conceivable dimensions. Because the first matter was passive, having no proper energy; it could not emanate by itself. It was caused by the intellect to proceed from the world soul which had to exert effort and show great care to facilitate for it to gush forth and become subsequently susceptible to accepting different forms."

(v) Al Tabi'ah (Nature) Nature is one of the powers of the world soul, the energy diffused throughout the sublunary world and effecting all bodies therein, organic and inorganic. It is the cause of motion, life, and change. It works wisely and uniformly. In this sense, it is the philosophical term for the religious concepts of divine will and Providence."

Here, with nature, ceases the influence of the intellect, since all subsequent emanations will tend to be more and more material, defective, and, consequently, unworthy of its care.

(vi) Al Jism al Mutlaq (The Absolute Body) When the world soul began, with the help of the intellect, to move the first matter in three directions, the first matter acquired the three dimensions (length, width, and depth) and became the absolute body or second matter. The second matter is no more a concept, an essence, or a quality denoting pure existence, as was the first matter, but a quantum, spherical in shape. This absolute body, or second matter, is the substance of which our world, as such, is made

(vii) The Spheres or the World of the Spheres In the seventh stage of emanation appeared the spheres which are not imaginary but spiritual, spherical, hollow, transparent, and concentric bodies. These spheres, which are eleven in number, vary in the thickness of their shells, in proportion to the magnitude of the planets with which they are inset. These spheres are: the spheres of the fixed stars, Saturn, Jupiter, Mars, the Sun, Venus, Mercury, and the Moon. All the heavenly bodies are made up of a fifth element, ether, and are not liable to generation and corruption.

(viii) The Four Elements-With the emanation of the four elements: fire, air, water, and earth, we come to the beings immediately under the sphere of the moon (within its orbit), to the sublunary world where the process of generation and corruption begins to take place.

Fire, air, water, and earth supposed to be elements by the Ikhwan al Safa like many Greek thinkers exist, free in nature, in minor spheres about the centre of the earth. Further, they espoused the view of the Ionians, and Thales (d. c. 545 B.C.) in particular, as against the Eleatics, that the four "elements" change into one another, water becomes air and fire; fire becomes air, water, earth, etc.

(ix) The Three Kingdoms In the closing stage of emanation appeared the three kingdoms: mineral, plant, and animal, which originated from the absolute interchange and proportional intermixture of the four elements.

Macrocosm and Microcosm: The early Greek thinkers conceived of the universe as one living being in which the phenomena and powers are correlated and governed hierarchically by a single general law. Democritus of Abdera (d. c. 370 B.C.) developed from that concept the Theory of Macrocosm and Microcosm which treated of man as a reduced model of the universe, and of the universe as the enlarged copy of man. His theory was accepted by the Ikhwan al Safa.

The Individual Soul (al Nafs al Juz'iyyah) and Its Fall: As soon as the world soul was called upon to care for individual beings, beginning with the spheres, its innumerable powers became distinct and independent but not detached, since detachability is a property of matter. In this sense individual souls, representing the infinite powers of the world soul, began to form. During a very long time these souls filled the world of the spheres and constituted the angels who animated the heavenly bodies. At first, they were aware of the grace which is bestowed by the intellect upon the world soul, of which they are the powers. They contemplated the intellect and performed the worship due to God. By and by, some of these individual souls began to forget much about their origin and office. This sin caused them to get farther and farther (though not in the sense of space and time) from God. The punishment was the fall of the sinful souls to our earth, to be tied to individual bodies in order to atone, by undergoing hardships, pain, and sorrow, for the sin they had committed in their heavenly abode. This was the metaphysical origin of life on earth.

The fall was described and explained symbolically by the Ikhwan al Safa. When God created the universe, He peopled it with spiritual incorporeal beings whose office was to praise and glorify God. These were; cognitive beings; they could witness fully the corporeal and the absolute and could conceive of every form and thought anywhere in the universe. The period during which this condition prevailed, since the creation, was called daur al kashfi or the period of exposition, as every being was exposed to every other being in every respect.

Towards the end of this period, God willed that daur al sitri, the period of concealment, should succeed and that the Absolute be hidden in a corporeal body which the faculties of the spiritual beings cannot penetrate. So, He created Adam in His own image and breathed in him the world soul and settled him in His paradise. Then God enjoined that all the spiritual beings, save a few archangels, should prostrate before him, worship him, and be at his command in the management of the world.

At the same time God warned Adam against eating from a certain tree. On the other hand, Satan (Iblis), one of the lesser leaders of the jinn who had aspired to be in place of Adam, was vexed by the honour bestowed on Adam. He refused to prostrate before Adam and be subordinate to him. Then he accosted God with the pretension: "I am better than he. Thou didst create me from fire and him from Clay." Afterwards he turned to Adam to avenge himself on him.

Knowing Adam's reality and frailty, Iblis could convince him that eating from the forbidden tree would disclose to him the names and grades of the archangels who were exempted from prostrating before him, would give him knowledge of the hereafter, and would render him immortal. When Adam realized what he had become, he was filled with boastfulness. At times he overshot himself and disclosed a part of the secret with him to some of those who were around him but were unworthy of this secret before the time assigned for such disclosure. This was Adam's crime curiosity and lust for power. Now, it was no more possible for Adam to stay with the angels who disavowed him because he showed a knowledge inconsistent with his physical appearance and which was even new and startling to them who, as spiritual beings, were supposed to know more than he. Even the animals and the other inhabitants of paradise were scared by his behaviour and abhorred him. Therefore, he was caused to fall to earth to lead on it the life of flesh, deprived of all the supernatural faculties accorded to him in the heavenly abode. With him also fell his wife and Iblis, so that the struggle may continue and be decided openly, and in a fair manner.

The fall of Adam represents, in the metaphysical system of the Ikhwan al Safa, the union of the individual souls with sublunary bodies. When an individual soul is caused to fall, it may be lucky enough to realize its mistake and repent readily. In this case its downward journey is interrupted and it is caused to turn back and regain its former place. The unlucky souls continue their fall towards the centre of the earth to be tied to an inorganic body, plant, beast, or man. We are concerned with the soul assigned to a man which is the least unlucky of all the falling souls.

When a soul falls, it enters the ovum which happens to be impregnated at the time of its fall. This soul in the ovum comes soon under the regimen of the planets. All planets, beginning with the farthest one, Saturn, influence the incubation of the soul turn by turn for a whole lunar month. After the completion of the third month the foetus comes under the influence of the sun, the king, of the planets, and life is breathed into it. The period of pregnancy is accepted by the Ikhwan al Safa to be (at least) seven complete lunar months, the number of the spheres of the then known planets.

The soul is prepared in this world through the medium of the body for the hereafter. Life in this world is only a means to an end: here the soul is enabled to attain perfection in order to be allowed to regain its former celestial life. The body is only the workshop of the soul, a temporary house, a shell, a mount necessary for a journey. Once the body is forsaken by the soul it becomes again a heap of solid matter akin to the constituent elements of the earth. But the body is as necessary for the soul as is the womb for the development of the foetus.

Death is welcome to the purified soul, since death means to it nothing more than that it has stopped using the body. With the death of the body the real life of the soul begins. Moreover, the soul cannot benefit by the knowledge acquired during its terrestial life except after the death of the body.

Lesser and Greater Resurrections, Paradise and Hell-With the death of the body occurs the first or lesser resurrection of the soul. All human souls are immortal: those which have attained perfection during their earthly life would be able to enjoy again the absolute being and happiness; those which have remained imperfect would be barred from entering heaven and remain suspended between heaven and earth with the devils dragging them on every side until they are forced back to the hollows of gloomy bodies and the bounds of physical nature.

In leaving the body, the soul leaves simultaneously the lesser hell which is the transient life on earth subject to generation and corruption, change and putrefaction. Greater hell is the eternal condemnation of the wretched soul to roam in the underworld, burdened with the accumulated ignorance and fettered with depression and pain. Paradise, on the other hand, is the vast space of heaven, where the righteous souls float in an infinite spread of light in perpetuance and immortality, in a state of happiness and grace.

When all the individual souls have left their bodies and are reunited with the world soul, the world soul would lose the reason for its independent existence: so it would return to God. The universe would cease, and there would remain one being: God. This is the greater resurrection: the closing of a manifestation of God.

Nature and the Sciences

The Ikhwan al Safa happened to compile in their "Epistles" the scientific materials available to them and, at the same time, support their esoteric doctrine. They tried to arrange these materials, thc scientific legacy of Greece since the earliest Ionian thinker, Thales of Miletus, in independent chapters. The picture which resulted was that of accumulation rather than of exposition, and never that of exhaustiveness and systematization. We do not know, however, what additions they made; but we are sure that they did give us a general account of the scientific life of the Muslims in the Middle Ages, with its bright and dark sides. Further, the "Epistles" supply us with a picture, though imperfect, of the ancient world of science.

(1) In arithmetic the Ikhwan al Safa depended in the, main, as they say, on Pythagoras and Nicomachus. "Pythagoras" must mean the Pythagorean school; Nicomachus was a late neo Pythagorean of Gerasa (present Jarash in Jordan) who flourished about the middle of the second Christian century. He elaborated the Pythagorean mathematics and wrote a book entitled Arithmatike eisogoge or "Introduction to Arithmetic," in which he maintained that "numbers had a pre existence in the spirit of the Creator before the formation of the universe. He wrote another book which the Ikhwan al Safa must have known and used: Arithmatika theologoumena or "Theology of Numbers," They also knew a book by Euclid on arithmetic called al Usul.

(2) Geometry has for its aim the training of the soul, by which it realizes promotion in knowledge from perception to conception, from the physical to the spiritual and from the concrete to the abstract. Geometry (Ar. handasah)is of two kinds: hissiyyah, tangible, sensible, or common plane and solid geometry which helps man to acquire skill in crafts; and `aqliyyah, intellectual or rational, namely: analytic and descriptive, which enables man to be versed in theoretical sciences. The Ikhwan al Safa knew Euclid and other writers on geometry from whom they drew their information on the subject.

To geometry belong the mysterious or magical figures, the smallest of which is composed of nine squares in three rows. In these squares are inserted the numbers 1 to 9 in a manner that any row, horizontal, perpendicular, or diagonal, must give the uniform sum of 15.

(3) The aim of the "Epistle" on music is to stimulate the souls, already instructed in mathematics, physics, psychics, and theology, to join the immortals in the vast space of heaven. Music itself is a spiritual art founded by wise men. It has a strong and varied effect on all souls. It is either soothing or exciting, gratifying or grieving. On this account, music is played to calm the sick and insane, to tranquillize a weeping child or to lull him to sleep. Even animals are subject to the effect of music. Music is also played in temples because of the touch of awe it possesses.

Pythagoras was said to have heard the sound of the moving spheres and planets. Since the motions of these spheres have regularity and ratios to one another, their sounds must have tunes which are of highest perfection and harmony. These tunes are intended for the inhabitants of the heaven. Pythagoras discovered the scale and essentials of music as a result of hearing the sounds of the heavenly bodies.

(4) The universe, say the Ikhwan al Safa, is made up of all the bodies in existence. It is finite and spherical in shape. Being is one solid body; it stuffs the whole space: it is the universe. Outside the universe there is neither Being nor Non Being, neither emptiness (vacuum) nor fullness, since the universe has no outside. On this they agree with the Eleatic Parmenides and his disciple Zeno; but they disagree with them fully on the question of motion. Parmenides and Zeno presumed that since the universe is completely replete, the movement of individual bodies is impossible. The view of the Ikhwan al Safa was: since the mass of the universe is not of the same density, the more dense may move through the less dense, as the fish swim in water and the birds fly in air.

The earth stands in the centre of the world; then come seven concentric sphere in which revolve the planets: the moon, Mercury, Venus, the sun, Mars, Jupiter, and Saturn. Finally comes the sphere of the fixed stars. The number of the stars which were determined by astronomical observation, including the seven planets, was one thousand and twenty nine. All the stars are luminous except the moon which receives its light from the sun.

The movement of the planets was explained by the rotation of the outer sphere clockwise: from east to west above the earth, and from west to east under the earth, once every day. The outer sphere carries the other spheres along with it. From this it follows that these spheres with their planets too should complete a revolution around the earth in one day. But the ancients noted that the planets have complicated movements: sometimes they appear to overtake the sun and continue their courses ahead of it; and sometimes the sun appears to overtake them. With the planets nearer the earth the moon, Mercury, and Venus this phenomenon was more conspicuous and gave rise to the theory of epicycles. This means that the orbits within the outer sphere are not homocentric with it, concentric or having one common centre, but eccentric, i. e., having independent centres.

Aristotle was in favour of homocentrieity; Claudius Ptolemy (d. 168 A.D), the Alexandrian astronomer, upheld the theory of epicycles. Unfortunately, the Ikhwan al Safa sided with Ptolemy and rejected, at the same time, the view that the heavenly bodies revolve from west to east, a view which seems to have had some upholders among the Pythagoreans.

Regarding the magnitudes of the stars, they showed some boldness. The earth, they said, is but a point in a large circle. The smallest planet has a size eighteen times that of the earth; the largest is one hundred and seven times.

They maintained, further, that the celestial bodies are neither heavy nor light. If any body, they argue, is in its specially assigned place in the spheres, it does not exert weight. It acquires weight, on the contrary, when it comes into the neighbourhood of other strange bodies, not of the same material (water in water or air in air, for example, has no weight). Weight, they say, is nothing but the mutual attraction and mutual repulsion in the face of resistance. We are reminded in this case of the artificial satellites and of the fact that they lose all weight as soon as they leave the zone of the gravity of the earth. In the same spirit, they declared also that the sun and the stars are neither hot nor cold.

The Ikhwan al Safa accepted the solar year to be of 365 1/4 days. On this basis they computed the revolutions of the planets around the earth: Saturn completes a revolution of its orbits in 29 years, 5 months and 6 days; Jupiter in 11 years, 10 months and 26 days; Mars in about 23 months; Venus in 584 days, and Mercury in 124 days only. The Ikhwan al Safa supplied us with data which enable us to construct formulae for the extension of the universe and for its volume which may be computed roughly at: 1,300,000,000 and 150,000,000,000,000,000,000,000,000 km., respectively or 13 x 108 and 15 x 1025. This is nothing to be compared with the real measurements, but it serves to give us an idea of the boldness of the Ikhwan al Safa in their age.

(5) The earth, say the Ikhwan al Safa is a sphere. Their proof is that any line on the surface of the earth or on the face of a river is an arch, and any portion of the sea is a part of the shell of a spherical body. George Sarton, the historian of science, holds that the idea of the sphericity of the earth is as old as Pythagoras; but he wonders how Pythagoras could arrive at a proof. He declares that Pythagoras must have postulated the sphericity of the earth out of wild boldness.

They believe also that the earth stands in the centre of the universe, suspended in the midst of the air, because it is in its special place within a space free from the attraction and repulsion of every other heavenly body. Although the Ikhwan al Safa were essentially Pythagorean, they rejected the Pythagorean view that the earth has two motions: a revolution around a central fire and a rotation on its axis. They believed, however, that it had a sway (forwards and backwards) on its axis, and that when it was created it was in motion; but afterwards it came to a standstill. It seems that they followed, in this view, Democritus who held that the earth had in the beginning a motion, but afterwards it came gradually to a standstill.

The earth is not solid or massive, but it is full of cavities. The solid parts of its interior are also of different densities. Further, it has no bottom, in the common meaning of the word; its bottom is its centre. So, wherever a man stands on the earth, his head is always towards the sky (above the earth) and his feet are always towards the bottom or centre of the earth. In spite of all this genial explanation, they believed that we live on one side of the earth only.

(6) In the two chapters on geography and meteorology, based principally on Meteorologica and other Greek works, the Ikhwan al Safa speak of the equator, of the polar zones where the winter is a night of six continuous months and the summer is a day of six continuous months, of the four seasons of longitude and time, of the mountains and their nature as reservoirs of water, and cognate topics. Their explanation of the eclipses is noteworthy, but their interpretation of the ebb and flow of tides is false: they believed that the rays of the moon heat the waters of the sea and cause their rise.

(7) In physics and chemistry the Ikhwan al Safa held, with Aristotle, the Theory of the Four Elements and rejected the atomic theory. They maintained also with the Ionian physicists that the so called four elements: fire, air, water, and earth, change into one another. Furthermore, when those four elements undergo intense heat and strong pressure inside the earth, they change into mercury and sulphur. If aerial moisture mixes with earth, it becomes mercury, a masculine element; if oily moisture mixes with earth, it changes into sulphur, a feminine element. From the further intermixture of sulphur and mercury, in different proportions, are formed all the mineral bodies: clay, glass, iron, copper, ruby, silver, gold, etc.

(8) The natural world is made up of three kingdoms: the mineral, plant, and animal kingdoms. Evolution rests on the view that every kingdom constitute the primary

matter and nourishing material for the next higher kingdom. Accordingly, the mineral kingdom must have come into existence long before that of plants. The plants came into existence before the animals; sea animals before the animals on land; the less developed before the more developed; and all animals were in existence ages before man. At the top of the animal kingdom appeared the qird(monkey, or ape) which bears so much resemblance to man in shape and behaviour.

There is also a spiritual evolution by which the human soul evolves from the soul of a child to that of an angel. At the age of fifty, the wise and cultivated man may attain the degree which enables him to receive inspiration, to become a messenger between the Intellect and his fellow men, to found doctrines, and to make laws. At this stage, he is a proxy of God on earth; he attains divinity and so worship is due to him.

Psychology

(1) The Soul The soul has three major faculties or powers, every one of which is called equally a soul.

(i) The vegetative or nutritive soul common to all living beings: plants, beast, and man alike. It is subdivided into three powers: that of nutritive proper, that of growth, and that of reproduction.

(ii) The animal, beastly, or sensitive soul belongs to beasts and men only. It is subdivided into two powers: locomotion and sensation. Sensation falls in turn in two categories: perception (sight, touch, etc.) and emotion. Emotion is either primitive (laughter, anger, etc.) or evolved (good food, social and political prestige, etc.).

(iii) The human (rational, thinking, or talkative) soul is restricted to man. These three faculties, together with their powers, work together and are united in man and likened to a tree with three boughs, every bough of which has several branches, and every branch many leaves and fruit. Comparison may also be made with a person who is a blacksmith, carpenter, and builder or who can read, write, and teach: he is one man with three faculties.

(2) The Brain, and the Heart The prevailing belief in ancient times was that the heart constituted the most important organ of the body: the centre of sensation, the seat of intelligence, and the house of life. Aristotle was also of this opinion. The Ikhwan al Safa decided in favour of the brain and held that it is the brain where the processes of perception, emotion, and conception develop.

(3) The Process of Thinking It begins in the five senses and continues in the brain. Fine nerves extend from the sense organs to different parts of the mass of the brain, where they form a net similar to a spider's web. Whenever the senses come in touch with sensible bodies, their temperament undergoes a change which is communicated soon, together with the abstract forms of those sensible bodies, to the imaginative zone in the front part of the brain. Next, the imaginative faculty passes the traces which the abstract forms have left on it to the reflective faculty, in the middle part of the brain, to ponder upon them and verify their indications; then, the indications are transmitted in turn to the retentive faculty (or memory) in the back part of the brain to be stored there until a recollection of them is needed. At the right time the relevant data are referred to the expressive or talkative faculty by which they are abstracted, generalized, and given the form expressible by the tongue to be received intelligibly by the ear.

Politics

(1) The Ikhwan al Safa had no interest in the theory of State or in the forms of government. Nor could they be influenced, in this respect, by Greek writers. The two worlds were totally different: Plato and Aristotle lived in City States; the Ikhwan al Safa lived in the great cities of an empire. At any rate, the Ikhwan al Safa believed that the State rests on two foundations: religion and kingship. A king is indispensable, though he may be a tyrant, if the State is to lead a secure and prosperous life. A group of wise men, however may do without a king.

(2) The indifference of the Ikhwan al Safa about the State was counterbalanced by their keen interest in al siyasat

al madaniyyah, a blend of civics and domestic economy, which bears more on the personal and communal behaviour of man.

Notes: As a rule, the Ikhwan al Safa preferred that their followers should practise celibacy. But since that was impracticable, marriage was enjoined to serve two purposes: first, that the race may continue a reason which was given by Aristotle too; and second, because there are people who cannot remain celebate.

A man of standing should be a kind of a ruler in his community. He should first exercise self control in the different situations through which he passes, because he who can control himself may be able to control others. Regarding his children and brothers, he should give them a fair, uniform but firm treatment from which he should allow no deviation except in circumstances not under his control.

People are governed easier and better if they have been accustomed to a certain way of government. As for other relatives of his servants, and dependants, he should be bounteous in their maintenance and meek in their treatment. But it is of no use to disclose to them any trouble or want of his.

This would impair his authority in their eyes without helping him in the least. If he was ever short of means, and consequently obliged to lay a restriction on his favours to them, he should try, to make them believe that he has done so on purpose and not because he has yielded to a certain pressure.

A man should choose his friends carefully and treat them with tact: know them well and betray none of his secrets to them. Further, he should appear always, before them, consistent in his opinion and behaviour, because they are expected to share with him his doctrines and way of life (the ultimate aim of the Ikhwan al Safa in making friends is to propagate their doctrines among these friends).

It is very important that the relatives of a leading personality should follow his doctrines and adopt his views, otherwise his friends would lose their enthusiasm for him. He should disclaim publicly any relative who proves to be at variance with him in the matter of doctrine.

Ethics

Muslims have always been more interested in morals and matters of conduct than in ethical theories, because Islam insists on good or righteous deeds as well as on good intentions. The Ikhwan al Safa's interest in ethics was confined to its bearing on their doctrine: acquiring theoretical knowledge and doing good in this life so that their souls may enjoy eternity and happiness in the hereafter. They start from the assertion that characters are either inborn or acquired. Inborn characters begin with the formation of the foetus in the womb, and they develop therein gradually under the influence of the planets. Innate characters, or virtues, are specialized aptitudes assigned to different organs. They enable the soul to act through every organ and produce the sensation, action, or craft particular to that organ without need for deliberation or choice. At one place the Ikhwan al Safa assume that inborn characters are uniformly good. At another, they maintain that they are bad, and, consequently, all religions were revealed to resist the innate characters of man and to reform them if possible.

After birth man begins to acquire virtues. He continues to do so until his death. There is in man an aptitude to do good, and with the same aptitude he can do evil. Character and behaviour are teachable.

Anything which should be done, if done as it should, to the extent to which it should, in the place where it should, at the time when it should, and in view of the end for which it should, is called good. And he who does that thin deliberately and with choice is called a wise man, a philosopher, and a perfect man. Good, for the masses, is that which religion has enjoined, and evil, that which religion has prohibited.

Acquired characters are determined and modified by the disposition of the body, climate of the land, and the contact of the children with their parents, tutors, comrades, and with the people in prominence. The different circumstances through which man usually passes are important factors in making people change from one character into another.

The Ikhwan al Safa urge their followers to be idealistic in their behaviour. The good they seek should be final and self sufficient. One should do good not because one expects from doing it, or for doing it, a benefit, nor because one expects to avoid some loss.

Education

As soon as a child is born, he comes under the influence of social factors for four complete years, during which he reaches a certain stage of intelligence and comprehension. After the fourth year the child begins to acquire his habits, knowledge, doctrines, crafts, and hobbies by imitation, as a result of his contact with those who happen to be around him. The masses copy the external behaviour of the dominant class.

Children are apt to use an analogy characteristic of them. They believe that their parents are perfect and that the conditions prevailing in their own homes are models for all the conditions elsewhere. On the practical side, children are more apt to master the arts, sciences, and crafts of their parents than those of strangers.

Knowledge is the abstraction of the knowable in the soul of the knower through the aid of a teacher. The aptitude to learn belongs to the soul alone. The end of teaching is to purify the souls of the taught and give them correct behaviour in order to prepare them for immortality and happiness in the hereafter. A science which does not lead to happiness in the hereafter is useless.

Every soul is potentially learned; the parents and tutors polish its aptitude and help it to become learned in action. A teacher is absolutely necessary, especially to common people.

The brain is able to store simultaneously all kinds of information, however diverse and contradictory they may be, since it stores their abstractions only. And in spite of the fact that the data stored in the brain fade gradually, and that some of them are sometimes totally forgotten, they do not annul one another.

Essentially, knowledge is never spontaneous; it must be taught and learnt. A teacher is simply a guide for the soul to knowledge. Knowledge is handed down traditionally through religious leaders, the Imams, whose ultimate source of knowledge is the Prophet, who acquires his knowledge from God by inspiration.

The Ikhwan al Safa touch at a thorny problem in education. They believe that neither the pupil may benefit from the tutor, nor the tutor may benefit from the pupil, unless there is a kind of intimacy between them. We know for certain that some kind of a reserved friendship is very useful in this respect. But the Ikhwan al Safa overshoot themselves and speak frankly of "the desire of grown up men for boys" as an incentive for effecting real education. Furthermore, they mention explicitly that such manners belong only to nations which esteem science, art, literature, and mathematics, like the Persians, the peoples of Mesopotamia and Syria as well as the Greeks. Nomads, who as a rule have no interest in science, art, etc., lack this desire.

The idea of Platonic love contaminated the Ikhwan al Safa as a result of their readings in Greek history in general and in the philosophy of Plato in particular. Plato advocated it especially in his Symposium. Sarton blames Plato and says of him: "Platonic love for him was the sublimation of paedcrasty; true love is called in the Symposium the right method of boy-loving". The Ikhwan al Safa condemn this desire, however, in all fields other than education. Plato too seems to have condemned it in a later work of his, Nomoi (The Laws), at least twice.

Religion

On the practical side of belief, the Ikhwan al Safa speak of religion and laws. The word for religion in Arabic is din, i. e., custom or obedience to one acknowledged head. Religion is a necessity as a social sanction for the government of the masses, for the purification of the soul, and also because all people are predisposed to religiousness and piety. In this sense, religion is one for all people and for all nations.

By Law (Ar. Shari'ah or namus, from the Greek word: nomos, law) the Ikhwan al Safa meant what we mean today by religion. Laws (religious) are different to suit different communities, groups, and even individuals. These laws are dictated by the wise men of every people for the benefit of their respective nations.

On this basis the Ikhwan al Safa declare that all metaphysical themes in the sacred books such as creation, Adam, Satan, the tree of knowledge, resurrection, the Day of

Judgment, hell, and paradise should be taken as symbols and understood allegorically. Only the masses, who cannot think adequately for themselves, understand these themes in their literal and physical sense. Themes of a lesser magnitude, as "He sendeth down water from the sky," should also be treated symbolically: water in this context being the Quran!

The Ikhwan al Safa were not satisfied with any of the existing religions; they, nevertheless, urged everybody to select one of them. To have a defective religion is better than to be a disbeliever, since there is an element of truth in every religion. Everybody should be left free to embrace the religion he chooses; he may also change his religion, perhaps often too, though he is expected to look for the best religion in his time. He should refrain, however, from contradictory opinions and false doctrines: a wise man does not embrace two contradictory religions at the same time.

There should be no compulsion in religion; compulsion should be effected only through the laws. This is so because religion is a self conviction felt in the heart. The laws of religions, on the contrary, are social orders, to abide by which is necessary for the maintenance of security and welfare of the community.

The Ikhwan al Safa formulated a definite attitude towards all existing religions, sects, and schools of theology. We shall content ourselves with their attitude towards Islam.

Islam is considered by them to be the religion par excellence: the best and most perfect of all religions. The Quran overruled all earlier revealed books. It, being the last, confirmed in them that which resembled its contents and abrogated that which was contrary to its precepts. Muhammad, peace be upon him, is the head of all the prophets and the last of them. He is the governor of all governors; in him has God united the elements of kingship and prophethood, so that his followers may enjoy the worldly as well as the spiritual glories.

9

AL-GHAZALI: METAPHYSICS A INTRODUCTION

Al-Ghazali occupies a position unique in the history of Muslim religious and philosophical thought by whatever standard we may judge him: breadth of learning, originality, or influence. He has been acclaimed as the Proof of Islam (hujjat al-Islam), the Ornament of Faith (zain al-din) and the Renewer of Religion (mujaddid).1 Al-Subki (d. 771/1370) went so far in his estimation of him as to claim that if there had been a prophet after Muhammad, al-Ghazali would have been the man. To be sure he gathered in his own person all the significant intellectual and religious movements of his time and lived over again in the inwardness of his soul the various spiritual phases developed by Islam. He was in turn a canon-lawyer and a scholastic, a philosopher and a sceptic, a mystic and a theologian, a traditionist and a moralist. His-position as a theologian of Islam is undoubtedly the most eminent. Through a living synthesis of his creative and energetic personality, he revitalized Muslim theology and reorientated its values and attitudes. His combination of spiritualization and fundamentalism in Islam had such a marked stamp of his powerful personality that it has continued to be accepted by the community since his time.

His outlook on philosophy is characterized by a remarkable originality which, however, is more critical than constructive. In his works on philosophy one is struck by a keen philosophical acumen and penetration with which he gives a clear and readable exposition of the views of the philosophers, the subtlety and analyticity with which he criticizes them, and the candour and open-mindedness with which he accepts them whenever he finds them to be true. Nothing frightened him nor fascinated him, and through an extraordinary independence of mind, he became a veritable challenge to the {581} philosophies of Aristotle and Plotinus and to their Muslim representatives before him, al-Farabi and ibn Sina. The main trends of the religious and philosophical thought of al-Ghazali, however, come close to the temper of the modern mind. The champions of the modern movement of religious empiricism, on the one hand, and that of logical positivism, on the other, paradoxical though it may seem, would equally find comfort in his works. The teachings of this remarkable figure of Islam pertaining either to religion or philosophy, either constructive or critical, cannot, however, be fully understood without knowing the story of his life with some measure of detail, for, in his case, life and thought were one: rooted in his own personality. Whatever he thought and wrote came with the living reality of his own experience.

LIFE

Abu Hamid Muhammad ibn Muhammad ibn Muhammad ibn Ta'us Ahmad al-Tusi al-Shafi'i, generally known simply by his nisbah al-Ghazali, was born in 450/1058 at Tabaran, one of the two townships of Tus, now in ruins in the neighbourhood of modern Meshed in Khurasan.

Al-Ghazali was not the first scholar of distinction in his family: there had been another abu Hamid al-Ghazali (d. 435/1043), his grand-uncle, who was a theologian and jurisconsult of great repute, possibly a model which he might have set before him in his ambitious youth. But he was early exposed to Sufistic influences. His own father was a pious dervish who according to al-Subki would not eat anything but what he could earn with his own hands {582} and spend as much time as he could in the company of the divines. Early left as an orphan, al-Ghazali was brought up and educated by a pious Sufi friend of his father along with his brother who later made a mark as a great mystic. While still a boy al-Ghazali began the study of theology and canon-law, with the express desire for wealth and reputation as he himself has acknowledged first in his native town under Shaikh Abmad ibn Muhammad al-Radhkhani al-Tusi and then at Jurjan under the Imam abu Nasr al-Isma'ili.

After his return from Jurjan he stayed for a while in Tas and possibly during this period studied Sufism under Ynsuf al-

Nassaj and perhaps even undertook some of the Sufistic exercises. At the age of about twenty he proceeded to the Nizamiyyah Academy of Nishapur to study under abu al-Ma'ali al-Juwaini known as Imam al-Haramain, the most distinguished Ash'arite theologian of the day, only fourth from al-Ash'ari himself in an apostolic succession of the Ash'arite teachers. The curriculum of the Academy included a wide range of subjects such as theology, canon-law, philosophy, logic, dialectics, natural sciences, Sufism, etc. Imam al-Haramain allowed full freedom of thought and expression to his pupils; they were encouraged to engage in debates and discussions of all kinds.

Al-Ghazali gave early proof of great learning and also of a tendency towards philosophizing. Imam al-Haramain described him as "a plenteous ocean to be drowned" and comparing him with two other pupils of his observed: "al-Khawafi's strong point is verification, al-Ghazali's is speculation, and al-Kiya's is explanation." In his debates with other students he showed great suppleness of mind and a gift for polemics. Not long afterwaidil he began to lecture to his fellow-students and to write books. But al-Ghazali was one of those rare minds whose originality is not crushed by their learning.-He was a born critic and possessed great independence of thought. It was verily during his studentship at the Nizamiyyah Academy of Nishapur that he became impatient of dogmatic teaching and freed himself from the bondage of authority (taqlid) and even showed the signs of scepticism.

During his stay at Niahapur, he also became a disciple to the Sufi abu 'Ali al-Fadl ibn Muhammad ibn 'Ali al-Farmadhi al-Tusi, a pupil of al-Ghazali's own uncle and of the reputed al-Qushairi (d. 465/1074). From al-Farmadhi al-Ghazali learnt more about the theory and practice of Sufism. He even practised rigorous ascetic and Sufistic exercises under his guidance but not to the desired effect. As he himself narrates, he could not attain to that stage where the mystics begin to receive pure inspiration from "high above." So he did not feel quite settled down in his mind. On the one hand, he felt philosophically dissatisfied with the speculative systems of the scholastic theologians and could not accept anything on authority, on the other, the Sufistic practices {583} also failed to make any definite impression on him for he had not received any sure results.

There is no doubt, however, that the increasing attraction of the Sufistic teaching, with its insistence upon a direct personal experience of God, added to al-Ghazali's critical dissatisfaction with dogmatic theology.

Al-Farmadhi died in 477/1084, and Imam al-Haramain in 478/1085. Al-Ghazali was then in his twenty-eighth year, ambitious and energetic; the fame of his learning had already spread in the Islamic world. He betook himself to the Court of Nizam al-Mulk, the great vizier of the Saljnq sovereign Malikshah (r. 465/1072-485/1092) and joined his retinue of canonists and theologians. Nizam al-Mulk by his munificent patronage of scholarship, science, and arts had gathered round him a brilliant galaxy of savants and learned men. He used to hold frequent assemblies for debate and discussion and al-Ghazali soon made his mark at these and was conspicuous for his skill in debate.

Al-Ghazali's profound knowledge of Muslim law, theology, and philosophy so much impressed Nizam al-Mulk that he appointed him to the Chair of Theology in the Nizamiyyah Academy (established 458-60/1065-67) at Baghdad in 484/1091. He was then only thirty-four. This was most coveted of all the honours in the then Muslim world and one which had not previously been conferred on anyone at so early an age.

As a professor in the Academy, al-Ghazali was a complete success; the excellence of his lectures, the extent of his learning, and the lucidity of his explanations attracted larger and larger classes including the chief savants of the time. Soon all Islam acclaimed his eloquence, erudition, and dialectical skill and he came to be looked upon as the greatest theologian in the Ash'arite tradition. His advice began to be sought in matters religious and political, and he came to wield influence comparable to that of the highest officials of the State.

Apparently, he attained to all the glory that a scholar could by way of worldly success, but inwardly he began to undergo an intellectual and spiritual crisis. {584} His old doubts and scepticism began to assail him once again and he became highly critical of the very subjects that he taught. He keenly felt the hollowness of the meticulous spinning of casuistry of the canon-lawyers. The systems of the scholastic theologians

(Mutakallimin) had no intellectual certainty, for they depended entirely on the acceptance of their initial dogmatic assumptions on authority. He denounced their over-emphasis on the doctrinal, for it led to a faulty representation of religion by reducing it to a mere mould of orthodoxy and catechism of dogmas.

The disputes of the scholastics amongst themselves he considered as mere dialectical logomachies which had no real relation with religious life. Al-Ghazali turned once again to the study of philosophy, this time as diligently and as comprehensively as he could, but found, like Kant, that it was impossible to build theology on reason alone. Reason was good so far as it went, but it could not go very far. The Ultimate, the Supreme Truth, could not be reached through it. Becoming keenly aware of the theological limitations of reason, he fell into a state of scepticism and lost his peace of mind. The hypocrisy of his orthodox teaching became unbearable and he found himself to be in a false position.

But all was not lost: he had some assurances that he could be delivered from this state of despair through the Sufi way. It was not that he now discovered that in Sufism lay the possibility for a direct encounter with reality; this fact he had been realizing over a period of years. He had made a theoretical study of Sufism and had even ventured into Sufistic exercises; only he had not advanced far enough into them. If he could consecrate himself to the Sufistic way of life through spiritual renunciation, sustained asceticism, and prolonged and deep meditation, he might have received the light he sought. But this meant in his case giving up his brilliant academic career and worldly position. He was by nature ambitious and had great desire for fame and self-glorification.

On the other hand, he was the most earnest seeker after truth. Besides, he had the anxiety to reach a secure faith which was accentuated by his thought of life after death. He remained in the throes of a severe moral conflict and in a spiritual travail for about six months beginning from Rajah 488/July 1095. He collapsed physically and mentally; appetite and digestion failed and he lost his power of speech. This made it easy for him to {585} to renounce his post as a professor. He left Baghdad in Dhu al-Qa'dah 488/ November 1095, ostensibly on a pilgrimage to Mecca: actuallv he went into seclusion to practise the ascetic and religious discipline of the Sufis in order to secure certainty for his mind and peace for his soul. He gave away all his fortune except some "trust funds" to maintain his family and proceeded to Syria.

For two years from 488/1095 to 490/1097 he remained in strict retirement in one of the minarets of the mosque of the Umayyads in Damascus, undergoing most rigorous ascetic discipline and performing religious exercises. He moved to Jerusalem for another period of meditation in the mosque of `Umar and the Dome of the Rock. After having paid his visit to the tomb of Abraham at Hebron, he went on pilgrimage to Mecca and Medina; then followed a long period of retreat at different places in holy shrines and mosques and wandering in deserts. After eleven years the life of a wandering dervish and scholar came to an end and he finally returned to his native town, Tus, in 499/1105.

Of his inner spiritual experiences in their experimental actuality, after he left Baghdad, al-Ghazali tells us almost nothing except that there were revealed to him in his periods of solitude things innumerable and unfathomable. Apparently, these experiences culminated in his acknowledgment of the authority of the Prophet and the complete submission to the truth revealed in the Quran. The first public sign of his recovery to orthodoxy is perhaps al-Risalah al-Qudsiyyah, written during his retreat in Jerusalem, where in all probability he was before 492/1099, for in Sha'ban of that year Jerusalem was captured by the Crusaders. This has heen inserted as Qawa'id al-`Aqa'id in the third chapter of the second book of his massive magnum opus Ihy?' ulm al-Din (The Revivification of the Sciences of Religion) in which he began to set down what he had learnt through his long periods of self-discipline and meditation. During his wanderings he not only kept on writing other {586} books besides Ihy?' but also resumed teaching from time to time. He keenly felt it incumbent upon him to crush heresy and unbelief around him and to call people back to the truth and moral power of Islam, both through writing and teaching: he virtually assumed the role of a moral and religious reformer. He began to devote himself more and more to the study of the traditions of the Prophet and make an extensive use of them for the purposes of edification and spiritual guidance.

On his return to Tus he once again gave himself to the life of retirement and contemplation, but very soon Fakhr al-Mulk, the son of his old patron, Nizam al-Mulk, who was the vizier to Sultan Sanjar, urged him to accept the chair of theology at the Maimunah Nizamiyyah College at Nishapur which he did after some hesitation in Dhu al-Qa'dah 499/August 1106. But he did not stay there long and retired once more to his home in Tns and established a madrasah at which he began to teach both theology and Tasawwuf. At the instance of the learned and the common people of Baghdad he was once again summoned by the Grand Vizier al-Said to take up teaching in the old Nizamiyyah Academy of Baghdad but al-Ghazali chose to remain at Tus. There he lived in peace with some personal disciples having charge of his madrasah. Every moment was filled with study and devotion till his death on the 14th of Jumada II 505/the 19th of December 1111. It was a beautifully complete and round life in which the end came to the beginning.

METHOD

The most important thing about al-Ghazali's system of thought is its method which may be described as that of the courage to know and the courage to doubt. The best expression of it is given in his famous autobiographical work, al-Munqidh min al-Dalal (The, Deliverer from Error), which he wrote some five years before his death. In al-Munqidh al-Ghazali makes {587} a critical examination of the methods of the various schools of thought current in his time in a manner closely similar to that of Descartes' (d. 1060/1650) in his Discours de la methods (1047/1637).

All kinds of knowledge, al-Ghazali held, should be investigated and nothing should be considered dangerous or hostile. For himself he said that he had embarked on the open sea of knowledge right from his adolescence setting aside all craven caution: "I poked into every dark recess and made an assault on every problem, I plunged into every abyss. I scrutinized the creed of every sect and I fathomed the mysteries of each doctrine. All this I did that I might distinguish between the true and the false. There was not a philosopher whose system I did not acquaint myself with, nor a theologian whose doctrines I did not examine. If ever I met a Sufi, I coveted to probe into his secrets; if an ascetic, I investigated into the basis of his austerities; if one of the atheistic zindiqs, I groped into the causes of his bold atheism."

Such was the courage of al-Ghazali to know. He was free from the parochialism of the dogmatic theologians of his day who would rather consign the books of the atheists and philosophers to flames than read them. But prepared though he was to listen to every creed and doctrine, he would accept none and doubt all. For one thing, he came to the conclusion that the greatest hindrance in the search for truth was the acceptance of beliefs on the authority of others and blind adherence to the heritage of the past. He remembered the traditional saying of the Prophet: "Every child is born with a sound disposition (fitrah); it is his parents who make him a Jew or a Christian or a Magian" and he was anxious to know what that sound disposition was before it suffered the impress of the unreasoned convictions imposed by others.

Indeed, he wanted to reconstruct all his knowledge from its very foundation and was led to make the following reflections: "The search after truth being the aim which I propose to myself, I ought in the first place to ascertain what are the bases of certitude. In the second place I ought to recognize that certitude is the clear and complete knowledge of things, such knowledge as leaves no room for doubt, nor any possibility of error." As one might foresee, this proposed test for certitude only led him to a series of doubts. No part of the knowledge he had acquired {588} hitherto could stand this rigorous test. He further observed, "We cannot hope to find truth except in matters which carry their evidence in themselves, i. e., in sense-perception and necessary principles of thought; we must, therefore, first of all establish these two on a firm basis." But he doubted the evidence of sense-perception; he could see plainly as Descartes did later that they so often deceive us. No eye can perceive the movement of a shadow, still the shadow moves; a small coin would cover any star yet the geometrical computations show that a star is a world vastly larger than the earth.

Al-Ghazali's confidence in sense-perception having been shaken, he turned to the scrutiny of what he called the necessary principles, but he doubted even these. Is ten more than three? Can a thing both be and not be at the same time or be both necessary and impossible? How could he tell? His doubt with regard to sense-perception made him very hesitant to accept the infallibility of reason. He believed in the testimony of senses till it was contradicted by the verdict of reason. Well, perhaps there is above reason another judge who if he appeared would convict reason of falsity and if such a third arbiter is not yet apparent it does not follow that he does not exist.

Al-Ghazali then considers the possibility that life in this world is a dream by comparison with the world to come; and when a man dies, things may come to appear differently to him from what he now beholds. There may be an order of reality different from this spatio-temporal order which may be revealed to a level of consciousness other than the so-called normal consciousness such as that of the mystics or the prophets. Such was the movement of al-Ghazali's thought, which though formulated a little artificially in the Munqidh was dramatic enough to make out a case for the possibility of a form of apprehension higher than rational apprehension, that is, apprehension as the mystic's inspiration or the prophet's revelation. {589}

Al-Ghazali's method of doubt or sceptical attitude did certainly have its historical antecedents. The Ash'arites' system of atomism, by reducing all categories except substance (jauhar) and quality ('ard) to mere subjectivities, virtually amounted to a form of scepticism. Even earlier the Mu'tazilites like al-Nazzam (d. 231/845) and abu al-Hudhail (d. 266/840) had formulated the principle of doubt as the beginning of all knowledge. But with al-Ghazali this was as much a matter of an inherent trait of his intellectual disposition as a principle.

One may be tempted to say that his keenly alert and sensitive mind, though, exposed from early youth to all the various intellectual and spiritual movements of the times such as scholasticism, rationalism, mysticism, etc., was not fully captured by any one single movement. Ambitious and self-confident, he had been in a way playing with the various influences rather than affected exclusively by anyone of them. His restless soul had always been trying to reach for what it had not attained. In his sincere and open search for absolute truth, he possibly remained oscillating for a long time between the moments of belief and disbelief-moments when he might have found comfort in his religious convictions with complete submission to the teachings of the Quran and the moments when his doubts and scepticism might have overwhelmed him, clamouring for indubitable certainty.

It is certainly very difficult to map the exact chronology of the spiritual development of such a complex mind as that of al-Ghazali's. The usual method of working out the history of the mental development of an author on the basis of the chronological order of his works is not possible in the case of al-Ghazali for our knowledge of his works is incomplete. both with regard to their extent and relative order, not to speak of exact dating. None of his works, not even {590} al-Munqidh which has often been compared with the Confessions of Augustine allows us a peep into the inward workings of his soul. It is merely a schematized description of his spiritual development and not an existential study of the "phenomenology" of his soul: he has simply arranged in a logical order what must necessarily have come to him in a broken and sporadic form.

Nevertheless, al-Munqidh is our most valuable source to determine al-Ghazali's relative position with regard to the various schools of thought around him. He had been moving through them all these years, studying them very closely in his quest for certainty, and of them he now gives us a critical evaluation in a summary fashion. He divides the various "seekers" after truth into the four distinct groups: Theologians, Mystics, Authoritarians Ta'limites), and Philosophers.

His criticism of the theologians is very mild. He himself had been brought up in their tradition and was thoroughly saturated into their system. It is doubtful if he ever parted company with them completely. He did not cease to be a theologian even when he became a mystic and his criticism of the philosophers was essentially from the standpoint of a theologian. Only he was dissatisfied with the scholastic method of the theologians, for it could not bring any intellectual certainty; their doctrines, he deemed, however, to be correct. His belief in God, Prophecy, and Last Judgment were too deeply rooted in him to be shaken altogether; his scepticism with regard to them, if at all, was a temporary phase; he only very much desired a confirmation of these fundamental beliefs either on some philosophical grounds or through some sort of first-hand experience. So far as the mystics were concerned, al-Ghazali found himself hardly in a position to level any criticism against them except for the extravagantly pantheistic utterances or antinomian tendencies of some of the intoxicated Sufis. They were essentially men of feeling (arbab al-ahwal) rather than men of words (ashab al-aqwal) and he had himself early realized the importance of experiences and states rather than that of definitions and dogmas. The claims of the mystics he knew could not be challenged by one who lacked their experiences.

Al-Ghazali held a very poor opinion of the pretensions of those whom he called the party of ta'lim or authoritative instruction also known as Ismail?iyyah and Batiniyyah. Theirs was a kind of Muslim popery or Montanist movement. {591} They renounced reason and held that truth can be attained only by a submissive acceptance of the pronouncements of an infallible Imam. This doctrine indeed was a part of the propaganda of the Fatimid Caliphate (297/909-555/1160) with its centre in Cairo and, thus, had its moorings in the political chaos of the day. Al-Ghazali's examination of the Taclimites was certainly due to his love for thoroughness in his search for truth, but perhaps he also wanted to make clear his position with regard to an ideology having political strings behind it.

It was the fourth class of the seekers of truth, namely, the philosophers, who engaged his attention most of all and troubled his mind more than anyone else.

10

ATTACK ON THE PHILOSOPHERS

INTRODUCTION

Al-Ghazali's critical examination of the method and doctrines of the philosophers is the most exciting and important phase of his intellectual inquiry. He was not at all against philosophical investigation as such. His early interest in philosophy is evidenced by the treatises that he wrote on logic such as MiÐyar al-`Ilm fi Fann al-Mantiq: "The Touchstone of Science in Logic" (quite an elaborate treatise) and Mihakk al-Nazar fi al-Mantiq: "The Touchstone of Speculation in Logic" (a smaller work). In the history of Muslim thought his is the first instance of a theologian who was thoroughly schooled in the ways of the philosophers; the doctors of Islam before him either had a dread of philosophy, considering it a dangerous study, or dabbled in it just to qualify themselves for polemics against the philosophers. But al-Ghazali very strongly realized that to refute a system before literally inhabiting it and getting thoroughly immersed into its very depths was to act blindly. "A man," he tells us, "cannot grasp what is defective in any of the sciences unless he has so complete a grasp of the science in question that he equals its most learned exponents in the appreciation of its fundamental principles and even goes beyond and surpasses them...." In all intellectual honesty he refrained from saying a word against the philosophers till he had completely mastered their systems.

He applied himself so assiduously to the study of the entire sweep of Greek philosophy current in his time and attained such a firm grasp of its problems and methods that he produced one of the best compendia of it in Arabic entitled as Maqasid al-Falasifah (The Intentions of the Philosophers). This compendium was such a faithful exposition of Aristotelianism that when it {592} came to be known to the Christian scholastics through a Latin translation made as early as 540/ 1145 by the Spanish philosopher and translator Dominicus Gundisalvus, it was taken to be the work of a genuine Peripatetic. Albert the Great (d. 679/1280), Thomas Aquinas (d. 673/1274), and Roger Bacon (d. 694/1294) all repeatedly mentioned the name of the author of the "Intentions of the Philosophers" along with ibn Sina and ibn Rushd as the true representatives of Arab Aristotelianism.

But never did Arab Aristotelianism find a more vigorous foe than al-Ghazali. His compendium in philosophy was merely propaedeutic to his Tah?fut al-Falasifah (The Incoherence of the Philosophers) in which he levelled a devastating attack on the doctrine of the Muslim Peripatetics with a dialectic as subtle as any in the history of philosophy. Al-Ghazali, for the purposes of his scrutiny, divided the philosophers into three main groups: The materialists (dahriyyun), the naturalists or the deists (tabi'iyyun), and the theists (il?hiyyun). The materialists completely dispensed with the idea of God and believed that the universe has existed eternally without a creator: a self-subsisting system that operates and develops by itself, has its own laws, and can be understood by itself. The naturalists or the deists, struck by the wonders of creation and informed of a running purpose and wisdom in the scheme of things while engaged in their manifold researches into the sciences of phenomena, admitted the existence of a wise Creator or Deity, but rejected the spirituality and immortality of the human soul. They explained the soul away in naturalistic terms as an epiphenomenona {593} of the body and believed that the death of the latter led to the complete non-existence of the former. Belief in heaven, hell, resurrection, and judgment they considered as old wives' tales or pious fictions.

Al-Ghazali discussed the theists at length for they, according to him, held a comparatively more final position and exposed the defects of the materialists and the naturalists quite effectively, thus saving him from doing so for himself. Socrates, Plato, and Aristotle he listed as theists but concentrated on Aristotle who had criticized all his predecessors and even had refuted his own teacher, excusing himself of this by saying:

"Plato is dear to us. And truth is dear, too. Nay, truth is dearer than Plato."

As far as the transmission of Aristotle's philosophy in Arabic was concerned, al-Ghazali found that none of the Muslim philosophers had accomplished anything comparable to the achievements of al-Farabi and ibn Sina. These two were Aristotle's most faithful and capable translators and commentators; the works of others were marked with disorder and confusion. Thus al-Ghazali came finally to concentrate on that philosophical thought of his day which had emerged from the writings of these two theistic philosophers (particularly ibn Sina) and applied himself to its examination in a systematic manner. He divided the philosophical sciences into mathematics, logic, physics, politics, ethics, and metaphysics, and went into their details in order to see if there really was anything false or untenable. He was most scientific in his approach: ready to accept whatever he found to be based on the evidence of factual data or susceptible of proof by argument in conformity with the principles of reason.

He had least hesitation in accepting as true much of what the philosophers taught with regard to their sciences of mathematics, logic, and physics; he even had no serious quarrel with them in the spheres of politics and ethics. The most grievous errors of the theistic philosophers, he found, consisted in their metaphysical views which, unlike mathematical and natural sciences, were not grounded in compelling reason or positive inquiry but on conjecture and fanciful speculations. Had their metaphysics been so very well grounded in sound reasoning as their mathematical sciences were, they would have agreed amongst themselves on metaphysical issues as they did on the mathematical ones. But, above all, what al-Ghazali saw to his dismay was that the philosophies of al-Farabi and ibn Sins, at points did violence without any philosophic warrant or justification to the principles of religion as enunciated in the Quran.

His empirical and theological spirit revolted very strongly against this. The positive facts of religion could not be sacrificed for sheer metaphysical speculations, nor could they be interpreted externally from the point of view of a preconceived system of philosophy. These had to be interpreted intrinsically and reckoned on their own grounds. The Muslim philosophers had failed to take this empirical standpoint. They had also been slow in realizing that notwithstanding a great breadth of outlook that the {594} study of Greek philosophy had brought to the Muslims, there was in the ultimate analysis quite a gulf between the inspiration of the Quranic teachings and the spirit of Hellenism. Carried away by their enthusiasm to bring a reconciliation between philosophy and religion, al-Farabi and ibn Sina, according to al-Ghazali, had so compressed the dogmas of Islamic religion within the moulds of Aristotelian and Plotinian systems as to fall either into a morass of inconsistencies or get implicated into heretical positions.

All this al-Ghazali brought out with most accomplished understanding and admirable skill, and with a "transcendental" dialectic as subtle as that of Kant's in his Tah?fut al-Falasifah which indeed is the most important of all his works from the point of view of our present study. Within less than a hundred years it called forth the most stimulating rejoinder (entitled Tah?fut al-Tah?fut) from the celebrated ibn Rushd and then a rejoinder of a rejoinder from Muslih al-Din Mustafa ibn Yusuf al-Bursawi generally known as Khwajah Zadah, a Turkish theologian who died in 893/1488. These works, particularly the first two, taken together epitomize the essential problems arising from the impact of classical philosophy on the teachings of religion.

Method and Problems of Tahfut: It is generally believed that al-Ghazali wrote his Tah?fut al-Fal?sifah during the period of his doubts, but in fact the work is essentially of a polemical nature and shows in him an odd combination of scepticism and ecstatic assurances. The general effect of the teaching of the philosophers, al-Ghazali felt, was so ruinous to the religious and moral life of the masses that his well-nigh apostolic humanism revolted against it and he dedicated himself to an open warfare against the philosophers. There is no doubt about the theological inspiration and the polemical spirit of the Tah?fut but then we add most emphatically that neither of them seriously affects the great philosophical value of this work. The modern reader cannot fail to be struck with clear anticipations of Hume (d. 1190/1776), Schleiermacher (d. 1250/1834), Ritschl (d. 1307/ 1889), and others, and even of the logical positivists of our day in some of the arguments and the general motif of the Tah?fut. His general position may be briefly described to be that the truths {595} of the positive facts of religion can neither be proved nor disproved, and to do otherwise leads the philosophers to take more often than not quite nonsensical positions.

Al-Ghazali assails the philosophers on twenty points (beginning with creation and ending with the last things) and endeavours to show that their dogmas of the eternity and the everlastingness of the world are false; their assertion that God is the creator of the world is dishonest for it is flagrantly inconsistent with their dogma of the eternity of the world; that they fail to prove the existence, the unity, the simplicity and the incorporeality of God or God's knowledge either of the universals or of the particulars; that their views with regard to the souls of the celestial spheres, and the spheres' knowledge of the particulars and the purpose of their movement are unfounded; that their theory of causation which attributes effects to the very nature of the causes is false; and that they cannot establish the spirituality of the soul, nor prove its immortality; and, finally, that their denial of the resurrection of the bodies in the life hereafter is philosophically unwarranted. Al-Ghazali charges the philosophers with infidelity on three counts, viz.,

(1) eternity of the world;

(2) denial of God's knowledge of the particulars, and

(3) denial of bodily resurrection.

For the rest their views are heretical or born of religious indifference. But in all they are involved in contradictions and suffer from confusion of thought.

The problem which al-Ghazali considers the most important is that of the eternity (qidam) of the world to which he allots the greatest space, almost a quarter of his book. This has been one of the most challenging and uncompromising problems in the conflict between religion and philosophy. The advocates of orthodoxy considered the eternality of the universe to be the most pernicious thesis of the philosophers and vehemently combated against it. Al-Ash'ari (d. 324/935) wrote a refutation of it in his Kitab al-Fusul which probably is the earliest scholastic treatise dealing with this question, and ibn Hazm (d. 457/1064) made the doctrine a dividing line between the orthodox and the heterodox sects. The orthodox could not possibly concede the philosophers' claim of the eternality of the world, for with them there is nothing eternal but God; all else is created (hadith).

To make anything co-eternal with God is to violate the strict principle of monotheism, for that infringes the absoluteness and infinity of God and reduces Him to the position of an artificer: a Demiurge. Virtually, the doctrine drives one to the materialists' position that the world is an independent universe, a self-subsistent system, which develops by itself, and can be understood by itself. All this was hard to swallow for a theologian like al-Ghazali.

The philosophers like al-Farabi and ibn Sina as Muslims did not deny that {596} God is an eternal creator of the universe, but as true Aristotelians believed that God's activity consists merely in bringing forth in the state of actuality the virtual possibilities inherent in the prime matter which was alleged to be co-eternal with Him. This was in conformity with the Aristotelian notion of change not as a passage from non-being into being, which would make it unintelligible, but as a process by which what is merely "potential being" passes over, through "form," into "actual being." So God as an eternal creator constantly combines matter with new forms; He did not create the universe out of sheer nothingness at a definite time in the past. As a corollary they believed in the infinity of time.

Al-Ghazali, on the other hand, in accordance with the obvious teachings of the Quran, firmly holds the position that the world was created by God out of absolute nothingness at a certain moment in the past which is at a finite interval from the present. He created not only forms but also matter and time along with them which had a definite beginning and hence is finite.

The two positions as outlined above readily remind one of Kant's thesis and antithesis in the first antinomy which present an impossible problem in the sense that conditions requisite for their verification or falsification are de facto impossible. One is tempted to say that al-Ghazali does recognize the impossibility of the problem for he clearly proclaims that he does not intend to defend his own position but only to refute that of the philosophers. This is true in general of all the other disputations in Tah?fut al-Fal?sifah. The arguments of the philosophers are presented with very considerable plausibility, but the dialectical skill and philosophical acumen which al-Ghazali employs to refute them are also overwhelming. Though the whole discussion is surcharged with a polemical spirit, yet one cannot fail to see that al-Ghazali's standpoint throughout remains highly scientific and logical; he does not succumb merely to verbal quibbles. He clearly says that he does not have any quarrel with the philosophers on the usages of terms.

Al-Ghazali's quarrel with the philosophers is because many of their particular arguments are logically false and the various positions that they take in their system as a whole are inconsistent with one another, but, above all, because some of their basic assumptions are unfounded. These assumptions, al-Ghazali proves most powerfully, can neither be demonstrated logically, nor are they self-evident through "intuition." Such, for example, is the assumption that every event has a cause or that causes produce their effects necessarily.

The {597} Muslim philosophers have accepted these assumptions merely in the dogmatic tradition of Aristotelian philosophy. The faulty reasonings of the philosophers or the inconsistencies in their positions are remediable but not so the uncritical acceptance of their assumptions. Al-Ghazali for himself is not prepared to accept any part of the Aristotelian system except the first principles of logic and rules of syllogism-nothing else until and unless it has logical coerciveness about it. On the other hand, he is not prepared to reject any of the doctrines of religion until and unless it is disproved with a similar logical rigour and cogency. Nothing is "possible" in philosophy till it is logically necessary, and nothing is "impossible" in religion till it is logically self-contradictory.

Apparently, this is a double-faced criterion to judge variously the truths of philosophic assumptions and those of religious assumptions, but from the point of view of philosophy of religion it is perfectly justified. Philosopher qua philosopher has to accept the facts of religion as given by religion; this is the sine qua non of any empirical philosophy of religion. Thus, in spite of the fact that al-Ghazali's whole polemic against the philosophers derives its inspiration from the Asst `arite theology, his method remains in its essentials purely philosophical, fulfilling in its own way some of the most important requirements of the modern and even contemporary approaches to the problems of the philosophy of religion.

These few observations with regard to al-Ghazali's method in the Tah?fut were necessary before we could enter into some of the detailed arguments which he gives in the refutation of the philoapphera' various positions.

Eternity of the World: The proof of the philosophers for the eternity of the world starts with certain assumptions with regard to the notions of cause and will. These they take to be true axiomatically: (1) Every effect has a cause. (2) Cause must be the action of some external force other than the effect. (3) Cause or an act of will when executed must immediately lead to the effeet. For world's coming from non-existence to existence there certainly should have been some cause; this cause could not be a physical cause for ex hypothe-si none yet existed. If this cause arose from an act of will by God at some specific time, then the divine will itself should have been determined by some other cause. This cause which led God to change His mind should certainly be outside His mind; but again this was not possible, for nothing outside Him yet existed. Thus, one is forced to conclude that either nothing ever arose from the being of God-which is not true, for the world does existor that the world must have been in existence from all eternity, as an immediate effect of His eternal will.

Al-Ghazali declines to subscribe to any one of the assumptions as stated {598} above and shows that belief in the origination of the world from the eternal will of God at a specific moment of time as chosen by Him involves no violation of the fundamental principles of logic. The assumptions of the philosophers, that every effect has a cause and that a cause is a force external to its effect, do not have a logical coerciveness about them. It is quite legitimate to believe that God's will does not have any cause or at least that this cause does not lie outside His will but in itself. Similarly, it is not logically necessary that the effect should follow a cause immediately, for it is not logically contradictory to hold the notion of "a delayed effect." It is possible to think that God's will is eternal and yet an object of that will has occurred at some period in time. Here a distinction should be made between the eternity of God's will and the eternity of the object of His will. God, for example, can eternally will that Socrates and Plato should be born at such and such a time and that the one should be born before the other. Hence it is not logically illegitimate to affirm the orthodox belief that God eternally willed that the world should come into being at such and such a definite moment in time.

But the philosophers point out a real difficulty here. According to them, it is impossible to find out a differentiating principle for God's eternal choice of a particular moment for the creation of the world. All moments of time are completely similar; how is it possible to choose between two completely similar things? Why, in short, was the world not created earlier or later than when it was created? One of the answers to this is that there arises no question of world's being created earlier or later, for time yet was not; time too was created along with the creation of the world, i. e., both world and time are finite in duration. Al-Ghazali adds further that should one assume with the philosophers that time is infinite, then at any present moment that infinite time has been brought to an end and a time that has an end is not infinite but finite. It is noteworthy that this is exactly the argument given by Kant in the thesis of his first antinomy.

Al-Ghazali's real standpoint, however, is that God just arbitrarily chose one particular moment rather than another for world's coming into being. We need ask no more about this choice, for God's will is completely undetermined. His will does not depend upon distinctions in the outside world, for it is itself the producer of all the distinctions therein. This creating of the distinctions in fact is the true significance of God's will. God chooses a particular moment for the creation of the universe as He chooses a particular direction for the movement of the spheres of the (Ptolemaic) heaven, in some cases from east to west, in others from west to east (as described in the Aristotelian astronomy) even when the reversal of directions would have made no difference. There is no way to explain God's choice either in one case or the other.

The difficulty posed by the philosophers arises because of their misguided attempt to understand the nature of divine will altogether in the terms of man's will. Certainly, God's will is not like man's, as God's knowledge is not like man's knowledge. So far as God's knowledge is concerned, the {599} philosophers avowedly admit that it differs from man's knowledge in so many respects that in their final position it becomes indeed an inexplicable mystery. God, according to them, possesses the knowledge of all the universals without this knowledge necessitating plurality, without its being additional to His essence, and without its multiplying in proportion to the multiplicity of the objects known. Some of them assert after Aristotle that God is the knower, the knowledge, and the known, and that the three are one. Should we judge all this by what applies to man's knowledge, it will be found to be an utter impossibility. While the philosophers admit that God's knowledge cannot be compared with man's knowledge, they insist upon drawing a comparison between God's will and man's will. This is exactly what al-Ghazali calls the incoherence of the philosophers and, according to him, their thought-system taken as a whole reveals quite a number of such incoherences. Indeed, the philosophers' very notion of eternal creation is self-contradictory and meaningless. Is it sense to speak of a creation of that which exists eternally? If God and the prime matter are both eternal existents, does it make sense to say that one is the cause of the other? Can the relation between two existents qua existents be regarded as a causal one?

Further, the philosophers put different constructions upon their notions of space and time. They assume time to be infinite and space to be finite, and yet consider time to be co-implicant of movement in space. Al-Ghazali insists rightly that one who believes in the finitude of space must in consistency assume the existence of finite time, particularly when one holds the Aristotelian position that space, time, and movement in space are all related to one another. And if they insist that it is impossible to think of empty space, they should equally realize that it is impossible to conceive of an empty time.

These are just a few of the inconsistencies of the philosophers pointed out by al-Ghazali in the course of his disputation with regard to the eternity of the world and they could be mentioned here only very briefly, considering the space at our disposal. One further point of criticism may, however, be added for its importance in the history of modern philosophy. Prior to its origination, the philosophers hold, the world must have either been possible (mumkin), or impossible (mumtani'), or necessary (wajib). It is impossible that it should have been impossible; for that which is impossible in itself is never brought into existence. Again, it is impossible for it to have been necessary in itself, for that which is necessary in itself is never deprived of existence. It follows then that the existence of the world must have always been possible in itself, otherwise it would never have come to be. This possibility cannot inhere in possibility itself, nor in the agent, nor in no-substratum, for the possible is that which is in the process of becoming actual. Hence the subject of possibility is some substratum which is susceptible of possibility, and this is matter. Now, this matter cannot be considered to have been originated. If it had been originated, the possibility of its existence would have preceded its {600} existence. In that case possibility would have existed in itself, but possibility existing in itself is unintelligible. Hence matter is eternal and it is only the passing over of the forms to matter which is originated.

In rebutting this highly sophisticated argument of the philosophers al-Ghazali points out in Kantian fashion that possibility like impossibility is a purely subjective notion to which nothing need correspond in reality. If possibility requires an existent to correspond to it, so would impossibility require something to correspond to it, but avowedly there is no existing thing in concrete reality to which impossibility may be referred. Hence possibility like impossibility is merely a concept; the assumption of an existing substratum to which this concept may be related is to have a metaphysical jump from mere thought to actual existence and is to commit as we understand now an ontological fallacy.

Theory of Emanation: The entire argument of the philosophers with regard to the eternity of the world is, thus, full of contradictions and unproved assumptions, but the most manifest of their inconsistencies and the sheer baselesaness of their assumptions become signally conspicuous when they come to explain the origination of the world from the being of God in the terms of the Plotinian Theory of Emanation. Plotinus considers the world to be a necessary outflow from the being of God like light from the sun or better as Spinoza described it later like the properties of a triangle from a triangle. Muslim philosophers' subscription to this view according to al-Ghazali is the clearest evidence that their verbal avowal of creation is a mere dissimulation and duplicity. The problem of emanation with the philosophers, however, arises because of their over-emphasis on the abstract unity and absolute perfection of God. Creation through an act of volition implies both will and knowledge, and these cannot be predicated of God as attributes apart from His essence without doing violence to His absolute unity. Further, both will and knowledge are limitations: will in particular implies a deficiency in a being who wills, for it means that he desires or wants to have that which he lacks. Hence the philosophers elaborated an ingenious theory of emanation which contrives to erect a cosmological staircase between the stable stillness of God's unity and the changing and varied multiplicity of the world. This staircase is constituted of a finely graded series of intelligences and souls of celestial spheres, each emanating from the other in an hierarchical fashion. The view that the celestial spheres are perfect and have souls and intelligences superior to that of man had the overwhelming authority of Aristotle and further it was possible and even fascinating to conceive of them in terms of angels as described by the theologians.{601}

The emanationism of the Muslim philosophers in the final analysis worked under two governing principles: First, it is not thinkable that from God who is a pure unity anything could proceed except that which is itself a unity. This gave rise to the formula: from one only one can follow. Secondly, being has two aspects: it is either necessary (wajib) or possible (mumkin); it is either essence or existence. In the case of God alone are essence and existence identical; in all other beings essence is separate from existence. From this it follows that all things are possible by their essence, and they become necessary by the existence given to them by God.

The first emanation from the existence of the First Principle (al-mabda' al-awwal), the Necessary Being, i. e., God, is the first intelligence which is numerically one. Its existence is possible in itself and necessary through the First Principle; further, it knows its own essence as well as the essence of the First Principle. From its twofold existence and two-fold knowledge springs a multiplicity of knowledge and existence.

The first intelligence, in fact, has three kinds of knowledge: of the First Principle, of its own essence in so far as it is necessary, and of its possible being. One might ask: What is the source of this three-foldness in the first intelligence when the principle from which it emanates is one?

The answer is: From the First Principle only one proceeds, i.e., the essence of the first intelligence by which it knows itself. Now, its knowledge of its principle is evidently necessary, although this necessity is not derived from that principle. Again, being possible in itself the first intelligence cannot owe its possibility to the First Principle but possesses it in its own self. Though only one should proceed from one, yet it is possible that the first effect may come to possess not from the First Principle but by itself certain necessary qualities which express some relation or negation of relation and give rise to plurality. Thus, from the three kinds of knowledge possessed by the first intelligence emanate three beings, but only one from each kind.

As it knows its principle there proceeds from it a second intelligence; as it knows its essence there proceeds from it the first soul of the highest sphere (which is the ninth heaven); and as it knows itself as possible in itself there proceeds from it the body of that sphere. In a similar fashion from the second intelligence emanates the third intelligence, the soul of the stellar sphere and the body of that sphere. From the third intelligence emanates the fourth intelligence, the soul of the sphere of Saturn and the body of that sphere. From the fourth intelligence emanates the fifth intelligence, the soul of the sphere of Jupiter and the body of that sphere. Now there are, according to the then current Ptolemaic system, only nine celestial spheres in all including the sphere of the fixed stars all in concentric circles with earth in the centre. So, starting from the First Principle the emanations proceed on till the last or the tenth intelligence appears and {602} with it the last sphere of the moon and its soul. The tenth intelligence, also called the active intellect, acts in our world. It produces the first matter which is passive and formless but which is the basis of the four elements from which all creatures arise.

The composition and decomposition of the elements is the cause of generation and corruption of all bodies. But all these transformations take place under the influence of the movement of the spheres. As the active intellect is the producer of matter, so it is the dispenser of forms, dator formarum. It gives to each matter its proper form and it also gives each body a soul (which in fact is its form) when that body is ready to receive it. Thus, active intellect is also the source of the existence of the human souls. But the human soul does not feel at home in its physical abode and yearns for nothing less than the First Principle Himself. Hence it starts its spiritual journey back to the original source traversing through the various stages of the intelligences of the spheres. This is a rounded though brief description of the emanationistic world-view so enthusiastically elaborated by the Muslim philosophers, by ibn Sina, for example, in both of his major works on philosophy, viz., Kitab al-Shifa and Kitab al-Najat and by al-Farabi in his al-Madanat al-Faailah.

Determinism implicit in this emanationistic world-view is so opposed to the theistic voluntarism of the Ash?arite world-view that al-Ghazali launches the moat vehement attack against it. His strictures against this grand cosmological construction made out of so many various foreign imported ideas are the strongest and the bitterest of all others that may be found in the entire Tah?fut. All this, he inveighs, is arbitrary reasoning, idle speculation; a wild guess work; darkness piled upon darkness. If someone says he saw things of this kind in a dream, it would be inferred that he was suffering from some disease. Even an insane person could not rest satisfied with such postulates. In our own times, to say nothing of the scientists, F. R. Tennant who may be described as an eminent "religious positivist" holds the theory of emanation more or leas in the same estimation.

Al-Ghazali's criticism of the emanatiorustic argument consists in showing, on the one hand, that it fails to account for the multiplicity and composition in {603} the universe and, on the other, that it does not at all succeed in safeguarding the absolute unity of God. If the formula ever so glibly repeated that from one only one proceeds should be observed strictly logically, then all the beings in the world would be units, each of which would be an effect of some other unit above it, as it would be the cause of some other unit below it in a linear fashion. But in fact this is not the case. Every object, according to the philosophers themselves, is composed at least of form and matter. How does a composite thing such as a body then come into existence? Does it have only one cause?

If the answer is in the affirmative, then the assertion that only one proceeds from one becomes null and void. If, on the other hand, a composite thing has a composite cause, then the same question will be repeated in the case of this cause so on and so forth till one arrives at a point where the compound necessarily meets the simple. This contact between the compound effect and the unitary cause wherever it occurs would falsify the principle that only one proceeds from one. Now, strictly speaking, all the existents in the universe are characterized by composition and only the First Principle, i. e., God, alone can be said to possess true simplicity or unity, for in Him alone there is the complete identity of essence and existence. This would lead us necessarily to the conclusion that either the principle of "only one from one" fails to account for the composition and multiplicity which is apparent in the universe or that even God does not possess a genuine unity. But the philosophers cloak the issue with their artificial subtleties and the grandiose constructions they put upon their emanationistic foundations.

What earthly and even unearthly relation is there, al-Ghazali questions rightly, between the first intelligence's having a possible existence and the body of the sphere of the second intelligence which is supposed to proceed from it? Neither logic nor experience can substantiate this wild supposition and as such it is no more than pure nonsense. Further, how is it possible that from two kinds of knowledge of the first intelligence, that is, knowledge of the First Principle and that of itself, should arise two kinds of existence, first, that of the second intelligence and, second, that of the soul of the highest sphere? How can the knowledge of a thing lead to the existence of a thing (as we would now put it after Kant) without committing an obvious ontological fallacy? How can the knower emanate from the knowing, al-Ghazali rightly wonders, as does F. R. Tennant, and like him deplores that of all the people, philosophers should believe in such mythical nonsense.

Even if the triplicity with which the philosophers characterize the first intelligence should be taken for granted (which indeed cannot be done) it fails to account for all that they want to deduce from it. The body of the highest sphere, which according to them proceeds only from one aspect of the essence of the first intelligence, is surely not unitary in nature but composite and that in three ways. {604} First, as stated above, it is composed of form and matter, as indeed all bodies are according to the philosophers' own admission. True, form and matter always exist conjointly in all bodies, yet they are so different from each other that one cannot be the cause of the other. Hence, form and matter of the body of the highest sphere require two principles for their existence and not one. A unitary aspect of the three-fold character of the first intelligence fails to account for it.

Secondly, the body of this sphere has a definite size. Its having a definite size is something additional to the bare fact of its existence. Certainly, it could have come into existence with a different size, bigger or smaller than what it is. Hence, over and above that which necessitated the existence of the body of the sphere, there should be an additional cause to account for the adoption of this particular size.

Thirdly, in the highest heaven, there are marked out two points as its poles, which are fixed. This fact was admitted by the philosophers in accordance with the Aristotelian astronomy. Now, either all the parts of the highest sphere are similar in which case it is impossible to explain why two points should be chosen in perference to all the others as its poles; or they are different, some of them possessing properties which are not possessed by the others. Hence, we require yet another aspect in the first intelligence to be the cause for differences in the various parts of the highest sphere which differences alone would justify the choice of two points therein to be the poles.

In view of what has been stated above, it is sheer "ignorance" on the part of the philosophers to hold that the body of the highest sphere has emanated only from one aspect of the essence of first intelligence. Either the principle that only one proceeds from one is true, in which case the first intelligence which is not a mere triplicity but a whole multiplicity remains unexplained, or this principle is an empty formula signifying nothing, and, thus, making it possible that "many may proceed from one." In the latter case the infinite variety and plurality of the world can be directly derived from the unity of God and there is no need to erect an emanationistic staircase between Him and the world.

The above principle certainly collapses when we come to the second intelligence, for it is supposed to be, in one of its aspects, the cause of the sphere of the fixed stars. These are twelve hundred or so (according to the then Greek or Arab astronomers' reekoning) and are different in magnitude, shape, position, colour, and in respect of their special function in nature, etc. Each one of these factors in every single star needs a separate cause as its {605} determinant (murajjih). All this necessitates a bewildering multiplicity in the second intelligence and also indirectly presupposes the same in the first intelligence in so far as the latter is the emanative cause of the former.

Should the above arguments fail to convince the philosophers, there is another way to show that the first intelligence is more than a mere triplicity. Is the self-knowledge of the first intelligence identical with its essence or other than it? It is not possible that it should be identical, for knowledge is not the same thing as that which is known. Hence, the first intelligence is not a triplicity but a quadruplicity, to wit: its essence, its knowledge of itself, its knowledge of the First Principle, and its being a possible existent by itself. To all these four aspects there can be added yet another, namely, its being a necessary being whose necessity is derived from an external cause. All this proves that the first intelligence has five aspects and not three, as arbitrarily assumed by the philosophers. Whether the first intelligence has five aspects or three, it certainly is not of purely unitary character according to the philosophers' own admission. This shows that there is something in the effect which is not present in the cause, i. e., the First Principle, and this is scandalous.

Not only does the formula that only one proceeds from one become shamefacedly invalid right at the outset, but further, according to al-Ghazali, the entire emanationistic line of argument does great violence to the concept of God's unity and, thus, nullifies the very purpose for which it is adopted. There is no reason, according to him, that the very arguments which the philosophers advance to establish the triple character of the first intelligence should not be applied to God Himself. One of the aspects of plurality in the first intelligence according to the philosophers is its being a possible existent by itself. It may be asked: Is its being possible identical with its existence or other than it? If it is identical, no plurality would arise from it. If it is other than its existence, then why should it not be possible to say that there is as much plurality in the First Principle, i. e., God Himself, for He not only has existence but is necessary in His existence ? The necessity of existence as such is other than existence itself. In truth, existence may be considered to be a generic concept divided into necessary and possible. If one specific difference is an addition to existence per se in one case, it should be considered so in the other also. If the philosophers insist that the possibility of existence is other than existence in the case of the first intelligence, through the same argument they should admit that necessity of existence is different from existence in the case of the First Principle. Similarly, al-Ghazali asks: Is the first intelligence's knowledge of its principle identical with its existence and with its knowledge of itself or other than the two ? If it is identical, then there will be no plurality in its nature. But if it is other than the two, then such a plurality exists also in the First Principle, for He too knows Himself as well as what is other than Himself. Thus, al-Ghazali contends that either there can be no plurality in the first intelligence or if it is there, then it is for the same reasons in the First Principle too, and, therefore, the beings characterized by diversity and plurality {606} would directly proceed from Him. Al-Ghazali forces this conclusion upon the philosophers through their own logic.

For himself al-Ghazali believes that: "The First Principle is an omnipotent and willing agent; He does what He wills, and ordains as He likes, and He creates the similar and dissimilar things alike, whenever and in whatever manner He wills? The impossibility of such a belief is neither a self-evident truth, nor a matter of inferential knowledge." 8 Al-Ghazali frankly and rightly confesses that the problem of God's relation with the universe in the final analysis remains ever beyond the comprehension of human understanding. The inquiry into the manner in which the world proceeded from God's will, he urges, is "an idle and aimless venture." The modus operandi of God's creative activity is wholly inexplicable and this inexplicability is inevitable; indeed, if it were explicable, it would not be "creative." Explanation in all its forms establishes some connection or similarity with what is experienced, whereas God's creativity is an activity through which the experients and what is experienced by them come to be. How can human comprehension envisage the mode of God's act of creation when it is itself the creature of that act?

The philosophers try to avoid the charge of plurality with regard to the First Principle so far as His knowledge is concerned by affirming that the First Principle does not know anything other than Himself and that His self-knowledge is the same thing as His essence; so the knowledge, the knower, and the object of knowledge are all one in Him. This indeed was originally the position of Aristotle according to whom God is describable as thought thinking itself. In Aristotle's own words, `... it must be itself that thought thinks, and its thinking is thinking on thinking." This view of God as reflective thought, reflective in the literal sense of turning back upon itself, has been subjected to severe criticism by al-Ghazali. According to him, self-knowledge of a literal and direct sort is An impossibility.

He argues with Plotinus that self-knowledge even in the case of God implies an epistemological subject-object dualism and, therefore, would impede the philosophers' thesis of the absolute unity of the First Principle. Not only the Aristotelian conception of God as thought thinking thought does not absolve the philosophers from introducing plurality in the First Principle, but further lends them into many more difficulties with regard to their emanationistic world-view. Consider, for example, the relative positions of the First Principle and the first intelligence in terms of their knowledge. The First Principle which is the emanative cause of the first intelligence does not know anything other than Himself, whereas the latter knows not only its cause but further knows itself and the three {607} effects which proceed from it, viz., the second intelligence, the soul of the highest sphere, and the body of that sphere.

It is a strange theory, al-Ghazali observes, which makes the effect have the knowledge of its cause but not the cause of its effect. The necessity of a cause possessing the knowledge of its effect is more compelling than the necessity of an effect possessing the knowledge of its cause. In fact, the philosophers make the first intelligence superior to and "nobler" than the

First Principle in so far as from the First Principle only one thing proceeds, while from the first intelligence three things proceed. Further, the First Principle does not know what prodeeds from Him; in fact, He does not know anything other than Himself, while the first intelligence knows itself, its cause, and its three effects. Al-Ghazali feels so bitter at the Aristotelian conception of God as thought thinking itself that he goes to the length of saying that the philosophers by limiting God's knowledge to the sphere of self-knowledge virtually reduce Him to the status of the dead.

God's Knowledge of the Particulars: Al-Ghazali is very emphatic and uncompromising with regard to the all-circumscribing knowledge of God: "God knows the creeping of the black ant upon the rugged rock in a dark night, and He perceives the movement of the mote in the midst of the air." Ibn Sina also subscribes to the view that God knows everything: "Nothing, not even as much as a particle of dust in the heavens or on the earth, remains hidden from His knowledge." Yet, interestingly enough, al-Ghazali does not hesitate to level a charge of infidelity against him on this score for, according to ibn Sina, though God knows all the particulars, He knows them only in a universal way. This means that God cannot have the perceptual knowledge of particular things but knows them by way of a universal knowledge. Ibn Sina realizes the difficulty of his position and so adds that the understanding of it needs great intellectual subtlety.

The reasons that he advances to deny perceptual knowledge to God are fully recognized by al-Ghazali. Perceptual knowledge is characterized both temporally and spatially, whereas God is above both time and space and so it is not possible to ascribe perceptual knowledge to Him. A particular event occurs at a particular moment of time and suffers change with the passage of time. Change in the object of perception implies a change in the content of perception itself which obviously leads to change in the subject of perception, i.e., in the percipient himself. But change in God is unthinkable; therefore, perception of a particular event is not {608} possible for Him. Similarly, to distinguish between one particular object and another in space is possible only through the senses and implies a special relation of a sensible thing to the percipient as being near to or far from him or in a definite position, and this is impossible where God is concerned. Hence, it is not possible for God to have perceptual knowledge of the particulars. His knowledge can only be that which rises above the particular "nows" and the particular "heres," that is to say, is of conceptual or universal nature.

Ibn Sina's position as briefly outlined above seems to be very well grounded in sound reasoning and is quite understandable, yet, according to al-Ghazali, it is so pernicious to religion that it altogether demolishes the entire edifice of religious Law (hence his charge of infidelity). The theory implies that God cannot know any new state that emerges in John-He cannot know that John has becomes an infidel or a true believer, for He can know only the unbelief or the belief of man in general in a universal manner and not in specific relation to individuals.

Yes, God cannot know Muhammad's proclaiming himself a prophet at the time when he did. And the same will be true of every other prophet, for God only knows that among men there are some who claim prophecy, and that such and such are their attributes; but He cannot know a particular prophet as an individual, for that is to be known only by the senses. There certainly is a point in what al-Ghazali says here for it is really difficult to show any relation between the temporal and the timeless, yet the above criticism of his is a little wide of the mark for it is based on a misinterpretation of ibn Sina's position. By the statement that God does not have perceptual knowledge of the particulars, ibn Sina does not mean to say that God does not have the knowledge of the particulars or that His knowledge is restricted only to that of the universals or general concepts. Ibn Sina insists that God does have knowledge of the particulars; only this knowledge comes to Him not through sensuous perception but through intellectual perception, not from moment to moment but eternally.

Ibn Sina starts with the Aristotelian conception that God has only self-knowledge but adds emphatically that His self-knowledge necessarily implies knowledge of all the existent things in the universe in so far as He is the principal or the ultimate source of them all. There is not a single existent particular which does not proceed from Him directly or indirectly and the existence of which does not become in some way necessary through Him. The coming into existence of particular events and objects is due to the action and interaction of the various causes but ultimately all these have to be traced back to the First Cause. God, the First Cause, has the full prescience of the working of the various causes which originate from Him, and knows the effects produced by them and the time involved in their occurrence and recurrence.

Thus, God knows the particular events even when they occur to a single individual under specific conditions and at particular times in so far as they are fully explicable in terms of general laws and all-pervasive causal nexus. This may be illustrated with reference to an analogous human situation. An astronomer {609} who has full understanding of the general laws governing the movements of the heavenly bodies can, through his proper calculations, describe the various phenomena such as the particular eclipses and the conjunctions of the stars.

The analogy, however, though helpful, cannot be stretched to an identity, for, strictly speaking, there is nothing in our experience to compare with divine knowledge. Our knowledge is liable to error and is fragmentary, whereas God's knowledge is infallible and all-embracing, so much so that the whole universe is known to Him in one single congruous manifestation which is not affected by time.

God is immediately aware of the entire sweep of history regarded as an ordered string of specific events in an eternal now. Further, God not only knows but is also the very ground of the objects that He knows. The universe proceeds from the essence of God verily because of His knowledge of the universe: the ideal representation of the universal system is the very cause of its emanation. Had God not known the universe with all its concrete particularities, the universe would never have come into being. This indeed is a very original and quite ingenious theory with regard to God's knowledge of the particulars. Yet it is undoubtedly of highly speculative nature and so al-Ghazali is all out to bring quite an arsenal of criticism against it with a dialectical analyticity and rigour not incomparable to those of the logical positivists of our own day. He is not at all prepared to accept any of the assumptions of the philosophers until and unless they should either be atatable in the form of analytical propositions or be verifiable through some kind of intuitive experience.

The attribution of knowledge to God as it is, but particularly that of "the other," cannot go without jeopardizing to some extent at least His absolute unity and simplicity which otherwise are so much emphasized, rather over-emphasized by the philosophers. Above all, the theory, like any of its kind, fails to relate in any satisfactory manner the eternality of God's knowledge with the tranaciency of human experience, which relation indeed is the very crux of religious experience. And so far as it suffers from the presuppositions of the intellectualistic-deterministic world-view of the philosophers, al-Ghazali simply has no patience with it. For one, it suggests a block universe such as makes little allowance if any at all even for the exercise of God's will. These are just a few general remarks to indicate the mode and the various lines of al-Ghazali's arguments against the philosophers; they may now be substantiated and amplified by listing some of the actual points of his criticism.

The statement that God's self-knowledge necessarily implies the knowledge of all the existent particulars in the universe cannot be logically validated, nor can it be verified on the basis of any analogous human experience. God's self-knowledge and His knowledge of others do not have the relation of logical entailment, for it is possible to imagine the existence of the one without imagining the existence of the other at the same time. Looking to our own experience it would be wrong to claim that man's knowledge of what is other than himself is identical with his self-knowledge and with his essence.

It may be said that God does not know other things in the first intention {610} (al-wajh al-awwal) but that He knows His essence as the principle of the universe and from this His knowledge of the universe follows in the second intention (al-wayh al-thani), i. e., by way of a logical inference. Now, the statement of the philosophers that God knows Himself directly only as the principle of the universe, according to al-Ghazali, is as much an arbitrary assumption as the earlier statement and is exposed to exactly the same kind of criticism. According to the philosophers' own admission, it would suffice that God should know only His essence; the knowledge of His being the principle of the universe is additional to it and is not logically implicated in it. Just as it is possible for a man to know himself without knowing that he is "an effect of God" (for his being an effect is a relation to this cause), even so it is possible for God to know Himself without knowing that He is the principle cr cause.

The principle or cause is merely the relation that He bears to His effect, the universe. His knowledge of His relation to the universe is not by any means entailed by His knowledge of His own essence. Do not the philosophers themselves in their doctrine with regard to the attributes of God affirm the possibility only of negative or relational statements about God on the plea that negations or relations add nothing to His essence? The knowledge of the relation, therefore, cannot be identical with the knowledge of the essence. Hence the philosophers' assumption that God knows His essence and thereby also knows Himself as the principle of the universe, remains unproved logically and unverified experientially. Al-Ghazali raises many more points of criticism of a similar nature which fully bring out the "positivistic" and "analytic" thrusts in his thought. This type of criticism should have been sufficient with al-Ghazali, for it served his purpose of refuting the philosophers quite effectively, but his religious calling and persuasion impell him to launch many more attacks on the philosophers. They do not aim so much at the complete smashing of the philosophers' arguments as to bring out either inconsistencies in their various positions or more so the difficulties of a religious nature in accepting them.

Al-Ghazali fully appreciates the motive of the philosophers in elaborating their theory with regard to the nature of God's knowledge of the particulars, which is no other than that of safeguarding the immutability and the unity of God. Eliminating the factor of time or change altogether in God's knowledge, however, has difficulties of its own which will be noted presently, but there is another aspect of the philosophers' treatment of the problem of God's knowledge which lands them into a morass of contradictions and annuls the very purpose for which it is belaboured, i. e., that of establishing the unity of God. Granted that God's knowledge remains unaffected by change, for it rises above the distinction of "is," "was" and "will," yet how can God's knowledge remain unaffected by the multiplicity and diversity of the objects that He knows? How can it be claimed that knowledge remains unitary even {611} when the things known are unlimited in number and are different, for knowledge has to conform to the nature of the things known? If the change in the objects of cognition necessarily presupposes change in the subject, multiplicity and difference in the former presuppose the same in the latter.

"Would that I could understand," says al-Ghazali, "how an intelligent person can allow himself to disbelieve the oneness of the knowledge of a thing whose states are divisible into the Past, the Present, and the Future; while he would not disbelieve the oneness of knowledge which relates to all the different Genera and Species. Verily the difference and the disparity among the diverse Genera and Species is more marked than the difference which may actually be found to exist among the states of a thing divisible in accordance with the division of time. If that difference does not necessitate multiplicity and difference, how can this do so either?"

Though the philosophers ascribe omniscience and foreknowledge to God, they make His knowledge a sort of mirror which passively reflects in an eternal now the details of an already finished sequence of events just as we in a particular present moment have the memory of a fixed and inalterable sequence of past events. Thus, God's knowledge of time is restricted only to the relational aspect of time, i. e., that of the sequence of before and after or of earlier and later. There is, however, another aspect of time which typically characterizes the human experience and forms its very essence, namely, that of the ever-fleeting, ever-changing now. This is the time which is born afresh at every moment, the time in which the future is perpetually flowing through the present into the past. Now, according to the philosophers' thesis of God's knowledge as explained above, in God's eternal being there can be no counterpart of the experience of this living time in which we humans move and act.

God may know, for example, that my acts of religious devotion are subsequent to my religious conversion, but He cannot know now that I am acting or have acted in such and such a way. So God in His supra-temporal transcendence would remain impervious to my religious solicitations, for I am eternally doomed to the tyranny of this ever-fleeting, ever-trembling now. Should this be true and should I come to realize it, I may cry in despair: "Of what use is God to me!" Such is the catastrophe to which the philosophers' over-emphasis upon the eternality and changelessness of God's knowledge leads through its very incumbent logic.

The problem of the relation of the eternality of God to {612} the temporality of human experience is almost an impossible problem and the philosophers of all times have stumbled over it. It may be suggested, however, that God is transcendental to both time and change and yet in some mysterious way immanent in it. Viewed superficially, this seems to be an apparent logical contradiction, but, adds al-Ghazali, the philosophers dare not point this out for they themselves have affirmed with regard to their doctrine of the eternity of the world that the world is eternal and yet at the same time subject to change.

The statement that God not only knows the universe but, further, that this knowledge is the very ground and the cause of the universe, though very significant in itself, is made by the philosophers essentially within the framework of their deterministic-emanationistic world-view and as such, according to al-Ghazali, involves them into an embarrassing predicament. There is no sense in talking about the knowledge of an agent when his action is a "natural action" in the sense that it follows from him necessarily and is not the result of his volition. We do not say that knowledge of light possessed by the sun is the requisite condition for the emanation of light from the sun, and this in fact is the analogy which the philosophers have employed to explain the procession of the world from the being of God.

Further, according to them, the universe has not been produced by God all at once but has proceeded from Him through "the intermediaries and the other consequences and the consequences of those consequences all indirectly connected with these intermediaries." Even if it should be granted that the necessary procession of something from an agent requires the knowledge by him of that which proceeds, God's knowledge at best would be only that of the first intelligence and of nothing besides. That which proceeds from something which proceeds from God may not be necessarily known to Him.

Knowledge is not necessary in the case of the indirect consequences of volitional actions; how can it be so in the case of the indirect consequences of necessary actions? Thus, the assertion of the philosophers that God's knowledge is the very ground and cause of that which He knows loses its entire significance because of its moorings in the Plotinian scheme of emanationism.

Through a strange irony of logic the emanationistic argument of the philosophers, instead of building a staircase between God and the world, creates almost an unbridgeable gulf between the two. It certainly leads to the conclusion that God is directly related only to the first intelligence, i.e., the first item of the series of emanations between God and the world; on the other hand, the world is directly related only to the lowest end of that series. Further, the argument makes the world an independent and autonomous system, which can be understood by itself because of its insistence on an inexorable causal necessity such as pervades the entire scheme of things.

This conception of a through and through causally determined universe rooted in the {613} intellectual-emanationistic metaphysics of the philosophers was so radically different from his own dynamic-occasionalistic world-view grounded in the theistic-voluntaristic metaphysics of the Ash'arite tradition that al-Ghazali declared a complete parting of the way with them. Their world-view, al-Ghazali made it clear, militates particularly against the fundamental Islamic doctrine of God's providence and omnipotence, and leaves no possibility for the happening of miracles such as turning of a rod into a serpent, denaturing fire of its capacity to burn, revivification of the dead, splitting of the moon (all so clearly referred to in the Quran). There certainly is no scope for the exercise of God's freewill in a universe in which there is no real becoming and in which the future is already given in the present as its necessary effect. Nor, in view of the reign of the inexorable law of causal necessity in such a universe, is there any possibility for the miracles, except those which can be "naturalized" through scientific explanation.

Causality: Al-Ghazali's desire to vindicate the truth of the religious position mentioned above led him to make a highly critical and acute analysis of the philosophers' concept of causality. This analysis, which bears a strikingly close similarity to that of Hume's, brings out clearly the most remarkable originality and acumen of al-Ghazali's thought. The problem that engaged him at the outset of his inquiry with regard to the seventeenth disputation in the Tah?fut is the problem of the alleged necessity of the causal connection as maintained and insisted on by the philosophers. He challenges the validity of this necessity right as he opens the discussion. "In our view," he asserts, "the connection between what are believed to be cause and effect is not necessary." The reason that he offers for the justification of his position is that the relation between cause and effect is not that of logical entailment. The affirmation of the one does not imply the affirmation of the other, nor does the denial of the one imply the denial of the other. Neither the existence nor the non-existence of the one is necessarily presupposed by the existence or the non-existence of the other. The relation between quenching of thirst and drinking, satiety and eating, burning and fire, or light and sunrise, etc., is not a necessary relation, for in no case does the one term logically imply the other. There is nothing logically contradictory in assuming that fire may not burn, and drinking may not quench thirst, and so on.

The alleged necessity of the causal connection is not logically warranted because through no amount of logical reasoning can we deduce the effect from {614} the cause. At best it is based on observation or experience. We observe that objects succeed one another or that similar objects are constantly conjoined. Now, this proves succession, not causation, or conjunction, not connection, The fire which is an inanimate object has no power to produce the effect of burning; "observation shows only that one is with the other and not that it is by it," i. e., the effect happens with the cause and not through it (`indahu la bihi).

The notion of necessity is valid only in the case of logical relations such as identity, implication, disjunction, etc. In the sphere of mere natural relations necessity has no scope. In the order of nature, unlike the order of thought, we deal merely with the contingent and alogical entities which remain unrelated to each other except in the minds of the perceiver. Objects as such are not connected with one another; only the ideas of them get connected in our mind by association. The relation between fire and burning is not a necessary relation, for it does not belong to the realm of necessity but to that of possibility such as may happen or may not happen depending on the will of God.

"It is only," al-Ghazali enunciates clearly, "when something possible is repeated over and over again (so as to form the Norm), that its pursuance of a uniform course in accordance with the Norm in the past is indelibly impressed upon our minds." Thus, if there is any semblance of necessity in the order of natural relations such as that of cause and effect, it is merely because the two terms which in nature remain extrinsic to each other, through constant repetition become conjoined in our consciousness. Causal necessity is just the habit of our mind: it is merely a psychological necessity and not a logical necessity. The psychological necessity differs from logical necessity in this that its denial like the latter does not involve us in a logical impossibility. Hence the miracles, such as the fire not burning the body of Abraham when he was thrown into it, are not impossible to think. Al-Ghazali insists that the denial of miracles can be justified only when it should be proved that they are logically impossible and where such proof is not forthcoming their denial is sheer ignorance and obduracy.

It is interesting to note further that al-Ghazali, in the course of his discussion of the principle of causality and the possibility of miracles, comes close to propounding the notion of the composite nature of a cause and also that of plurality of causes. Cause he understands to be the sum total of many contributory factors, some of which are positive while others negative, and all of which have to be considered in conjunction. Take the case of a man seeing a coloured object: he should possess sound vision, he should open his eyes, there should be no obstruction between the eyes and the object of vision, the object should be a coloured one, the atmosphere should be not dark but have sufficient light, etc. Any one condition by itself cannot be taken to be a cause and a single negative condition such as the blindness of the {615} person or the darkness of atmosphere may make the cause non-operative though logically not impossible.

The relation of cause and effect is based on observation and observation as such does not rule out the possibility that the same effect might follow some cause other than the apparent one. Even where we recognize that there are many causes for the same effect, we cannot limit the number of causes just to those which we ourselves have observed. So there are many causes for the same effect and a cause is a sum total of many conditions. In view of this it is not possible to negate an effect on the negation of one particular cause but on the negation of all the various causes. This latter possibility, however, is emphatically discounted by al-Ghazali so far as we are concerned, for it presupposes a complete and exhaustive knowledge of all the causes and their conditions, which knowledge we humans can never come to possess. Moreover, causes by themselves are inert entities; will and action cannot be attributed to them. They act only through the power and agency of God. The only will is the absolutely free-will of God which works unconstrained by any extraneous law or incumbency except the self-imposed law of contradiction. Thus, the things to which God's power extends include mysterious and wonderful facts such as "elude the discernment of human sensibility." Indeed, God's power extends to all kinds of logical possibilities such as turning of a rod into a serpent, or the revivification of the dead. For the same reason it is not impossible for Him to bring about the resurrection of bodies in the life hereafter and all other things with regard to paradise and hell which have been mentioned in the Quran. To deny them is both illogical and irreligious. One may add that, according to al-Ghazali, not only all miracles are natural but also all nature is miraculous. Nature, however, seems to be pervaded by a causal nexus only because as a rule God does not choose to interrupt the continuity of events by a miracle; it is possible, however, that Ile might intervene at any moment that He deems fit. Such a standpoint may make one sceptical of the phenomena of nature, but it may equally lead one to an acute mystical sense of the presence of God to all things. Scepticism of this kind and mysticism need not always be antithetical-the former may as well lead to the latter. This indeed is said to have had happened in the case of al-Ghazali. {616}

11

MYSTICISM IN ISLAMIC PHILOSOPHY

INTRODUCTION

It will not be quite true to say that al-Ghazali's final resort to Sufi-mysticism was merely the result of his disillusionment with philosophy and dissatisfaction with scholastic theology. This is only a part of the truth; his own confessional statement to this effect in al-Munqidh seems to be rather an over-statement of the actual facts. Sufistic influences had all along been working upon his mind right from his early childhood. We need only recall that his father was a pious dervish and his guardian a Sufi devout, that in his youth he studied1 and even practised Sufism first under Yusuf al-Nassaj in Tus and then under al-Farmadhi at Nishapur and that his own brother Ahmad al-Ghazali (d. 520/1126) made a name as a great Sufi. It is not improbable that he should have also learnt of Sufism from his teacher Imam al-Haramain, for it is reported that the Imam himself had been the pupil of the renowned Sufi abu Nu'aim al-Isfahani (d. 430/1038). So al-Ghazali's eventual adoption of the Sufi way of life was in reality a continuation of these early influences and not simply the consequence of his failure to find the philosophical solution of theological problems.

Further, it has to be emphasized that, in spite of his explicit official denunciation of philosophy, al-Ghazali could never completely part company with it. His Sufi-mysticism was as much influenced by his thorough study of philosophy as by theology; in its final development it was the mysticism of a philosopher and a theologian. There is a marked note of Hellenic thought in his mystical doctrines and even the tracings of Neo-

Platonism, and yet paradoxical though it may seem they remain circumscribed within the limits of orthodoxy. His is surely a sober kind of mysticism carefully eschewing all kinds of pantheistic extravagances and severely criticizing the antinomian tendencies of the intoxicated Sufis.

On the one hand, he tried to make mysticism orthodox and, on the other, orthodoxy mystical. It is the mystical element in religion, he insisted, which is most vital and makes religious life a reality. Both to the philosophers {617} and the scholastic theologians he brought home the fact that the basis of all religious certainty is the first-hand living experience of God. He indeed did his best to vitalize the Law and the doctrine of Islam through this emphasis on the living religious experience, and this is evident from the very title of his magnum opus, Ihy?' `Ulum al-Din (Revivification of the Sciences of Religion). But the mystical teaching of al-Ghazali found in Ihy?', meant for all to read, must be studied in conjunction with what is given in his other works dealing more specially with the Sufi doctrine such as Mishkat al-Anwar, al-Ma'rif al-`Aqliyyah, Muk?shafat al-Qulab and the like.

The theory developed in these works represents what may be labelled as theosophical mysticism and this cannot be properly understood without reference to al-Ghazali's specific views about the nature of God and the human soul. From the point of view of our present study his mystical views with regard to God and soul may be profitably compared with those of the philosophers, i. e., al-Farabi, ibn Sina, and their followers.

GOD

The philosophers have particularly emphasized the absolute unity of God. No positive attributes can be ascribed to God for that leads to the subject-predicate dualism. Even existence can only be referred to Him. He is above all distinctions and above all the categories of thought. This overemphasis on unity shorn of all qualities reduces God to a mere contentless inanity. He becomes an ineffable, indescribable, impredicable something. Such is the result of the dialectic of the philosophers' monistic reductionism. As mentioned in the preceding chapter, some (if them, following Aristotle, have described God as thought thinking thought. That which He knows comes into being emanating from the over-effulgence of His Being, but He does not positively will anything, for willing implies a need-a deficiency. He recognizes only Himself or at best His first emanent, the first intelligence, and, thus, is purely transcendent to this world of change and multiplicity.

Like the philosophers, al-Ghazali lays stress on the unity of God: God is the sole-existent and the ultimate cause and ground of all being, the only self-subsisting reality. Yet He possesses the fullness of being, all the attributes mentioned in the Quran inhere in Him, only the modality of this inherence is rationally unknowable. We should, however, understand that all His attributes are spiritual. He is perfect goodness and perfect beauty: the supreme object of love. He is the light of lights, the eternal wisdom, the creative truth, but above all He is the eternal will.

To the philosophers God is primarily thought or intelligence, but to al-Ghazali He is primarily a will which is the cause of creation. "The First Principle," he says, "is an omnipotent and willing agent, He does what He wills, and ordains as He likes, and He creates the similar and dissimilar things alike, whenever and in whatever manner He wills." So Ultimate Reality is {618} essentially will. The entire choir of the heavens and the furniture of the earth are the direct work of God, produced out of sheer nothingness simply through His terrific "Be." God has created the universe through His will, sustains it through His will, and one day will let it pass away by His will. According to the philosophers, God wills the world because He thinks of it. According to al-Ghazali, "God has cognizance of the world because He wills it and in His willing it."

Like the philosophers, al-Ghazali also emphasizes the transcendent aspect of God. He is exalted beyond the limitations of space and time, for He is the creator of space and time. He was before time and space were. But He is also immanent in this apatio-temporal order; His eternal wisdom and supreme beauty manifest themselves through the wonders and glory of His creation. His eternal will is in action throughout the universe; it is in the swing of the sun and the moon and in the alternation of day and night. Everywhere around is the touch and working of God. Al-Ghazali's God is not the Absolute of the philosophers who is bleak and cold, but a personal God, a living

God. He desires intercourse with His creatures and makes it possible for them to enter into fellowship with Himself through prayer and contemplation and, above all, through the gift of mystical gnosis.

SOUL

The difference between al-Ghazali and the philosophers with regard to the nature of the soul is not so very well marked. He only insists, like Kant, that the philosophers through their rational arguments cannot give any conclusive proof for the spirituality, substantiality, unity, immortality, etc., of the human soul. His attack on the philosophers on this issue is as incisive and analytic as that of Kant but probably more violent. He actually smashes one by one all the ten arguments which he himself expounds as forcefully as they could be in favour of their thesis. Like Kant again, he does not disagree with their basic position but only with their method. He even joins the philosophers in their refutation of the position of some of the scholastic theologians, who maintained that the soul is a kind of subtle body or an accident and not a substance. What is more and rather strange, while determining the place of the soul in the realm of beings, al-Ghazali talks the very language of {619} the Neo-Platonic philosophers.

His cosmological triad of the divine world (`?lam al-malakat), the celestial world (`?lam al-jabrat), and the material, phenomenal world (`alam al-mulk w-al-shahadah) runs closely parallel to that of Plotinus consisting of the universal mind, the universal soul, and matter. Like Plotinus, he seems to vouchsafe that the human soul belongs to `?lam al-jabar?t, i.e., midway between the divine world and the material world, and so is neither purely eternal like the former nor merely temporal like the latter but partakes of them both.

Al-Ghazali's conception of the human soul, however, is essentially based on the teachings of the Quran and the Tradition. The interesting thing about this conception is that it runs parallel to his conception of God. Soul like God is a unity and like Him it is primarily and essentially a will. Further, as God is both transcendent to and immanent in the universe so is soul with reference to body. "Man is made in the image of God," is a saying of the Holy Prophet and it is twice stated in the Quran that "Allah breathed into man of His own spirit." The soul is a mirror illumined by the divine spark reflecting the qualities and even the essence of God. "Not only are man's attributes," says al-Ghazali, "a reflection of God's attributes but the mode of existence of man's soul affords an insight into God's mode of existence...." Knowledge of the self is the key to the knowledge of God, for so is the oftquoted tradition: "He who knows himself knows his Lord." "Both God and soul," al-Ghazali adds, "are invisible, indivisible, unconfined by space and time, and outside the categories of quantity and quality: nor can the ideas of shape, colour, or size attach to them...."

The soul of man is different from everything else in the sensuous world. There are two worlds: the world of command (amr) and the created world (khalq). Everything devoid of quantity and dimension belongs to the world of amr. Soul belongs to the world of amr also because it proceeds from the command of God: "Say, the spirit proceedeth at the command of my Lord"

12

INFLUENCE OF MUSLIM THOUGHT ON THE EAST

INTRODUCTION

Gibbon describes the rise and expansion of Islam as one of the most memorable revolutions which has impressed a new and lasting character on the nations of the world. Beginning with a small following, ill-equipped financially and militarily, Islam turned out eventually a mighty force, wielding its sceptre of authority over a world greater than that of Alexander the Great, greater than that of Rome, and that too acquired in a very much shorter period. Hardly fifty years had passed since Prophet Muhammad was commissioned by God to spread His gospel of truth when the Muslims planted the banner of Islam on the confines of India on the one side, and on the shores of the Atlantic on the other. Islam began to spread after the migration (hijrah) of the Prophet from Mecca to Medina. Conversions took place on an unprecedented scale. The new ideology inspired the Arabs as no other ideology had done before; it filled their hearts with longings both mundane and supramundane and enabled them to accomplish in an incredibly short time what would have otherwise required centuries of well-planned and well-calculated strategy.

The amazing success of the Arab nation was due not only to their organization, zeal, and aspiration, but also and in a large measure to the unifying action of Islam and the inspiring and revolutionary nature of its social programme and its ability to lead the masses out of the hopeless situation created by the decay of the antique civilizations of Greece, Rome, Persia, China, and India,' and to the all-powerful influence of the

Quran. None can deny the inherent faith of the early Muslims in the ultimate triumph of their cause, actuated as that faith was, not by the baser motives of power, but by the idea of establishing the Kingdom of God on earth.

In the opinion of Georges Rivoire the objective of the Muslim conquests was the construction of a universal State which "recognized no distinctions of race, nor of social conditions, the only rule it insisted upon was equal justice and fraternity." Naturally, the physically suffering and morally disjointed masses found in Islam a promise of liberation and salvation.

To the places they conquered the Muslims carried not only the flag of Islam but also culture, philosophy, and the study of nature all of which had their source in the Quran and the Sunnah.

In what follows, an attempt will be made to trace the course of intellectual revolution which Muslim thought brought about in Persia, Turkey, China, India, and Indonesia.

PERSIA

Islam was introduced to the land of Persia in 7/628 by the Prophet Muhammad himself, when through an epistle addressed to Khusrau Parviz, the then Persiah monarch, he extended an invitation to him and his subjects to embrace Islam: to affirm the unity of God and the apostleship of Muhammad,

to do good and to refrain from evil. In olden times no king, much less a Persian potentate, would receive a direct communication from an unknown person without getting flared up, the act being regarded as an instance of insolence and sacrilege. Accordingly, the Prophet's letter was torn to pieces and his emissary expelled with ignominy and disgrace. On hearing this, the Prophet felt sad and prophesied an early downfall of Khusrau's Empire. It was during the rule of the first Caliph that, as a response to this insult, the Muslim forces, under the leadership of General Sa'd, invaded Persia and inflicted a terrible defeat on the Persian army in the battle of Qadisiyyah. This battle served as a prelude to a series of defeats which the Persians suffered at the hands of the Arabs and which sealed their fate in a short period of ten years after the delivery of the Prophet's letter. King Yazdigird, a lad of eighteen, was probably the last ruler to make a futile attempt against the Muslims. His Chinese and Turkish mercenaries deserted him on the first onslaught of the Arabs, while he was himself plundered and assassinated by a villager in whose hut he had taken refuge after fleeing from the battlefield.

In the first/seventh century the Persian Empire like the Byzantine Empire was tottering under the crushing weight of despotism. Persecutions born of religious dissensions were the order of the day. Zoroastrianism was the State religion and its priests, not content with the spiritual authority they enjoyed by virtue of their office, also held positions of trust and responsibility in the administration of the State. A campaign of vilification followed by persecutions started against the adherents of the older forms of religion in Persia, among which ranked Jews, Christians, Buddhists, Sabaeans, Gnostics, and Manichaeans. All the older faiths and creeds longed to breathe freely and freshly in an atmosphere of toleration and comradeship which they eventually found in the teachings of Islam. Not only was it enjoined by Islam that the Christians and Jews must be treated with fairness and consideration because of their being the "People of the Book," but according to the clear directions of the Prophet the Zoroastrians were also to be treated at par with them, and hence entitled to the same privileges and concessions as enjoyed by the Muslims. All that was required of the non-Muslims was payment of a nominal poll-tax for the security they enjoyed under the Muslim rule. In return they were exempted not only from the payment of zakat, the State tax which every Muslim had to pay, but also from military service. Those non-Muslims who entered the military service had not to pay the poll-tax.

The conquest of Persia by the Arabs brought relief to the Christians. Earlier, the Sassanid kings had fomented bitter struggles between the Jacobites and the Nestorians; they had also been persecuting the Christian sects within their domains because of the Christian aggression from abroad. King Khusrau II ordered a general persecution of the Christians as he had suffered a defeat at the hands of Heraclius, a Christian monarch. The masses also welcomed the new creed. The Zoroastrian priests held in contempt the working classesartisans, mechanics, labourers, agriculturists-who defiled fire, earth, and water in pursuance of their trades and professions. The labouring classes in the Zoroastrian society had the same miserable lot as the Sudras in the casteridden Hindu society. In the new faith of the conquerers, the common man found a panacea to most of the social ills from which he had so terribly suffered. Islam recognizes no distinctions of caste and occupation; it gives no preference to one class of individuals over another save on the basis of merit; and advocates a theory of human brotherhood which transcends geographical and political limits.

With the downfall of the Sassanid dynasty, Zoroastrianism lost its powerful support. In the altered circumstances it found it extremely difficult to hold its own against the contending forces competing for supremacy. To its spiritual bankruptcy may be added the social confusion for which its priests were chiefly responsible. The Zoroastrian masses welcomed the new faith because of its liberalism, dynamism, and absence of parochialism. They were also drawn towards it because of the many similarities between their faith and the new one. Instead of Ahura Mazdah and Ahriman, they found Allah and Iblis; they also got their angels and demons, their stories about the creation of man and his resurrection, about heaven and hell and about sundry things similar to those they found in their own religion. Besides all this, they discovered that the ethics of Islam was not very different from theirs. Under the Muslim rule they began to enjoy a remarkable degree of toleration; their religious practices were respected and their fire-temples safeguarded.3

Besides the causes enumerated above for the spread of Islam in Persia mention may also be made of the marriage of Shahrbanu, a daughter of Yazdigird-the last monarch of the Sassanid dynasty-with Husain, the son of 'Ali. Consequently, in the descendants of Husain and Shahrbanu,the Persians could see the heirs to their ancient kings. This also accounts to some extent for the rise of Shi'ism as a separate sect in Persia and the devotion of the Persians to the 'Alids. Islam lost its alien character and appealed to the patriotic feelings of the average Persian, as he felt that, in addition to other advantages, he gained through the aforesaid marriage alliance a reassertion of his native values and traditions.

Persia had a remarkable culture and a highly developed civilization many centuries before the advent of Islam. In olden times, she was the cradle of thoughts and beliefs which supplied religion and philosophy to Persians and non-Persians. She was also the centre of a mighty political organization, and her theories of statecraft and administration became a model to the Turks. The intellectual aspect of the pre-Muslim Persian culture was determined by the philosophies of Zoroaster, Mani, and Mazdak-more or less dualistic despite a tinge of monotheism. The pre-Sassanian thought indicated a tendency towards monotheism, especially in Zoroaster, but the tendency became a dominant feature of Persian thought, almost an indubitable truth, only after the Muslim conquest. The dualism of Good and Evil yielded place to the dualism of God and matter.

The 'Abbasid Caliphate provided the most congenial atmosphere to the development of philosophy. As a result of Muslim influence, the Persians became the leaders of thought. Among the names of the foremost Persian thinkers may be mentioned those of ibn Miskawaih, ibn Sina, al-grhazali, Fakhr alDin Razi, Nasir al-Din Tasi, Mulla Sadra. The encyclopedists, I1i_hwan al-Safa, though not original in their contributions, are also worthy of mention. They had among them some good scholars like Zaid, son of Rifa'a, abu SulAiman Muhammad of Bust, 'Ali of Zanjan, abu Ahmad Mihrajani and 'Aufi.4 Persian Sufism also contains some very great names such as abu Said ibn abi al-Khair, 'Attar, Jalal al-Din Rilmi, Sa'di, Hafiz, al-Jili, and Jami.

From Persia, Islam spread to China, Turkey. Afghanistan, India, and Indonesia.

CHINA, TURKEY, AND AFGHANISTAN

Islam was carried over to China by Muslim merchants. It was firmly planted there by Arab troops who fought for Su Tsung (139/756) and settled in China after the successful conclusion of the war.

Arnold thinks that there is no direct evidence of any proselytizing activity on the part of the Muslims in China. The entire Muslim population of the land consists of the descendants of the immigrants from Arabia, Persia, Turkey, and other Muslim territories as a result of Mongol conquests.5 The number of Muslims in China is estimated at about thirty million.6 The Chinese Muslims have, however, identified themselves with the rest of their countrymen, in spite of their religious differences.

The Afghans believe that they were invited to Islam by Khalid bin Walid in the first/seventh century. But the earliest record of their conversion to Islam dates from the reign of al-Mamdn (198-218/813-833) when a king of Kabul was converted to Islam. His successors, however, reverted to Buddhism. Afghanistan was won for Islam in 258/871 by Ya'qub bin Laith, but Islamic ideas did not catch the imagination of the masses until after the conquest of the country by Subuktigin and Mahmfd of Chaznah.

The invasion of Chingiz Khan on Muslim Asia is regarded as the greatest calamity that has ever fallen on the human race. Like the huge waves of a mighty cyclone, it swept over the lands of Bukhara, Khiva, Khurasan, Iraq, and Russia. Not only did Chingiz Khan plunder whatever he laid his hands on, but he also destroyed seats of learning and the precincts of Islamic civiliza. tion. After his death, his Empire was divided among his sons. Persia fell to the lot of Tuli, one of whose descendants, Hulagu, was destined to found a dynasty which lasted for about a century and a half. The official religion of the Mongols was Shamanism, which, being a primitive type of religion, could not hold its own against the organized religions prevalent in the lands over which the Mongols ruled. Islam had the least chance of success as the Mongols had established their kingdom on the ruins of the Muslim Empire. But it is one of the surprises of human history that the conquered became the conquerors. The Mongols eventually accepted Islam-a religion the annihilation of which they had planned. With the conversion of the Mongol king to Islam this religion got a chance of spreading to Turkestan, Siberia, and Russia.

The Turks originally inhabited certain parts of Central Asia, particularly Mongolia, Siberia, and Turkestan. They did not profess any of the Semitic or non-Semitic faiths. They worshipped, like most primitive tribes of Asia, the sky, the earth, and water. Their religion lay in deifying the forces of nature and propitiating them by offerings, magic, and incantations. Before their acceptance of Islam they had come under the influence of Buddhism, Manichaeism, Judaism, and Christianity. But none of these creeds could win them over permanently to its side. It was Islam which they accepted finally in the fourth/tenth century. Several reasons have been advanced for the triumph of Islam, but the most cogent one out of these, according to G. L. Lewis, "was the fact that acceptance of Islam automatically conferred citizen rights in a vast and flourishing civilisation." 7

It was towards the middle of the seventh/thirteenth century that a small band of nomad Turks migrated from Khurasan under Sulaiman Shah. Driven by Mongols they hoped to find shelter in Asia Minor. In the rulers of this area they found people of a kindred race, the Saljugian Turks, whose kingdom was disintegrating due to disputes of succession and invasions from Central Asia. Taking advantage of the decadent conditions, Ertoghrul and Dundar, two sons of Sulaiman, established themselves in a territory ceded by the Saljugs in recognition of their military assistance. To `Uthman, the son of Ertoghrul, however, goes the credit of laying a secure foundation for the Turkish Empire.

Though the Saljugs were nomad tribesmen, they evinced keen interest in the civilizations of the Persians and the Greeks with whom they came in contact. During the sixth/twelfth century, Anatolia, Quniyah, and Erzerum became covered with architectural designs inspired by the Persian and the Greek art, They also "encouraged religious thinkers and philosophers. The famous Jalal al-Din Riimi flourished under their auspices in Quniyah, and so did others of the Sufi school." 9

The Ottoman Turks who replaced the Saljugs were no less ardent in furthering the cause of learning and literature. It is said about `Ut-hman that as he lay on his death-bed, he advised his sons to "promote the learned to honour... and whatsoever place thou hearest of a learned man, let honour, magnificence, and clemency attend him."9 Ottoman literature is very extensive, comprising every species of letters then current. Among the earlier poets may be mentioned Ghazi Fadil, Shaikhi, Mir 'Ali Shir Nawa'i, Abmad Pasha, Najati, Dhati, Zainab, Mihri, and ibn Kamal. They wrote lyrics, and also thoughtful poems explaining the knotty problems of life through allegories and stories of animals and birds. Among the later poets who give evidence of greater poise and balance may be mentioned Fudiili, Bagi, Nefi, Nabi, and Nadim. They introduced new strains and new modes of thinking in poetry. Among the prosewriters, the names of 'Ali Chalabi, Avliya Efendi, Katib Chalabi may be mentioned. They wrote on history, chronology, geography, travels, and other subjects.'°

All this shows that, like other Muslim countries, Turkey espoused the cause of learning and literature. The incentive was, however, provided by the religion of Islam, which the Turks had finally accepted.

INDIA

The impact of Islam on Hinduism is a phenomenon of remarkable significance. It is regretted that the Western writers as well as those of India (with the sole exception of Dr. Tara Chand) have in their works either ignored this fact altogether or assigned to it an insignificant place in the history of Indian thought. In this section, it is intended to bring out the extent and significance of those ideas and beliefs which had their source in Muslim philosophy and religion and which in course of time, through personal contacts, religious disputations, discussions, and exchange of views, coloured and changed to a very substantial degree the complexion of Hindu thought and gave it a new orientation and direction.

There is no denying the fact that the Muslims were also influenced by Hinduism in some very important respects. They borrowed from the Hindus some aspects of mysticism and some mores, especially their caste-system, funeral and birth rites, marriage customs, untouchability which they practised against sweepers, and a host of other things-good and bad-which it is needless to enumerate. But the main tenets of the Hindu creed had no influence on Muslim ideology and code of life. No Muslim thinker of any importance has ever accepted the doctrines of transmigration, incarnation, karma, and polytheism in any shape or form, and these doctrines constitute the very soul and spirit of Hinduism. On the contrary, monotheistic ideas of the Muslims together with their belief in the universal brotherhood of mankind were adopted by the Hindus which they bandied about as of Hindu origin. Indian philosophy after the first/seventh century has evinced keener interest in monotheism and tasteless society; it has also laid less emphasis on ritualism and negativism in life. This change may be due to several sociological and technological forces among which the advent of Islam in India must be ranked as a major factor of great cultural and philosophical importance. In the event of two cultures meeting together the dominant one pushes the weaker one to the periphery and occupies the centre itself. Something of the same sort happened in the case of Hindu culture and beliefs. In the ideological struggle which ensued Muslim infiltration into India, the native culture, finding itself unequal to the incoming one, had to relinquish the central position.

In what follows an attempt will be made to explain very briefly this remarkable phenomenon. After a short historical survey of the cultural contact, Muslim influence will be traced first up to Sankara, then from Sankara to Ramanuja, and lastly from Ramanuja down to the present times.

Cultural Contacts: The impact of Islam on Indian culture, thought, and religion was felt as early as the second/eighth century if not earlier. The writings of Muslim historians and travellers show that it was in South India, on the Malabar Coast, that the Muslims who were often preachers of their faith first settled as traders. Akbar Shah Khan" reports of the tomb of a Companion of the Prophet, named Tamim Ansari at Mylapur, twelve miles south of Madras. Islam also penetrated Ceylon, Ibn Battutah found the tombs of several preachers and saints in Ceylon during his travels. He mentions the names of Shaikh 'Abd Allah Hanif, Shaikh 'Uthman, and Baba Tahir among others.

Historical evidence proves unmistakably that the first Arab fleet appeared on Indian waters in 15/636 and was repulsed. But about the end of the first/ seventh century, says Rawlinson, the Muslim Arabs settled on the Malabar Coast, and this fact is corroborated by Francis Day in his Land o/ the Permals, and by Sturrock in his South Kanara and Madras Districts Manuals. Humayun Kabir writes, "Innes, in his Malabar and Anjangode District Gazetteer, quotes an inscription of a tomb from Kollam of one 'Ali who died there in 166/788. Further circumstantial evidence is offered by the revolt in 141/ 758 of a colony of Muslims established at Canton in China. It is obvious that this colony could not have been founded without intermediate stations, of which the Malabar Coast was likely to be one. Caldwell picked up near Kayalapattan in Tinnevelly, near the mouth of the Tamraparni, a number of Arab coins bearing dates from 71/690."

Mubammad bin Qasim invaded Sind in 94/712. The expedition was despatched by I,Iajjaj, the viceroy of Iraq and Iran of the Umayyad dynasty. As a result of the conquest of Sind, Islam came to exercise a potent influence on Indian thought and culture. This part of India remained the Far Eastern territory of the Caliphate till 267/880 when the Caliphate began to decline. The kingdom of Ghhaznah founded by Subuktigin who conquered Peshawar in 380/990 was a direct result of the weakening of the Caliphate. The aggressive policy of Subuktigin was followed by his ambitious and energetic son Mabmdd and by a series of Mughul, Tartar, Khurasani, and Afghan leaders. It was never the intention of the Muslim invaders to spread or work for their religion. A large number of the natives were converted to Islam not because of the political domination of the Muslims but for other reasons, among which may be ranked the missionary activities of the Sufi thinkers and the intolerable economic condition of the masses coupled with the ignorance of their own religion.

The most important cause of the conversion was, however, the simplicity of the Islamic doctrine: the brotherhood it proclaims, and the equal status it accords to Sudras and non-Siidras alike. Even at the early stages the influence was so great that Dr. Titus mentions eleven out of the several Hindu sects in which a definite mixture of Hindu and Muslim notions and practices prevailed" K. A. Nilkanta admits monotheism and democratic spirit of Islam as potent factors in the evolution of religio-philosophic culture in India and traces in the strictly monotheistic doctrines of Nanak the influence of Islam."

It has been observed that Sind formed an outlying province of the Caliphate till 267/880. During this period and particularly during the reigns of al-Mansnr, al-Harun, and al-Mamiin attempts were made to understand Indian thought. From Sind, Hindu pundits came to the Court of al-Mansur and presented to him Brahmasiddhanta and Khandakhadyaka, famous astronomical works of Brahmagupta. Both of these were translated into Arabic. A great impetus to this cultural understanding was afforded by the ministerial family of the Barmakids, who were patrons of Hindu learning in the Court of Harun al-Rashid. According to al-Biruni, this family came from Balkh where an ancestor of theirs was an official in a Buddhist temple. Arab scholars were sent by this family to India to study Indian thought, while Indian scholars were invited to the Court of Baghdad to explain Hindu learning. In the fifth/eleventh century al-Muwaffiq and al-Birdni visited India with the object of understanding Indian medicine, astronomy, and philosophy. Al-Biruni was the first to translate Sattkhya of Kapila into Arabic. He also translated Yoga Sutra by Patanjali and introduced Bhagvad-Gita to the Muslims.

The Hindus also evinced eagerness for understanding Muslim religion and thought. Baladhuri writes in the Futuh al-Buldan that during the reign of Harun al-Rashid, a Hindu rajah requested the Caliph to send a scholar to him to expound and discuss the fundamentals of Islam. Mas'udi, a historian, reports that when he arrived in India in 302/914 he found a Brahmani ruler supremely interested in religious discussions. Whenever this ruler heard of a Muslim arriving in his territory he would invite him and entered into religious discussion with him.'s

From the First/Seventh Century to o6arikara.-Intercommunication of such an active nature could not but influence the thoughts and beliefs of both the communities. Indian philosophy would have been substantially different from what it is today, had Islam with its "militant democracy," "liberal rationalism," and "uncompromising monotheism" not entered the arena of Indian thought. There would have been, in all probability, no proofs for the existence of God such as we find in Udavana's Kusumdnjli written in the fourth/tenth century, nor would there have been gankara about whom Humayun Kabir observes, "Historical factors do not exclude the possibility of 8ankara's acquaintance with the elements of Islamic thought."16 "It is necessary to repeat that most of the elements in the southern school of devotion and philosophy taken singly were derived from ancient systems, but the elements in their totality and in their peculiar emphasis betray a singular approximation to Muslim faith and therefore make the argument for Islamic influence probable."19 Even today there is a group of ~ainkara's followers who do not cremate but bury their dead in the Islamic way.

All the Mu'tazilites, with the solitary exception of al-Jabiz, had discussed philosophy and propounded their theories, before 8ahkara was born in the last quarter of the second/eighth century. Even al-Jdbiz would have died before 8ankara, had he not lived up to the age of ninety. The Mu'tazilites were Unitarians par excellence. They would not admit the attribution of eternal qualities to God, for that would mean the existence of other eternals besides the eternal God. 8ahkara too was an uncompromising monist, believing God to be one and the only reality, all else being illusion. In the writings of 8ahkara one finds an increasing emphasis on the unity of God which some people have regarded as an extension of the ancient monotheism of the Upanisads.

But this explanation has failed to satisfy a good many Orientalists who find in ~ankara's works "something pertaining to the semitic religions especially."'s Abu al-Hudhail, a prominent Mu'tazilite, appears to be a precursor of those Hindu monists who maintained that God could be described only in negatives. Abu al-Hudhail, however, admitted, quite contrary to his fundamental position, that God is knowing, loving, and powerful. The other Mu'tazilites were quick to discover the inconsistency and denied, therefore. all positive attributes to the Supreme Reality. In their hands God became unpredicable as well as unknowable, more of an abstract, impersonal, and absolute principle at the back of the universe than a God conceived as a person with whom any contact could be established. They did believe in the possibility of the beatific vision but strongly repudiated all forms of anthropomorphism.

The majority of the Mu'tazilites were atomists. The universe, they thought, was composed of atoms which were indivisible entities. They divided the physical world into substance and accidents or atoms and bodies. Strict determinism, according to them, governed physical phenomena, while freedom of action characterized human beings.

As we have shown in previous chapters, the Mu'tazilites believed in the cult of reason and endeavoured to reconcile the doctrines of Islam with rationalistic views then prevalent. Quite a good many of them enjoyed State patronage. Bis_hr, the son of Mu'ammar, was a favourite of the Caliph alMamiin during whose reign efforts were made to understand Hindu thought and culture through discussions and translations of religious literature. In theological and philosophical discussions, the protagonists of different views had complete freedom to express themselves. It is not unlikely that in this free exchange of ideas the Hindu participants returned to their homeland with quite a number of rationalistic doctrines having their origin in the Mu'tazilite mode of thought.

Communication is rarely one-sided; in free and frank exchange of ideas the traffic is more often than not two-sided. The Mu'tazdites could not satisfy the masses because of their exclusive concern with reason and their seemingly unorthodox views. The As_h'arites protested against the religious rationalism of the Mu'tazilites and advocated a middle path between philosophy and orthodoxy. They refuted the Mu'tazilite views, even while they modified the orthodox doctrine. They rejected the Greek and Oriental philosophies, proved Islamic doctrines by the dialectical method, and refuted non-Islamic religions as well as some sects of Islam. Al-As_h'ari, al-Bagillani, alJuwaini, al-Ghazali. Fakhr al-Din al-Razi, and ibn Taimiyyah wrote in defence of Islamic theology and in refutation of Greek and particularly Aristotelian thought. Al-As_h'ari was born in c. 260/873, while al-Ghazali, in whose hands the Ash'arite theology reached its final triumph; was born in 450/1058. AlGhazali was convinced that the philosophical theory could not form the basis of religious thought and that it was by revelation alone that the essentials of religion could be known. Al-Ghazali asserted that revelation was quite enough and that its ultimate truth could be ascertained only by the experience of the individual. Through ecstasy one could become a knower and receive, so to say, direct communication from God.

In addition to the Mu'tazilites, Ash'arites, and al-Ghazali who touched almost on all problems of philosophical and religious interest and whose theories found a way to the Indian soil through various channels some of which we have mentioned above, there was a long, unbroken line of Sufis, beginning with the early Companions of the Prophet who, like the Prophet himself, set a model for the Sufis by their intense zeal and enthusiasm for the cause of Islam, by their piety, and by the austere life they led. The Sufis, among whom may be counted Ibrahim bin Adham (d. 160/783), Fad[bin 'Iyad (d. 185/901),

Rabi'ah al-Adwiyyah (d. 1851802), were orthodox Muslims with no pantheistic bias; they revelled, however, in self-abandonment, fervent piety, and quietism, carried to the extreme. Rabi'ah conceived of prayer as a free and intimate intercourse with God. Her prayers indicate spontaneous outpouring of her heart to God. Says she, in one of her prayers, "0 my Lord, if I worship Thee from fear of hell, burn me in hell, and if I worship Thee from hope of paradise, exclude me thence, but if I worship Thee for Thine own sake, then withhold not from me Thine Eternal Beauty."

From oaAkara to Ramanuja.-By the time of Ramanuja, who was born in 407/1016, a host of Muslim thinkers and Sufis-some of the best philosophers that Islam has ever produced-had expounded and elaborated their thoughts in fine systems. It is very unlikely that their thoughts and theories should have failed to influence Indian thought through religious discussions and philosophical disputations which, as we have seen, took place on a wide scale both on the Indian soil and in the Courts of the Caliphs. Evidence is not wanting to show that some of the controversies which figured so prominently in Indian philosophy, after Islam had firmly entrenched itself on the Indian soil, were nothing more than echoes of Muslim thought, in some cases well in others more blatantly expressed.

Sufism now entered a new phase of its development. Asceticism still remained important but it was subordinated to theosophical and gnostic speculations. This position is discernible in the sayings of Ma'riif al-Karkhi (d. 200/815), abu Sulaiman al-Darani (d. 236/850), and Dhu al-Nun Misri. According to Nicholson, Dhu al-Nun is the source of Neo-Platonic elements in Islamic thought. Abu Yazid al-Bistami (d. 260/874) was the first Sufi to propound the doctrine of /and', and in his teaching Sufism became practically identified with pantheism. Husain bin MansOr, commonly known as al-Hallaj (b. 244/857), famous for his saying, "I am the Truth," had travelled in East Iran, Gujerat (India), and Central Asia. He maintained that the soul which is immaterial and immortal suffers from its alignment with the body, that the Supreme Being is incomprehensible by the human intellect and imagination, and that union with the Ultimate Reality is possible through suffering. Mansur was not appreciated by his contemporaries owing to some of his unorthodox utterances as a result of which he was executed. It was al-'Dhazali, however, who won recognition for Sufism in Islam.

Apart from the fact that Sufi doctrines and practices must have found their way to India along with other ideas of Muslim origin, there is irrefutable historical evidence to show that Muslim Sufis came in the wake of Muslim conquerors and traders and attracted the people of India by the purity and sublimity of their lives. They transmitted, by their personal contacts and discussions, their whole ideology and the way of life as understood by them and their counterparts in other parts of the Muslim world. Ibn Hajar 'Asgalani mentions in his al-Isabah ft Tamyiz al-Sahdbah a certain Baba Rattan who accepted Islam and visited Mecca twice. He was perhaps the earliest Indian Sufi. A little later came 'Abd Allah known as Baba Khaki, who died in 101/ 719 and was buried in Pakdaman cemetery in Lahore. Another saint was Sayyid Salar Mas'ud~,hazi Mian who, in 425/1033, met a martyr's death at the age of nineteen and was buried in Bharaich in the United Provinces. In the same century there came to India another saint of very great eminence and of far greater historical significance than any of his predecessors. He was 'Ali al-Hujwiri, popularly known as Data Ganj Bakhs_h, the writer of the wellknown work, Katb/ al-Mahjitb.

Amongst the Muslim thinkers who flourished between the second/eighth and fifth/eleventh centuries may be mentioned al-Kindi (c. 185/830-260/873), the first philosopher of the Arabs, more renowned as a mathematician and astrologer; al-Farabi (258/870-339/950), who adopted the Neo-Platonic doctrine of emanation; al-Razi (251/865-313/925), the celebrated Muslim physician, physicist, chemist, and philosopher; Miskawaih (d. 421/1030), a Persian moralist, philosopher, and physicist; and ibn Sina (370/980-428/1037), the representative of purer Aristotelianism.

The philosophical thought that had developed from al-Kindi to ibn Sina, that is, before Ramanuja's time, was transplanted in India by the early Muslims, who, in the opinion of Tara Chand, "were men of high rank... who lived and laboured in India, and through their personal contact and influence spread the ideas of Islamic philosophy and mysticism through the length and breadth of India." As a result of this impact, theism became pronounced in Indian philosophy; one comes across proofs for the existence of God for the first time in Udayana's Ku8maiijali. The Kusumdnjali or the Hindu proof of the existence of God was written in the fourth/tenth century. Keith says, "To Udayana doubtless belongs the credit of making theism a principal tenet of the school, though we have no reason to suppose him the inventor of the doctrine." The same is true of the Vai,esika. Radhakrishnan observes, "The Vaifesika has been regarded as non-theistic. Kanada... the author of the Vai4esika Sutras... does not mention God, but later commentators felt that the immutable atoms could not by themselves produce an ordered universe unless a presiding God regulated their activities. The authorship of the Vedas and the convention of the meaning of words require us to postulate a prime mover. The world cannot be explained by the activities of the atoms alone or by the operation of karma. The system, therefore, adopts the view of God which is found in Nydya."

In Indian philosophy the Nyaya and the Vai.esika are generally treated together, but these systems in fact never formed a single unitary doctrine before the middle of the third/ninth century. Keith puts the date of the syncretism of these two systems in the year 285/898 when Vaeaspati composed his Nyayasucini-bandhu.S3 A clear exposition of the combined doctrine is, however, to be found in Udayana "whose date, after many vicissitudes of opinion, is definitely fixed at 374/984 by his own statement in the Laksanavli.... Much more famous is his Kusumdnjali which is the classic exposition of the proof of God."

It is worth remembering that the Nyaya and the Vaiaieska were combined together to form a single system, after Islam had penetrated deep into the Indian sub-continent. Both the systems were atheistic and atomistic to begin with, but later they took a theistic turn as a result of Muslim influence.

From Ramanuja up to Date.-Ramanuja (b. 407/1016), a Hindu reformer of southern India, advocated the worship of God with devotion and faith. He recognized love as the guiding principle for the relation not only between man and God but also between man and man. Consequently, all man-made barriers including those of caste were to be discarded and the doors of religiont hrown open to all, irrespective of social position arising from caste or colour. Ramanuja admitted S`ndras to temples, emphasized self-surrender (prapatti), and adoration of the guru (guru bhakti). His emphasis on selfsurrender and love of the guru can be traced to Buddhism and Upanisadism but his acceptance of monotheism and the stress he laid upon it was entirely due to the inspiration he received from the new faith which was then being preached to the people by Muslim saints like Nathad Wali, for the erection of whose mosques land was granted by the Hindu king Kun-Pandya

While not denying the influence of Buddhism and Upanisadism on the philosophy of Ramanuja, it can be maintained that Islam could have supplied to the Bhakti leader both the idea of submission to the will of God and that of adoration of the spiritual guide. As for adoration of the guru, Ramanuja could have got the clue from the writings of the Sufis and also from his personal contacts with them. The objective of bhakti, according to Ramanuja, is not the realization of nirvana, but eternal blessedness in the presence of God-a Sufistic belief and not a Buddhistic view. His recommendation of a tasteless society in which Siidras should suffer no indignity because of their birth and his throwing the doors of temples open to the low-caste are a clear evidence of profiting by Muslim religion and Muslim practices.

In the sixth/twelfth century there arose two sects in the South which clearly revealed the influence of Islam. They were the Lingayats and the Siddharis. The Lingayats worshipped one God, who, according to them, reveals Himself, as the world-teacher (`Allamah Prabhu). The leader of the movement, Basava, was regarded as an incarnation of Shiva, an `Altdmah Prabhu, whose divinity passed on to his successors and representatives. As love was considered to be the first creation of God, bhakti or devotion was taken to be the ideal of life. This ideal was attainable through treading a path of austerity, resignation, and concentration on God. The Lingayats made no sacrifices, kept no fasts, did not go on pilgrimages, and discarded purification ceremonies. There was no caste and no differences based on birth or sex. Marriage was voluntary, widows were permitted to remarry, the dead were buried, and the doctrine of transmigration of the soul was not believed in.

Siddharis, a group of philosophical rhymists, were more uncompromising in their monotheistic beliefs than the Lingayats. They rejected the authority of the Vedas and Ssastras and also the theory of metempsychosis. Like the Sufis, they described the Ultimate Reality as Light and conceived of the end of life to be an absorption in God. The Siddharis were also alchemists, and followed Phu al-Nun Misri in this respect.

The religious reform movement started in the South spread to the North from the eighth/fourteenth century onward. The Muslim conquest of Northern India by the end of seventh/thirteenth century ushered in an era of unprecedented revolution in traditional Hindu thought, From the eighth/fourteenth century onward, we find the religious leaders of the North rejecting certain elements of the ancient creed and exhibiting a strong tendency to imbibe new ideas and theories. Indian architectural designs show a borrowing of certain features from the Arab and Persian styles of architecture; Indian paintings are influenced by the Central Asian and Persian techniques; in Indian literature a common medium arises in the form of Urdu, while Indian technical and scientific disciplines give evidence of a considerable use of terminology and information contained in Muslim works.

In the realm of thought the same phenomenon is evident. Ramananda, who flourished in the first half of the ninth/fifteenth century, is by many regarded as a bridge between the Bhakti movement of the South and that of the North. He travelled far and wide in search of knowledge and had teachers from the various sects of Hinduism, but his soul remained discontented till he came in contact with Muslims in Benares. Followers of all religions were welcome to his creed. He admitted to his sect disciples from both sexes.

From the teachings of Ramananda arose two schools, one represented by Tulsidasa and the other by Kabir, the former being conservative and the latter radical, but each was concerned in its own way with the evolution of a religion acceptable to the Hindus and Muslims alike. Both lay stress upon devotion; condemned externalia of religion, rituals, and ceremonies; protested against dogma and authority; and maintained that "the divine disclosed itself in the human race as a whole. Kabir was introduced to Hindu philosophy and religion by Ramananda, but he spent a considerable part of his time in the company of the Sufis. Kabir hated caste distinctions, rejected the authority of the six schools of the Indian philosophy, pooh-poohed the theory of the transmigration of souls, and repudiated the doctrine of reincarnation.

In his teachings Kabir was indebted to the Sufis. His central theme was that God cannot be comprehended through intellect but that He can be approached only through bhakii, i. e. to say, through devotion and ecstatic trance. He held that the essence of God is light and thus came close to the fundamental position of the Sufis. Nicholson finds many points of resemblance between his views about the universe expounded in his first Ramaini and the notions of al-Jili and Badr al-Din hid. According to Tara Chand, Kabir made an attempt to reproduce, as in Muslim philosophy, the scheme of nine spheres through which the whole creation develops. The goal of human life is the realization of union with God for which purpose the services of a guru are absolutely essential. Consequently, utmost care is to be exercised in the selection of a guru. The guru directs the soul of the disciple along the right path, disciplines his self, and brings him in the living presence of God. Kabir never recommended renunciation, in spite of his concern with God, and remained till the end of his life a weaver. No doubt, he prescribed a rigorous path of self-discipline, even prophesied disappointments and frustration for the pilgrims, but nowhere did he teach complete withdrawal from the world.

In the latter half of the ninth/fifteenth century was born a redoubtable champion of monotheism in a small village of the Punjab. His parents gave him the name of Nanak and the subsequent generations remember him as Guru Nanak for his piety, cosmopolitanism, and spiritual leadership. He laid the foundation of Sikhism on principles which show clearly and unmistakably the influence of Islamic ideology, beliefs, and practices. Guru Nanak felt that he was commissioned by the Almighty to launch a campaign for monotheism and a life of righteousness. He condemned polytheistic beliefs and practices, preached non-sectarianism, and admitted no caste distinctions. His ethics, unlike that of the Hindus, was life-affirming, practical, and to some extent puritanical. He recommended righteous living, fear of God, and the obedience of a guru-all

Muslim principles-in order to attain salvation which to him was the blending of the light of the soul with that of God. Nanak realized like the Sufis that God, being incomprehensible through the intellect, can be approached through humility and through understanding one's worthlessness and inadequacies. Despite his love for God, he would allow no anthropomorphic characterization of the Deity, though he remembered Him lovingly sometimes as a husband and sometimes as a bride to relate Him intimately to his own soul31 Guru Nanak did believe in the transmigration of souls and also in hell. Not satisfied with the punishment which the sinners were destined to suffer through repeated births in lower forms, he threatened them with dire punishments as described in the Quran in the parable of hell. Guru Nanak's debt to Islam was so great and his teachings so well steeped in Sufi lore that, according to Tara Chand, "the fact of the matter is that it is much harder to find how much exactly he drew from the Hindu scriptures.

His rare references to them lead one to imagine that Nanak was only superficially acquainted with the Vedic and the Purdnic literature."98 In his insistence on the unity and brotherhood of mankind and in his condemnation of idol-worship, caste distinctions, and ritualism, Guru Nanak was as good a Muslim as any other Muslim. It is a pity that the later Gurus were drawn into a whirlpool of politics as a result of which a peace-loving Church was converted into a militant society.

Kabir, Tulsidasa, and Guru Nanak were followed by a host of Hindu thinkers and reformers in the tenth/sixteenth and eleventh/seventeenth centuries who promoted and furthered what in essence were the fundamental principles of Islam. Tuka Ram, a Maratha saint, conceived of God on lines identical with those of Kabir, rejected Vedic sacrifices, idol-worship, and caste,33 while Chaitanya, a Brahman by caste, loved the Muslims so much that he had several Muslim disciples. Caitanya preached the unity of God, insisted on love and devotion, song and dance and ecstatic trance for union with God. It can be easily seen that Chaitanya's teachings bore a close resemblance to those of the Sufis.

Coming to modern times, we notice two important movements of the Arya Samaj and the Brahmo Samaj. The former, despite its opposition to Islam, preaches what in reality is the essence of Islam. Swami Dayanand (vide his Satydrath Parka_sh), the founder of the Arya Samaj movement, denounced idol-worship and ritualism as a corruption of the pure Hindu religion. He also condemned hereditary caste-system and instead favoured functional castes. What is remarkable about him is that he indefatigably preached the doctrine of monotheism which in his opinion could be derived from the Vedas and other sacred books of the Hindus. That monotheism is deducible from the Vedas, may be true. It does not, however, contradict Islam; rather, it ratifies the basic standpoint of Islam that God has been revealing Himself to different nations. Hence if monotheism is found in the Vedas, it would not be surprising to a Muslim. What is, however, surprising is Swami Dayanand's emphasis on this doctrine which is lacking in the pre-Islamic literature of India.

The Brahmo-Samajists have discarded the theory of rebirths. They are also opposed to ritualism, image-worship, and caste-system.

In addition to these two movements in modern Hinduism, there is the Rama-Krishna religious reconstruction movement and the Theosophical

Society following a religious and social programme; each of these bears close resemblance to Muslim faith and practice. From India Islam goes to Indonesia.

INDONESIA

Before the advent of Islam, the Indonesian Archipelago, the biggest country after China in the Far East and the seventh among the great countries of the world, was ruled over for about a thousand years by the Hindus, who went there as traders in the first or second century A.D. and eventually became rulers through their effective diplomacy and practical common sense. According to Pandit Jawahar Lal Nehru, the first Hindu immigrants to Indonesia belonged to Southern India. Being traders they settled on coasts and traded with different lands in sundry articles of daily use. They also brought with them their religion which, because of its superiority, could not fail to influence the natives. There is, however, no historical evidence to show whether it was Buddhism or Hinduism that first came to Indonesia. The Hindus never cultivated the art of history in the early centuries, nor did they devise canons for sifting recorded or oral evidence, with the result that their early history is nothing but a mass of fairy tales founded upon imagination, makebelieve, or hearsay with no solid rock of facts to stand upon.

The early Hindu settlers in Indonesia have left no record of theirs; consequently, it is difficult to determine the chronological order of Hindu cults and beliefs as they found their way into this new land. It is, however, conjectured that the form of Buddhism first to enter the Archipelago was Hinayana and that after a considerable period of time the other form of Buddhism, Mahayana, was also introduced. In the Majaphit period when Hindu culture and Hindu domination were at their highest a new religion arose, which was the result of the fusion of Brahmanism and Buddhism, incorporating in itself some strands of indigenous thoughts and feelings.

In spite of the political and commercial domination of the Hindus, the country as a whole was never converted to Hinduism. In Java, Hinduism had its strongest centre, while Buddhism had the greatest number of its adherents in Sumatra, Malaya, and a few other adjoining and adjacent islands.

A large part of the Archipelago, however, remained untouched by Hinduism and continued to revel in idolatry and nature-worship. In a large majority of the islands, life went on as usual-the same round of festivals, customary observances, and rituals, showing no sign of foreign influence or changed socio-political conditions. Life in these areas was hemmed in by countless superstitions and irrational fears-the products of ignorance and idol-worship. Multiplicity of superstitions led to the creation of innumerable deities, each deity being held responsible for a particular phase of human life or nature. Homage was paid to gods and goddesses out of fear, for their displeasure could bring about disaster, infertility, epidemics, floods, death, and what not. Consequently, an elaborate ritual, performed meticulously, was required to keep the deities on the right side. Often the ritual was so complicated that a specially trained agency was called for to perform it strictly in accordance with set practices and established laws. There arose thus a priestly class whose function it was to help invoke the sympathy of gods and goddesses through incantations, charms, sacrifices, and offerings-all of these practised and performed in a characteristic manner and style.

Wherever Hinduism was in ascendancy the Brahmans assumed the functions of priests and arrogated to themselves the power which none else but a person endowed with supernatural powers could have. The priestly class came to wield, in course of time, not only spiritual but also temporal power through their association with Courts and princes, for the kings needed divine help as much as ordinary mortals. Anxious to keep their power intact, the priests transmitted their knowledge only to their kith and kin. Very often the recipient of the information was the son of the priest who was initiated into the art of performing ceremonies and trained in them with the utmost exactitude and care, for a slight error or omission would bring about the wrath of a god instead of pleasing him. Thus, the priestly class became hereditary, enjoying special privileges and prerogatives.

The society was split up into two classes, with the priestly class at the top, dominating and exploiting the other by its cleverness, sophistry, and chicanery. Because of his colossal ignorance, political servitude, and economic insufficiency, the common man contented himself with the life and fortunes of a serf or an underling.

Hinduism accentuated the prejudice of class distinction; it gave a fillip to idolworship; it augmented rather than diminished the number of deities; and above all it introduced ahirisa, a life-negating ethics and a life-renouncing philosophy. The natural outcome of this attitude was extension in the field of superstition, an acute sense of individual and collective insecurity together with moral and spiritual bankruptcy on a wide scale.

Islam entered the arena when Hinduism was at the zenith of its glory. The latter was armed with the might of political domination; it had its missionaries all over the Archipelago, who had converted thousands of the natives to their faith; and it had firmly entrenched itself on the soil by its cultural superiority, commercial leadership, and marital relationships. Islam had to fight against heavy odds. There was no political power to launch a campaign against the Indonesian Hindu rulers. In the middle of the seventh/ thirteenth century when

Islam got a foothold in Sumatra, the Muslims all over the world had fallen on evil days. The Fatimids who ruled over the Arab countries, Egypt, and Africa were in a process of disintegration; the `Abbasids were on their last legs; Persia was the vantage ground for self interested upstarts; while Spain, once the pride of Muslim culture and philosophy, had forgotten its traditions and was in the throes of death, surrounded as it was by the Christian hordes who were bent upon giving it a short shrift. In India the Slave dynasty was replaced by the)ihhaljis, who were busy at that time setting their own house in order and had little time to look to other peoples' affairs. It is evident that under these circumstances no Muslim power was in a position to lend a helping band to any campaign, much less to one which had no connection with territorial aggrandizement or imperialistic expansionist programme.

On the Indonesian soil no gun was fired, nor any sword drawn for the propagation of Islam. Arnold says, "The history of the Malay Archipelago during the last six hundred years furnishes us with one of the most interesting chapters in the story of the spread of Islam by missionary efforts.... In every instance, in the beginning, their work had to be carried on without any patronage or assistance from the rulers of the country, but solely by the force of persuasion, and in many cases in the face of severe opposition, especially on the part of the Spaniards.."

Several causes have been listed by historians for the slow and spontaneous spread of Islam throughout Indonesia, but it must be admitted that there is yet no established theory to account for this remarkable phenomenonunique in the annals of history for its methodology and success.

A common explanation for the religious conquest of Indonesia by Islam is offered in terms of the commercial relations which the Muslim merchants from India established in the middle of the seventh/thirteenth century with the Indonesians. These merchants, it is said, married Indonesian women and secured thereby a respectable position for themselves. In course of time the Indonesian wives together with the slaves of their household furnished a nucleus for the acceptance and spread of Islam. A little reflection will, however, show that this explanation is no better than a myth and needs to be exploded in the interest of truth. Before exhibiting the hollowness of the explanation, it is interesting to note that even so great an authority as Arnold37 seems to subscribe to it. He quotes approvingly from Padre Gainza who says, "The better to introduce their religion into the country, the Muhammadans adopted the language and many of the customs of the natives, married their women, purchased slaves in order to increase their personal importance, and succeeded finally in incorporating themselves among the chiefs who held the foremost rank in the state. Since they worked together with greater ability and harmony than the natives, they gradually increased their power more and more, as having numbers of slaves in their possession, they formed a kind of confederacy among themselves and established a sort of monarchy, which they made hereditary in one family.

Though such a confederacy gave them great power, yet they felt the necessity of keeping on friendly terms with the old aristocracy, and of ensuring their freedom to those classes whose support they could not afford to dispense with." To this quotation Arnold adds, "It must have been in some such way as this that the different Muhammadan settlements in the Malay Archipelago laid a firm political and social basis for their proselytising efforts. They did not come as conquerors, like the Spanish in the sixteenth century, or use the sword as an instrument of conversion; nor did they arrogate to themselves the privileges of a superior and dominant race so as to degrade and oppress the original inhabitants, but coming simply in the guise of traders they employed all their superior intelligence and civilisation in the service of their religion...."

This explanation along social lines founded on respect and prosperity is invalidated, according to C. A. 0. van Nieuwenhuijze, by the fact "that the type of trade which the foreign Muslims conducted was by no means alien or new to the Indonesian society."39 The same point of view is presented with much rigour and empirical data by Comp. J. C. van Lour 40 to whom the inquisitive reader may turn for further elucidation and clarification.

The object of the refutation is not to deny the role of the early Muslim traders in the dissemination of Islamic beliefs and practices; it is rather to assign to them a proper place in the situation which was extremely complex and comprised far more potent factors than trade and marital relationships. The traders were no better than carriers of a culture or a world-view which could not have gained ground in spite of their zeal and fervour, had it not the strength to stand on its own legs.

Another explanation for the peaceful penetration of Islam into Indonesia is to be found in the socio-political conditions of the urban society which was powerfully influenced by the caste-system that had been introduced by Hinduism. Priesthood had divided the society into two watertight compartments. This and like differences were supported and in a way accentuated by the caste-system which the Hindus had brought with them and introduced. Hinduism not only ratified bifurcation in the Indonesian society, it also multiplied the then existing divisions, for Hinduism admits of four classes and not only two in society. These divisions based originally on professions became hereditary so that no person, howsoever talented he might be, could change his caste. A person born in a dra home could by no means shed the social stigma attached to him for having been born in a low-caste home. Intelligence, integrity, talent, and hard work were of no avail in face of the inflexibility of the caste-system. The worst to suffer in this system were those who stood at the lowest rung; they were the most oppressed and the most exploited, but the others too with the exception of the priestly and the Brahmanical class had to suffer different kinds of social indignities and disabilities.

The non-priestly classes, particularly the lower ones, found in Islam a panacea to the ills which like a miasma were eating up the very fabric of the society. Since Islam recognizes no distinctions which divide man from man and recommends a classless and tasteless society, it captured the imagination of the Indonesians, who embraced the new religion to reassert their dignity as human beings and to re-acquire democratic rights to live as free individuals unhampered by artificial man-made restrictions. The conception of the universal brotherhood of mankind together with the basic equality of all human beings, which Islam advocates so vehemently, proved a dynamite for the foundations of the social structure of Hinduism. Accordingly, Hinduism crumbled like a house of cards and the Indonesian masses, particularly those living in the urban areas, accepted the new faith in large numbers. From the harbour towns and coastal areas, where the grip of the caste-system was the strongest and the most pinching, Islam spread inland.

Another reason for the success of Islam is to be discovered in the simplicity of the creed that it preaches. It makes no metaphysical presuppositions as is done, for instance, by Buddhism, nor does it demand credence in too many transcendental beings as is the case with Hinduism. Islam is unencumbered by theological subtleties. It simply asserts the godhead of one God and the prophethood of Muhammad and that of others.

The fundamental tenets of Islam are, thus, the fundamental demands of the human intellect. Professor Montet says, "Islam is a religion that is essentially rationalistic in the widest sense of this term considered etymologically and historically.... This fidelity to the fundamental dogma of the religion, the elemental simplicity of the formula in which it is enunciated... are so many causes to explain the success of Muhammadan missionary efforts. A creed so precise, so stripped of all theological complexities and consequently so accessible to the ordinary understanding, might be expected to possess and does indeed possess a marvellous power of winning its way into the consciences of men."

Hinduism never accorded with the genius of the Indonesians in spite of the Hindus' long cultural contact with them and their equally long political domination. The average Hindu Indonesian wore his creed like a veneer which left his soul as well as his body almost naked. He yearned for a creed more in line with his natural cravings and intellectual demands. When Islam presented itself as a rival to Hinduism and heathenism, it quickly acquired victory by the force of its logic and the rationality of its demands.

Another factor which may have contributed to the success of Islam is its theory of human society which releases man from his narrow geographical grooves and makes him a member of the community (ummale) of Islam. National loyalties and political affiliations are subordinated to the larger interests of the Muslim community as a whole. Not only does this conception emancipate an individual from the prison of self-interest and parochialism, it also provides an anchor-sheet for the forlorn and the neglected.

A convert, after having lost his kinship with his clan, can save himself from the pangs of loneliness by conjuring up his association with a bigger whole which recognizes neither territorial limits nor clannish bonds. A thing of this kind is not to be found in other religions, much less in Hinduism, torn as it is by its caste-system, family distinctions, and the practice of untouchability.

Islam has not only the idea of ummah to put an individual in a wider perspective, it has still another idea nobler and richer in content for the rehabilitation and re-establishment of the lonely and the forsaken. This idea is to be found in mysticism which promises to place man in the lap of Infinity. It is said that in the beginning the Indonesians were attracted by the mysticism of Islam rather than by any of its other aspects.

In addition to the reasons enumerated above, one very potent reason for the propagation and success of Islam in foreign lands, particularly in Indonesia, Malay, Indo-China, and the Philippine Islands, was the enthusiasm and sincerity with which Islam was presented by the early Muslim mystics who migrated to these islands of their own accord and settled there temporarily or permanently.

Generally, they accompanied the Muslim traders or came in their wake. The first thing they did was to acquaint themselves with the local dialect; this was necessary for transmission and exchange of ideas.

After acquiring proficiency in the native language, the Sufis started propagating Islam among the influential and the rich, believing that reform of these would rid the society of most of the ills from which it suffered, and that their conversion would be followed by those of the masses.

The unlettered and the unsophisticated people which formed the bulk of the society looked up to their chiefs and nobles for guidance and inspiration. Not able to make a decision themselves, they imitated the high-ups in all matters. Hence the success of a religious ideology among the upper classes, the Sufis thought, would work for the spiritual regeneration.

The Sufis built mosques which often had schools attached to them. From these centres of learning were delivered courses of lectures on Muslim theology, culture, philosophy, and history. Mysticism has a philosophy of a very high order. It replaces the cold formalism of the Shari'ah by an intense and passionate longing for the all-loving God and ensures the purification of the heart by treading a well-regulated Path. The Subs regarded prayers, fasting, and pilgrimage as means and not ends to be cultivated and pursued for their own sake. But they knew that the means were as much necessary for the spiritual uplift of a person as the attainment of the end. And, therefore, the early mystics who took upon themselves the burden of carrying the message of God to the four corners of the world stressed the performance of religious duties, such as offering prayers, fasting, going on a pilgrimage, etc., along with acts of supererogation for winning the pleasure of God.

A brief historical sketch of the growth and development of mysticism in Islam has been provided in an earlier chapter and, therefore, need not be repeated here. Suffice it to say that by the end of the seventh/thirteenth century when Islam was imported to Indonesia and other adjacent islands, the theory of mysticism had received its final touches at the hands of the leading Muslim thinkers and divines. According to a number of Orientalists, the best of Muslim religion is to be found in its mysticism.

Maulana Burhan al-Din is said to have been the first Muslim to preach his faith to the islanders. He belonged to the Qadiriyyah order of Sufism which is named after 'Abd al-Qadir al-Jilani (470/1077-561/1166), a saint whose writings, generally orthodox in content, have a tendency to mystical interpretation of the Quran. The Maulana also belonged to the Shafi'iyyah sectone of the four legal schools of Muslim theology named after Imam al-Shafi'i who effected a synthesis of the strict adherence to Tradition of the Malikii with the Hanafl method of giyds, that is to say, with the analogical deduction. Abu Hanifah, the founder of the Hanafi legal school, made free use of his own judgment in deciding between traditions, while Malik ibn Anas maintained the exclusive validity of the accepted traditions. Al-Shafi'i carved a via media between these two modes of approach and attempted a synthesis.

Maulana Burhan al-Din was, thus, steeped in the best traditions of Islam. He followed the Shari'ah and was affiliated to the most tolerant and progressive school of Sufism, a school which was neither too liberal nor yet too conservative. The Muslims of the Archipelago at present belong predominantly to the Shafi'iyyah sect and this is due to the teachings of the Maulana.

It is interesting to note that the Shafi'iyyah sect was predominant on the Coromandel and the Malabar Coasts of India when the Muslim traders from these areas first landed in Sumatra and introduced their culture and religion. It may be conjectured in the absence of any historical record that the Maulana belonged to India and travelled with or came in the wake of the Indian Muslim traders who also belonged mostly to the Shafi'iyyah sect as well as to the Qadiriyyah school of mysticism.

Among the Muslim rulers of Sumatra, Sultan Alimad worked ceaselessly for the glory of Islam. During his reign as well as during that of his descendants Muslim missionaries were sent far and wide. Wherever they went, they built mosques and schools to provide permanent centres of devotion and learning. The schools also served as community centres where matters of common interest were discussed.

The King al-Malik al-Z, whir, a descendant of Sultan Abmad, was fond of holding discussions with theologians, and his Court was thronged with men of learning and letters. We have it on the authority of ibn Battiitah that the king had summoned two jurisconsults from Persia for discussion and clarification of some religio-legal issues knowing of the fact how the new religion was introduced, but this much can be inferred from the present cultural condition of the islands that there existed strong traces of Indian and Arabian influence in the life and literature of the inhabitants.

Their religion is predominantly Shafl'iyyah, but their culture is steeped in Arabian lore and learning. The Muslim kings of the Moluccas rendered yeoman's service to the cause of Islam by instituting centres of Muslim culture, literature, history, and philosophy. During the reign of Mansur, the Malayan language adopted the Arabic script. Ancient Indian Muslim literature was transliterated into Malayan Arabic script. Manefir also introduced Islamic constitution in the country, though not completely, for he kept intact the old system of taxation, general administration, and fishing; yet in all other matters he made an attempt to follow the ShAfi'iyyah jurisprudence, social polity, and details of administration.

Islam spread to Java through the efforts of the trading mystics of Malay, particularly of Maulana Malik Ibrahim, an Indian national of Gujerat district. The Maulana was not only a Sufi of high order but also a scholar of the first rank and a Hakim of no mean repute. He cured a Hindu dignitary who subsequently embraced Islam and is counted among the nine saints of Java. He is known as Raden Rahmat.

The other saints belonged either to the rich Hindu families or to the defunct Majaphit dynasty. All of them without exception led a life of simplicity, piety, and high religious fervour. They converted thousands to Islam by their example and teaching. A mosque was built where the nine saints met occasionally to discuss matters of common interest.

The converts also congregated there to discuss their problems and difficulties. Deputations from foreign lands were also received in this mosque. This shows that the mosque was not only a centre of devotion but also a community centre dedicated to multipurpose activities. So great was the religious ardour that the Muslim converts of Java entertained a keen desire to visit the holy places of Islam; one of them, Sunan Gunang by name, went for pilgrimage to Mecca where he learnt the principles of Islam from Arab teachers, and came back to Java full of enthusiasm for the new faith.

It will take several pages to recount the story of the spread of Islam in other islands of Indonesia. Suffice it to say that its propagation was nothing but a peaceful penetration through the efforts of traders, mystics, and preachers-both native and foreign.

Before the advent of Islam, Java had been ruled by Majaphit, a Hindu dynasty, which had fallen on evil days; as a result, the country had become divided into a number of principalities, each owing allegiance to its own chieftain. The people followed either Hinduism or Buddhism, but very often their religion was an admixture of both with a strong overtone of animism and belief in magic and sorcery.

The condition of other islands was no better. The Hindus whose early contacts with the Archipelago were of purely commercial nature soon developed colonial and imperialistic designs in the land" and started a process of "Hinduization," which gave birth to a caste-system as rigid as that in India and provided in addition an appeal to the deification of kings and the ruling class.

After the downfall of the Majaphit dynasty in the ninth/ fifteenth century the Muslim rule was firmly established in Java and other islands till the conquest of the Archipelago by the Dutch towards the end of the tenth/ sixteenth century. For about two hundred years the Muslims remained at the helm of affairs and contributed substantially to the cultural development of the country.

They tried to rid literature of absurd and obscene stories about gods and goddesses; they worked for the amelioration of the society, and introduced, through translation of Arabic and Persian books, a system of philosophy, mysticism, jurisprudence, and ethics, which had its roots in Muslim thought and religion. That the Indonesian literature of the preMuslim period was utterly nonsensical, superstitious, and obscene, has been testified by Crawford and also by Dr. Richards.

The latter maintains that the purpose of such literature was simply to humour the princely class by its esoteric and fictitious nature. The Muslim rulers replaced it by healthy literature. Sultan Agung, a ruler of Mataram (1022/1613-1055/ 1645), wrote a treatise on philosophy, morals, and statecraft; the eldest son of an Egyptian scholar, 'Allamah ibn Hajar al-Hutami, wrote a monumental book on mysticism entitled Sirat al-Mus_hldgin; `Allamah Nur al-Din compiled a historical work called Bustdn al-Salutin, while Tan Muhammad, a premier of Malaya during the reign of Sultan 'Abd al-Jalil, wrote a historical account of the rulers of Malaya and Sumatra.

Besides original publications, a host of Persian and Arabic works were translated. Al-Gbazali's al-Isrdr was translated by 'Abd al-Samad. Sikandar Nanaeh and Mathnatoi of Maulana

Rum and Tuhtat al-Ahrdr of Jami were also rendered into the Malayan language.

The impact of-translations and original works on theology, morals, philosophy, and culture of the Indonesians was tremendous. It paved the way to a new type of literature which attempted to deduce morals from stories in which the principal actors and characters were birds, animals, and trees.

These anecdotes were written on the pattern of the aforesaid Malhnawi of Maulana Rum and Mantiq al-Tair of `Attar, and helped to inculcate a healthy attitude towards world and its affairs. Instead of ahimsa and life-negating ethics, emphasis was now laid upon effort, struggle, and achievement. Renunciation was eschewed in favour of community living, and a tasteless society was preached for in place of a caste-ridden one. Spiritual values were extolled as against the commercial ones. All this led to a great awakening among the masses. The Indonesians realized as never before that they were connected with one another by ties which transcend caste, creed, and colour.

BIBLIOGRAPHY

Abdali, M.R. : *Scientific Thought in Islam*, Pious Publications, Hyderabad, 2001.

Abdul, Hamid Siddiqui : *The Life of Muhammad (PBUH)*, Islamic Pub., New Delhi,1997.

Abdullah, Muhammad : *Islamic Prayers,* Idara Ishaat-e-Diniyat Pvt. Ltd, New Delhi, 1999.

Ahmed, Hasanuddin : *A Handbook of Muslim Belief,* Goodword Books Pvt. Ltd., New Delhi, 1995.

Ahmad, Ilyas : *Social Contract and the Islamic State,* Urdu Publishing House, Allahabad, 1940.

Amery, Reeves : *The Anatomy of Peace,* Oxford, New York, 2001.

Amini, Mualana Taqi : *Fundamentals of Ijtihad,* Idaara-I-Adabiyat, Delhi, 1986.

Arnold and Guillaume : *The Legacy of Islam,* Oxford University Press, London, 1949.

Arnold, Sir Thomas : *The Caliphate,* MacMillan, London, 1965.

Arnold, T. W. : *Preaching of Islam*, Luzac & Co., London, 1913.

Atta, Mohiuddin : *Abu Bakr,* Feroz Pub., Lahore, 1999.

Aurobindo, Sri : *The Foundations of Islamic Culture,* New York, 1973.

Bagley, R.R.C. : *Ghazzali's Book of Counsel for Kings,* Oxford, New York, 1964.

Baloch, N. A. : *Great Books of Islamic Civilization,* Kitab Bhavan, New Delhi, 2001.

Bawer, Raymond : *The New Man in Soviet Social Psychology,* Oxford, New York, 1990.

Bhatia, H. S. : *Studies in Islamic law, Religion and Society,* Deep & Deep Publications, New Delhi, 1997.

Brigadier, Gulzar Ahmed : *The Battles of the Prophet of Allah (PBUH)*, Aziz Pub., Islamabad, 2001.

Calverley, Edwin Elliot : *Worship in Islam*, University of Madras, Madras, 1925.

Dawud, Rahbar : *God of Justice*, Mac & Jac Pub., Leiden, 1960.

Edward, Mortimer : *Faith and Power, the Politics of Islam*, Oxford, New York, 2002.

Ernst, Carl W. : *Teaching of Sufism*, Deep & Deep, New Delhi, 2000.

Fatima, T. : *Islamic Law and Judiciary*, Deep & Deep Publications, New Delhi, 2001.

Friedmann, Yahanan : *Tolerance and Coercion in Islam : Interfaith Relations in the Muslims Traditions*, Cambridge, New York, 1990.

Gairdner, W.H. Temple : *Al-Ghazzali's Mishkatul-Anwar : the Niche for Lights*, Oxford, London, 1915.

Gins Berg, M. : *Evolution and Progress*, William Heinemann Ltd., London, 1982.

Halepota, A.J. : *Philosophy of Shah Waliullah*, Feroz Pub., Lahore, 1986.

Haq, M. Anwarul : *The Faith Movement of Mawlana Muhammad Ilyas*, Country Pub., London, 1972.

Harun, Yahya : *Islam : the Religion of Ease*, Goodword Books Pvt. Ltd., New Delhi, 1993.

Hasan, M. : *Hadrat Ali Murtada (R.A.A.)*, Kitab Bhavan, New Delhi, 2003.

Husain, Wahed : *Administration of Justice during the Muslim Rule in India*, Kitab Ghar, New Delhi, 1977.

Husaini, Waqar : *Islamic Thought*, Goodword Books Pvt. Ltd., New Delhi, 1999.

Hussain, M. Hadi : *Imam Abu Hanifah : Life and Work*, Kitab Bhavan, New Delhi, 2001.

Imamuddin, S. M. : *Arab Muslim Administration*, Kitab Bhavan, New Delhi, 1984.

Inge, R. : *Philosophy of Plotinus*, MacMillan, London, 1918.

Jalbani, G. N. : *Teachings of Hazrat Shah Waliyullah*, Kitab Bhavan, New Delhi, 1997.

Jamila, Khatun : *The Face of God,* Adam Pub., New Delhi, 1996.

Kalerji : *From War to Peace,* Oxford, New York, 1991.

Karpinski, L.C. : *Algebra of al-Khwarizmi,* Oxford, New York, 1915.

Khalifa, Abdul Hakim : *The Islamic Ideology,* Fortune Books,London, 1993.

Khan, N. M. Yamin : *God Soul and Universe in Science and Islam,* Kitab Bhavan, New Delhi, 1993.

Landau, R. : *The Philosophy of the Ibn Arabi,* Century Pub., London, 1959.

Levy, Reuben : *The Social Structure of Islam,* Cambridge University Press, New York, 1993.

MacDonald, D.B. : *Development of Muslim Theology,* New Century Pub., London, 1903.

Maudoodi, S.A.A. : *Islami Riyasat,* Islamic Book Foundation, New Delhi, 1999.

Mohiuddin, Ahmad : *Saiyid Ahmad Shahid,* Modern Pub., Lucknow, 1975.

Muir, Sir William : *The Caliphate, its Rise, Decline and Fall,* Oxford, Edinburgh, 1915.

Muir, William : *Early Caliphate,* Oxford, New York, 1970.

Najjar, Fauzi M. : *The Islamic State : a Study in Traditional Politics,* Oxford, New York, 1967.

Narayan : *Pan Islamism,* MacMillan, New York, 1953.

Oudha, Abdul Qadir : *Criminal Law of Islam,* Kitab Bhavan, New Delhi, 1999.

Pearson, M. M. : *Pious Passengers : the Hajj in Earlier Times,* Sterling Publishers Pvt. Ltd., New Delhi, 1999.

Poole, Lane, S. : *The Mohammedan Dynasties,* MacMillan & Co., London, 1895.

Qureshi, A. Iqbal : *Islam and the Theory of Interest,* Kitab Bhavan, New Delhi, 1994.

Rahim, Abdur : *Principles of Islamic Jurisprudence,* Kitab Bhavan, New Delhi, 1994.

Rizvi, Hasan Askari : *Islami Reassertion : a Socio Political Study,* Progressive Publishers, Lahore, 1981.

Rodinson, Maxime : *Islam and Capitalism,* Penguin, London,1974.

Saxena, K.P. : *Human Rights: Perspective and Challenges,* Lancers Books, New Delhi, 1996.

Schacht, J. : *The Origins of Muhammadan Jurisprudence,* Clarendon Press, Oxford, 1953.

Shehadi, F. : *Ghazzali's Unique Unknowable God,* MacMillan & Co., London, 1964.

Smith, M. : *Al-Ghazzali : the Mystic,* MacMillan & Co., London, 1944.

Stanton : *Teaching of the Quran,* Discovery Publishing House, New Delhi, 1989.

Stern, S.M. : *Fatimid Decrees,* Faber and Faber, London, 1964.

Syed, M. H. : *Islam and Science,* Anmol Publications, New Delhi, 2003.

Titus, M. : *Indian Islam,* Milford, New Delhi, 1979.

Ullah, M. : *Administration of Justice in Islam,* Kitab Bhavan, New Delhi, 1990.

Valliuddin, Mir : *The Quranic Sufism,* Motilal Banarsi Das Publishers, New Delhi, 1989.

Walker, Benjamin : *Foundation of Islam : the Making of World Faith,* Rupa & Co., New Delhi, 2001.

Watt, W.M. : *Islamic Surveys,* Edinburgh University Press, Edinburgh, 1999.

Wensick, A.E. : *A Handbook of Early Muhammadan Traditions,* Luzac & Co., Leiden, 1960.

Wolfson, H.A. : *The Philosophy of the Kalam,* Oxford, London, 1976.

Yousuf, Abbas Hashmi : *Rasul (PBUH),* Adam Pub., New Delhi, 2001.

Yusuf, S.M. : *Economic Justice in Islam,* Kitab Bhavan, New Delhi, 1988.

Zahid, Malik : *Subjects of Quran,* Kitab Bhavan, New Delhi, 1998.

Zaydan, Jurji : *History of Islamic Civilization,* Kitab Bhavan, New Delhi, 1994.

INDEX

N

O

P

□□□